Frommer's 96

Las Vegas

by Rena Bulkin

Macmillan • USA

ABOUT THE AUTHOR

Rena Bulkin began her travel-writing career when she set out for Europe in search of adventure. She found it writing about hotels and restaurants for the *New York Times* International Edition. She has since authored 15 travel guides to far-flung destinations.

MACMILLAN TRAVEL

A Simon & Schuster Macmillan Company
1633 Broadway
New York, NY 10019

Find us online at **http://www.mcp.com.mgr.travel** or
on America Online at Keyword **SuperLibrary**

ISBN 0-02-860878-X
ISSN 0899-3262

Editor: Douglas Stallings
Production Editor: Pete Fornatale
Design by Michele Laseau
Digital Cartography by Ortelius Design and John Decamillis
Maps copyright © by Simon & Schuster, Inc.

SPECIAL SALES

Contents

List of Maps

AN INVITATION TO THE READER

In researching this book, I discovered many wonderful places. I'm sure you'll find others. Please tell me about them, so I can share the information with your fellow travelers in upcoming editions. If you were disappointed with a recommendation, I'd love to know that, too. Please write to:

Rena Bulkin
Frommer's Las Vegas '96
Macmillan Travel
1633 Broadway
New York, NY 10019

AN ADDITIONAL NOTE

Please be advised that travel information is subject to change at any time, and this is especially true of prices. We therefore suggest that you write or call ahead for confirmation when making your travel plans. The authors, editors, and publisher cannot be held responsible for the experiences of readers while traveling. Your safety is important to us, however, so we encourage you to stay alert and be aware of your surroundings. Keep a close eye on cameras, purses, and wallets, all favorite targets of thieves and pickpockets.

WHAT THE SYMBOLS MEAN

✪ Frommer's Favorites

Hotels, restaurants, attractions, and entertainment you should not miss.

⑤ Super-Special Values

Hotels and restaurants that offer great value for your money.

The following abbreviations are used for credit cards:

AE	American Express	EU	Eurocard
CB	Carte Blanche	JCB	Japan Credit Bank
DC	Diners Club	MC	MasterCard
DISC	Discover	V	Visa
ER	enRoute		

Introducing Las Vegas

Las Vegas is a city designed for overindulgence—an anything-goes kind of place where you're encouraged to eat too much (at lavish low-priced buffets), drink too much (liquor is gratis at gaming tables), spend too much, and sleep too little. Leave your real life back home. In this 24-hour, neon-lit playground, you can leer at sexy showgirls prancing around in topless costumes, hoot and holler at the craps tables, even watch a volcano erupting while you're walking down the street. Traditionally this is the place to let it all hang out. Jimmy Durante—the first performer at the Flamingo—demolished a $1,600 piano on opening night just for kicks. And this was nothing compared to the high jinks of Flamingo owner Bugsy Siegel and his cohorts.

More than Chicago, it's Sinatra's kind of town, offering more superstar entertainment every night of the week than any other city in the world. It would seem that every performer ends up in Las Vegas at some time or other. Even such unlikely people as Noël Coward, Woody Allen, Bob Dylan, Buster Keaton, the Beatles, Luciano Pavarotti, and Orson Welles have played the Strip's showrooms. And Las Vegas audiences have witnessed many great moments in entertainment history. For instance:

In 1962 former President Harry Truman, in town to address the American Legion, joined Jimmy Durante in a piano duet at the Sands.

Elvis and Liberace once appeared together at the Riviera (Elvis played piano, Liberace guitar, and they donned each other's flamboyant costumes for the occasion).

Paul Anka and Wayne Newton surprised pal Tony Orlando by joining him onstage during his opening night at the Riviera in 1977 and belting out his trademark song, "Tie a Yellow Ribbon," for an ecstatic audience.

A year after Gracie Allen retired, Jack Benny—in full drag—performed in her stead one night with George Burns at the Sahara Congo Room.

And it was only years later that audiences realized they had witnessed entertainment history in the making when Judy Garland brought her 9-year-old daughter Liza onstage at the Flamingo in 1957.

Major sporting events take place on a regular basis—from championship boxing matches to championship poker playoffs, not to mention bizarre daredevil feats such as Evel Knievel's near-fatal motorcycle jump over the fountains fronting Caesars Palace.

Impressions

*It is highwayman and whore on the desert road, a city . . . dedicated to
waste and excess, heartless . . . a town where probably nothing good
or worthwhile has ever happened, nor ever will . . .*
                              —Trevor Fishlock, *Americans and Nothing Else*

*In some ways Las Vegas is still the wild West. For me, that's part of
the attraction. This town is the closest thing to an unstructured
society . . . anywhere in the world.*   —Steve Wynn

And then there's gambling. Fortunes are won and lost (usually lost)
on a roll of the dice. But we all secretly believe we'll beat the odds and
sail out of town with big bucks (preferably in a limo)—like the young
bride on her honeymoon who hit the jackpot to the tune of $1 mil-
lion after playing the slots at Caesars for just 3 minutes! Such stories
abound, and even sober folks can contract gambling fever upon hear-
ing them . . . not to mention watching the electronic billboards on the
Strip displaying ever increasing multimillion-dollar progressive slot
jackpots. A little more than a decade ago $1 slot machines caused a sen-
sation in the casinos. Today—in sumptuous high-roller precincts—you
can bet $1,500 on a single pull! On the other hand, you can still find
penny slots in some downtown casinos.

But even if you don't want to gamble, you can have a great vacation
here. Plush hotels, which charge only about half the amount of their
counterparts in other cities, offer numerous resort facilities—immense
pools, tennis, health clubs, and more. Shows are reasonably priced.
Food is cheap (a full prime-rib dinner can be had for under $5). And
many great attractions are within easy driving distance—magnificent
desert canyon vistas at Red Rock and Valley of Fire, pine-forested
Mount Charleston, Hoover Dam (an awe-inspiring engineering feat
even in today's high-tech world), and the recreational pleasures of
Lake Mead among them. Or you can just stroll the Strip at night and
enjoy the world's most spectacular sound and light show.

It's amazing to think that just 100 years ago all you would have
found here was a desert wilderness.

1 Frommer's Favorite Las Vegas Experiences

- **A Stroll on the Strip After Dark:** You haven't really seen Las Vegas
  until you've seen it at night. This neon wonderland is the world's
  greatest sound and light show. Begin at Circus Circus, where you'll
  find circus acts and carnival games, and continue—if your energy
  holds out—as far as the Luxor for a narrated barge cruise on the
  "Nile." Make plenty of stops en route to take in the ship battle at
  Treasure Island, see the Mirage volcano erupt, and enjoy the light,
  sound, and water show at Bally's.

- **A Creative Adventures Tour:** Char Cruze provides personalized
  tours that unlock the mysteries of the desert canyons and make

regional history come vibrantly alive. I can't think of a better way to spend a day than exploring canyons with her.

- **A Visit to the Magic and Movie Hall of Fame:** This delightful attraction offers hours of solid entertainment for just a few dollars. Following a very good magician/ventriloquist show, you'll tour dozens of fascinating magic-related exhibits enhanced by video clips of actual performances.

- **Dinner at the Palace Court:** This stunning French restaurant at Caesars Palace offers haute cuisine graciously served in opulent surroundings. Plan after-dinner drinks at the adjoining piano bar, where a retracting skylight opens to starry skies—one of the most romantic spots in town.

- **An Excursion to Mount Charleston:** Especially in summer, the scenic drive to the mountains, which ends at a charming restaurant nestled in a pine forest, is a delight. Spend the day here hiking, horseback riding, or just kicking back. If you don't feel like going back right away, stay the night at the Mount Charleston Hotel.

- **Cirque du Soleil:** You haven't really seen Cirque du Soleil until you've seen it at Treasure Island, where the showroom is equipped with state-of-the-art sound and lighting systems, and where Steve Wynn has provided a seemingly infinite budget for sets, costumes, and high-tech special effects. It's an enchantment.

- **An evening in Glitter Gulch:** Set aside an evening to tour downtown hotels and take in the Fremont Street Experience. Stay on to see *Country Fever* at the Golden Nugget.

- **A Sunday Champagne Brunch:** Especially leisurely and lavish are those featured at Bally's, Caesars Palace, and the Golden Nugget. The Sunday brunch at the Sheraton Desert Inn is in a class by itself.

- **A Trip to Lake Mead:** Book a night at Lake Mead Lodge, using it as a base to explore Hoover Dam and the 1.5-million-acre Lake Mead National Recreation Area. An engineering marvel in the 1930s, the dam is still damned impressive. After your tour, you can enjoy swimming, boating, fishing, scuba diving, rafting, and canoeing here. Take a scenic breakfast, lunch, or dinner cruise aboard a Mississippi-style paddlewheeler.

- **Catching Your Favorite Headliners:** As soon as you arrive in town, pick up a show guide and see who's playing during your stay. Las Vegas offers an unparalleled opportunity to enjoy your favorite entertainers.

- **Shopping the Forum at Caesars Palace:** This is an only-in-Vegas shopping experience—an arcade replicating an ancient Roman streetscape, with classical piazzas and opulent fountains. The central "Fountain of the Gods" features animatronic statues of Bacchus, Venus, and others. The result is Rodeo Drive meets the Roman Empire.

- **Hiking and Picknicking at Valley of Fire State Park:** More thrilling natural wonders—majestic sandstone canyons, cliffs, rock formations, and Native American petroglyphs—to explore.

- **Seeing Siegfried & Roy:** I'd as soon miss their show at the Mirage as go to India and skip the Taj Mahal. See it!

- **Playing Craps at a Casino:** The most exciting casino action is always at the craps tables, where bettors bond over fast-paced play.

2   The City Today and Tomorrow

Las Vegas is on a roll. In the works at press time are many new projects. On the site where the Dunes stood for decades, Steve Wynn's billion-dollar 3,000-room Bellagio will evoke a small Italian village resort on the shores of a 15-acre "Lake Como."

His Mirage Resorts corporation, in partnership with Circus Circus Enterprises, is also behind the 3,024-room Monte Carlo, which will occupy 43 acres on the south end of the old Dunes property. Its architecture will reflect the belle époque in France with a magnificent neo-classic facade. Illusionist Lance Burton, currently at the Hacienda, will headline in the showroom.

The MGM Grand has teamed up with Primadonna Resorts to create the Big Apple–themed 2,100-room New York-New York on the northwest corner of Tropicana Avenue and The Strip. It will reproduce on its premises the Empire State Building, Central Park, the Statue of Liberty, and other N.Y.C. landmarks and feature a Coney Island theme park with a water flume ride and a major roller coaster.

The French motif at Bally's $420 million, 2,500-room Paris Casino Resort will be reflected in replicas of the Eiffel Tower (this one a 50-foot structure crowned by a restaurant and an observation lookout), the Arc de Triomphe, the Champs-Elysées, the Paris Opera House, Parc Monceau, and the Seine. A working winery and a gondola ride are also in the works, while a Paris Metro station will herald a connection to the monorail that links Bally's and the MGM Grand.

Bob Stupak's 1,149-foot Stratosphere Tower—which will be topped by a revolving restaurant/cocktail lounge and the world's highest roller coaster—is already beginning to dominate the Las Vegas skyline. The tower, which will also contain a thrill ride called the Space Shot, will adjoin a 1,500-room hotel housing a vast World's Fair–themed casino, four wedding chapels, a child-care center, and a 160,000-square-foot entertainment retail complex à la The Forum Shops at Caesars Palace.

In addition, many existing properties are being expanded.

Circus Circus has purchased the Hacienda (and some 120 surrounding acres) with plans to add one or two additional hotels—all of which will be linked by monorails to the Luxor and Excalibur.

The Rio will be spending $185 million to add 1,015 suites as well as larger gaming, dining, and retail facilities. Plans also include a second hotel and casino on 22 acres of land adjoining the current property.

Harrah's recently announced plans for a $150-million expansion to include a renovation of its facade, an enlarged casino, new restaurants, and a 35-story tower with almost 700 rooms and suites.

A 225,000-square-foot Roman Great Hall will be added to the dazzling ancient Roman streetscape of The Forum Shops at Caesars Palace and will include 37 new stores and two restaurants as well as an IMAX simulator and an "Atlantis Odyssey" attraction. Also upcoming at Caesars: a new entertainment attraction called "Caesars Magical Empire," which will include magic-themed dinner shows and a sound and light extravaganza.

At the Las Vegas Hilton, a 40,000-square-foot entertainment complex called "Star Trek: The Experience"—created in conjunction with Paramount Parks, is nearing completion. Visitors will assume the identities of Starfleet or alien crew members to participate in a high-tech interactive adventure. Then they can eat at a 24th-century Cardassian restaurant or gamble in a 20,000-square-foot casino.

Finally, the Sahara is under new ownership and slated for a much-needed total renovation. The new proprietors will also construct an as-yet-unnamed sister hotel on vacant land across the Strip.

As Las Vegas history continues to be written, one can only wonder, "What will they think of next?"

3 A Look at the Past

For many centuries the land that would become Nevada was inhabited only by several Native American tribes—the Paiute, Shoshone, and Washoe. It wasn't until 1826 that white men set foot in the future state, and not until 1829 that Rafael Rivera, a scout for Mexican traders, entered a verdant valley nurtured by desert springs and called it Las Vegas ("the meadows"). From 1831 to 1848 these springs served as a watering place on the Old Spanish Trail for trading caravans plying the route between Santa Fe and the California coast. Explorer, soldier, and pathfinder Col. John C. Frémont (for whom the main thoroughfare downtown is named) rested near the headwaters of Las Vegas Springs on an overland expedition in 1844. A decade later Congress established a monthly mail route through Las Vegas Springs. And in 1855 Mormon leader Brigham Young sent 30 missionaries to Las Vegas to help expand Mormonism between Salt Lake City and southern California. Just north of what is today downtown (what would these missionaries think if they could see it now?) the Mormon colony built an adobe fort and dwellings. They raised crops, baptized Paiutes, and

Dateline

- **Prehistory**
Archaeological studies show humans occupying Las Vegas region from 3000 B.C. Hunter-gatherers called the Anasazi ("the ancient ones") live here from the 1st century A.D.

- A.D. 1150 Anasazi leave the area. Nomadic Paiutes become the dominant group.

- **1829** Expedition of Mexican traders camping 100 miles from the present site of Las Vegas send

continues

scout Rafael
Rivera to explore
the surrounding
desert. He
discovers a
verdant oasis—
Las Vegas
Springs.

■ **1831–48** Artesian
spring waters of
Las Vegas serve as
a watering place
on the Old
Spanish Trail.

■ **1855** Mormon
colony of 30
missionaries
establishes
settlement just
north of today's
downtown.
Unsuccessful in
its aims, the
colony disbanded
in 1858.

■ **1861** President
James Buchanan
authorizes
formation of
the territory
of Nevada.

■ **1864** President
Lincoln proclaims
Nevada 36th state
of the Union. Las
Vegas, however, is
still part of the
Territory of
Arizona.

■ **1865** Gold
prospector
Octavius D. Gass
builds Las Vegas
Ranch—the first
permanent
settlement in
Las Vegas—
on site of the
old Mormon
fort.

continues

mined lead in the nearby mountains. However, none of these ventures proved successful, and the ill-fated settlement was abandoned after just 3 years.

The next influx into the area came as a result of mining fever in the early 1860s, but this soon subsided. However, gold prospector Octavius Decatur Gass stayed behind and, in 1865, built the 640-acre Las Vegas Ranch using structures left by the Mormons as his base. Since Gass controlled the valley's water, he finally found "gold" offering services to travelers passing through. Gass planted crops and fruit orchards, started vineyards, raised cattle, established cordial relations with the Paiutes (he even learned their language), and served as a legislator. This became the first significant settlement in the area. By 1900 the Las Vegas valley had a population of 30.

A TENT CITY IN THE WILDERNESS

The city of Las Vegas was officially born in 1905 when the Union Pacific Railroad connecting Los Angeles and Salt Lake City decided to route its trains through this rugged frontier outpost, selected for its ready supply of water and the availability of timber in the surrounding mountains. On a sweltering day in May, 1,200 townsite lots were auctioned off to eager pioneers and real estate speculators who had come from all over the country. The railroad depot was located at the head of Fremont Street (site of today's Amtrak station). Championing the spot was Montana senator William Clark, who had paid the astronomical sum (for that time) of $55,000 for the nearby Las Vegas Ranch and springs. The coming of a railroad more or less ensured the growth of the town. As construction began, tent settlements, saloons, ramshackle restaurants, boardinghouses, and shops gradually emerged. The early tent hotels charged a dollar to share a double bed with a stranger for eight hours! Early businesses flourished serving railroad men and prospectors from nearby mining operations.

By present-day standards, the new town was not a pleasant place to live. Prospectors' burros roamed the streets braying loudly, generally creating havoc and attracting swarms of flies. There were no screens, no air conditioners, no modern showers or baths (the town's bathhouse had but one tub) to ameliorate the fierce summer heat. The streets were rutted with dust pockets up to a foot deep that rose in great gusts as stage coaches, supply wagons, and 20-animal mule teams careened over them. It was a true pioneer town, complete with saloon brawls and shoot-outs. Discomforts notwithstanding, gaming establishments, hotels, and nightclubs—some of them seedy dives, others rather luxurious—sprang up and prospered in the Nevada wilderness. A red-light district emerged on Second Street between Ogden and Stewart avenues. And gambling, which was legal until 1909, flourished.

THE EIGHTH WONDER OF THE WORLD

For many years after its creation, Las Vegas was a mere whistlestop town. That all changed in 1928 when Congress authorized the building of nearby Boulder Dam (later renamed Hoover Dam), bringing thousands of workers to the area. In 1931 gambling once again became legal in Nevada, and Fremont Street's gaming emporiums and speakeasies attracted workers from the dam. Upon the dam's completion, the Las Vegas Chamber of Commerce worked hard to lure the hordes of tourists who came to see the engineering marvel (it was called "the eighth wonder of the world") to its casinos. Las Vegas was about to make the transition from a sleepy desert town to "a town that never sleeps." But it wasn't until the early years of World War II that visionary entrepreneurs began to plan for its glittering future.

LAS VEGAS GOES SOUTH

Contrary to a popular conception, Bugsy Siegel didn't actually stake a claim in the middle of no-where—he just built a few blocks south of already existing properties. Development a few miles south of downtown on Highway 91 (the future Strip) was already under way in the 1930s, with such establishments as the Pair-O-Dice Club and the Last Frontier. And in 1941 El Rancho Vegas, ultraluxurious for its time, was built on the same remote stretch of highway (across the street from where the Sahara now stands). According to legend, Los Angeles hotelier Thomas E. Hull had been driving by the site when his car broke down. Noticing the extent of passing traffic, he decided to build there. Hull invited scores of Hollywood

■ **1867** Arizona cedes 12,225 square miles to Nevada, which assumes its present shape. Las Vegas is now in Nevada.

■ **1880s** Due to mining fever, the population of Nevada soars to more than 60,000 in 1880. The Paiutes are forced onto reservations.

■ **1895** San Franciscan inventor Charles Fey creates a three-reel gambling device—the first slot machine.

■ **1905** The railroad connecting Salt Lake City and Los Angeles routes its trains through Las Vegas and auctions off 1,200 lots in the official townsite.

■ **1907** Fremont Street—the future "Glitter Gulch"—gets electric lights.

■ **1909** Gambling is made illegal in Nevada, but Las Vegas pays little heed.

■ **1911** William Howard Taft, first American president to pass through Las Vegas, waves at residents from his train.

continues

- **1928** Congress authorizes Hoover Dam 30 miles away, bringing thousands of workers to the area. Later, Las Vegas will capitalize on hundreds of thousands who come to see the engineering marvel.
- **1931** Gambling is legalized once again.
- **1932** The 100-room Apache Hotel opens Downtown.
- **1933** Prohibition is repealed. Las Vegas's numerous speakeasies become legit.
- **1934** The city's first neon sign lights up the Boulder Club downtown.
- **1941** The luxurious El Rancho Las Vegas becomes the first hotel on the Strip. Downtown, the El Cortez opens.
- **1944** Major star Sophie Tucker plays the Last Frontier, which had opened a year earlier.
- **1946** Benjamin "Bugsy" Siegel's Flamingo extends the boundaries of the Strip. Sammy Davis, Jr. debuts at the Last

continues

glitterati to his grand opening, and El Rancho Vegas soon became the hostelry of choice for visiting film stars. Beginning a trend that still continues today, each new property tried to outdo existing hotels in luxurious amenities and thematic splendor. In 1943 the Last Frontier (the Strip's second hotel) created an authentic western setting by scouring the Southwest in search of authentic pioneer furnishings for its rooms, hiring Zuni craftsmen to create baskets and hangings, and picking up guests at the airport in a horse-drawn stagecoach. The Last Frontier also presaged a new era when it brought stage and screen star Sophie Tucker to its showroom for a 2-week engagement in 1944 with much attendant hoopla. Tucker's train was met with a parade, and "the last of the red-hot mammas" was conveyed to the hotel in a fire truck. Las Vegas was on its way to becoming the entertainment capital of the world.

Las Vegas promoted itself in the 1940s as a town that combined Wild West frontier friendliness with glamour and excitement. As Chamber of Commerce president Maxwell Kelch aptly put it in a 1947 speech, "Las Vegas has the impact of a Wild West show, the friendliness of a country store, and the sophistication of Monte Carlo." Throughout the decade, the city was largely a regional resort—Hollywood's celebrity playground. Clara Bow and Rex Bell (a star of westerns) bought a ranch in Las Vegas where they entertained such luminaries as the Barrymores, Norma Shearer, Clark Gable, and Errol Flynn. The Hollywood connection gave the town glamour in the public's mind. So did the mob connection (something Las Vegas has spent decades trying to live down), which became clear early on when notorious underworld gangster Benjamin "Bugsy" Siegel (with partners Lucky Luciano and Meyer Lansky) built the fabulous Flamingo, a tropical paradise and "a real class joint." Hollywood people found the gangsters glamorous and vice versa—and the public was entranced by both. In 1947 the Club Bingo opened across the street from El Rancho Vegas, bringing a new game to town. The Thunderbird, the fourth hotel on the Strip, opened in 1948.

A steady stream of name entertainers followed Sophie Tucker into Las Vegas, adding to the city's tourist appeal. In 1947 Jimmy Durante opened the showroom at the Flamingo. Other headliners of the 1940s included Dean Martin and Jerry Lewis, comedian Jack Carter, tap-dancing legend Bill "Bojangles" Robinson, the Mills Brothers (who first recorded "Bye-Bye Blackbird"), skater Sonja Henie, Frankie Laine, Vic Damone, and Joe E. Lewis. Future Las Vegas legend Sammy Davis, Jr. debuted at El Rancho Vegas in 1945.

While the Strip was expanding, Downtown kept pace with new hotels such as the El Cortez, the Nevada Biltmore, the Golden Nugget, and the Eldorado Club. By the end of the decade, Fremont Street was known as "Glitter Gulch," its profusion of neon signs proclaiming round-the-clock gaming and entertainment.

THE 1950S: BUILDING BOOMS AND A-BOMBS

Las Vegas entered the new decade as a city (no longer a frontier town) with a population of about 50,000, its future as a tourist mecca ensured by postwar affluence and improved highways. Photographs indicate that Las Vegas was more glamorous in the 1950s than it is today. Men donned suits and ties, women floor-length gowns, to attend shows and even for casino gambling. Hotel growth was phenomenal. The Desert Inn, which opened in 1950 with headliners Edgar Bergen and Charlie McCarthy, brought country club elegance (including an 18-hole golf course and tennis courts) to the Strip. In 1951 the Eldorado Club downtown became Benny Binion's Horseshoe Club, which would gain fame as the home of the annual World Series of Poker. A year later, the Club Bingo entered a new incarnation as the African desert-themed Sahara (with camels guarding its portals), and the Sands emerged to further brighten the star-studded Strip. One of the Sands's major backers was Copacabana nightclub owner Jack Entratter who, being well connected in showbiz, brought major talent and stunning showgirls to its Copa Room. In 1954 the Showboat sailed into a new area east of Downtown. Although people said it could never last in such a remote location, they were wrong. The Showboat not only innovated buffet meals and a bowling alley (106 lanes to date) but offered round-the-clock bingo. In 1955 the Last Frontier became the New Frontier and the Côte d'Azur–themed Riviera became the ninth big

Frontier. Downtown (dubbed "Glitter Gulch") gets two new hotels—the Golden Nugget and the Eldorado.

- **1947** United Airlines inaugurates service to Las Vegas.
- **1948** The Thunderbird becomes the fourth hotel on the Strip.
- **1950** The Desert Inn adds country club panache to the Strip.
- **1951** The first of many atom bombs is tested in the desert just 65 miles from Las Vegas. An explosion of another sort takes place when Sinatra debuts at the Desert Inn.
- **1952** The Club Bingo (opened in 1947) becomes the desert-themed Sahara. The Sands' Copa Room enhances the city's image as an entertainment capital.
- **1954** The Showboat pioneers buffet meals and bowling alleys in a new area of Downtown.
- **1955** The Strip gets its first

continues

high-rise hotel—
the nine-story
Riviera—which
pays Liberace the
unprecedented
sum of $50,000
to open its
showroom. The
Riviera is the
ninth hotel on
the Strip. A
month later, the
Dunes becomes
the 10th.

■ **1956** The
Fremont opens
downtown, and
the Hacienda
becomes the
southernmost
hotel on the
Strip.

■ **1957** The Dunes
introduces
bare-breasted
showgirls in its
*Minsky Goes to
Paris* revue. The
most luxurious
hotel to date, the
Tropicana, opens
on the Strip.

■ **1958** The 1,065-
room Stardust
opens as the
world's largest
resort complex
with a spectac-
ular show from
France, the *Lido
de Paris.*

■ **1959** The Las
Vegas Conven-
tion Center goes
up, presaging the
city's future as a
major convention
city. Another
French produc-
tion, the still-
extant *Folies*

continues

hotel to open on the Strip. Breaking the ranch-style mode, it was, at nine stories, the Strip's first high-rise. Liberace, one of the hottest names in show business, was paid the unprecedented sum of $50,000 a week to dazzle audiences in the Riviera's posh Clover Room. The Dunes opened immediately after, topped by a 30-foot fiberglass sultan; the 15-story Fremont Hotel Downtown became the highest building in Las Vegas; and the Hacienda extended the boundaries of the Strip by opening 2 miles south of the nearest re-sort. Elvis appeared at the New Frontier in 1956 but wasn't a huge success; his fans were too young to fit the Las Vegas tourist mold. In 1957 the Tropicana joined the Hacienda at the far end of Las Vegas Boulevard. Billing itself as "the Tiffany of the Strip," it offered 40 tropically lush acres and a musical extravaganza starring Eddie Fisher. In 1958 the $10 million, 1,065-room Stardust upped the spectacular stakes by importing the famed *Lido de Paris* from the French capital. It became one of the longest run-ning shows ever to play Las Vegas. The Stardust was also the first hotel to bring massive serious neon to the Strip in the form of a 216-foot sign emblazoned with more than 7,000 feet of neon tubing and 11,000 lamps. The year after it opened it absorbed the Royal Nevada next door.

Throughout the 1950s most of the above-mentioned hotels competed for performers whose followers spent freely in the casinos. The advent of big-name Strip entertainment tolled a death knell for glamorous nightclubs in America; owners simply could not compete with the astro-nomical salaries paid to Las Vegas headliners. Major '50s stars of the Strip included Rosemary Clooney, Nat King Cole, Peggy Lee, Milton Berle, Judy Garland, Red Skelton, Ernie Kovacs, Abbott and Costello, Ray Bolger, Tommy and Jimmy Dorsey, Fred Astaire and Ginger Rogers, the Andrews Sisters, Zsa Zsa Gabor, Marlene Dietrich, Billy Eckstine, and Gordon McRae. Two performers whose names have ever since been linked to Las Vegas—Frank Sinatra and Wayne Newton—made their debuts. Mae West not only performed in Las Vegas, but cleverly bought up a half mile of desolate Strip frontage between the Dunes and the Tropicana.

Competition for the tourist dollar also brought nationally televised sporting events such as the

PGA's Tournament of Champions to the Desert Inn golf course (the winner got a wheelbarrow filled with silver dollars). In the 1950s the wedding industry helped make Las Vegas one of the nation's most popular venues for "goin' to the chapel." It was and is easy. Nevada requires no blood test or waiting period. Celebrity weddings of the 1950s that sparked the trend included singer Dick Haymes and Rita Hayworth, Fernando Lamas and Arlene Dahl, Joan Crawford and Pepsi chairman Alfred Steele, Carol Channing and TV exec Charles Lowe, and Paul Newman and Joanne Woodward.

On a grimmer note, the '50s also heralded the atomic age in Nevada, with nuclear testing taking place just 65 miles northwest of Las Vegas. A chilling 1951 photograph shows a mushroom-shaped cloud from an atomic bomb test visible over the Fremont Street horizon. Throughout the decade, about one bomb a month was detonated in the nearby desert.

THE 1960S: THE RAT PACK . . .

The very first month of the new decade made entertainment history when the Sands hosted a 3-week "Summit Meeting" in the Copa Room presided over by Chairman of the Board Frank Sinatra with Rat Pack cronies Dean Martin, Sammy Davis, Jr., Peter Lawford, and Joey Bishop. President Dwight Eisenhower, Nikita Khrushchev, and Winston Churchill were all invited. They didn't attend, but showroom guests who witnessed the Rat Pack's antics are probably still dining out on the stories. No other Las Vegas show tickets have ever been more coveted or difficult to obtain. One night Sinatra picked up Sammy Davis, Jr. bodily and said, "Ladies and gentlemen, I want to thank you for giving me this valuable NAACP trophy." He then dropped Davis into the lap of a man in a ringside seat who happened to be Senator John F. Kennedy. Davis looked up and quipped, "It's perfectly all right with me, Senator, as long as I'm not being donated to George Wallace or James Eastland." The Rat Pack returned to the Copa stage in 1961 for an onstage birthday party for Dean Martin with a 5-foot-high cake in the shape of a whiskey bottle. Martin threw the first slice, and a food fight ensued. The riotous clan kept Las Vegas amused during most of the decade.

Bergére, opens at the Tropicana.

- **1960** The Rat Pack, led by Chairman of the Board Frank Sinatra, hold 3-week "Summit Meeting" at the Sands. A championship boxing match—the first of many—takes place at the Convention Center. El Rancho Las Vegas, the Strip's first property, burns to the ground.

- **1963** McCarran International Airport opens. Casinos and showrooms are darkened for a day as Las Vegas mourns the death of President John F. Kennedy.

- **1965** The 26-story Mint alters the Fremont Street skyline. Muhammad Ali defeats Floyd Patterson at the Las Vegas Convention Center.

- **1966** The Aladdin, the first new hotel on the Strip in 9 years, is soon eclipsed by the unparalleled grandeur of Caesars Palace.

continues

The Four Queens opens Downtown. Howard Hughes takes up residence at the Desert Inn. He buys up big chunks of Las Vegas and helps erase the city's gangland stigma.

■ **1967** Elvis Presley marries Priscilla Beaulieu at the Aladdin, the city's all-time most celebrated union.

■ **1968** Circus Circus gives kids a reason to come to Las Vegas.

■ **1969** The Landmark and the International (today the Hilton) open within a day of each other on Paradise Road. Elvis Presley makes a triumphant return headlining at the latter.

■ **1971** The 500-room Union Plaza opens Downtown on the site of the old Union Pacific depot.

■ **1973** The ultraglamorous 2,100-room MGM Grand assumes the mantle of "world's largest resort." Superstars of magic, Siegfried & Roy,

continues

On November 25, 1963, Las Vegas mourned the death of President John F. Kennedy with the rest of the nation. Between 7am and midnight, all the neon lights went off, casinos stood empty, and showrooms were dark.

The building boom of the '50s took a brief respite. The Strip's first property, the El Rancho Vegas, burned down in 1960. And the first new hotel of the decade—the first to be built in 9 years—was the exotic Aladdin in 1966. A year after it opened the Aladdin hosted the most celebrated Las Vegas wedding of all time when Elvis Presley married Priscilla Beaulieu. In 1966 Las Vegas also hailed Caesar—Caesars Palace, that is—a Lucullan pleasure palace whose grand opening was a million-dollar, 3-day Roman orgy with 1,800 guests. Its Carrara marble repro-ductions of ancient temples, heroic arches, and classical statuary were a radical departure from the more ersatz glitz of earlier Strip hotels. Also in the '60s, the Mint and the Four Queens altered the Downtown skyline.

. . . AND A PACK RAT

During the '60s negative attention focused—with good reason—on mob influence in Las Vegas. Of the 11 major casino hotels that had opened in the previous decade, 10 were believed to have been financed with mob money. Attorney General Robert Kennedy ordered the Department of Justice to begin serious scrutiny of Las Vegas gaming operations. Then, like a knight in shining armor, Howard Hughes rode into town. He was not, however, on a white horse. Ever eccentric, he arrived (for security rather than health reasons) in an ambulance. The reclusive billionaire moved into a Desert Inn penthouse on Thanksgiving Day 1966 and did not set foot outside the hotel for the next 4 years! It became his headquarters for a $300 million hotel- and property- buying spree, which included the Desert Inn itself (in 1967). Hughes was as "bugsy" as Benjamin Siegel any day, but his pristine reputation helped bring respectability to the desert city and reverse its gangland stigma. People generally believed that if the gaming business was truly shady, Howard Hughes would not be in it. Hughes purchased the Sands along with half a dozen other hotels and casinos, the airport, an airline, and a local TV station. Topless showgirls and hookers were not welcome at his properties, and showroom comedians were warned to "keep it clean." For decades he provided fodder for Strip performers. "You're wondering why I don't have a drink in my hand?" Frank Sinatra asked a Sands audience one night. "Howard Hughes bought it."

Las Vegas became a family destination in 1968 when Circus Circus burst on the scene with the world's largest permanent circus and a "junior casino" comprising dozens of carnival midway games on its mezzanine level. In 1969 the Land-mark and the dazzling International (today the Hilton) ventured into a new area of town— Paradise Road near the Convention Center. That same year Elvis made a triumphant return to Las Vegas at the International's showroom and went on to become one of the city's all-time legendary performers. His fans had come of age.

Hoping to establish Las Vegas as "the Broad-way of the West," the Thunderbird Hotel pre-sented Rodgers and Hammerstein's *Flower Drum Song*. It was a smash hit. Soon the Riviera picked up *Bye, Bye, Birdie,* and, as the decade progressed, *Mame* and *The Odd Couple* played at Caesars Pal ace. While Broadway played the Strip, produc-tion shows such as the Dunes's *Casino de Paris* became ever more lavish, expensive, and techni-cally innovative. Showroom stars of the 1960s included "Funny Girl" Barbara Streisand and funny ladies Phyllis Diller and Carol Burnett, Little Richard (who billed himself as "the bronze Liberace"), Louis Armstrong, Bobby Darin, the Supremes, Steve Allen, Johnny Carson, Bob Newhart, the Smothers Brothers, and Aretha Franklin. Liza Minnelli filled her mother's shoes, while Nancy Sinatra's boots were made for walk-ing. And Tom Jones wowed 'em at the Flamingo.

THE 1970S: MERV, MIKE, MGM & MAGIC

In 1971, the 500-room Union Plaza opened at the head of Fremont Street on the site of the old Union Pacific Station. It had what was, at the time, the world's largest casino, and its showroom specialized in Broadway productions. The same year talk show host Merv Griffin began taping at Caesars Palace, taking advantage of a ready supply of local headliner guests. He helped popu-larize Las Vegas even more by bringing it into America's living rooms every afternoon. Rival Mike Douglas soon followed suit at the Las Vegas Hilton.

- debut at the Tropicana.
- **1975** A flash flood causes more than $1 million in damages.
- **1976** Fittingly, pioneer aviator Howard Hughes dies aboard a plane en route to a Houston hospital. Martin and Lewis make up after a 20-year feud.
- **1978** Leon Spinks dethrones "the Greatest" (Muhammad Ali) at the Las Vegas Hilton. Crime-solver Dan Tanna (Robert Urich) makes the streets of "Vega$" safer—and better known.
- **1979** A new international arrivals building opens at McCarran International Airport.
- **1980** McCarran International Airport embarks on a 20-year, $785 million expansion program. Las Vegas celebrates its 75th birthday. A devastating fire destroys the MGM Grand, leaving 84 dead and 700 injured. Bally's takes over the property.

continues

- **1981** Siegfried & Roy begin a record-breaking run in their own show, *Beyond Belief,* at the Frontier.
- **1982** A Las Vegas street is named Wayne Newton Boulevard.
- **1985** Another child-oriented attraction, Wet 'n Wild, opens on the Strip.
- **1989** Steve Wynn makes headlines with his spectacular Mirage, fronted by an erupting volcano. He signs Siegfried & Roy to a 5-year $57 million showroom contract (since extended)!
- **The 1990s** The medieval Arthurian realm of Excalibur opens as the new "world's-largest-resort" title holder with 4,032 rooms, a claim it relinquishes when the MGM Grand's new 5,005-room megaresort/theme park opens in 1994.—Other new Strip residents in 1994 are the Luxor, a 2,500-room, 30-story Egyptian-themed pyramid, and

continues

The year 1973 was eventful: The Holiday Inn (today Harrah's) built a Mississippi riverboat complete with towering smokestacks and foghorn whistle which was immediately dubbed "the ship on the Strip." Dean Martin headlined in the celebrity room of the magnificent new MGM Grand, named for the movie *Grand Hotel.* More than 800 tons of marble were imported from Italy just for the fountain at the front entrance, and sculptors in three Italian towns were kept busy for 2 years making columns and statues for the property. Facilities included everything from a jai alai fronton to the largest shopping mall in the state. And over at the Tropicana, illusionists extraordinaire Siegfried & Roy began turning women into tigers and themselves into legends in the *Folies Bergére.* Several years later they moved on to *Hallelujah, Hollywood,* and the *Lido de Paris.* Whatever show they were in became (and remains to this day) the hottest ticket in town.

Two major disasters hit Las Vegas in the 1970s. First, a flash flood devastated the Strip, causing more than $1 million in damage. Hundreds of cars were swept away in the raging waters. Second, gambling was legalized in Atlantic City. Las Vegas's hotel business slumped as fickle tourists decided to check out the new East Coast gambling mecca.

On a happier note, audiences were moved when Frank Sinatra helped to patch up a 20-year feud by introducing Dean Martin as a surprise guest on Jerry Lewis's 1976 Muscular Dystrophy Telethon at the Sahara. Martin and Lewis hugged and made up. Who would balk Sinatra?

As the decade drew to a close, Dan Tanna began investigating crime in glamorous "Vega$," an international arrivals building opened at McCarran International Airport, and dollar slot machines caused a sensation in the casinos. Hot performers of the '70s included José Feliciano, Ann-Margret, Tina Turner, Englebert Humperdinck, Ben Vereen, Bill Cosby, Sonny and Cher, Tony Bennett, the Neils (Diamond and Sedaka), Joel Grey, Mel Tormé, Bobby Darin, Johnny Carson, Gregory Hines (with his brother and dad), Donny and Marie, the Jackson 5, Gladys Knight and the Pips, and that "wild and crazy guy" Steve Martin. Debbie Reynolds introduced her daughter Carrie with a duet performance before a Desert Inn audience. Shirley MacLaine began an incarnation at the Riviera. And country was now cool; the names Johnny Cash, Bobby Gentry, Charlie Pride, and Roy Clark went up in marquee lights.

Steve Wynn's Treasure Island, based on the novel by Robert Louis Stevenson.

THE 1980S: THE CITY ERUPTS!

Las Vegas was booming once again. McCarran Airport began a 20-year, $785 million expansion program. In 1980 a devastating fire swept through the MGM Grand, leaving 84 dead and 700 injured. Shortly thereafter, Bally acquired the property and created a cheerful megaresort with so many facilities you need never leave. It billed itself as the "city within a city."

Siegfried & Roy were no longer just the star segment of various stage spectaculars. Their own show, *Beyond Belief,* ran for 6 years at the Frontier, playing a record-breaking 3,538 performances to sellout audiences every night. It became the most successful attraction in the city's history.

In 1989, Steve Wynn made Las Vegas sit up and take notice. His gleaming white and gold Mirage was fronted by five-story waterfalls, lagoons, and lush tropical foliage—not to mention a 50-foot volcano that dramatically erupted, spewing great gusts of fire another 50 feet into the air every 15 minutes after dark! Inside were dolphin and royal white tiger habitats, a rain forest under a 90-foot atrium dome, and a 20,000-gallon simulated coral reef aquarium whose residents included six sharks and 1,000 colorful tropical fish. Wynn gave world-renowned illusionists Siegfried & Roy carte blanche—and more than $30 million—to create the most spellbinding show Las Vegas had ever seen (don't miss it).

Stars of the '80s included Eddie Murphy, Don Rickles, Roseanne Barr, Bob Newhart, Dionne Warwick, Paul Anka, the Captain and Tennille, Donna Summer, Rich Little, George Carlin, David Brenner, Barry Manilow, Bernadette Peters, Flip Wilson, and Diahann Carroll. Country continued to be cool, as evidenced by frequent headliners Willie Nelson, Kenny Rogers, Dolly Parton, Crystal Gale, Merle Haggard, Mickey Gilley, Kris Kristofferson, and Barbara Mandrell. Joan Rivers posed her famous question "Can we talk?" and bug-eyed comic Rodney Dangerfield complained he "got no respect."

THE 1990S: KING ARTHUR MEETS KING TUT

The decade began with a blare of trumpets heralding the rise of a turreted medieval castle fronted by a moated drawbridge and staffed by jousting knights and fair damsels. Excalibur's interior had so many stone castle walls that a Strip comedian quipped "it looks like a prison for Snow White." Like Circus Circus (same owner), it abounds in family attractions—carnival games, puppet shows, jugglers, magicians, high-tech thrill cinemas, and a major show called *King Arthur's Tournament* which is geared to youngsters. Excalibur reflects the '90s marketing trend to promote Las Vegas as a family vacation destination.

Three sensational megahotels have opened on the Strip since 1993, and they're all running at close to 100% occupancy—as are older properties benefiting from the visitor excitement they've generated. They include the *Wizard of Oz*–themed MGM Grand Hotel, backed by a full theme park (it ended Excalibur's brief reign as the world's largest resort); the Luxor Las Vegas, a gleaming 30-story reflective bronze pyramid, prefaced by a Sphinx and a 191-foot obelisk (inside is a full-scale reproduction of King Tut's tomb); and Steve Wynn's Treasure Island, replicating an 18th-century pirate village overlooking Buccaneer Bay—scene of fierce hourly combat between a British frigate and a pirate vessel.

On October 27, 1993, a quarter of a million people crowded onto the Strip to witness the implosion of the 37-year-old Dunes Hotel. Vegas-style, it went out with a bang. Later that year a unique pink-domed 5-acre indoor amusement park, Grand Slam Canyon, became part of the Circus Circus Hotel. In 1995 the Fremont Street Experience was completed, revitalizing Downtown Las Vegas; closer to the Strip, rock restaurant magnate Peter Morton opened the Hard Rock Hotel, billed as "the world's first rock 'n' roll hotel and casino."

4 Famous Las Vegans

Benny Binion (1904–89)   This feisty Texan, who misspent his youth punching cattle, horse trading, running illegal craps games, and bootlegging, came to Las Vegas in 1947 with a suitcase full of money. He bought a casino, renamed it the Horseshoe, and made it famous for the highest limits in town and the annual World Series of Poker. When he died, Binion was a casino czar worth $100 million. His family are still major players in town.

Nicholas "Nick the Greek" Dandolos (1893–1966)   America's most famous gambler, Nicholas Andrea Dandolos was a reckless high-stakes player who became a Las Vegas legend. At 18, Nick went to Montreal and—with some inside information—quickly accumulated half-a-million dollars at the racetrack. He blew it just as quickly in Chicago at cards and dice. He is said to have won and lost more than $500 million in his lifetime. He spurned offers of hotel partnerships that would have made him financially independent. Raking in house percentages, he claimed, would have robbed him of the thrill of betting. He died broke.

Jackie Gaughan (b. 1920)   A Nebraskan who ran a bookie joint in an Omaha cigar store, Gaughan started out in Las Vegas by buying a

Impressions

Benny often found it necessary to arbitrate business differences with a .45 automatic.
—Article about Benny Binion, founder of Binion's Horseshoe Hotel and Casino, in *Texas Monthly* (Oct. 1991)

> ## Las Vegas Advisor
>
> Professional gambler and longtime Las Vegas resident Anthony Curtis, author of *Bargain City: Booking, Betting, and Beating the New Las Vegas,* knows all the angles for stretching your hotel, restaurant and—most important—gaming dollar. His 12-page monthly newsletter, the *Las Vegas Advisor,* is chock-full of insider tips on how to maximize your odds on every game, which slot tournaments to enter, casino promotions that represent money-making opportunities for the bettor, where to obtain the best fun books, which hotel offers a 12-ounce margarita for 99¢ or a steak dinner for $2, what are the best buffet and show values in town, and much, much more. Subscribers get $240 worth of coupons for discounts on rooms, meals, show tickets, and car rentals, along with free slot plays, two-for-one bets, and other perks. I would recommend it to regular Vegas visitors. A subscription is $45 a year, a single issue $5. To subscribe call 800/244-2224 or send a check to Las Vegas Advisor, 3687 Procyon St. Las Vegas, NV 89103.

3% interest in the Boulder Club in 1946. In 1951 he bought a 3% interest in the Flamingo. He went on to run the city's only race and sports book, the Saratoga, until 1959. In 1963 he bought the El Cortez. He now owns six Downtown Las Vegas properties, including the Gold Spike, the Plaza, Las Vegas Club, the Western Hotel & Bingo Parlor, and the Showboat. His son Michael owns the Barbary Coast and the Gold Coast.

Howard Hughes (1905–76)   Howard Hughes was the man who gave Las Vegas respectability. The richest man in America, he arrived in town in 1966 at a time when the Justice Department had begun focusing on mob involvement in Nevada gaming operations. Eccentric though he was (he hated sunlight and had the windows of his Desert Inn accommodations blacked out), his casino- and hotel-buying spree was a public relations bonanza for Las Vegas. The gambling public trusted him, and they began to trust Las Vegas casinos. During his 4-year residency, he became Nevada's largest employer, putting 8,000 people on his payroll. At one time his seven casinos accounted for 17% of the state's gaming revenues.

Impressions

They printed a lot of crap about Ben. He just wanted to be somebody. He used to pal around with Clark Gable, Gary Cooper, Cary Grant, and a lot of other big stars. I used to copy a lot of Ben's mannerisms when I played gangsters. Ben and the other tough guys . . . they were like gods to me. Ben had class, he was a real gentleman, and a real pal.
        —Movie star George Raft on his pal Benjamin "Bugsy" Siegel

Kirk Kerkorian (b. 1917)   The self-made son of Armenian immigrants who fled a Turkish massacre by cattle boat, Kerkorian grew up in California, where he dropped out of school in the eighth grade. He was a successful amateur boxer and a World War II army pilot. After the war, he started his own airline, beginning with one used C-47; when he sold the company in 1969 he walked off with $104 million. He built the International Hotel and bought the Flamingo, both of which he eventually sold to Hilton. He went on to build the MGM Grand in the 1970s (today Bally's). In 1993, he made another "grand" statement—the billion-dollar *Wizard of Oz*–themed MGM Grand megaresort and adjacent theme park. Next project: the 2,100-room New York-New York. Kerkorian is also Chrysler Corporation's largest single shareholder.

Thomas "Amarillo Slim" Preston (birthdate unknown)   In May 1972, Thomas Preston, a colorful Texas cattle rancher with a slow drawl, loped off with $60,000 at Binion's third World Series of Poker. Preston is a legendary gambler who has made—and won—many bizarre bets. He beat daredevil Evel Knievel at golf using a hammer instead of a club, outplayed Minnesota Fats at pool using a broom handle for a cue, and topped a Ping-Pong champ using a Coke bottle for a paddle.

Benjamin "Bugsy" Siegel (1906–47)   A nefarious underworld kingpin, Siegel opened his dream hotel—the mob-financed $6 million Flamingo—in December 1946. He was gunned down in Los Angeles six months later at the home of his girlfriend, Virginia Hill. Although he was never convicted of any crime (witnesses tended to suffer mysterious deaths), Siegel once boasted to fellow casino owner Del Webb that he had killed 20 men. His suite in the Flamingo had extra-thick walls, a secret trapdoor, and four exits.

Steve Wynn (b. 1942)   Wynn, whose father owned a chain of East Coast bingo parlors, first got into Las Vegas real estate by purchasing a small parking lot next to Caesars. Later he sold it back to Caesars and used the money to bankroll his purchase of the Golden Nugget in 1969. In 1989 Wynn's $620 million Mirage revolutionized the Strip with Disneyesque attractions such as dolphin and tiger habitats, an indoor rain forest, and an erupting volcano. In 1993 he followed this up with Treasure Island, another Strip extravaganza property with a swashbuckling pirate theme. And a third Steve Wynn Strip hotel called Bellagio is going up at this writing.

2

Planning a Trip
to Las Vegas

Las Vegas isn't a destination that requires a great deal of advance planning. However, you might want to read through the sightseeing and excursions chapters (7 and 11) in order to figure out how you want to budget your time, and call or write the organizations below for advance information.

1 Information

For advance information call or write the **Las Vegas Convention and Visitors Authority,** 3150 Paradise Rd., Las Vegas, NV 89109 (☎ 702/892-0711). They can send you a comprehensive packet of brochures, a map, show guide, events calendar, and attractions list; help you find a hotel that meets your specifications; and answer any questions. Or stop by when you're in town. They're open daily 8am to 5pm.

Another excellent information source is the **Las Vegas Chamber of Commerce,** 711 E. Desert Inn Rd., Las Vegas, NV 89109 (☎ 702/735-1616). Ask them to send you their *Visitor's Guide,* which contains extensive information about accommodations, attractions, excursions, children's activities, and more. They can answer all your Las Vegas-related questions, including those about weddings and divorces. They're open Monday to Friday 8am to 5pm.

And for information on all of Nevada, including Las Vegas, contact the **Nevada Commission on Tourism,** Capitol Complex, Carson City, NV 89701 (☎ 800/638-2328). They send out a comprehensive information packet on Nevada.

2 When to Go

Since most of a Las Vegas vacation is usually spent indoors, you can have a good time here year-round. The most pleasant seasons, as you'll see from the chart below, are spring and fall, especially if you want to take in some of the outdoor attractions described in chapters 7 and 11. Weekdays are slightly less crowded than weekends. Holidays are always a mob scene accompanied by high hotel prices. Hotel prices also

What Things Cost in Las Vegas	U.S. $
Taxi from the airport to the Strip	8–12.00
Taxi from the airport to Downtown	15–18.00
Minibus from the airport to the Strip	3.50
Minibus from the airport to Downtown	4.75
Double at Sheraton Desert Inn (very expensive)	155–175.00
Double at Luxor Las Vegas (expensive)	59–139.00
Double at the Sahara (moderate)	55–85.00
Double at Motel Six (budget)	35.99–47.99
Three-course dinner at Palace Court for one without tax or tip (very expensive)	70.00
Three-course dinner at Chin's for one without tax or tip (expensive)	35.00
Three-course dinner at Stage Deli for one without tax or tip (moderate)	20.00
Three-course dinner at Chili's for one without tax or tip (inexpensive)	15.00
All-you-can-eat buffet dinner at Circus Circus	4.99
All-you-can-eat buffet dinner at Caesars Palace	13.25
Bottle of beer	2.25
Coca-Cola	1.50
Cup of coffee	1.50
Roll of ASA 100 Kodacolor film, 36 exposures	4.70
Show ticket for the *Great Radio City Spectacular* cocktail show (including two drinks, tax, and gratuity)	28.29
Show ticket for *Enter the Night* (including two drinks and tax; gratuity extra)	26.90
Show ticket for headliners at Caesars (including tax and gratuity, drinks extra)	45–75.00
Show ticket for *Siegfried & Roy* (including two drinks, tax, and gratuity)	78.35

skyrocket when big conventions and special events are taking place. Call the **Las Vegas Convention and Visitors Authority** (☎ 800/ 332-5333) to find out if a major convention is to be held during your trip; if so, you might want to change your date.

One thing you'll hear again and again is that even though Las Vegas gets very hot, the dry desert heat is not uncomfortable. This is true. The humidity averages a low 22%, and even on very hot days there's apt to be a breeze. Also, except on the hottest summer days, there's relief at night when temperatures often drop as much as 20°.

Temperatures (°F) in Las Vegas

	Jan	Feb	Mar	Apr	May	June	July	Aug	Sept	Oct	Nov	Dec
Average	44	50	57	66	74	84	91	88	81	67	54	47
High	55	62	69	79	88	99	105	103	96	82	67	58
Low	33	39	44	53	60	68	76	74	65	53	41	36

LAS VEGAS CALENDAR OF EVENTS

You may be surprised that Las Vegas does not offer as many annual events as most tourist cities. The reason: Las Vegas wants people in the casinos, not off at Renaissance fairs and parades. When in town, check the local paper and call the **Las Vegas Convention and Visitors Authority** (☎ 702/892-0711), **Las Vegas Events** (☎ 702/731-2115), or the **Chamber of Commerce** (☎ 702/735-1616) to find out about other events scheduled during your visit.

January

- **The PBA Invitational.** The Showboat Hotel, 2800 Fremont St. (☎ 702/385-9150), hosts this major bowling tournament every January.

April

- **The World Series of Poker.** This famed 21-day event takes place at Binion's Horseshoe Casino, 128 Fremont St. (☎ 702/382-1600), in late April and early May, with high-stakes gamblers and show-biz personalities competing for six-figure purses. There are daily events with entry stakes ranging from $125 to $5,000. To enter the World Championship Event (purse $1 million), players must put up $10,000. It costs nothing to go watch the action.
- **Senior PGA Tour Las Vegas Senior Classic.** This 4-day event in late April or early May takes place at the Tournament Players Club (TPC), 1700 Village Center, in nearby Summerlin. For details and driving information, call 702/382-6616.

May

- **Helldorado.** This Elks-sponsored western heritage celebration takes place over a 10-day period in mid-May. It includes a western dress ("be seen in jeans") parade, a vast carnival midway, bull riders, a trail ride, a barbecue, and four major Professional Rodeo Cowboys Association (PRCA) rodeos at the Sam Boyd Stadium, located at Boulder Highway and Russell Road. For information call the Elks Lodge (☎ 702/870-1221) or check the local papers. The ticket office number is 702/895-3900.

Factoid

In 1995, Don Harrington entered a satellite event at the World Series of Poker for just $220, won his way into the $10,000 buy for the Championship Event, and went on to win the $1 million prize.

September

- **Oktoberfest.** This boisterous autumn holiday is celebrated from mid-September through the end of October at the Mount Charleston Resort (☎ 702/386-6899 or 800/955-1314) with music, folk dancers, sing-alongs around a roaring fire, special decorations, and Bavarian cookouts.

October

- **PGA Tour Las Vegas Invitational.** This 5-day championship event, played early in the month on three local courses, is televised by ESPN. For details call 702/382-6616.

December

- ✪ **National Finals Rodeo.** This is the superbowl of rodeos, attended by close to 170,000 people each year. The top 15 male rodeo stars compete in six different events: calf roping, bulldogging, Brahman bull riding, team roping, saddle bronc riding, and bareback bronc riding. And the top 15 women compete in barrel racing. An all-around "Cowboy of the Year" is chosen. In connection with this event, hotels book country stars in their showrooms, and there's a cowboy shopping spree—the NFR Cowboy Christmas Gift Show, a trade show for western gear—at Cashman Field.

    Where: At the 17,000-seat Thomas and Mack Center of UNLV. **When:** For 10 days during the first 2 weeks of the month. **How:** Order tickets as far in advance as possible by calling 702/895-3900.

- **Las Vegas Bowl Week.** A championship football event in mid-December pits the winners of the Mid-American Conference against the winners of the Big West Conference. The action takes place at the 32,000-seat Silver Bowl (☎ 702/731-2115 for ticket information). There are championship basketball and hockey games the same week at the Thomas and Mack Center (☎ 702/895-3900 for ticket information).

- **New Year's Eve.** This is a biggie (reserve your hotel room early). Downtown, Fremont Street is closed to traffic between Third and Main streets, and there's a big block party with two dramatic countdowns to midnight (the first is at 9pm, midnight on the East Coast). Of course, there are fireworks.

    There's also a big New Year's Eve gala at the Mount Charleston Resort (☎ 702/386-6899 or 800/955-1314). Make dinner reservations early and book a cabin for the night (☎ 702/872-5500). See chapter 11 for details.

3 Tips for Special Travelers

FOR THE DISABLED   Write or call **The Independent Living Program,** Nevada Association for the Handicapped, 6200 W. Oakey Blvd., Las Vegas, NV 89102 (☎ 702/870-7050). They can recommend hotels and restaurants that meet your needs, help you find a personal attendant, advise about transportation, and answer all questions.

In addition, the **Nevada Commission on Tourism,** Capitol Complex, Carson City, NV 89701 (☎ 800/638-2328), offers a free accommodations guide to Las Vegas hotels that includes access information.

Some nationwide resources include two helpful travel organizations—**Accessible Journeys** (☎ 610/521-0339 or 800/TINGLES) and **Flying Wheels Travel** (☎ 507/451-5005 or 800/535-6790)— offer tours, cruises, and custom vacations worldwide for people with physical disabilities; Accessible Journeys can also provide nurses/ companions to travelers. **The Guided Tour Inc.** (☎ 215/782-1370 or 800/783-5841) has tours for people with physical or mental disabilities, the visually impaired, and the elderly.

Mobility International USA, P.O. Box 10767, Eugene, OR 97440 (☎ 503/343-1284), offers accessibility and resource information to its members and has many interesting travel programs for the disabled. Membership ($25 a year) includes a quarterly newsletter called *Over the Rainbow.*

There's no charge for help via telephone (accessibility information and more) from the **Travel Information Service** (☎ 215/456-9600). Another organization, the **Society for the Advancement of Travel for the Handicapped (SATH),** 347 Fifth Ave., Suite 610, New York, NY 10016 (☎ 212/447-7284) charges $5 for sending requested information.

Recommended books: A publisher called **Twin Peaks Press,** Box 129, Vancouver, WA 98666 (☎ 360/694-2462), specializes in books for people with disabilities. Write for their *Disability Bookshop Catalog,* enclosing $5.

Amtrak (☎ 800/USA-RAIL) provides redcap service (at all major stations), wheelchair assistance, and special seats with 72 hours' notice. The disabled are also entitled to a 25% discount on one-way regular coach fares. Documentation from a doctor or an ID card proving your disability is required. Amtrak also provides wheelchair-accessible sleeping accommodations on long-distance trains, and guide dogs are permitted and travel free of charge. Write for a free booklet called *Amtrak's America* from Amtrak Distribution Center, P.O. Box 7717, Itasca, IL 60143, which has a section on services for passengers with disabilities. *Note:* If you will need help with bags on arrival, arrange it with Amtrak when you reserve. The Las Vegas station has no redcap service.

Greyhound (☎ 800/752-4841) allows a disabled person to travel with a companion for a single fare. Call at least 48 hours in advance to discuss this and other special needs.

Airlines don't offer special fares to the disabled. When making your flight reservations, ask where your wheelchair will be stowed on the plane and if your guide dog may accompany you.

FOR SENIORS   Always carry some form of photo ID that includes your birthdate so you can take advantage of discounts wherever they're offered. And it never hurts to ask.

If you haven't already done so, consider joining the **American Association of Retired Persons** (☎ 202/434-2277). Annual membership costs $8 per person or couple. You must be at least 50 to join. Membership entitles you to many discounts. Write to Purchase Privilege Program, AARP Fulfillment, 601 E St. NW, Washington, DC 20049, to receive their *Purchase Privilege* brochure—a free list of hotels, motels, and car-rental firms nationwide that offer discounts to AARP members.

Another good source of reduced-price information is *The Discount Guide for Travelers Over 55* by Caroline and Walter Weinz (E. P. Dutton).

Elderhostel is a national organization that offers low-priced educational programs for people over 55 (your spouse can be any age; a companion must be at least 50). Programs are generally a week long, and prices average about $335 per person, including room, board, and classes. For information on programs in Nevada call or write Elderhostel headquarters, 75 Federal St., Boston, MA 02110 (☎ 617/426-8056), and ask for a free catalog.

Amtrak (☎ **800/USA-RAIL**) offers a 15% discount off the lowest available coach fare (with certain travel restrictions) to people 62 or over.

Greyhound also offers discounted fares for senior citizens. Call your local Greyhound office for details.

FOR FAMILIES Las Vegas in the '90s is doing its utmost to promote itself as a family vacation destination. Kids just adore the place. Everything for them is geared to having fun; nothing is educational. See the "Especially for Kids" suggestions in chapter 7. A few general suggestions to make traveling with kids easier:

If they're old enough, let the kids write to various tourist offices for information and color brochures. If you're driving, give them a map on which they can outline the route. Let them help decide your sightseeing itinerary.

Although your home may be toddler-proof, hotel accommodations are not. Bring blank plugs to cover outlets, and whatever else is necessary.

Carry a few simple games to relieve the tedium of traveling. Packing snacks will also help and save money. If you're using public transportation (Amtrak, airlines, bus), always inquire about discounted fares for children.

Children under 12, and in many cases even older, stay free in their parents' rooms in most hotels. Look for establishments that have pools and other recreational facilities (see "Family-Friendly Hotels" in chapter 5).

4 Getting There

BY AIR

THE MAJOR AIRLINES

The following airlines have regularly scheduled flights into Las Vegas (some of these are regional carriers, so they may not all fly from your

Las Vegas & Environs

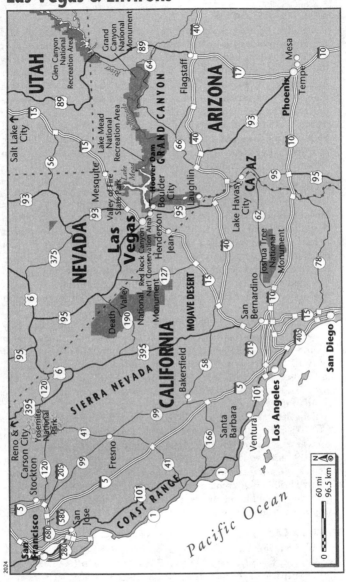

point of origin): **Alaska Airlines** (☎ 800/426-0333), **America West** (☎ 800/548-8969), **American** (☎ 800/433-7300), **American Trans Air** (☎ 800/543-3708), **Continental** (☎ 800/525-0280), **Delta** (☎ 800/221-1212), **Frontier** (☎ 800/432-1359), **Hawaiian** (☎ 800/367-5320), **Northwest** (☎ 800/225-2525), **Reno Air** (☎ 800/736-6247), **Southwest** (☎ 800/435-9792), **TWA** (☎ 800/221-2000), **United** (☎ 800/241-6522), and **USAir** (☎ 800/428-4322).

FINDING THE BEST AIRFARE

Generally, the least expensive fares (except for special packages and special-promotion discount fares you see announced in newspaper travel sections) are **advance-purchase fares** that involve certain restrictions. For example, in addition to paying for your ticket 3 to 21 days in advance, you may have to leave or return on certain days, stay a maximum or minimum number of days, and so on. Also, advance-purchase fares are often nonrefundable. Nonetheless, the restrictions are usually within the framework of one's vacation plans, and savings of $500 and more are not unusual. You can also save money by booking airline packages, which are discussed later in this chapter in "Money-Saving Packages."

THE LAS VEGAS AIRPORT

Las Vegas is served by **McCarran International Airport,** 5757 Wayne Newton Blvd. (☎ 702/261-5743), just a few minutes' drive from the southern end of the Strip. It's a big, modern airport, and rather unique in that it includes a vast casino area with more than 700 slot machines. Although these are reputed to offer lower paybacks than hotel casinos (the airport has a captive audience and doesn't need to lure repeat customers), I can never resist the lure of throwing in a few quarters on arrival. And happily, getting to your hotel from the airport is a cinch.

   Bell Trans (☎ 702/739-7990) runs 20-passenger minibuses daily between the airport and all major Las Vegas hotels and motels almost around the clock (4:30am to 2am). Buses from the airport leave about every 10 minutes. For departure from your hotel, call at least 2 hours in advance. The cost is $3.50 per person each way to Strip and Convention Center area hotels, $4.75 to downtown properties (any place north of the Sahara Hotel and west of I-15).

   Even less expensive are **Citizen's Area Transit (CAT)** buses (☎ 702/CAT-RIDE). The no. 302 bus departs from the airport and stops at or close to most Strip and Convention Center area hotels. The no. 109 bus goes from the airport to the Downtown Transportation Center at Casino Center Blvd. and Stewart Ave. The fare for the no. 302 is $1.50, 50¢ for seniors and children. *Note:* If you have heavy luggage, you should know that you might have a long walk from the bus stop to your door (even if it's right in front of your hotel).

RENTING A CAR

All of the major car-rental companies are represented in Las Vegas. I always rent from **Allstate** (☎ 702/736-6148 or 800/634-6186), the least expensive of the airport-based car-rental agencies. Their fleet of more than 1,500 vehicles includes—besides the usual mix—an inventory of 15 passenger vans, four-wheel drives, jeeps, minivans, sports cars, and convertibles. I've always found this local family-owned company (the largest independent operator in Las Vegas) friendly and competent; they're open 24 hours. And they've agreed to offer my readers a **20% discount off regular rental rates** at any Allstate location (just show the agent your copy of this book). In addition to McCarran Airport, there are Allstate car desks at the Aladdin, Hacienda, Riviera,

---

I Do, I Do

More than 100,000 weddings take place in Las Vegas each year. If you feel ready to take the plunge, call **Las Vegas Weddings and Rooms** (☎ 800/488-MATE), a one-stop shop for wedding services. They'll find a chapel or outdoor garden that suits your taste (not to mention such only-in-Vegas venues as the former mansions of Elvis Presley and Liberace), book you into a hotel for the honeymoon, arrange the ceremony, and provide flowers, a photographer (or videographer), wedding cake, limo, car rental, music, champagne, balloons, and a garter for the bride. They even have a New Age minister on call who can perform a Native American ceremony. Let Las Vegas Weddings arrange your honeymoon stay—sightseeing tours, show tickets, and meals, as well.

Sahara, Stardust, and Jackie Gaughan's Plaza hotels, and the company offers free pickup anywhere in Las Vegas.

Other companies with outlets in Las Vegas include **Alamo** (☎ 800/327-9633), **Avis** (☎ 800/367-2847), **Budget** (☎ 800/922-2899), **Dollar** (800/826-9911), **Enterprise** (☎ 800/325/8007), **Hertz** (☎ 800/654-3131), and **National** (☎ 800/227-7368).

BY TRAIN

If you arrive on **Amtrak** (☎ 702/386-6896 or 800/USA-RAIL), you'll be at the depot right downtown, at Main and Fremont Streets. From there, you can take a taxi to your hotel or board CAT bus no. 301 at the **Downtown Transportation Center,** 300 Casino Center Blvd., at Stewart Avenue (five blocks away) to Strip hotels. A taxi to the Strip will cost about $11 to $15. The bus fare is $1.50.

BY BUS

Greyhound buses (☎ 702/384-9561, or 800/231-2222 for reservations and information) connect the entire country with Las Vegas. Their downtown terminal (200 S. Main St., at Carson Street) is adjacent to the Amtrak station. Once again, you can take a taxi or catch the no. 301 bus at the Downtown Transportation Center to Strip hotels. The bus fare structure tends to be complex, but the good news is that when you call to purchase a ticket in advance, the agent will always give you the lowest fare options. Advance-purchase fares, booked 3 to 21 days prior to travel, can save you up to 50%.

BY CAR

The main highway connecting Las Vegas with the rest of the country is I-15; it links Montana, Idaho, and Utah with southern California. From the East Coast, take I-70 or I-80 west to Kingman, Arizona, and then U.S. 93 north to Downtown Las Vegas (Fremont Street). From the south, take I-10 west to Phoenix and then U.S. 93 north to Las Vegas. From San Francisco, take I-80 east to Reno and then

Driving Distances to Las Vegas (in miles)

Chicago	1,766
Dallas	1,230
Denver	759
Los Angeles	269
New York City	2,564
Phoenix	286
Salt Lake City	421
San Francisco	586

U.S. 95 south to Las Vegas. Be sure to read the driving precautions under "By Car" in chapter 4's "Getting Around" section.

MONEY-SAVING PACKAGES

When you make reservations on any airline, also inquire about money-saving packages that include hotel accommodations, car rentals, tours, and so forth, with your airfare.

For instance, a **Delta Dream Vacation** package leaving from New York, priced at about $369 to $389 (per person based on double occupancy) includes round-trip coach air transportation, two nights accommodations at your choice of several major casino hotels (these prices were for the Tropicana), a rental car for 24 hours, airport transfers, and bonus discounts and admissions. Prices vary according to the season, as do seat availability and hotel choices, and whether you travel midweek or on the weekend, etc. Since even an advance-purchase round-trip fare between New York and Las Vegas is, as I write, $518 per person, it seems almost insane not to book a less expensive package that includes so many extras. For details on Delta packages, consult your travel agent or call the airline directly (☎ 800/872-7786).

Similar packages are available from such airlines as **American** (☎ 800/321-221), **America West** (800/356-6611), and **USAir** (☎ 800/455-0123), all of which also offer packages directly or through a travel agent.

3

For Foreign Visitors

This chapter will provide some specifics about getting to the United States as economically and effortlessly as possible, plus some helpful information about how things are done in Las Vegas—from receiving mail to making a local or long-distance telephone call.

1 Preparing for Your Trip

ENTRY REQUIREMENTS
DOCUMENT REGULATIONS

Canadian nationals need only proof of Canadian residence to visit the United States. Citizens of the United Kingdom, Japan, and most Western European countries need only a current passport. Citizens of other countries, including Australia and New Zealand, usually need two documents: a valid passport with an expiration date at least 6 months later than the scheduled end of their visit to the United States and a tourist visa, available at no charge from a U.S. embassy or consulate.

To get a tourist or business visa to enter the United States, contact the nearest American embassy or consulate in your country; if there is none, you will have to apply in person in a country where there is a U.S. embassy or consulate. Present your passport, a passport-size photo of yourself, and a completed application, which is available through the embassy or consulate. You may be asked to provide information about how you plan to finance your trip or show a letter of invitation from a friend with whom you plan to stay. Those applying for a business visa may be asked to show evidence that they will not receive a salary in the United States. Be sure to check the length of stay on your visa; usually it is six months. If you want to stay longer, you may file for an extension with the Immigration and Naturalization Service once you are in the country. If permission to stay is granted, a new visa is not required unless you leave the United States and want to reenter.

MEDICAL REQUIREMENTS

No inoculations are needed to enter the United States unless you are coming from, or have stopped over in, areas known to be suffering from epidemics, particularly cholera or yellow fever.

If you have a disease requiring treatment with medications containing narcotics or drugs requiring a syringe, carry a valid signed generic prescription from your physician to allay any suspicions that you are smuggling drugs. The prescription brands you are accustomed to buying in your country may not be available in the United States.

CUSTOMS REQUIREMENTS

Every adult visitor may bring in, free of duty: 1 liter of wine or hard liquor; 200 cigarettes or 100 cigars (but no cigars from Cuba) or 3 pounds of smoking tobacco; and $100 worth of gifts. These exemptions are offered to travelers who spend at least 72 hours in the United States and who have not claimed them within the preceding 6 months. It is altogether forbidden to bring foodstuffs (particularly cheese, fruit, cooked meats, and canned goods) and plants (vegetables, seeds, tropical plants, and so on) into the country. Foreign tourists may bring in or take out up to $10,000 in U.S. or foreign currency with no formalities; larger sums must be declared to Customs on entering or leaving.

INSURANCE

Unlike most other countries, the United States does not have a national health system. Because the cost of medical care is extremely high, we strongly advise all travelers to secure health coverage before setting out on their trip. You may want to take out a comprehensive travel policy that covers (for a relatively low premium) sickness or injury costs (medical, surgical, and hospital); loss or theft of your baggage; trip-cancellation costs; guarantee of bail in case you are arrested; costs of accident, repatriation, or death. Such packages (for example, "Europe Assistance" in Europe) are sold by automobile clubs at attractive rates, as well as by insurance companies and travel agencies and at some airports.

MONEY

The U.S. monetary system has a decimal base: One American dollar ($1) = 100 cents (100¢). Dollar bills commonly come in $1 (a buck), $5, $10, $20, $50, and $100 denominations (the last two are not welcome when paying for small purchases and are usually not accepted in taxis or at subway ticket booths). There are six coin denominations: 1¢ (one cent or "penny"); 5¢ (five cents or "nickel"); 10¢ (ten cents or "dime"); 25¢ (twenty-five cents or "quarter"); 50¢ (fifty cents or "half dollar"); and the $1 pieces (both the older, large silver dollar and the newer, small Susan B. Anthony coin).

Traveler's checks in U.S. dollars are accepted at most hotels, motels, restaurants, and large stores. Sometimes picture identification is required. American Express, Thomas Cook, and Barclay's Bank traveler's checks are readily accepted in the United States.

Credit cards are the method of payment most widely used: Visa (BarclayCard in Britain), MasterCard (EuroCard in Europe, Access in Britain, Diamond in Japan), American Express, Discover, Diners Club, enRoute, JCB, and Carte Blanche, in descending order of acceptance. You can save yourself trouble by using "plastic" rather than cash or traveler's checks in almost all hotels, motels, restaurants, and retail stores. A credit card can also serve as a deposit for renting a car, as proof of identity, or as a "cash card," enabling you to draw money from automatic-teller machines (ATMs) that accept them.

If you plan to travel for several weeks or more in the United States, you may want to deposit enough money into your credit-card account to cover anticipated expenses and avoid finance charges in your absence. This also reduces the likelihood of your receiving an unwelcome big bill on your return.

You can telegraph money, or have it telegraphed to you very quickly using the **Western Union** system (☎ 800/325-6000).

SAFETY

While tourist areas are generally safe, crime is on the increase everywhere, and U.S. urban areas tend to be less safe than those in Europe or Japan. Visitors should always stay alert. This is particularly true of large U.S. cities. It is wise to ask the city's or area's tourist office if you're in doubt about which neighborhoods are safe.

Remember also that hotels are open to the public, and in a large hotel, security may not be able to screen everyone entering. Always lock your room door—don't assume that once inside your hotel you are automatically safe and no longer need be aware of your surroundings.

DRIVING

Safety while driving is particularly important. Question your rental agency about personal safety, or ask for a brochure of traveler safety tips when you pick up your car. Obtain written directions, or a map with the route marked in red, from the agency showing how to get to your destination. And, if possible, arrive and depart during daylight hours.

Recently more and more crime has involved cars and drivers. If you drive off a highway into a doubtful neighborhood, leave the area as quickly as possible. If you have an accident, even on the highway, stay in your car with the doors locked until you assess the situation or until the police arrive. If you are bumped from behind on the street or are involved in a minor accident with no injuries and the situation appears to be suspicious, motion to the other driver to follow you. Never get out of your car in such situations.

If you see someone on the road who indicates a need for help, do not stop. Take note of the location, drive on to a well-lighted area, and telephone the police by dialing 911. Park in well-lighted, well-traveled areas if possible.

Always keep your car doors locked, whether attended or unattended. Never leave any packages or valuables in sight. If someone attempts to rob you or steal your car, do not try to resist the thief/carjacker—report the incident to the police department immediately.

2   Getting to the U.S.

Travelers from overseas can take advantage of the APEX (advance purchase excursion) fares offered by all the major U.S. and European carriers. Aside from these, attractive values are offered by Virgin Atlantic from London.

A number of U.S. airlines offer service from Europe to the United States. If they do not have direct flights from Europe to Las Vegas, they can book you straight through on a connecting flight. You can make reservations by calling the following numbers in London: **American** (☎ 0181/572-5555), **Continental** (☎ 4412/9377-6464), **Delta** (☎ 0800/414-767), and **United** (☎ 0181/990-9900).

And of course many international carriers serve LAX and/or San Francisco International Airport. Helpful numbers to know include **Virgin Atlantic** (☎ 0293/747-747 in London), **British Airways** (☎ 0345/222-111 in London), and **Aer Lingus** (☎ 01/844-4747 in Dublin or 061/415-556 in Shannon). **Qantas** (☎ 008/177-767 in Australia) has flights from Sydney to Los Angeles and San Francisco; you can also take United from Australia to the West Coast. **Air New Zealand** (☎ 0800/737-000 in Auckland or 643/379-5200 in Christchurch) also offers service to LAX. Canadian readers might book flights on **Air Canada** (☎ in Canada 800/268-7240 or 800/361-8620), which offers direct service from Toronto, Montreal, Calgary, and Vancouver to San Francisco and Los Angeles.

The visitor arriving by air, no matter what the port of entry, should cultivate patience and resignation before setting foot on U.S. soil. Getting through immigration control may take as long as 2 hours on some days, especially summer weekends, so have your guidebook or something else to read handy. Add the time it takes to clear customs and you will see you should make a very generous allowance for delay in planning connections between international and domestic flights—figure on 2 to 3 hours at least.

In contrast, for the traveler arriving by car or by rail from Canada, the border-crossing formalities have been streamlined to the vanishing point. And for the traveler by air from Canada, Bermuda, and some places in the Caribbean, you can sometimes go through Customs and Immigration at the point of departure, which is much quicker.

3 Getting Around the U.S.

On their transatlantic or transpacific flights, some large U.S. airlines offer special discount tickets for any of their U.S. destinations (American Airline's Visit USA program and Delta's Discover America program, for example). The tickets or coupons are not on sale in the United States and must be purchased before you leave your point of departure. This system is the best, easiest, and fastest way to see the United States at low cost. You should obtain information well in advance from your travel agent or the office of the airline concerned, since the conditions attached to these discount tickets can be changed without advance notice.

International visitors can also buy a **USA Railpass,** good for 15 or 30 days of unlimited travel on Amtrak. The pass is available through many foreign travel agents. Prices in 1996 for a 15-day pass are $245 off-peak, $355 peak; a 30-day pass costs $350 off-peak, $440 peak (peak is June 17 to August 21). (With a foreign passport, you can also buy passes at some Amtrak offices in the United States including locations in San Francisco, Los Angeles, Chicago, New York, Miami,

Boston, and Washington, D.C.) Reservations are generally required and should be made for each part of your trip as early as possible.

Visitors should also be aware of the limitations of long-distance rail travel in the United States. With a few notable exceptions (for instance, the Northeast Corridor line between Boston and Washington, D.C.), service is rarely up to European standards: delays are common, routes are limited and often infrequently served, and fares are rarely significantly lower than discount airfares. Thus, cross-country train travel should be approached with caution. Amtrak does serve Las Vegas.

The cheapest way to travel the United States is by bus. Greyhound/Trailways, the sole nationwide bus line, offers an **Ameripass** for unlimited travel for 7 days (for $179), 15 days (for $289), and 30 days (for $399). Bus travel in the United States can be both slow and uncomfortable, so this option is not for everyone. In addition, bus stations are often located in undesirable neighborhoods. Happily, the one in Las Vegas is conveniently located downtown.

FAST FACTS: For the Foreign Traveler

Automobile Organizations Auto clubs will supply maps, suggested routes, guidebooks, accident and bail-bond insurance, and emergency road service. The major auto club in the United States, with 955 offices nationwide, is the American Automobile Association (AAA). Members of some foreign auto clubs have reciprocal arrangements with the AAA and enjoy its services at no charge. If you belong to an auto club, inquire about AAA reciprocity before you leave. The AAA can provide you with an International Driving Permit validating your foreign license, although drivers with valid licenses from most home countries don't really need this permit. You may be able to join the AAA even if you are not a member of a reciprocal club. To inquire, call 619/233-1000. In addition, some automobile rental agencies now provide these services, so you should inquire about their availability when you rent your car.

Business Hours Offices are usually open weekdays from 9am to 5pm. Banks are open weekdays from 9am to 3pm or later and sometimes Saturday morning. Shops, especially those in shopping complexes, tend to stay open late: until about 9pm weekdays and until 6pm weekends.

Climate See "When to Go" in chapter 2.

Currency See "Preparing for Your Trip" earlier in this chapter.

Currency Exchange The "foreign-exchange bureaus" so common in Europe are rare in the United States. They're at major international airports, and there are a few in most major cities, but they're nonexistent in medium-size cities and small towns. Try to avoid having to change foreign money, or traveler's checks denominated other than in U.S. dollars, at small-town banks, or even at branches in a big city; in fact leave any currency other than U.S. dollars at home (except the cash you need for the taxi or bus ride home when you return to your own country); otherwise, your own currency may prove more nuisance to you than it's worth.

Las Vegas casinos can exchange foreign currency, usually at a good rate.

Drinking Laws   The legal age to drink alcohol is 21.

Electric Current   The United States uses 110–120 volts, 60 cycles, compared to 220–240 volts, 50 cycles, as in most of Europe. Besides a 100-volt converter, small appliances of non-American manufacture, such as hairdryers or shavers, will require a plug adapter, with two flat, parallel pins. The easiest solution to the power struggle is to purchase dual voltage appliances which operate on both 110 and 220 volts and then all that is required is a U.S. adapter plug.

Embassies/Consulates   All embassies are located in Washington, D.C. Listed here are the West Coast consulates of the major English-speaking countries. The Australian Consulate is located at 611 N. Larchmont, Los Angeles, CA 90004 (☎ 213/469-4300). The Canadian Consulate is at 300 South Grand Ave., Suite 1000, Los Angeles, CA 90071 (☎ 213/346-2700). The Irish Consulate is located at 655 Montgomery St., Suite 930, San Francisco, CA 94111 (☎ 415/392-4214). The New Zealand Consulate is at 12400 Wilshire Blvd., Los Angeles, CA 90025 (☎ 310/207-1605). Contact the U.K. Consulate at 11766 Wilshire Blvd., Suite 400, Los Angeles, CA 90025 (☎ 310/477-3322).

Emergencies   Call **911** for fire, police, and ambulance. If you encounter such traveler's problems as sickness, accident, or lost or stolen baggage, call Traveler's Aid, an organization that specializes in helping distressed travelers. In Las Vegas, there is an office in McCarran International Airport (☎ 702/798-1742), which is open daily from 8am to 5pm. Similar services are provided by Help of Southern Nevada, 953 E. Sahara Ave., Suite 23B, at Maryland Parkway in the Commercial Center on the northeast corner (☎ 702/369-4357). Hours are Monday to Friday, from 8am to 4pm.

Holidays   On the following national legal holidays, banks, government offices, post offices, and many stores, restaurants, and museums are closed: January 1 (New Year's Day), third Monday in January (Martin Luther King, Jr. Day), third Monday in February (Presidents' Day), last Monday in May (Memorial Day), July 4 (Independence Day), first Monday in September (Labor Day), second Monday in October (Columbus Day), November 11 (Veterans Day/Armistice Day), fourth Thursday in November (Thanksgiving Day), and December 25 (Christmas Day). The Tuesday following the first Monday in November is Election Day.

Legal Aid   If you are stopped for a minor infraction (for example, of the highway code, such as speeding), never attempt to pay the fine directly to a police officer; you may be arrested on the much more serious charge of attempted bribery. Pay fines by mail, or directly into the hands of the clerk of the court. If accused of a more serious offense, it is best to say and do nothing before consulting a lawyer. Under U.S. law, an arrested person is allowed one telephone call to a party of his or her choice. Call your embassy or consulate.

Mail   You may receive mail c/o General Delivery at the main post office of the city or region where you expect to be. The addressee must pick it up in person, and must produce proof of identity (driver's license, credit card, passport).

Mailboxes are blue with a red-and-white logo, and carry the inscription U.S. MAIL. Within the United States, it costs 20¢ to mail a standard-size postcard. Letters that weigh up to 1 ounce cost 32¢, plus 23¢ for each additional ounce. A postcard to Mexico costs 30¢, a $1/2$-ounce letter 35¢; a postcard to Canada costs 30¢, a 1-ounce letter 40¢. A postcard to Europe, Australia, New Zealand, the Far East, South America, and elsewhere costs 40¢, while a letter is 50¢ for each $1/2$ ounce.

Medical Emergencies   See "Emergencies" above.

Taxes   In the United States there is no VAT (value-added tax) or other indirect tax at a national level. There is a $10 Customs tax, payable on entry to the United States, and a $6 departure tax. Sales tax is levied on goods and services by state and local governments, however, and is not included in the price tags you'll see on merchandise. These taxes are not refundable.

Telephone and Fax   Pay phones can be found on street corners, as well as in bars, restaurants, public buildings, stores and at service stations. Some accept 20¢, most are 25¢. If the telephone accepts 20¢, you may also use a quarter (25¢) but you will not receive change.

In the past few years, many American companies have installed "voice-mail" systems, so be prepared to deal with a machine instead of a receptionist if calling a business number. Listen carefully to the instructions (you'll probably be asked to dial 1, 2, or 3 or wait for an operator to pick up); if you can't understand, sometimes dialing zero will put you in touch with an operator within the company. It's frustrating even for locals!

For long-distance or international calls, it's most economical to charge the call to a telephone charge card or a credit card; or you can use a lot of change. The pay phone will instruct you how much to deposit and when to deposit it into the slot on the top of the telephone box.

For long-distance calls in the United States, dial 1 followed by the area code and number you want. For direct overseas calls, first dial 011, followed by the country code (Australia, 61; Republic of Ireland, 353; New Zealand, 64; United Kingdom, 44; and so on), and then by the city code (for example, 71 or 81 for London, 21 for Birmingham, 1 for Dublin) and the number of the person you wish to call.

Before calling from a hotel room, always ask the hotel phone operator if there are any telephone surcharges. There almost always are, and they often are as much as 75¢ or $1, even for a local call. These charges are best avoided by using a public phone, calling collect, or using a telephone charge card.

For reversed-charge or collect calls and for person-to-person calls, dial 0 (zero, not the letter "O") followed by the area code and number you want; an operator will then come on the line, and you should specify that you are calling collect, or person-to-person, or both. If your operator-assisted call is international, immediately ask to speak with an overseas operator.

Telephone Directory   The local phone company provides two kinds of telephone directories. The general directory, called the "white pages," lists businesses and personal residences separately, in alphabetical order. The first few pages are devoted to community-service numbers, including a guide to long-distance and international calling, complete with country codes and area codes.

The second directory, the "yellow pages," lists all local services, businesses, and industries by type, with an index at the back. The listings cover not only such obvious items as automobile repairs by make of car, or drugstores (pharmacies), often by geographical location, but also restaurants by type of cuisine and geographical location, bookstores by special subject and/or language, places of worship by religious denomination, and other information that a visitor might otherwise not readily find. The yellow pages also include city plans or detailed area maps, often showing postal ZIP codes and public transportation.

For local directory assistance ("Information"), dial 411; for long-distance information dial 1, then the appropriate area code and **555-1212.**

Most hotels have fax machines available for their customers and there is usually a charge to send or receive a facsimile. You will also see signs for public faxes in the windows of small shops.

Time   Nevada is on Pacific time, which is 3 hours earlier than on the U.S. East Coast. For instance, when it is noon in Las Vegas, it is 3pm in New York and Miami; 2pm in Chicago, in the central part of the country; and 1pm in Denver, Colorado, in the midwestern part of the country. Nevada, like most of the rest of the United States, observes daylight saving time during the summer; in late spring, clocks are moved ahead 1 hour and then are turned back again in the fall. This results in lovely long summer evenings, when the sun sets as late as 8:30 or 9pm.

Tipping   Some rules of thumb: bartenders, 10–15%; bellhops, at least 50¢ per bag, or $2–$3 for a lot of luggage; cab drivers, 10% of the fare; chambermaids, $1 per day; checkroom attendants, $1 per garment; hairdressers and barbers, 15–20%; waiters and waitresses, 15–20% of the check; valet parking attendants, $1; showroom maître d's, see chapter 10 for details; casino dealers, a few dollars if you've had a big win.

4

Getting to Know
Las Vegas

Located in the southernmost precincts of a wide, pancake-flat valley, Las Vegas is the biggest city in the state of Nevada. Treeless mountains form a scenic backdrop to hotels awash in neon glitter. For tourism purposes, the city is quite compact.

1 Orientation

TOURIST INFORMATION

All major Las Vegas hotels provide comprehensive tourist information at their reception and/or sightseeing and show desks. Other good information sources are: the **Las Vegas Convention and Visitors Authority,** 3150 Paradise Rd., Las Vegas, NV 89109 (☎ 702/892-0711, daily 8am to 5pm); the **Las Vegas Chamber of Commerce,** 711 E. Desert Inn Rd., Las Vegas, NV 89109 (☎ 702/735-1616, Monday to Friday 8am to 5pm), and, for information on all of Nevada, including Las Vegas, the **Nevada Commission on Tourism,** Capitol Complex, Carson City, NV 89710 (☎ 800/638-2328).

FOR TROUBLED TRAVELERS

The **Traveler's Aid Society** is a social-service organization geared to helping travelers in difficult straits. Their services might include reuniting families separated while traveling, providing food and/or shelter to people stranded without cash, or even emotional counseling. If you're in trouble, seek them out. In Las Vegas there is a Traveler's Aid office at McCarran International Airport (☎ 702/798-1742). It's open daily from 8am to 5pm. Similar services are provided by **Help of Southern Nevada,** 953 E. Sahara Ave. (suite 23B), at Maryland Parkway in the Commercial Center at the northeast corner (☎ 702/369-4357). Hours are Monday to Friday 8am to 4pm.

CITY LAYOUT

Nothing could be simpler than the layout of Las Vegas—especially the three areas of interest to tourists.

THE STRIP

The Strip is probably the most famous 3½-mile stretch of highway in the nation. Officially Las Vegas Boulevard South, it contains most of the top hotels in town and offers almost all of the major showroom entertainment. It extends from just below Tropicana Avenue at the southernmost end—where you'll find the MGM Grand, Tropicana, Excalibur, Luxor, and Hacienda hotels—to Sahara Avenue, where the Sahara hotel anchors the northern boundary.

CONVENTION CENTER

This is a sort of eastern addition to the Strip that has grown up around the Las Vegas Convention Center. Las Vegas is one of the nation's top convention cities, attracting about 2.7 million conventioneers each year. The major hotel in this section is the Las Vegas Hilton, but in recent years Marriott has built Residence Inn and Courtyard properties here, the Debbie Reynolds Hotel & Casino has opened, and many excellent smaller hotels and motels are arrayed southward along Paradise Road. All of these offer close proximity to the Strip.

DOWNTOWN

Also known as "Glitter Gulch" (narrower streets make the neon seem brighter), Downtown Las Vegas, which is centered on Fremont Street between Main and 9th Streets, was the first section of the city to develop hotels and casinos. For the most part, it's more casual than the Strip—a "just-folks" kind of place—and the room rates are generally lower. There are exceptions, however—notably the gleaming white, palm-fringed Golden Nugget, which looks like it belongs in Monte Carlo. And with the advent of the revitalizing Fremont Street Experience (see chapter 7 for details), Downtown is becoming more upscale these days. Still, it remains easier to find casinos offering low minimum bets Downtown. Should you want to go casino-hopping, this area is more compact and the hotels closer together. Las Vegas Boulevard runs all the way into Fremont Street downtown (about a 5-minute drive). The area between the Strip and Downtown is a seedy stretch dotted with tacky wedding chapels, bail-bond operations, pawn-shops, and cheap motels.

2 Getting Around

I can't think of any tourist destination that is easier to navigate than Las Vegas. The hotels are the major attractions and they're clustered in two different areas—on and around the Strip/Convention Center area and Downtown. Even first-time visitors will feel like natives after a day or two.

BY PUBLIC TRANSPORTATION

The no. 301 bus operated by **Citizens Area Transit** (☎ 702/ CAT-RIDE) plies a route between the Downtown Transportation Center (at Casino Center Boulevard and Stewart Avenue) and a few miles beyond the southern end of the Strip. The fare is $1.50 for adults, 50¢ for seniors (62 and older) and children 5 to 17, and free

Las Vegas at a Glance

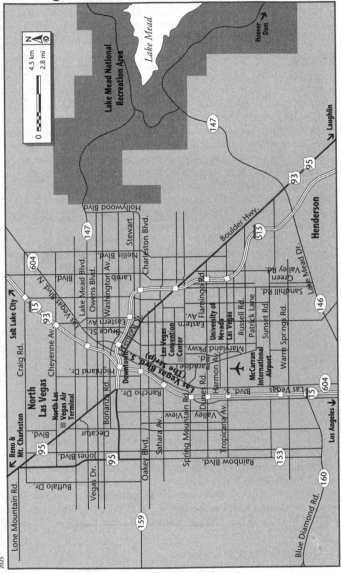

for those under 5. CAT buses run 24 hours a day and are wheel-chair-accessible. Exact change is required, but dollar bills are accepted.

Or you can hop aboard a classic streetcar replica run by **Las Vegas Strip Trolley** (☎ 702/382-1404). These old-fashioned dark-green vehicles have interior oak paneling and are comfortably air-conditioned. Like the buses, they run northward from the Hacienda, stopping at all major hotels en route to the Sahara, and then looping back via the

Las Vegas Hilton. They do not, however, go Downtown. Trolleys run every 20 to 30 minutes daily between 9:30am and 2am. The fare is $1.20 (under 5 free), and exact change is required.

BY CAR

Although it is possible to get around in Las Vegas without a car, I love to have one at my disposal. Parking is a pleasure, since all casino hotels offer valet service. That means that for a mere $1 tip you can park right at the door. And in sweltering summer heat, the valet will bring back your car with the air-conditioning already turned on. Furthermore, though bus tours are available to nearby attractions, a car lets you explore at your own pace rather than according to a tour schedule. See "Renting a Car" in chapter 2 for information and toll-free numbers of companies with offices in Las Vegas.

In town, traffic on the Strip is often bumper-to-bumper. If it's especially heavy, you often make better time using Paradise Road, which runs parallel to the Strip on the east.

Since driving on the outskirts of Las Vegas—for example, coming from California—involves desert driving, you must take certain precautions. It's a good idea to check your tires, water, and oil before leaving. Take at least 5 gallons of water in a clean container that can be used for either drinking or the radiator. Pay attention to road signs that suggest when to turn off your car's air conditioner. And don't push your luck with gas—it may be 35 miles, or more, between stations. If your car overheats, do not remove the radiator cap until the engine has cooled, and then remove it only very slowly. Add water to within an inch of the top of the radiator.

BY TAXI

Since cabs line up in front of all major hotels, the easiest way to get around town is by taxi. Cabs charge $2.20 at the meter drop and 30¢ for each additional one-fifth of a mile. A taxi from the airport to the Strip will run you $8 to $12, from the airport to Downtown $15 to $18, and between the Strip and Downtown about $7 to $10. You can often save money by sharing a cab with someone going to the same destination (up to five people can ride for the same fare).

If you want to call a taxi, any of the following companies can provide one: **Desert Cab Company** (☎ 702/376-2688), **Whittlesea Blue Cab** (☎ 702/384-6111), and **Yellow/Checker Cab/Star Company** (☎ 702/873-2000).

FAST FACTS: Las Vegas

Ambulances   See "Emergencies," below.

Area Code   702

Babysitters   Contact **Around the Clock Child Care** (☎ 702/365-1040 or 800/798-6768). In business since 1985, this reputable company clears its sitters with the Health Department, the sheriff, and the FBI and carefully screens references. Charges are $36 for

4 hours for one or two children, $7 for each additional hour, with surcharges for additional children and on holidays. Sitters are on call 7 days a week, 24 hours a day, and they will come to your hotel. Call at least 2 hours in advance.

Banks   Banks are generally open 9 or 10am to 3pm, and most have Saturday hours. See also "Cash and Credit," below.

Car Rentals   See "Getting Around," above.

Cash and Credit   It's extremely easy—too easy—to obtain cash in Las Vegas. Most casino cashiers will cash personal checks and can exchange foreign currency, and just about every casino has a machine that will provide cash on a wide variety of credit cards.

Climate   See "When to Go" in chapter 2.

Convention Center   Las Vegas is one of America's top convention destinations. Much of the action takes place at the **Las Vegas Convention Center,** 3150 Paradise Rd., Las Vegas, NV 89109 (☎ 702/892-0711). The largest single-level convention center in the world, its 1.6 million square feet includes 96 meeting rooms. And this immense facility is augmented by the **Cashman Field Center,** 805 Las Vegas Blvd. N., Las Vegas, NV 89101 (☎ 702/386-7100). Under the same auspices, Cashman provides another 100,000 square feet of convention space.

Currency Exchange   Most Las Vegas hotels can exchange foreign currency. There's also a currency exchange desk run by Travelex in the ticketing area on the first level of McCarran International Airport.

Dentists and Doctors   Hotels usually have lists of dentists and doctors should you need one. In addition, they are listed in the Centel Yellow Pages.

For dentist referrals you can also call the **Clark County Dental Society** (☎ 702/255-7873), weekdays 9am to noon and 1 to 5pm; when the office is closed, a recording will tell you whom to call for emergency service.

For physician referrals, call **Desert Springs Hospital** (☎ 702/733-6875). Hours are 8am to 4pm.

Driving   See "Getting Around—By Car" earlier in this chapter.

Drugstores   See "Pharmacies (Late-Night)" below.

Emergencies   Dial 911 to contact the police or fire departments or to call an ambulance.

Emergency services are available 24 hours a day at **University Medical Center,** 1800 W. Charleston Blvd., at Shadow Lane (☎ 702/383-2000); the emergency room entrance is on the corner of Hastings and Rose streets. **Sunrise Hospital & Medical Center,** 3186 Maryland Pkwy., between Desert Inn Road and Sahara Avenue (☎ 702/731-8080), also has a 24-hour emergency room.

Eyeglass Repair   A company whose name is its phone number, (☎ 702/732-EYES) (24 hours a day), has several branches in Las

Vegas; the most convenient one is at 3507 S. Maryland Pkwy., across the street from the Boulevard Mall. During store hours (Monday to Saturday, 9am to 6pm), call this store directly at 702/732-3758. They offer same or next-day service. Prices are very reasonable.

Highway Conditions For recorded information, call 702/ 486-3116.

Hot Lines **The Rape Crisis Center** (☎ 702/366-1640), **Suicide Prevention** (☎ 702/731-2990), **Poison Emergencies** (☎ 702/ 732-4989).

Information See "Visitor Information" earlier in this chapter.

Libraries The largest in town is the Clark County Library branch at 1401 Flamingo Rd., at Escondido Street, on the southeast corner (☎ 702/733-7810). Hours are Monday to Thursday 9am to 9pm, Friday and Saturday 9am to 5pm, Sunday 1 to 5pm.

Liquor and Gambling Laws You must be 21 to drink or gamble. There are no closing hours in Las Vegas for the sale or consumption of alcohol, even on Sunday.

Newspapers and Periodicals There are two Las Vegas dailies— the *Las Vegas Review Journal* and the *Las Vegas Sun*. The *Review Journal's* Friday edition has a helpful "Weekend" section with a comprehensive guide to shows and buffets. And at every hotel desk, you'll find dozens of free local magazines, such as *Vegas Visitor, What's On in Las Vegas, Showbiz Weekly,* and *Where To in Las Vegas,* that are chock-full of helpful information.

Parking Valet parking is one of the great pleasures of Las Vegas. When you visit a hotel for its casino, restaurants, or show, you can pull right up to the door and have the valet take your car. It's well worth the dollar tip (given when the car is returned) to save walking a city block from the far reaches of a hotel parking lot, particularly when the temperature is over 100°. Another summer plus: the valet will turn on your air-conditioning, so you don't have to get in an "oven on wheels."

Police For nonemergencies call 702/795-3111. For emergencies call 911.

Post Office The most convenient post office is immediately behind the Stardust Hotel at 3100 Industrial Rd., between Sahara Avenue and Spring Mountain Road (☎ 702/735-2525). It's open Monday to Friday 8:30am to 5pm. You can also mail letters and packages at your hotel, and there's a full-service U.S. Post Office in the Forum Shops in Caesars Palace.

Rest Rooms Las Vegas is one of the few places where finding a public rest room is not impossible. Just look in the casino (but they're sometimes difficult to find). Someone will direct you if you ask.

Safety In Las Vegas vast amounts of money are always on display, and criminals find many easy marks. Don't be one of them. At gaming tables and slot machines, men should keep wallets well concealed and out of the reach of pickpockets, and women should keep handbags in plain sight (on laps). Outside casinos, popular spots for pickpockets and thieves are restaurants and outdoor shows, such as the volcano at Mirage or at the Treasure Island pirate battle. Stay alert. Unless your hotel room has an in-room safe, check your valuables in a safety-deposit box at the front desk.

Show Tickets   See chapter 10 for details on obtaining show tickets.

Taxes   Clark County hotel room tax is 8%; the sales tax is 7%.

Taxis   See "Getting Around—By Taxi" earlier in this chapter.

Time Zone   Las Vegas is in the Pacific time zone, 3 hours earlier than the East Coast, 2 hours earlier than the Midwest.

Weather and Time   Call 702/734-2010.

Weddings   Las Vegas is one of the easiest places in the world to tie the knot. There's no blood test or waiting period, the ceremony and license are inexpensive, chapels are open around-the-dock, and your honeymoon destination is right at hand. More than 100,000 marriages are performed here each year. Get a license Downtown at the **Clark County Marriage License Bureau,** 200 S. 3rd St., at Bridger Avenue (☎ 702/455-3156). Open 8am to midnight Monday to Thursday and from 8am Friday through midnight Sunday. On legal holidays they're open 24 hours. The cost of a marriage license is $35, the cost of the ceremony, another $35.

Among the many famous folk who've married here: Roger Vadim (to both Brigitte Bardot and Jane Fonda), Elvis and Priscilla Presley, Frank Sinatra and Mia Farrow, Mickey Rooney (several times), and—a few couples who are still together at this writing—Paul Newman and Joanne Woodward, Bruce Willis and Demi Moore, and Steve Lawrence and Eydie Gorme.

Wedding chapels abound, and there's something for every taste (yes, you can have an Elvis impersonator perform your wedding) and pocketbook. The most romantic settings are at Mount Charleston or on a boat on Lake Mead (see chapter 7). One of the most popular chapels is the historic **Candlelight Wedding Chapel,** 2855 Las Vegas Blvd. S. (☎ 702/735-4179 or 800/962-1818). The Candlelight, along with most other Las Vegas wedding chapels, can meet requests (with enough advance notice) to stage your wedding in a limousine, a hot-air balloon, in a nearby canyon, or in almost any eccentric setting you can think of. A service called **Las Vegas Weddings and Rooms** (☎ 800/488-MATE) can give you a full rundown on the various options.

5

Accommodations in Las Vegas

Las Vegas has more than 88,000 hotel and motel rooms, of which more than 12,000 were completed since 1993. And another 12,000 rooms are under construction at this writing. Why the building boom? Although Las Vegas already has substantially more rooms than most big cities, its annual occupancy rate (close to 85%) is also far higher than the national average. And as one of America's top convention cities, it frequently fills existing hotels to the bursting point. Booking well in advance is recommended.

The city's accommodations profile is rather unique. Here the hotel norm is a 24-hour megaresort (9 of the 10 largest hotels in the world are located in Las Vegas) with 6 to 10 restaurants, lavish entertainment showrooms and lounges, shopping arcades, fully equipped health clubs, swimming pools, and—most important—vast casinos. These megaresorts charge considerably less for rooms than do equivalent properties in other major cities. The price of a room in a deluxe Las Vegas hotel would be equivalent to what you would pay at a *M* hotel in any other tourist mecca. The reason: The casino is the raison d'être for most properties here; therefore, *I* hotel rooms are a lure for visitors.

GETTING THE MOST FOR YOUR HOTEL DOLLAR

When the town is overflowing with visitors, top rates are charged, and there's little you can do about it. However, when business isn't quite so brisk, you can cut deals. Using toll-free numbers, call around town and ask reservations clerks if they can undercut the first rates quoted. Often, they will. A hotel makes nothing on an empty room. Hence, though they don't bruit it about (for obvious reasons), most hotels would rather reduce rates than leave a room unoccupied. Whatever rate you agree upon, ask for a confirmation number (written confirmation if possible) and check the rate again when you register at the hotel. Also, always inquire about reduced-price packages when you reserve.

If you're willing to chance it, an especially advantageous time to secure reduced rates is late in the afternoon or early evening on the day of your arrival when a hotel's likelihood of filling up with full-price bookings is remote.

Important Information About Las Vegas Hotel Rates

You'll notice quoted rates vary dramatically. For instance, the Mirage lists its standard room rates as $79 to $349! The reason: Rates soar during holidays and when major conventions are in town. If you have some flexibility in planning the dates of your vacation, you can save quite a bit. Call the **Las Vegas Convention and Visitors Authority** (☎ 800/332-5334) to find out if an important convention is scheduled at the time of your planned visit; if so, you might want to change your date.

Another anomaly here: While in many cities hotels offer reduced weekend rates, in Las Vegas rates are lower Sunday to Thursday.

Sometimes you can get into the most exclusive hotels at surprisingly low rates. Since almost all properties have toll-free numbers, it's worth your while to call around.

RESERVATIONS SERVICES

If you get harried when you have to haggle, use a free service offered by **City-Wide Reservations,** 2929 E. Desert Inn Rd., Suite 20, Las Vegas, NV 89121-3604 (☎ 702/794-4481 or 800/733-6644). They'll find you a hotel room in your price bracket that meets your specific requirements. Because they book rooms in volume, they are able to get discounted rates. Not only can they book rooms, but they can arrange packages (including meals, transportation, tours, show tickets, car rentals, and other features) and group rates.

The **Las Vegas Convention and Visitors Authority** also runs a room reservations hot line (☎ 800/332-5334), which can be helpful. They can apprise you of room availability, quote rates, contact a hotel for you, and tell you when major conventions will be in town.

WHAT THE PRICE CATEGORIES MEAN

The following price categories represent the average rack rate you can expect to be quoted for a double room on an average night (i.e., *not* when the Consumer Electronics Show is in town, *not* on New Year's Eve). Your *actual* rate may be a little less than this if you stay only Sunday through Thursday and a little more than this if you stay Friday and Saturday. And please be sure to check the actual rates in the hotel listings to see where in this category your hotel stands:

Very Expensive	More than $100
Expensive	Between $75 and $100
Moderate	Between $50 and $75
Inexpensive	$50 and Under

Of course, you can expect significant savings if you book a money-saving package deal, like those described in chapter 2. And on any given night when business is slow, you might be able to stay at a "very expensive" hotel for a "moderate" price.

1   Best Bets

- **Best for Conventioneers/Business Travelers:** The **Las Vegas Hilton,** adjacent to the Las Vegas Convention Center and the setting for many on-premises conventions, offers extensive facilities along with helpful services such as a full business center.

- **Best Elegant Hotel:** Country club elegance is the keynote of the **Sheraton Desert Inn.** In its European-style casino, gaming tables are comfortably spaced, the glitzy glow of neon is replaced by the glitter of crystal chandeliers, and the scarcity of slot and video poker machines eliminates the usual noisy jangle of coins. Extensive facilities are complemented by attentive personal service. This is the most prestigious hotel address in town.

- **Best Archetypically Las Vegas Hotel: Caesars Palace** continues to embody the excess and excitement that is Las Vegas—from the overstated magnificence of its classical Roman facade to the orgiastic ambience of its Bacchanal Room. Catering to a sophisticated, upscale clientele, Caesars houses a spectacular Rodeo Drive–style shopping arcade and an impressive roster of restaurants. Its extensive facilities are matched by classy service: Once, when I was standing in a long line at the registration desk, gratis champagne was served.

- **Best Swimming Pool:** Almost every Las Vegas hotel has a stunning pool area. The **Flamingo Hilton** boasts a 15-acre Caribbean landscape with three pools, Jacuzzis, water slides, swan- and duck-filled ponds, a grove of 3,000 palms, waterfalls, fountains, lagoons, and islands of flamingos and African penguins. Similarly lush is the **Tropicana,** whose offerings also include a swim-up bar/blackjack table.

- **Best Health Club:** Like sumptuous swimming pools, deluxe state-of-the-art health clubs are the rule in Las Vegas hotels. Most exclusive (fee is $18 per visit) and extensively equipped is the club at the **Mirage,** offering a full complement of machines—some with individual TVs (headphones are supplied), free weights, private whirlpool rooms as well as a large whirlpool and saunas, a thoroughly equipped locker room, and comfortable lounges in which to rest up after your workout. Guests are given gratis terry robes. An adjoining salon offers every imaginable spa service. Steve Wynn works out here almost daily, as do many celebrity guests.

- **Best for Twentysomethings Through Baby Boomers:** The **Hard Rock Hotel,** billing itself as the world's "first rock 'n' roll hotel and casino" and "Vegas for a new generation," sent out invitations to its opening on casino chips bearing the image of Jimi Hendrix. Need I say more?

- **Best Interior:** I love walking into the verdant tropical rain forest at the **Mirage.** A massive coral-reef aquarium behind the registration desk and the on-premises tiger habitat further enhance this property's natural ambience, and well-designed paths also make the casino extremely easy to navigate.

- **Best for Families:** The centrally located and low-priced **Circus Circus** has almost unlimited activities for kids—ongoing circus acts, a vast video-game arcade, a carnival midway, and a full amusement park. The **MGM Grand** houses a full Youth Center, a first-rate facility for kids 3 to 16. This is the only hotel in town to offer full child care.

- **Best Rooms:** The **Rio's** tropically themed and spacious suites are the most beautiful in town. Decorated in resort hues with half-canopy beds, they offer large dressing rooms, gorgeous baths, wraparound sofas, and upholstered chaise longues. Picture windows provide panoramic views of the Strip. Many people consider the Rio the most appealing hotel in Las Vegas.

- **Best Noncasino Hotel:** The very upscale **Alexis Park Resort** is the choice of many visiting celebrities and headliners. Many of its rooms have working fireplaces and/or Jacuzzis, and guests are cosseted with can-do concierge service. I also like the **Residence Inn by Marriott,** where apartment-like accommodations are equipped with full kitchens and living room areas, many with working fireplaces.

- **Best Casinos:** My favorite places to gamble are the **Mirage** (lively, beautiful, and not overwhelming), the **Sheraton Desert Inn** (where the intimate casino is reminiscent of sophisticated European gaming houses), and the **Hard Rock** (where you can bet to a beat). For sports fans, **Harrah's** sports pit equipped with TV monitors airing athletic events is a favorite.

- **Best Downtown Hotel:** The **Golden Nugget,** evoking an elegant resort on the French Riviera, is exceptionally appealing in every aspect—from its sun-dappled interior to an opulent, European-style casino. Also notable is the New Orleans–themed **Showboat,** its slightly out-of-the-way location (not a problem if you have a car) offset by a delightful interior, a friendly staff, cheerfully decorated low-priced rooms, and special features such as a bingo parlor and bowling alley.

2 Choosing a Hotel

There are basically three areas of town of interest to visitors: The Strip, the Convention Center & Paradise Road (both east of the Strip), and Downtown. Since it's only a 5-minute ride by car between Downtown and Strip hotels (the Convention Center is more or less in between), there's no such thing as a bad location if you have access to a car. If money is no object, only a $10 cab ride separates the Strip from Downtown.

However, for those of you depending on public transportation, while the bus ride between Downtown and the Strip is short in distance, it can be long in time stuck in traffic. You should also be aware that the buses become quite crowded once they reach the strip and may pass by a bus stop if no one signals to get out and the driver does not wish to take on more passengers. Without a car, your ease of movement between areas of town is, therefore, limited.

Personally, I like to stay on the Strip, but others prefer the more casual Downtown ambience. If you've never seen Las Vegas before, I'd suggest staying on the Strip and checking out Downtown for possible future visits.

Another factor in your choice is whether to stay at a casino or noncasino hotel. A casino hotel, especially a major one, is a kind of multifacility city-within-a-city that offers nonstop gaming, shows, and excitement. It can be great if you're the kind of person who thrives at the heart of the action. If you'd rather visit the action but then retire to more tranquil surroundings at night, choose a noncasino hotel. The hotel that gives you the best of both worlds is the Sheraton Desert Inn—a refined casino hotel with a country-club atmosphere.

HOTELS BY LOCATION

ON OR NEAR THE STRIP

Algiers (No Casino, *I*)
Bally's (Casino, *E*)
Barbary Coast (Casino, *M*)
Caesars Palace (Casino, V*E*)
Carriage House (No Casino, *E*)
Center Strip Inn (No Casino, *I*)
Circus Circus (Casino, *I*)
Desert Inn (Casino, V*E*)
Excalibur (Casino, *I*)
Flamingo Hilton (Casino, *E*)
Hacienda (Casino, *M*)
Harrah's (Casino, *M*)
Holiday Inn Boardwalk (Casino, *M*)
Imperial Palace (Casino, *M*)
La Quinta (No Casino, *M*)
Luxor Las Vegas (Casino, *E*)
Maxim (Casino, *M*)
MGM Grand (Casino, *E*)
Mirage (Casino, V*E*)
Rio Suites (Casino, *E*)
Riviera (Casino, *E*)
Sahara (Casino, *E*)
Sands (Casino, *E*)
Stardust (Casino, *M*)
Treasure Island at the Mirage (Casino, V*E*)
Tropicana (Casino, *M*)
Vagabond Inn (No Casino, *M*)
Westward Ho (Casino, *I*)

NEAR THE CONVENTION CENTER/ EAST OF THE STRIP

Alexis Park (No Casino, *E*)
Best Western Mardi Gras Inn (Casino, *M*)
Courtyard Marriott (No Casino, *M*)
Debbie Reynolds (Casino, *M*)
Emerald Springs Holiday Inn (No Casino, *M*)
Fairfield Inn by Marriott (No Casino, *M*)
Hard Rock Hotel (Casino, *E*)
La Quinta Inn (No Casino, *M*)
Las Vegas Hilton (Casino, V*E*)
Motel 6 (No Casino, *I*)
Residence Inn by Marriott (No Casino, *E*)
Super 8 (Casino, *I*)

DOWNTOWN

California (Casino, *I*)
Days Inn (Casino, *M*)
El Cortez (Casino, *I*)
Golden Nugget (Casino, *E*)
Fitzgerald's (Casino, *I*)
Four Queens (Casino, *I*)
Freemont (Casino, *I*)
Jackie Gaughan's Plaza (Casino, *M*)
Lady Luck (Casino, *M*)
Showboat (Casino, *M*)

Key to abbreviations: *I=Inexpensive; M=Moderate; E=Expensive; VE=Very Expensive.*

3   On or Near the Strip—Hotels with Casinos

VERY EXPENSIVE

The category "very expensive" is a bit misleading. These are among the top hotels in town, most of them offering vast casinos, a wide array of restaurants, glamorous showrooms, and many facilities. But the rates they charge are comparable to "high moderate" in other major cities. Even if you're staying elsewhere, read through these listings; some of the hotels described below are sightseeing attractions in their own right. You don't have to stay there to take advantage of their posh restaurants, casinos, and showrooms.

✪ Caesars Palace

3570 Las Vegas Blvd. S., just north of Flamingo Rd., Las Vegas, NV 89109 ☎ **702/ 731-7110** or 800/634-6661. Fax 702/731-6636. 1,305 rms, 190 suites. A/C TV TEL. $100–$175 single, $115–$190 double, $450–$7,500 suite. Extra person $20. Children under 12 stay free in parents' room. AE, DISC, JCB, MC, V. Free parking (self and valet).

Designed to reflect the decadent grandeur of ancient Rome, Caesars has been a major player on the Strip since it opened in 1966. This world-class resort is a Roman pleasure palace where guests are greeted by gladiators and centurions, classical marble statuary graces public areas, and cocktail waitresses are costumed as goddesses. Its several entrances are graced by 18 spectacular fountains (Evel Knievel once attempted to jump over them on a motorcycle), Roman temples, heroic arches, golden charioteers, and elegant driveways lined by 50-foot Italian cypresses. Caesars pioneered the "people mover" concept, using moving walkways to convey visitors from the Strip into the hotel. Today there are three of these conveyances, leading to the casino, the OMNIMAX™ Theatre, and the Forum Shops—a Rodeo Drive–style shopping complex.

Accommodations occupy three towers, and there are too many decorator schemes to describe here. You'll likely enjoy lavish bath facilities with marble flooring, European fixtures, and oversized marble tubs (about half are Jacuzzis). Art in the rooms keeps to the Greco-Roman theme (some have classical sculptures in niches), furnishings tend to neoclassic styles, and design elements such as Roman columns, pilasters, and pediments are common. Many rooms have four-poster beds with mirrored ceilings, and all are equipped with three phones (bedside, bath, and desk) and hotel information stations. All rooms have private safes.

Dining: Caesars has a well-deserved reputation for superior in-house restaurants. There are nine in the hotel, plus dining facilities in the Forum shopping area. All are highly recommended.

The hotel's premier restaurant, the exquisite **Palace Court,** can hold its own with prestigious gourmet dining rooms anywhere in the country. See chapter 6 for details.

A second gourmet room, **Bacchanal,** re-creates a multicourse Roman feast in fittingly sumptuous surroundings, complete with scantily clad "wine goddesses." See chapter 6 for details.

Neros, specializing in prime aged steaks and fresh seafood, also features chicken, veal, and lamb dishes. An extensive wine list complements the menu. The restaurant's octagonal design is a contemporary interpretation of the Spanish Mudejar style, with an eight-pointed star radiating from the ceiling and tiered copper walls forming a gleaming inverse pyramid. There's also terrace seating overlooking the casino. Dinner only; entrees $19.50 to $36.

Just off the casino is Caesars elegant Japanese restaurant, **Ah'So,** fronted by an oak-floored terrace lit by paper lanterns. Inside, seating areas under pine and cherry trees are divided by arched bridges that span flower-bordered streams, and a waterfall cascades over faux lava rock. Fixed-price multicourse teppanyaki dinners are $49.50 per person.

The pretty crystal-chandeliered **Primavera,** with pink-cloth-covered tables, bamboo fan-back chairs, and ficus trees in big terra-cotta pots, has a wall of Palladian windows overlooking the pool. Alfresco terrace seating under white canvas umbrellas is especially lovely at night when poolside trees are lit by tiny lights. Open breakfast, lunch, and dinner, its menu features homemade pasta and specialties from all regions of Italy. Lunch entrees $9.50 to $16.50, dinner entrees $11.50 to $29.50.

Empress Court, fronted by a two-story double-balustrated stair-case encircling a koi pond, is aquatically themed from its coral reef aquarium to its etched-glass fish-motif room dividers. Seating is in black lacquer chinoiserie chairs at elegantly appointed tables, and Chinese dulcimer music enhances the ambience. The menu offers first-rate Cantonese cuisine and specializes in fresh seafood. Dinner only; most entrees are $12 to $20; multicourse fixed-price dinners $40 to $55 per person.

In **Cafe Roma,** Caesars 24-hour coffee shop, murals of pastoral Roman landscapes behind arches create a scenic window effect. This is a very comfortable restaurant, offering international buffets and a menu that runs the gamut from filet mignon to seafood enchiladas, from kung pao chicken to burgers, salads, and sandwiches.

La Piazza Food Court is a great choice for families. See chapter 10 for details.

The lavish **Caesars Palace Palatium Buffet** is described more fully in chapter 6.

Restaurants in the Forum Shops arcade include **Spago** (Wolfgang Puck's famed establishment), **The Palm,** and the **Stage Deli**—all discussed in chapter 6—as well as **Bertolini's** (a good Italian restaurant), **Planet Hollywood,** and **Boogie's Diner of Aspen** (for great milk shakes and burgers).

There are several casino lounges, among them the **Discus Bar** in the Forum Casino and the **Galleria Lounge** near the baccarat area. The **Olympic Lounge** and **La Piazza Lounge** offer nightly entertainment in the Olympic Casino; the **Neptune** pool bar is open seasonally. See also **Cleopatra's Barge,** a nightclub, in chapter 10.

Services: 24-hour room service, shoeshine, complimentary gaming lessons.

Accommodations
On the Strip and Paradise Road

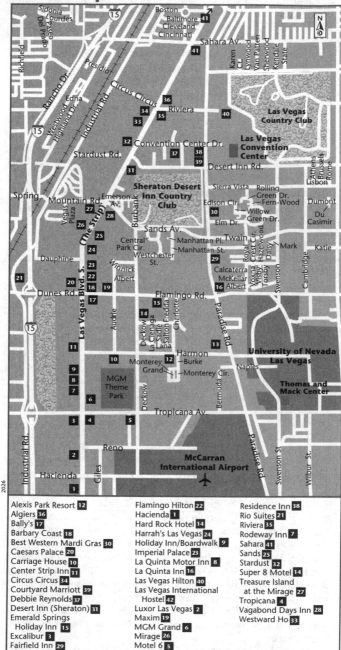

Alexis Park Resort 12	Flamingo Hilton 22	Residence Inn 38
Algiers 36	Hacienda 1	Rio Suites 21
Bally's 17	Hard Rock Hotel 14	Riviera 35
Barbary Coast 18	Harrah's Las Vegas 24	Rodeway Inn 7
Best Western Mardi Gras 30	Holiday Inn/Boardwalk 9	Sahara 41
Caesars Palace 20	Imperial Palace 23	Sands 25
Carriage House 10	La Quinta Motor Inn 8	Stardust 32
Center Strip Inn 11	La Quinta Inn 16	Super 8 Motel 14
Circus Circus 34	Las Vegas Hilton 40	Treasure Island
Courtyard Marriott 39	Las Vegas International	at the Mirage 27
Debbie Reynolds 37	Hostel 42	Tropicana 4
Desert Inn (Sheraton) 31	Luxor Las Vegas 2	Vagabond Days Inn 28
Emerald Springs	Maxim 19	Westward Ho 33
Holiday Inn 15	MGM Grand 6	
Excalibur 3	Mirage 26	
Fairfield Inn 29	Motel 6 5	

Facilities: Three casinos, four outdoor tennis courts and pro shop, two extensive shopping arcades (see chapter 9), state-of-the-art video arcade, American Express office, full-service unisex salon, tour and show desks, car-rental desk.

Caesars' magnificent Olympic-size swimming pool, focal point of the exquisitely landscaped "Garden of the Gods," was inspired by the Pompeii Baths of Rome. Shaped like a Roman shield and surrounded by classical statuary, it is tiled with Carrara marble and dramatically lit by a colonnade of stately lamps. A 28-foot diameter whirlpool spa centered by a marble statue of Venus adjoins. A second pool with three large fountains and "lounging islands" is located on the upper level of the garden. The Roman Tower health spa offers extensive workout equipment as well as a steam room, sauna, whirlpool, tanning beds, massage, aromatheraphy, facials, and a sundeck.

✪ Sheraton Desert Inn Resort & Casino

3145 Las Vegas Blvd. S., between Desert Inn Rd. and Sands Ave., Las Vegas, NV 89109. ☎ **702/733-4444** or 800/634-6906. Fax 702/733-4744. 280 rms, 438 suites. A/C TV TEL. $155–$175 single or double, $205–$235 minisuite, $300–$2500 suite. Extra person $25. Children under 12 stay free in parents' room. Inquire about golf, spa, and other packages. AE, CB, DC, DISC, JCB, MC, V. Free parking (self and valet).

Many people consider the Sheraton Desert Inn the most prestigious address on the Strip. Country-club elegance is the keynote here: The emphasis is on extensive resort facilities, fine restaurants, and first-rate service; when you reserve a room here, you can arrange restaurant reservations and show tickets anywhere in town, car rentals, golf times, and more in the same phone call. The property occupies 200 exquisitely landscaped acres of rock gardens, flower beds, duck ponds, waterfalls, and tree-shaded lawns. Strolling the grounds is almost like visiting a botanical garden or arboretum. The hotel opened in 1950, with Edgar and Charlie McCarthy premiering in the showroom. Howard Hughes (and later his estate) owned the hotel from 1967 to 1988, and he lived here in the late 1960s. It is my favorite Las Vegas Hotel.

Stunning rooms and suites—named for famous golf courses and tennis stadiums—offer substantial comfort. The most luxurious accommodations, in the nine-story St. Andrews Tower, are being renovated at this writing as the Desert Inn further enhances its upscale profile; they will be contemporary in decor and will feature spacious marble baths with Jacuzzi tubs. Less *E* rooms in the 14-story Augusta Tower are also lovely; they're done up in subtle blue-gray tones, with bleached oak furnishings and upholstered headboards. Baths have large dressing rooms. Headliners, high rollers, and other well-heeled people prefer the Wimbledon Building's duplex suites, with private pools or 4,000-square-foot penthouses. A luxurious 98-suite tower, now nearing completion, will offer 12 poolside lanai suites. All Desert Inn rooms offer superior bath toiletries; you'll find an iron and full-sized ironing board in the closet.

Dining: The opulent **Monte Carlo Room** has been one of the city's most highly regarded dining rooms for several decades. Also notable here is the Chinese restaurant **Ho Wan.** See chapter 6 for details on both—and the most lavish brunch in town.

Portofino—with oak and marble floors, brass urns filled with flowers and foliage, and large Carrara marble room dividers—overlooks the casino. Its spacious semi-circular booths are upholstered in rich brown velvet. Northern Italian cuisine is featured. Only dinner is served; entrees are $19.50 to $32.50, pasta dishes $9.75 to $14.

La Promenade, a delightful, plant-filled 24-hour coffee shop with a 30-foot window wall overlooking the pool, offers seating in comfortable upholstered booths and armchairs under immense fringed gold-silk umbrellas. You can order anything here from a grilled kosher frank with fries to a broiled lobster tail. There are also Asian specialties.

The stone-walled **Champions Deli,** on the golf course, serves deli fare—pastrami and corned beef sandwiches and the like. A posh new steakhouse is also in the works. The **Starlight Theatre,** a plush casino lounge, offers name entertainment at night, sporting events (on a large-screen TV) during the day. It's one of two casino bars.

Services: 24-hour room service, concierge, shoeshine.

Facilities: Casino, tour and show desks, car-rental desk, beauty salon/barbershop, shops (men's and women's clothing, gifts and sundries, jewelry, logo items), golf and tennis pro shops.

Golf Digest calls the verdant, palm-studded 18-hole golf course one of America's top resort courses (more about this in chapter 7).

But even if it has no casino or golf course, the Desert Inn could function as a luxury spa retreat, offering water-therapy programs (there are hot, warm, and cool tubs), private whirlpools with recliner seats, tanning beds, steam rooms, and sauna, and all the treatments one would expect in a world-class spa. It's not all pampering. The cardiovascular fitness center has a range of machines, free weights, a small pool and sun deck, aerobics classes, and a jobbing parcourse with exercise stations. You can relax, post-workout, in a TV lounge. The hotel has a large swimming pool in a garden setting with adjoining whirlpool, poolside snack/cocktail bar, and pool sundries shop. And there are five tournament-class tennis courts—all lit for night play; expert instruction and practice ball machines are available. And, finally, there are two shuffleboard courts.

✪ Mirage

3400 Las Vegas Blvd. S., between Flamingo Rd. and Sands Ave., Las Vegas, NV 89109. ☎ **702/791-7111** or 800/627-6667. Fax 702/791-7446. 3,044 rms, 279 suites. A/C TV TEL. Single or double $79–$199 Sun–Thurs, $159–$349 Fri–Sat and holidays; $250–$3,000 suite. Extra person $30. AE, CB, DC, DISC, MC, V. Free parking (self and valet).

Steve Wynn's gleaming white and gold Mirage redefines the word "spectacular" in a town where spectacular is a way of life. Occupying 102 acres, it's fronted by more than a city block of cascading waterfalls and tropical foliage centering on a very active "volcano," which, after dark, erupts every 15 minutes, spewing fire 100 feet above the lagoons below! Step inside the hotel and you're in a verdant rain forest—a 90-foot domed atrium where paths meander through palms, banana trees, waterfalls, and serene pools. And behind the front desk is a

53-foot, 20,000-gallon simulated coral reef aquarium stocked with more than 1,000 colorful tropical fish, including six sharks.

In addition, the hotel has a habitat for rare white tigers belonging to performers Siegfried & Roy, and another for seven Atlantic bottle-nose dolphins—a site of fascinating educational tours. The Mirage corporation has been active in protesting fishing practices harmful to dolphins and serves only "dolphin-safe" tuna in its restaurants. And no furs are sold in Mirage boutiques.

Mirage rooms, among the most aesthetically tasteful in town, are decorated in warm, peachy earth tones with upscale furnishings and lovely prints (botanicals and others) gracing the walls. Beds have shuttered backboards framed by curtains; dressing areas offer lighted cosmetic mirrors; and luxurious marble baths are equipped with hair dryers. Oak armoires hide 25-inch TVs, and phones are equipped with fax and computer jacks. Further up the price scale are super-deluxe rooms with whirlpool tubs.

Dining: Kokomo's, situated in the tropical rain forest atrium, offers seating under bamboo-thatched roofing and trellised bougainvillea vines. Comfortable upholstered rattan furnishings and candlelit tables—some overlooking lagoons and waterfalls—are set amid lofty palms and giant ferns. The menu features steaks, chops, prime rib, and seafood, supplemented by burgers and tropical salads at lunch. All meals are served; lunch entrees $7 to $14.75, dinner entrees mostly $22 to $33.50.

Mikado, under a starlit sky at night, offers diners a candlelit setting with a sunken tropical rock garden, lotus pond, and sheltering pines. Teppanyaki cooking is featured along with à la carte Japanese specialties and a sushi bar. Dinner only; entrees mostly $16 to $30.

At **Moongate,** also under a starlit sky, seating is in an open courtyard defined by classical Chinese architectural facades and tiled roof-lines. White doves perch on cherry tree branches, and intricately hand-carved walls frame a moongate tableau. The menu offers Cantonese and Szechuan specialties. Dinner only; entrees mostly $16 to $30.

A cobblestone passage evoking a European village street leads to **Restaurant Riva,** a very pretty dining room decorated predominantly in peach tones, with raw silk wall coverings and upholstery. Candlelit at night, its walls are hung with gilt-framed still-life paintings and its windows with swagged draperies. Sophisticated northern Italian fare is served. Dinner only; entrees $14 to $32.

Off the same quaint street is the **Bistro,** a charming belle-époque setting with rich mahogany paneling, art nouveau designs on mirrored walls, Toulouse-Lautrec-style murals, and pink-cloth-covered tables lit by shaded brass oil lamps. Fare is French/continental, Dinner only; entrees mostly $22.50 to $34.

The circular **California Pizza Kitchen,** under a thatch-roofed dome, is in the center of the casino overlooking the race and sports book. A bank of video monitors lets you follow the action while dining on oak-fired pizzas with toppings ranging from duck sausage to goat cheese. Calzones, salads, and pasta dishes are served here, too. All entrees under $11.

Impressions

Supercalafragilisticexpialadocious!
—Governor Bob Miller's reaction upon first visiting the Mirage

The **Caribe Café** is the Mirage's festive 24-hour coffee shop, and it adheres to the tropical theme with bamboo furnishings upholstered in bright tropical colors, murals of jungle foliage, and planters of birds of paradise. It's designed to evoke an open-air Caribbean village. Even the entranceway is lined with faux banana palms and mango trees.

Additional food and beverage facilities include **Coconuts,** an attractive ice-cream parlor; the **Paradise Café,** an alfresco terrace with umbrella tables overlooking the pool (drinks and light fare are served); the **Lagoon Saloon** in the rain forest, specializing in tropical drinks (the bartop is a glass-covered beach strewn with seashells) and offering live music; the **Baccarat Bar,** where a pianist entertains nightly; the poolside **Dolphin Bar,** and the **Sports Bar** in the casino. See also "Buffets and Sunday Brunches" in chapter 6.

Services: 24-hour room service, overnight shoeshine on request, morning newspaper delivery.

Facilities: Casino, car-rental desk, shops (designer boutiques for men and women, *Siegfried & Roy* and Cirque du Soleil merchandise, costume jewelry, gifts, activewear), unisex hairdresser and salon offering all beauty services (waxing, body treatments, facials, and much more), state-of-the-art video-game arcade, business-services center. A free tram travels between the Mirage and Treasure Island almost around the clock.

The Mirage health club is the most extensive hotel facility in town, offering a large selection of machines, Gravitron, free weights, sauna, steam, whirlpool, and massage.

Waterfalls cascade into the hotel's immense swimming pool (it has a quarter-mile shoreline) in a lush tropical setting where lagoons link palm-lined islands. Kids will enjoy the big pool slides. Free swimming lessons and water aerobics classes take place daily. Private poolside cabanas equipped with phones, free drinks, refrigerators, misting systems, rafts, and radios can be rented for $85 a day. Guests enjoy preferred rates at the highly rated 18-hole championship course of the Mirage Golf Club.

✪ Treasure Island at the Mirage

3300 Las Vegas Blvd. S., at Spring Mountain Rd., Las Vegas, NV 89109. ☎ **702/ 894-7111** or 800-944-7444. Fax 702/894-7446. 2,688 rms, 212 suites. A/C TV TEL. Single or double $159–$179 Sun–Thurs, $109–$239 Fri–Sat; $129–$500 suite. Extra person $30. Children under 3 stay free in parents' room. Inquire about packages. AE, CB, DC, DISC, JCB, MC, V. Free parking (self and valet).

In 1989 Steve Wynn brought a lava-spewing volcano to the Strip to front his spectacular Mirage. What could he possibly do for an encore? Everyone found out in 1993, when he lowered the gangplank to unveil Treasure Island—an 18th-century Caribbean pirate village based on the writings of Robert Louis Stevenson. The Strip in front of the hotel has been transformed into a long wooden dock overlooking Buccaneer Bay, where live sea battles between two full-scale ships— the pirate vessel *Hispaniola* (its prow adorned with a pair of fierce-looking dragons) and the proud but battle-scarred British frigate HMS *Britannia*—take place at regular intervals. The village facade behind the bay is made up of ramshackle waterfront structures representing a merchant's house, bakery, tinmaker, and other village shops. Towering above is the hotel itself—a 36-story peach and stucco building with white-shuttered windows. Within, public areas all maintain the pirate theme.

Rooms are decorated in soft hues (there are five different color schemes). Nautically themed prints, maps, and astrological charts adorn the walls. Floor-to-ceiling windows provide great views of the Strip, pool, or mountains. Especially desirable are corner rooms with windows on two sides.

Dining: The hotel's premier restaurant, the **Buccaneer Bay Club,** is described in chapter 6, as are its buffet offerings.

The Plank, designed on the unlikely theme of a pirate's library, comprises a warren of cozy rooms where books and curios are displayed in leaded-glass cases. Its ambience is a mix of gleaming brass, polished burl, and musty leather-bound volumes. The menu features seafood and mesquite-grilled steaks and prime rib. Dinner only is served; entrees are $13.50 to $26.

The Black Spot Grille, its name notwithstanding, is an Italian "sidewalk cafe" set off from the shopping arcade by lacy iron grillwork. The Italian village ambience derives from a Venetian *putti* (cherub) fountain, stucco walls painted peach, festival lanterns strung overhead, and faux bougainvillea draped from terra-cotta eaves. Polished granite tables are lit by shaded lamps. Lunch and dinner are served; almost all menu items are under $10.

The very comfortable **Lookout Café,** Treasure Island's 24-hour coffee shop, has an arched beamed ceiling suggestive of a ship's underdeck. Straw-plastered walls are hung with muskets, daggers, and pirate booty from the seven seas; amber broken-bottle sconces provide soft lighting; and a wall of windows overlooks the lushly landscaped pool. The menu supplements typical coffee-shop fare with entrees such as grilled orange roughy with red bliss potatoes. From 4pm to midnight, a full prime rib dinner is $9.95.

Sharing a space just across from Mutiny Bay (the video-game arcade) are **Sweet Revenge** (an ice-cream/frozen yogurt parlor) and **Smugglers Cantina** (for light Mexican fare). Both of these pleasant eateries are off the casino. And the **Island Snack Bar** offers light foods and nonalcoholic specialty drinks by the pool.

Factoid

Every television set in every room at Steve Wynn's Treasure Island hotel has a channel that runs the movie *Treasure Island*—24 hours a day.

Captain Morgan's Lounge is described in chapter 10. The **Battle Bar,** in the casino near the race and sports book, airs athletic events on TV monitors overhead and offers live music nightly except Monday. More importantly, it provides patio seating overlooking Buccaneer Bay; for the best possible view of the ship battle, arrive at least 45 minutes prior to the show and snag a table by the railing. Two other very attractive bars also serve the casino. And in the pool area is the simpatico **Island Bar** offering frozen specialty drinks such as a "banana split" (a yummy concoction of amaretto, crème de banane, fresh pineapple, and coconut cream); it's cooled by a misting system in summer.

Services: 24-hour room service, limo rental, foreign currency exchange, shoeshine (in men's room in the lobby and casino).

Facilities: Casino, tour and sightseeing desks, car rental desk, travel agency, Mutiny Bay (an 18,000-square-foot Moorish castle-themed, state-of-the-art video game arcade fronted by talking pirate skeletons and encompassing a carnival midway; one highlight is a full-size Mazda Miata motion-simulator ride), two wedding chapels, full-service unisex salon (days of beauty are an option), and a shopping arcade (for details, see chapter 9). A state-of-the-art spa offers a full complement of machines, exercise bikes, and free weights; sauna, steam, whirlpools, and massage; on-site trainers; TVs and stereos with headsets; and anything you might need in the way of work-out attire or grooming and shower accessories. A large free-form swimming pool with a 230-foot loop slide has a beautifully landscaped sundeck area amid palms and flower beds. There's a kiddie pool and whirlpool, and cabanas (equipped with overhead fans, small refrigerators, phones, cable TVs, rafts, tables, and chairs) can be be rented for $60 a day. A free tram travels between Treasure Island and the Mirage almost around the clock.

EXPENSIVE

This category generally includes multi-facility megahotels that are similar to the "very expensive" properties.

✪ Bally's

3645 Las Vegas Blvd. S., at Flamingo Rd., Las Vegas 89109. ☎ **702/739-4111** or 800/634-3434. Fax 702/794-2413. 2,549 rms, 265 suites. A/C TV TEL. $89–$169 single or double; concierge floor $30 additional (including breakfast); $289–$393 suite. Extra person $15. Children 18 and under stay free in parents' room. AE, CB, DC, JCB, MC, V. Free parking (self and valet).

Bally's recently completed a $38 million renovation, which included the construction of a megaresort-to-megaresort monorail that whisks passengers from its downstairs shopping level (a bit of a hike from the casino) to the MGM Grand. More noticeable is its elaborate new facade—a plaza containing four 200-foot people movers that transport visitors to and from the Strip via a neon-lit coil arch structure surrounded by cascading waters, neon-lit pylons, and lush landscaping. Light, sound, and water shows take place here every 20 minutes after dark.

The hotel's new theme is "a touch of class." You'll notice that Bally's is one of the most cheerful hotels on the Strip the minute you step from its glittering porte-cochere entranceway into its light and airy casino with colorful confetti-motif carpeting and brilliant neon display. Also inviting is a whimsical mural of Las Vegas scenes behind the front desk. A virtual "city within a city," as self-contained as the Biosphere, Bally's offers a vast array of casino games, superb restaurants, entertainment options, shops, and services. During your Las Vegas stay, you will never need to step outside.

Large rooms are decorated in teal, mauve, and earth tones with dark wood furnishings. All have sofas. TVs offer video checkout, and even credit card cash-advance capability. Guests on the 22nd floor (a concierge level) have the use of a plush private lounge—the setting for gratis continental breakfasts and evening hors d'oeuvres/open bar. They also enjoy added amenities such as nightly turndown, gratis spa admission, and morning newspaper delivery.

Dining: Seasons, its interior modeled after a grand salon at Versailles, is an ornate setting of crystal chandeliers, gilded plaster-work and trellising, and elegantly draped private alcoves backed by gilt-framed mirrors. Diners are seated in Louis XIII–style chairs at beautifully appointed white-linen-covered and flower-bedecked tables. The cuisine is continental, and entrees are mostly $22.75 to $29.95.

Bally's Steakhouse has an ambience of substantial comfort. Gleaming brass chandeliers are suspended from a gorgeous oak and mahogany ceiling, and diners are seated at crisp, white-linened tables in leopardskin-upholstered booths and black leather armchairs. A traditional steak and seafood menu is featured. The fare is first-rate, complemented by an extensive wine list. Dinner only is served; entrees are $17.50 to $28.50.

Al Dente—attractively decorated in turquoise, sienna, beige and jade—has an expanse of marble flooring, art-deco maple and black lacquer columns, colorful abstract glass lighting fixtures, and stucco walls covered with beautiful modernist hangings. Planters of greenery create intimate dining areas. Its menu offers delicious pastas, thin-crust pizzas with California-style toppings, and other Italian entrees. Only dinner is served; entrees are $14.75 to $26.95, most pastas under $15, pizzas $8.75 to $12.

Las Olas is a charming candlelit Mexican eatery fronted by a lounge with a tiered fountain. The dining area has adobe peach walls hung with rugs and embroideries, displays of Mexican statuary and pottery in wall niches, and Aztec-motif carpeting. A mariachi band entertains during dinner. Dinner entrees run $8.50 to $17.95. Las Olas also serves Mexican and American breakfasts and lunches.

The **Coffee Shop,** bright and cheerful with red and turquoise upholstered chairs at bleached oak tables and colorful murals of street scenes on the walls, is Bally's 24-hour facility. It offers all the expected Vegas coffee-shop fare from snacks to full-course meals as well as Italian specialties.

The mermaid-themed **Bubbles Bar** serves the casino. In addition, **On the Rocks,** a poolside bar with a lovely terrace cooled by ceiling fans, specializes in tropical drinks and wines by the glass. And the **Terrace Café,** a seasonal poolside eatery with colorful umbrella tables under a green awning, offers light fare during the day. See also the buffet listings in chapter 6.

Services: 24-hour room service, guest-services desk, shoeshine, foreign-currency exchange.

Facilities: Casino, tour and show desks, car-rental desk, small video-game arcade, shopping arcade (see chapter 9), wedding chapel, men's and women's hair salons, state-of-the-art health spa (full complement of Universal and Life Fitness equipment, rowing machines, Lifecycles, treadmills, steam, sauna, whirlpools, massage, tanning bed, facials, salt rubs, and more), eight nightlit tennis courts and pro shop (lessons available), two basketball courts. A gorgeous palm-fringed sun- deck surrounded by lush tropical plantings centers on an Olympic-size swimming pool—one of the most beautiful in Las Vegas. There's a whirlpool, and guests can rent private cabanas with stocked refrigerators, TVs, ceiling fans, rafts, and private phones for $60 to $85 a day.

Flamingo Hilton

3555 Las Vegas Blvd. S., between Sands Ave. and Flamingo Rd., Las Vegas, NV 89109. ☎ **702/733-3111** or 800/732-2111. Fax 702/733-3353. 3,642 rms, 180 suites, 201 time-share units. A/C TV TEL. $69–$205 single or double, $250–$580 suite. Extra person $16. Children 18 and under stay free in parents' room. Inquire about packages and time-share suites. AE, CB, DC, DISC, ER, JCB, MC, V. Free parking (self and valet).

The Flamingo has changed a great deal since Bugsy Siegel opened his 105-room oasis "in the middle of nowhere" in 1946. It was so luxurious for its time that even the janitors wore tuxedos. Jimmy Durante was the opening headliner, and the wealthy and famous flocked to the tropical paradise of swaying palms, lagoons, and waterfalls. Today the Flamingo is a senior citizen on the Strip with a colorful history but a fresh, new look—one enhanced by a recent $130-million renovation and expansion. Siegel's "real class joint" is better than ever.

Rooms—occupying six towers—are variously decorated. Some are done up in shades of soft blue and peach for a resort look enhanced by pretty fabrics, light painted-wood furnishings, and lovely water-colors of tropical scenes. Other color schemes focus on soft earth tones, forest green, or coral. All accommodations offer in-room safes; TVs have in-house information and gaming-instruction stations, a keno channel, video checkout, message retrieval, and account review.

Dining: The Old West–themed **Beef Barron,** heralded by golden steer heads and a mural of a cattle roundup, bills itself as "a steakhouse forged in the spirit of our first great cattle ranchers." It has western art on the walls, steer-horn chandeliers, a mounted display of antique guns, and potted cacti. Dinner only; entrees $17.75 to $27.

Fronted by a tiered terra-cotta fountain, **Alta Villa** is designed to suggest an Italian village, with a vaulted ceiling, a trellised grape arbor under a painted sky, lots of plants, and grapevine-motif carpeting on flagstone floors. A pretty ceramic-tiled exhibition kitchen is a focal point. A traditional Italian menu offers pizzas, pastas, and entrees such as scampi in garlic butter, and chicken cacciatore or piccata. Dinner only; entrees $12.95 to $17.50 (pastas and pizzas $5.50 to $11).

Peking Market's interior simulates an open marketplace in a bustling Chinese city. Corrugated tin roofing, rough-hewn beams and columns, rattan-shaded hanging lamps, and shelves crammed with canned foodstuffs—not to mention a mural of an actual Chinese market—enhance the illusion. A central wood-burning brick oven casts a warm glow. Dinner only; entrees mostly $11 to $17.50. A four-course early bird dinner served from 5 to 7:30 pm is $8.50.

The **Flamingo Room**—adorned with murals of flamingos, flamingo sculptures, and glass etched with flamingos—is a posh candlelit precinct proffering piano-bar music at dinner. One of the draws here is an extensive salad bar where leafy greens and pasta salads are supplemented by smoked whitefish and salmon, crab salad, marinated chicken breast, peel-and-eat shrimp, and much more ($8.25 alone, $4.25 with an entree). The menu highlights steak and seafood dishes. The Flamingo Room also serves full American breakfasts. Open for breakfast and dinner daily; dinner entrees $9.95 to $17.50.

Hamada of Japan is a softly lit, teak-beamed restaurant centering on a small rock garden. Some of the seating is at teppanyaki grill tables, and there's also a sushi bar. Come by for a Japanese breakfast of fresh salmon, raw egg, sticky beans, rice, soup, pickles, vegetables, and seaweed ($12, including tax and tip). Open for all meals; lunch entrees $7.50 to $19.50, dinner entrees $7.50 to $26 (full teppanyaki dinners $13.95 to $22.95).

Lindy's Deli, a 24-hour coffee shop, is attractively decorated in southwestern colors (mauve, teal, and peach) with painted wood sculptures and pretty paintings. In addition to typical Las Vegas coffee-shop fare, it offers appetizing smoked fish platters (salmon, whitefish, sturgeon) with bagels and cream cheese, corned beef and pastrami sandwiches, matzo ball soup, and other traditional Jewish deli items.

Bugsy's Deli, featuring hero sandwiches and Italian desserts, along with other light fare, is a casual self-service eatery just off the casino. The **Pool Grille** serves up sandwiches, burgers, salads, and other light fare items along with desserts such as crème brûlée and key lime pie. And a **snack bar** serves the race and sports book area. **Bugsy's Bar,** festooned with orange and pink neon flamingo feathers, occupies a central position in the casino. And the **Rainbow Bar,** off the casino, has a wall of windows overlooking palm trees and waterfalls. The Flamingo's **Paradise Garden Buffet** is described in chapter 6.

Services: 24-hour room service, guest services desk, multilanguage services (interpreters are available for more than 35 languages; gaming guides are available in 6 languages).

Facilities: Casino, car-rental desk, tour and show desks, full-service beauty salon/barber shop, wedding chapel, four nightlit championship tennis courts with pro shop and practice alley (tennis clinics and lessons are available), shopping arcade (see chapter 9 for details). Three gorgeous swimming pools—along with two Jacuzzis, water slides, and a kiddie pool—are located in a 15-acre Caribbean landscape amid lagoons, meandering streams, fountains, waterfalls, a rose garden, and islands of live flamingos and African penguins. Ponds are filled with ducks, swans, and koi, and a grove of 3,000 palms graces an expanse of lawn. A health club offers a variety of machines, free weights, sauna, steam, a TV lounge, and hot and cold whirlpools. Exercise tapes are available, and spa services include massage, soap rub, salt glow, tanning beds, and oxygen pep-up.

✪ Luxor Las Vegas

3900 Las Vegas Blvd. S., between Reno and Hacienda aves., Las Vegas, NV 81119. ☎ **702/262-4000** or 800/288-1000. Fax 702/262-4452. 2,276 rms, 250 suites. Single or double $59–$139 Sun–Thurs, $109–$139 Fri–Sat. Concierge level $159, Jacuzzi suite $199–$250, other suites $500–$800. Extra person $10. Children under 12 stay free in parents' room. AE, CB, DC, DISC, MC, V. Free parking (self and valet).

Perfectly suited to its desert setting is the Luxor—a 30-story bronze pyramid fronted by an ornately carved 191-foot obelisk and guarded by a 10-story replica of the Sphinx of Giza. Inside, visitors can gaze at murals tracing 4,000 years of Egyptian history on narrated barge cruises along the "River Nile," which flows for 3,000 feet along the interior perimeter of the property. Throughout the hotel, ornamentation authentically replicates paintings, hieroglyphics, and artifacts from historic Egyptian sites. High-speed "inclinator" elevators run on a 39-degree angle, making the ride up to your room a bit of a thrill. At night, the eyes of the sphinx shoot lasers that interact with the obelisk and lagoon, holographic images appear on a water screen on the Karnak Lagoon, and "Re," a 315,000-watt light beam (the most powerful on earth) searches the heavens from the pyramid's apex (ancient Egyptians believed that their souls would climb the sides of a pyramid and ascend to the afterlife on a beam of light).

The Luxor's rooms are among the most attractive in town. Handsome faux-marquetry furnishings of mahogany- and amber-stained maple are painted with cartouches (symbolic signatures of Cleopatra and Alexander the Great) and hieroglyphics; walls are decorated with Egyptian friezes and bas-relief art, and attractive Egyptian-motif print fabrics complement deep teal carpeting. Sloped window walls remind you you're in a pyramid. *Note:* Most baths have showers only—no tubs. Especially desirable are a group of suites with glamorous art-deco elements, private sitting rooms, refrigerators, and—notably—Jacuzzis by the window (enabling you to soak under the stars at night). Floors 28 through 30 comprise a concierge level where the rates include continental breakfast, afternoon hors d'oeuvres, and an open bar; guests enjoy a private lounge, upgraded services and amenities, and their own concierge.

Dining: The Luxor's **Manhattan Buffet** is discussed in chapter 6. To enter **Isis,** the hotel's gourmet room, you'll pass through a colonnade of caryatid statues. Within, replicas of artifacts from King Tutankhamen's tomb are on display in glass cases, and a golden statue of Osiris forms a visual centerpiece. Diners—most of them ensconced in plush semicircular booths—are seated at candlelit tables under a domed turquoise ceiling studded with gold stars. A harpist plays during dinner. Entrees are listed under their Egyptian names.

The **Sacred Sea Room,** decorated in Egypt-evocative hues (turquoise, sienna, and tan), has gold walls adorned with murals and hieroglyphics depicting fishing on the Nile. Turquoise mosaic tiles on the ceiling suggest ocean waves, and the dining-at-sea ambience is further enhanced by a central ship's hull and mast and turquoise booths and tablecloths. Fresh- and salt-water seafood arrives daily from both coasts. Dinner only; entrees range from $12.95 to $21.95.

Papyrus, a Trader Vic's–like tropical setting, seats diners in high-backed bamboo and rattan chairs amid lush palms, Polynesian sculptures, native spears, and colorful stuffed birds. Bamboo eaves are draped with bougainvillea, laminated rattan tables are lit by candle lamps, and a rear wall replicates a Mayan ruin. The cuisine is eclectic Asian/Pacific Rim. Dinner only; entrees are $6.95 to $14.95.

The futuristic **Millennium High-Energy Café** on the attraction level—decorated in bold patterns and colors with red and blue neon tubing and faux-industrial finishes—serves space-age-monikered light fare. Beer, wine, and specialty drinks are available. Open daily 11am to 11pm.

The 24-hour **Pyramid Café**—with a double row of booths flanked by palm trees and foliage—is Egyptian-themed, with hieroglyphic-motif upholstery fabrics; Egyptian friezes, sculptures, and murals; and columns with scarab designs from the Temple of Luxor. The setting suggests the interior of a pyramid. Like the decor, the menu has an Egyptian theme with a small nod to Middle Eastern cuisine. Most menu items, however, are of the burger/salad/pasta/steak/seafood Las Vegas hotel coffee-shop genre.

The casino-level **Nile Deli,** paradoxically offering kosher-style fare—pastrami or corned beef on rye, chicken soup, bagel and lox platters—on the banks of the Nile, is open daily from 7am to 11pm. And there's a **Swensen's Ice Cream** shop on the attraction level.

The plush **Nefertiti's Lounge** is described in chapter 10. The **Obelisk Bar** and **Anteroom Lounge** serve the casino. **Tut's Hut**—a pink neon-rimmed lounge with bamboo columns and upholstered rattan furnishings—specializes in Polynesian drinks and Otemanu Hot Rock samplers (seafood, tenderloin, chicken, pork, or vegetables grilled at your table and served with plum, peanut, mustard, and teriyaki dipping sauces). The **Sportsbook Lounge,** adjoining the race and sports book, airs sports action on TV monitors overhead. And the **Oasis Terrace & Bar** provides poolside food and drinks.

Services: 24-hour room service, foreign-currency exchange, shoeshine.

Facilities: Casino; full-service unisex hair salon; complete spa and health club (with a full range of machines, free weights, steam, sauna, and Jacuzzi; massage, facials, herbal wraps, and other beauty treatments available); VirtuaLand, an 18,000-square-foot video arcade that show-cases Sega's latest game technologies; car-rental desk; tour/show/sightseeing desks. An immense palm-fringed swimming pool (palms even grow right in the pool), outdoor whirlpool, kiddie pool, pool-accessories shop, and luxurious cabanas (cooled by misting systems and equipped with rafts, cable TVs, phones, ceiling fans, tables and chairs, chaise longues, and refrigerators stocked with juices and bottled water) that rent for $75 a day.

✪ MGM Grand Hotel, Casino & Theme Park

3799 Las Vegas Blvd. S., at Tropicana Ave., Las Vegas, NV 89109. ☎ **702/891-7777** or 800/929-1111. Fax 702/891-1112. 4,254 rms, 751 suites. A/C TV TEL. $69–$119 single or double; concierge floor $79–$129 single or double with breakfast; $99–$2,500 suite. Extra person $10. Children under 12 stay free in parents' room. AE, DC, DISC, MC, V. Free parking (self and valet).

Sprawling over 112 acres, Kirk Kerkorian's billion-dollar *Wizard of Oz*–themed megaresort is the world's largest—an immense emerald-green monolith fronted by an 88-foot green-eyed golden sculpture of the MGM lion which doubles as an entranceway at its southeast corner. Visitors enter into a vast white-marble-floored lobby (the most impressive in town). Its registration desk is backed by the world's largest video wall, with 80 42-inch TV monitors apprising registering guests of hotel happenings. The casino—which includes a seven-story replica of Emerald City, with 75-foot green crystal spires—is the size of four football fields.

And the hotel's "backyard" is a 33-acre theme park (see chapter 7). A monorail connects this property with Bally's (see details in that hotel's listing above), and pedestrian skywalks link it with the Tropicana, Luxor, and Excalibur.

The rooms in MGM's quartet of 30-story towers are decorated in four distinct motifs. Most glamorous are the Hollywood rooms furnished in two-tone wood pieces (bird's-eye maple on cherry), with patterned gold bedspreads, gold-flecked walls (hung with gilt-framed prints of Humphrey Bogart, Marilyn Monroe, and Vivien Leigh as Scarlett), gilded moldings, and beds backed by mirrored walls. Oz-themed rooms have emerald-green rugs and upholstery, silver and gold star-motif wallpaper, bright poppy-print bedspreads, and tassled green drapes; walls are hung with paintings of Dorothy and friends. In the Casablanca rooms—decorated in earth tones (rust, taupe, sage) with shimmery fabrics and pecan/walnut furnishings and moldings—artworks depict Moroccan scenes such as an Arab marketplace. And the cheerful Old South rooms feature 18th-century–style furnishings, floral-print bedspreads and curtains, and faux-silk beige damask walls hung with paintings of southern belles and scenes from *Gone with the Wind.* All rooms offer gorgeous marble baths.

Impressions

There was a magic in this place. It was like stepping back into the frontier. Casino owners were king. They owned the town. They were glamorous. They had beautiful women and lots of money.

—Steve Wynn, on Las Vegas when he visited as a boy

Dining: Three cutting-edge stars in the Las Vegas culinary galaxy—the **Wolfgang Puck Café, Charlie Trotter's,** and **Mark Miller's Coyote Café**—are detailed in chapter 6. In addition, the following dining facilities comprise a restaurant row between the casino and the theme park.

The plush **Sir Reginald's Steak House**—with its rich mahogany beams and paneling, candlelit, white-linened tables with red napery; and tufted red leather booths—strikes a whimsical note at its entrance: a formally dressed canine (Sir Reginald) next to an oil portrait of his beautiful showgirl wife Foxey (a fox). Their story is detailed in the menu, which includes steak and seafood entrees. Dinner only; entrees mostly $12.95 to $24.95 (more for lobster).

Dragon Court is fronted by a pair of textured gold wall coverings adorned with tassled braid, and purple and gold fleur-de-lis pattern carpeting. Eclectic Chinese entrees are featured. Dinner only; entrees $7.50 to $24 (most under $15).

The inviting circus-themed **One-Liners Food Court**—with seating under an orange-and-yellow tent top—houses McDonald's, Hamada's Orient Express, Mamma Ilardo's Pizzeria, Nathan's (hot dogs and fries), and a Häagen-Dazs ice cream outlet that also features espresso and cappuccino. It is conveniently near the video-game arcade/carnival midway.

The **Stage Deli Express,** a cafeteria-style offshoot of the New York original, serves up traditional deli sandwiches; seating overlooks race and sports book action. **Benninger's,** off the casino, provides gourmet coffees and scrumptious fresh-baked pastries (great bear claws here). In addition, there are many restaurants and fast-food eateries in the theme park (details in chapter 7). The **Oz Buffet** is described in chapter 6. And another 24-hour New York–style deli, as yet unnamed, is in the works.

The **Center Stage Lounge,** the **Betty Boop Lounge,** and **Santa Fe Lounge**—all of them offering entertainment—are described in chapter 10. The circular **Flying Monkey Bar** serves the Emerald City casino. A talking robotic horse and jockey spout sports data at the **Turf Club Lounge** in the race and sports book area.

Services: 24-hour room service, foreign-currency exchange, guest-relations desk, shoeshine (in men's rooms).

Facilities: World's largest casino; MGM Grand Adventures Theme Park; state-of-the-art health spa and health club (with hot and cold whirlpools, a full complement of machines, sauna, steam, aerobics classes, a luxurious lounge and full supply of toiletries; massages, facials, sea-salt scrubs, herbal wraps, and many other beauty treatments are available); full-service unisex hair/beauty salon; four night-lit tennis courts with pro shop (lessons available); huge, beach-entry swimming pool with waterfall; a vast sundeck area with a Jacuzzi, pool bar, and cabanas equipped with cushioned chairs and towels that rent for $20 per day; a 30,000-square-foot video arcade (including virtual reality games); carnival midway with 33 games of skill; business center; florist; shopping arcade; two wedding chapels (in the theme park); show/sports event ticket desks; car-rental desk; sightseeing/tour desks; America West airline desk.

The **MGM Grand Youth Center,** a first-rate facility for children ages 3 to 16, has separate areas for different age groups. The center has a playhouse and tumbling mats for toddlers, a game room, extensive arts and crafts equipment, video games, a dining area, and a large-screen TV/VCR for children's movies. Accompanied by professional counselors, youngsters can visit the theme park or the swimming pool, take excursions to nearby attractions, have meals, and participate in all sorts of entertainment and activities (☎ 702/891-3200) for details and prices.

✪ Rio Suite Hotel & Casino

3700 W. Flamingo Rd., at I-15, Las Vegas, NV 89103. ☎ **702/252-7777** or 800/752-9746. Fax 702/253-6090. 1,555 suites. A/C TV TEL. Single or double $85 Sun–Thurs, $103–$150 Fri–Sat and holidays. Extra person $15. Children under 12 stay free in parents' room. Inquire about golf packages. AE, CB, DC, MC, V. Free parking (self and valet).

The Rio's gorgeous palm-fringed facade heralds a luxurious tropical resort—an ongoing "carnivale" enhanced by turquoise and pink neon lighting within and Brazilian music emanating from the Ipanema Bar. Casino carpeting is strewn with Rio resort motifs—confetti, maracas, streamers, and seashells—and there's a sandy "beach" out back. You won't miss the Strip, at this lively casino hotel and, in any case, it's just a few minutes away. After dark, the Rio emits powerful laser beams visible for 15 miles.

The Rio's spacious suites (each one is at least 600 square feet) are, unequivocally, the most stunning accommodations in town. The original suites are decorated in resort hues (peach, mauve, turquoise, coral) with splash-of-color accents; they feature bamboo furnishings, half-canopy beds, paintings of parrots and toucans in jungle settings, and beautiful tropical floral-print bedspreads and drapes. Newer Tower suites—done up in teal and burgundy, with handsome teak furnishings and lovely chintz fabrics—are equally appealing. Each suite has a large dressing room, a stunning bath (with full-length mirror and cosmetic lighting), big closets, a wraparound sofa, coffee table, and upholstered chaise longue. Picture windows provide panoramic views of the Strip. As for in-room amenities, you'll find an in-room safe, marble-topped refrigerator, and coffeemaker. Some suites are equipped with two phones.

Dining: Fiore, the Rio's premier restaurant, and its first-rate buffet are described in chapter 6.

The elegant **Antonio's** centers on a marble-columned rotunda in which a crystal chandelier is suspended from a recessed ceiling that resembles a Mediterranean sky. Other focal points are an exhibition kitchen and a magnificent marble display table brimming with tempting antipasto selections. Tables are exquisitely appointed. The menu features Italian entrees. Only dinner is served; most entrees are $17.95 to $24.95 (less for pasta).

Buzio's Oyster Bar offers a simpatico resort setting with glossy wood floors, seating in rattan chairs, and window walls overlooking the palm-fringed pool. Massive alabaster chandeliers and flowering plants are suspended from a lofty canvas-tent ceiling, a marble counter faces an exhibition kitchen where white-hatted chefs prepare food, and light jazz forms a pleasing audio backdrop. The menu features pan-roasted oysters and shrimp, seafood pastas, chowders, seafood salads, steamers, and raw oysters. Open Sunday to Thursday 11am to 11pm, Friday and Saturday 11am to 1am; entrees $8.95 to $15.95.

The Beach Café, also overlooking the swimming pool and sandy beach, is the Rio's 24-hour facility. It's tropically festive, with bright-red tufted-leather booths, colorful awnings and patterned canvas umbrellas, and pretty paintings of tropical scenes framed by shutters for a *trompe l'oeil* effect. Besides regular coffee-shop fare, the cafe features Mexican, Italian, Jewish deli, and Polynesian/Chinese specialties. Delicious fresh-baked desserts are a plus.

The two-story **All American Bar & Grille** is warmly inviting and filled with Americana. Mahogany-paneled walls are adorned with sporting paraphernalia and vintage advertising signs; there's a torch-bearing Statue of Liberty; and the 50 state flags hang over the bar, while American flags fly from lofty mahogany rafters. TV monitors over the bar broadcast sporting events. The menu features burgers, salads, and sandwiches at lunch; dinner options include steaks, seafood, and a choice of 27 domestic beers and selected wines by the glass. Lunch items $5.95 to $13.75 (most under $8), dinner entrees $8.95 to $23.95.

Toscano's Deli, off the casino, not only looks like a New York delicatessen but serves up a creditable pastrami or corned beef on rye. It also features pizza and pastas.

The **Ipanema Bar** and **Mambo Bar** in the casino are described in chapter 10. Another casino bar is under a fantasy coral reef with fish swimming overhead. Drinks, tropical and otherwise, are available poolside from the attractive open-air **Coco-Bana** or a service window off Buzio's Oyster Bar.

Services: 24-hour room service, guest-services desk, foreign-currency exchange, shoeshine, complimentary shuttle bus to/from the MGM and the Forum Mall.

Facilities: Casino, car-rental desk, tour and show desks, unisex hair salon (all beauty services, including massage and facials), small video arcade, fitness room (stair machine, rowing machine, Lifecycle, four-station exercise machine), shops (gifts, clothing for the entire family, logo merchandise). The Rio has two swimming pools, one shaped like an angelfish, the other a nautilus shell with a sand bottom (extending to a beach) and a waterfall. Three whirlpool spas nestle amid rocks and foliage, there are two sand volleyball courts, and blue-and-white-striped cabanas (equipped with rafts and misting coolers) can be rented for $8 per hour or $25 per day.

Riviera Hotel & Casino

2901 Las Vegas Blvd. S., at Riviera Blvd., Las Vegas, NV 89109. ☎ **702/734-5110** or 800/834-6753. Fax 702/794-9451. 1,978 rms, 158 suites. A/C TV TEL. $59–$95 single or double, $125–$500 suite. Extra person $20. Inquire about "Gambler's Spree" packages. AE, CB, DC, MC, V. Free parking (self and valet).

Opened in 1955 (Liberace cut the ribbon and Joan Crawford was official hostess of opening ceremonies), the Riviera is styled after

Factoid

What hotel was Martin Scorsese's movie Casino (starring Robert De Niro, Joe Pesci, and Sharon Stone) filmed at?

—The Riviera

the luxurious casino resorts of the Côte d'Azur. Its original nine stories made it the first "high-rise" on the Strip. Several towers later, the present-day Riviera is as elegant as ever.

Accommodations are richly decorated with handsome mahogany furnishings and burgundy or teal bedspreads with matching gold-tasseled drapes. Half the rooms here offer pool views. Amenities include in-room safes and cable TVs with pay-movie options and an in-house information station.

Dining: Kristofer's, a candlelit steak and seafood restaurant overlooking the pool, has a tropical look with rattan chairs at copper-topped bamboo tables, overhead fans, and potted ferns. An exhibition kitchen adds excitement. Prix-fixe dinners run $19.95 to $25.95. The adjoining lounge serves poolside fare. Dinner only.

Ristorante Italiano, under a simulated starlit sky, has a window wall backed by murals of Venice. Decorated in burgundy and mauve, it's a romantic setting with framed Italian art reproductions adorning brick walls and seating in roomy tapestry-upholstered booths. Classic Italian specialties are featured. Dinner only; most entrees $10.95 to $23.50 (veal and lobster dishes are pricier).

Kady's is the Riviera's very cheerful 24-hour restaurant, with white tile walls, marble-topped tables, and seating in bright leather-upholstered red, blue, and yellow booths. A wall of windows overlooks the pool, and poolside, there's patio seating. Along with the usual coffee-shop fare, Kady's menu offers Jewish deli specialties.

Rik' Shaw (don't ask me what the punctuation means) features Chinese fare in an elegant candlelit room with crystal chandeliers and mirrored columns. Mauve velvet walls are hung with gilt-framed Chinese paintings. The fan-shaped menu offers traditional Cantonese specialties. Dinner only; entrees $9.50 to $22.95 (most under $15).

An excellent choice for families is the **Mardi Gras Food Court** which, unlike most of its genre, is extremely attractive. White canvas umbrella tables, Toulouse–Lautrec-style murals, and etched-glass dividers combine to create a comfortable French cafe ambience. Your food choices include a Burger King, pizza, tacos, rotisserie chicken, Chinese fare, deli sandwiches, gyros and falafel, ice cream and frozen yogurts, and fresh-baked pastries. The Food Court is adjacent to the video-game arcade, so you can relax over espresso while the kids run off and play. Open daily 10:30am to midnight.

See also the buffet listings in chapter 6. There are two casino bars, **Delmonico's** and **Le Bistro Lounge;** the latter offers nightly live entertainment (see chapter 10).

Services: 24-hour room service, shoeshine.

Facilities: Casino (one of the world's largest), large arcade with carnival and video games, well-equipped health club (full complement of machines, free weights, steam, sauna, tanning, facials, salt/soap rubs, massage), Olympic-size swimming pool and sundeck, wedding chapel, beauty salon/barbershop, comprehensive business-services center, America West airlines desk, tour and show desks, car-rental desk, shops (see chapter 9 for details), two Har-Tru tennis courts lit for night play. A unique feature here: a wine-tasting booth operated by Nevada's only winery.

Sands Hotel Casino

3355 Las Vegas Blvd. S., just south of Sands Ave., Las Vegas, NV 89109. ☎ **702/ 733-5000** or 800/634-6901. Fax 702/733-5624. 675 rms, 40 suites. A/C TV TEL. $65–$145 single or double, $200–$2,000 suite. Extra person $10. Children under 12 stay free in parents' room. AE, CB, DC, DISC, MC, V. Free parking (self and valet).

The Sands, which opened in 1952 with new wings added here and there, is a familiar Las Vegas landmark. New York show producer and Copacabana nightclub owner Jack Entratter was one of its original backers, and he used his show-biz contacts to bring superstar entertainment and gorgeous showgirls to the Copa Room stage. Jimmy Durante, Red Skelton, Debbie Reynolds, Jerry Lewis, and the famed "Rat Pack" were among those who made regular appearances, and Frank Sinatra married Mia Farrow here eons ago. Entratter's efforts not only put the Sands on the map but helped establish Las Vegas as America's entertainment capital.

From the street you'll see only a scalloped 18-story white circular tower. Less visible are 10 smaller units named after famous racetracks— Hollywood Park, Aqueduct, Belmont, and others—situated over a wide expanse of palm-fringed gardens. Some tower rooms have textured faux-silk wall coverings adorned with prints of classical composers, traditional dark oak furnishings, plush rust-colored armchairs, green carpeting, and floral-pattern bedspreads and drapes. Others substitute plum carpeting and upholstery and display sports-themed artwork. Although the tower is circular, the rooms are sizable (not little wedges), with large mirrors behind the beds to enhance the spacious feeling. The rooms on the top four floors have balconies. The garden rooms—almost all with furnished patios or balconies—are decorated in soft resort pastels with bleached oak and painted off-white furnishings. Mirrored dressing areas are a plus. All Sands accommodations have large double closets or spacious armoires and phones with call waiting. The tower rooms have wet bars and tubs with marble seats. *Note:* Future plans call for a new 1,500-room tower.

Dining: The **Xanadu Steak House** has a warmly comfortable ambience with seating in plush teal booths and banquettes discreetly aglow in lavender and green neon. Glass bricks, a recessed ceiling, and gleaming copper decorative elements—all awash in red neon—provide a futuristic contrast to walls adorned with sprigs of cherry blossoms. Prix-fixe meals here (a terrific value) include all the trimmings and cost $18.95; only dinner is served.

The posh **Regency Ristorante**—softly illuminated by candles, frosted-glass sconces, and flattering pink light emanating from a cove ceiling—is highlighted by a large silk-flower display atop a pedestal.

Tables are beautifully appointed, cut-glass dividers create intimate dining areas, and a mirrored ceiling and arched mirrors add elegant gleam. Entrees include traditional Italian steak, veal, chicken and pasta dishes; seafood lasagne is a house specialty. Dinner only; most entrees $19.50 to $24.95 (more for steak and lobster, less for pasta).

The 24-hour **Shangri-La Café** centers on a rock fountain under a domed skylight where animated birds perch on the branches of a tree. Walls are embellished with murals of the magical Himalayan kingdom described by James Hilton in *Lost Horizon,* and the recessed sky ceiling is rimmed by a thin band of purple neon. In addition to its regular coffee-shop fare, Shangri-La offers a full Chinese menu from 5 to 11pm daily.

The **Snack Bar** in the casino offers light fare—pizza, sandwiches, hot dogs, 99¢ shrimp cocktails, danish and coffee—from 6am to 12:30am. One casino bar is called **Northern Exposure,** another is located in the race and sports book area, and the **Winners Circle Lounge** offers live nightly entertainment. See the buffet listings in chapter 6.

Services: 24-hour room service.

Facilities: Casino, tour and show desks, car-rental desk, shops (gift shop, men's and women's clothing, logo items), beauty salon,

---

🎠 Family-Friendly Hotels

Circus Circus *(see p. 81).*   My first choice if you're traveling with the family is centrally located on the Strip. Its mezzanine level offers ongoing circus acts daily from 11am to midnight, dozens of carnival games, and an arcade with more than 300 video and pinball games. Behind the hotel is a full amusement park.

Excalibur *(see p. 82).*   Also owned by Circus Circus, Excalibur features a whole floor of midway games, a large video-game arcade, crafts demonstrations, free shows for kids (puppets, jugglers, magicians), and thrill cinemas. It has child-oriented eateries and shows (details in chapter 10).

Luxor Las Vegas *(see p. 61).*   Another Circus Circus property. Kids will enjoy VirtuaLand—an 18,000-square-foot video arcade that showcases Sega's latest game technologies. Another big attraction here is the "Secrets of the Luxor Pyramid"—a high-tech adventure/thrill ride utilizing motion simulators and IMAX™ film.

The MGM Grand Hotel, Casino & Theme Park *(see p. 63).*   This *Wizard of Oz*–themed resort is backed by a 33-acre theme park and houses a state-of-the-art video arcade, a carnival midway, and an Emerald City adventure and magic show. A unique offering here is a youth center for hotel guests ages 3 to 16, with separate sections for different age groups. Offerings range from a playhouse and tumbling mats for toddlers to extensive arts and crafts equipment for the older kids.

nine-hole putting green. There are two swimming pools (one quite large) in a verdant tropical setting amid trees, shrubbery, stretches of neatly manicured lawn, and flower beds. A smallish men's and women's health club (men have somewhat more facilities, including a Universal 21-station unit and a stair machine) offers treadmills, Lifecycles, rowing machines, and cross-country ski machines. Both sections also feature whirlpools, sauna, steam, and massage.

MODERATE

Most of my Las Vegas listings fall into this category, and, once again, the hotels quoted here are much cheaper than moderately priced properties in other tourist meccas.

Barbary Coast Hotel & Casino

3595 Las Vegas Blvd. S., at Flamingo Rd., Las Vegas, NV 89109. ☎ **702/737-7111** or 800/634-6755. Fax 702/737-6304. 184 rms. A/C TV TEL. Single or double $75 Sun–Thurs, $100 Fri–Sat and holidays. Extra person $10. Children under 12 stay free in parents' room. AE, CB, DC, DISC, JCB, MC, V. Free parking (self and valet).

Evoking the romantic image of turn-of-the-century San Francisco, the Barbary Coast enjoys a terrific Strip location. The casino is adorned with $2 million worth of magnificent stained-glass skylights and the extremely charming Victorian-style rooms make for an opulent setting. The latter, decorated in shades of rose and gray, have half-canopied brass beds, gaslight-style lamps, oak moldings, period-look wallpapers, lace-curtain-trimmed windows, and pretty floral carpets. All accommodations include little sitting parlors with entrances framed by floral chintz curtains.

Dining: Michael's, the Barbary Coast's premier restaurant, is flamboyantly Victorian—an intimate dining room entered via frosted etched-glass doors, with white marble floors, red satin damask wall coverings, plush red velvet booths, and a gorgeous stained-glass dome overhead. A pink rose graces every elegantly appointed table. The menu highlights steaks and seafood. Dinner only; entrees $25 to $65.

The **Victorian Room,** open 24 hours, is another attractive turn-of-the-century venue, with multipaned beveled mirror walls, stained-glass windows and skylights, and seating in red tufted-leather booths. Its extensive menu runs the gamut from burgers to broiled Alaskan crab legs; in addition, Chinese entrees are offered at lunch and dinner.

There's also a **McDonald's** on the premises—a rather nice one with an oak-beamed ceiling, beveled mirrors, and a stained-glass sign—open almost round-the-clock. And two bars serve the casino.

Services: 24-hour room service, shoeshine.

Facilities: Casino, Western Union office, tour and show desks, gift shop.

Hacienda Hotel & Casino

3950 Las Vegas Blvd. S., between Tropicana Ave. and Russell Rd., Las Vegas, NV 89119. ☎ **702/739-8911** or 800/634-6713. Fax 702/798-8289. 1,090 rms, 50 suites. A/C TV TEL. Single or double $38–$68 garden room, $68–$98 tower room; $125–$350 suite. Extra person $8. Children 12 and under stay free in parents' room. AE, CB, DC, DISC, MC, V. Free Parking (self and valet).

Note: The Hacienda had just been acquired by new owners (the Circus Circus group) at press time, so you should expect to see changes in the offing by our next edition.

This south-of-the-border–themed hotel at the southern end of the Strip still offers warm hospitality and pleasant surroundings. Unlike most Las Vegas hotels, its entrance does not lead directly into a casino but into a charming terra-cotta–floored lobby where white stucco archways are colorfully embellished with paintings of tropical birds, flowers, and fruit. To your right is a 20-foot waterfall with live palms and tropical plantings under a skylight. And when you do enter the casino, it's an attractive, low-key facility decorated with garland friezes rather than neon.

Rooms in the North Tower sport rust or gray-blue color schemes with brass-accented walnut furnishings and quilted paisley bedspreads. Rooms in the South and Central towers have sturdy oak furnishings, but their colors, artwork, and Aztec-print bedspreads and drapes combine to create a southwestern feel. A flagstone passageway lined with tropical plants, bamboo, and cacti meanders through the garden-room area; these rooms, in six low buildings grouped around the pool, also maintain a southwest theme. All Hacienda room TVs offer pay-movie options, video checkout, and an in-house information channel.

Dining: The **Charcoal Room** is an intimate steak-and-seafood restaurant with semicircular black tufted-leather booths, candlelit white linened tables, and Mexican-themed gilt-framed oil paintings on wide-plank pine walls. Amber lighting emanates from wrought-iron lamps. Flambé specialties, prepared tableside, add excitement. Dinner only; entrees $12.95 to $21.95.

The southwestern-motif **Cactus Room,** a 24-hour restaurant, has peach adobe walls, with Mexican artifacts and terra-cotta pots of cacti set in arched stucco niches. Many Mexican entrees are offered as well as the requisite coffee-shop fare, and from 4pm to 2am there are low-priced specials featuring a choice of prime rib, crab legs, or fried chicken.

El Grande Buffet, served in a "Mexican courtyard" with wrought-iron railings, ficus trees, and ceramic-tiled food stations, offers all-you-can-eat meals at breakfast, lunch, dinner, and Sunday brunch.

The **New York Pasta Company** is cozy and cheerful, with candlelit tables covered in red-and-white checkered cloths, lace-curtain-draped windows, and a brick wall lined with oak wine casks. Its menu features pizzas, pastas, and traditional Italian entrees. Dinner only; entrees $6.50 to $14.95 (most under $10).

A pizza shop, deli, and frozen yogurt vendor are in the shopping arcade. There are two casino bars—the **Bolero Lounge,** featuring live entertainment nightly, and the 24-hour **Island Cantina,** offering 64-ounce "megaritas."

Services: Room service 6:30am to 1:30pm and 4:30 to 11pm, guest-services desk (also functions as show- and car-rental desk).

Facilities: Casino, shops (men's and women's clothing, jewelry, gifts, liquor, logowear), video-game arcade, beauty salon, night-lit tennis court, clover-shaped swimming pool and sundeck in a lush garden setting.

Camperland, a nicely landscaped 20-acre RV park on the premises, has spaces for 363 vehicles. In addition to complete hookups, it offers a nearby convenience store, playground, swimming pool, rest rooms, showers, picnic tables/barbecue grills, and coin-op laundry facilities. The rate is $14.95 to $19.95 per night, including full hookup. For details call 702/739-8911.

⑤ Harrah's Las Vegas

3475 Las Vegas Blvd. S., between Flamingo and Spring Mountain rds., Las Vegas, NV 89109. ☎ **702/369-5000** or 800/634-6785 or 800/HARRAHS. Fax 702/369-5008. 1,675 rms, 36 suites. A/C TV TEL. $50–$250 single or double. Extra person $15. Children 12 and under stay free in parents' room. AE, CB, DC, DISC, ER, MC, V. Free parking (self and valet).

Harrah's glittering Mississippi riverboat facade—complete with 185-foot smokestacks and a foghorn that sounds at frequent intervals—has been a Las Vegas landmark since 1973. The centrally located "ship on the Strip" is docked at Jackson Square, a French Quarter–themed shopping area.

At this writing, a new 35-story tower is in the works, which will add 644 rooms and 50 suites, 22,000 square feet of casino space, and two new restaurants.

My favorite Harrah's rooms, in the 35-story Captain's Tower, are decorated in peach and teal with bleached oak furnishings and verdigris accents. Prints by Renoir, Van Gogh, and Degas hang in the hallways—a rare note of culture in this town. Spacious mini-suites in this section, offering large sofas and comfortable armchairs, are especially desirable. In the 23-story Riverboat Tower, the carpets are gray or teal, the furnishings mahogany, with print bedspreads adding a splash of color. All room TVs offer hotel information and keno channels, pay movies, Nintendo, and video account review and checkout.

Dining: The plush **Claudine's Steak House** seats diners in roomy floral-tapestry-covered booths at candlelit tables. There are gorgeous brass candelabra chandeliers overhead, peach watered-silk walls are hung with Renoir-like paintings, and intimate seating areas are created by cut-glass and grass dividers. It all adds up to a romantic turn-of-the-century setting for continental/steak-and-seafood meals. Dinner only; most entrees $17.95 to $24.95. After you dine, relax over drinks in the adjoining piano bar lounge.

The garden-themed **Veranda,** Harrah's 24-hour coffee shop, is softly lit, with lots of faux foliage, framed botanical prints, and pretty floral carpeting. An extensive menu offers all the expected Las Vegas coffee-shop fare.

An "old salt" mannequin guards the entrance to **Joe's Bayou,** a Creole/seafood restaurant. Nautically themed, with amber ship's lanterns suspended over candlelit tables, the decor consists of riverboat paintings, fishnets, and racks of oars. Dinner only; entrees $8.95 to $15.95.

All That Jazz simulates a French Quarter street. Its walls reproduce the facades of shuttered New Orleans townhouses with wrought-iron balconies and window boxes; trees and streetlamps enhance the illusion. Jazz emanates from a player piano at night. With breakfast, you'll visit a gratis fruit, cereal, and pastry bar; Italian dinner entrees ($5.95 to $7.95) include soup, salad bar, and dessert bar.

Similar in decor is the **Court of Two Gators,** a bar/lounge off the casino with ivied walls and a lofty skylight ceiling. Its dance floor is popular at night when live bands play jazz and oldies. In the lobby are a **TCBY** and a cappuccino/espresso/pastry cart for quick breakfasts. And, finally, there's a **Race & Sports Book Bar** with an adjoining snack bar called the **Derby Deli.** See also the buffet listings in chapter 6.

Services: 24-hour room service (including a special pizza and pasta menu), complimentary gaming lessons.

Facilities: Casino, car-rental desk, tour and show desks, nice-sized video-game arcade, coin-op laundry, shops (see chapter 9 for details), unisex hair salon, wedding chapel. Harrah's has a beautiful Olympic-size swimming pool and sundeck area with a whirlpool, kids' wading pool, cocktail and snack bar, and poolside shop selling T-shirts and sundries. The hotel's health club is one of the best facilities on the Strip, offering Lifecycles, treadmills, stair machines rowing machines, lots of Universal equipment, free weights, whirlpool, steam, sauna, and massage; there are two TVs and a VCR for which aerobic exercise tapes are available.

Holiday Inn Casino Boardwalk

3750 Las Vegas Blvd. S., between Harmon and Tropicana aves., Las Vegas , NV 89109. ☎ **702/735-2400** or 800/HOLIDAY. Fax 702/739-8152. 202 rms. A/C TV TEL. Single or double $65–$105 Sun–Thurs, $85–$150 Fri–Sat. Extra person $10. Children 19 and under stay free in parents' room. AE, CB, DC, DISC, JCB, MC, V. Free parking at your room door.

You can't miss this Holiday Inn. Its unique new facade, fronted by a 100-foot sign, replicates New York's Coney Island, complete with roller coaster, ferris wheel, and a parachute jump—all with mannequin passengers. Newly renovated rooms are spanking clean standard hotel units. In the works are a 440-room tower and a brand-new casino which will contain 650 slot/video poker games, 20 table games, and a sports book. The already-extant amusement park–themed casino, notably cheerful and festive, has $1 minimum blackjack tables.

Dining: The **Cyclone Coffee Shop,** a 24-hour facility, is decorated with murals of the Coney Island Boardwalk and adorable roller coaster–motif lighting fixtures. It features vast portions and low-priced specials. Fresh-baked doughnuts and immense cinnamon buns are appealing here. A deli in the casino proffers pastrami sandwiches and the like. And a full restaurant and buffet room are under construction.

Services: 24-hour room service.

Facilities: Casino, two swimming pools, gift shop, RV and truck parking, coin-op washers/dryers, tour and show desks. Guests can use health club facilities nearby.

Imperial Palace

3535 Las Vegas Blvd. S., between Sands Ave. and Flamingo Rd., Las Vegas, NV 89109. ☎ **702/731-3311** or 800/634-6441. Fax 702/735-8578. 2,412 rms, 225 suites. A/C TV TEL. $49–$99 single or double, $79–$149 "luv tub" suite, $159–$499 other suites. Extra person $15. Inquire about packages. AE, DC, DISC, MC, V. Free parking (self and valet).

The blue pagoda-topped Imperial Palace, its shoji-screenlike facade patterned after Japanese temple architecture, is one of the world's largest hotels. Its Asian theme continues inside, with a dragon-motif ceiling and giant wind-chime chandeliers in the casino. A unique feature here is the Imperial Palace Auto Collection of more than 750 antique, classic, and special-interest vehicles spanning a century of automotive history (details in chapter 7).

Rooms, decorated in tones of beige and tan, have bamboo-motif beds and furnishings highlighted by bright tropical-look curtains and paintings. TVs offer in-house information channels, video message review and checkout, and pay-per-view movies. If you so desire, you can rent a "luv tub" suite with an enormous faux-marble bath (ample for two) and a canopied bed with a mirrored ceiling.

Dining: Embers, the Imperial Palace's gourmet room, is a plus venue with oak-framed mirrors adorning burgundy silk–covered walls, spacious candlelit booths, and a smoked-mirror ceiling with recessed pink neon. The menu features many steak and seafood entrees; there are also pasta dishes, and flambé desserts are a specialty. Dinner only; entrees $10.95 to $28 (most under $18).

The Ming Terrace, fronted by a bamboo ricksha, achieves additional Eastern ambience from Chinese screens and painted fans. Candles in fluted-glass holders provide soft lighting. The menu features Mandarin, Cantonese, and Szechuan specialties. Dinner only; most entrees $8.75 to $20.95.

The **Rib House** is a rustic setting with exposed brick walls, wood-bladed fan chandeliers overhead, and heavy oak dividers defining seating areas. Light from frosted-glass sconces, candlelit tables, and a working fireplace casts a warm, cozy glow. Barbecued ribs and chicken are specialties. Dinner only; entrees $9.95 to $16.95.

The Seahouse, a casual nautically themed restaurant under a beamed ceiling, seats diners in captain's chairs. Low lighting emanates from brass ship's lanterns and candlelit tables. Fresh seafood entrees are featured, but if you're not a fish fancier you can order filet mignon béarnaise or charbroiled chicken breast with sautéed mushrooms. Dinner only; entrees mostly $11.95 to $16.95.

The 24-hour **Teahouse** has pagoda eaves overhead, bamboo furnishings, and booths separated by shoji-screen dividers. It offers (in addition to the usual burgers, salads, sandwiches, and full entrees) buffet brunches weekdays ($5.95) and champagne Sunday brunches ($6.50) from 8am to 3pm. A great buy here is a prime rib and champagne dinner featured nightly from 5 to 10pm for $8.25.

Pizza Palace—a cheerful eatery with wine-barrel facades adorning cream stucco and exposed-brick walls, red-and-white checkered tablecloths, big tufted-leather booths, and stained-glass lighting fixtures—serves regular and deep-dish pizzas, Italian sandwiches, and pasta dishes. An antipasto salad bar is a plus. Open 11am to midnight; entrees $3.75 to $10.30, the latter for a large pizza with three toppings.

The **Emperor's Buffet,** on the third floor, has a South Seas decor composed of thatched roofing, bamboo and rattan paneling, Polynesian carvings and totems; seating is in sea-green leather booths. Breakfast is served 7 to 11am ($3.99); lunch 11am to 4pm ($4.99), dinner 5 to 10pm ($5.99).

Betty's Diner, in the shopping arcade, serves sandwiches, pizza, nachos, hot dogs, malts, and ice-cream sundaes. **Burger Palace** is attractively decorated with sports-themed murals. Adjoining it is the **Sports Bar** where you can follow the races over cocktails. There are a total of 10 cocktail bars/lounges in the hotel, including the **Mai Tai Lounge** on the main floor and the **Poolside Bar** (both specializing in exotic Polynesian drinks), and the **Ginza, Geisha, Sake,** and **Kanpai** bars serving the casino.

Services: 24-hour room service, gratis gaming lessons, shoeshine in casino.

Facilities: Casino, health club (machines, free weights, sauna, steam, massage, tanning, TV lounge), show and tour desks, car-rental desk, travel agency, unisex hairdresser, wedding chapel, video-game arcade, shopping arcade (gifts, women's fashions, a western shop, logo items, souvenirs). An Olympic-size swimming pool is backed by a rock garden and waterfalls, and its palm-fringed sundeck area also has a Jacuzzi.

Maxim

160 E. Flamingo Rd., between the Strip and Koval Lane, Las Vegas, NV 89109. ☎ **702/731-4300** or 800/634-6987. Fax 702/735-3252. 757 rms, 38 suites. A/C TV TEL. Single or double $49–$69, Sun–Thurs, $75–$98 Fri–Sat; $175–$305 suite. Extra person $10. Children under 4 stay free in parents' room. AE, DC, MC, V. Free parking (self and valet).

Just a short walk from the heart of the Strip, the Maxim is a friendly property that has doubled in size since its 1977 opening. The rooms and public areas are currently undergoing a multimillion-dollar renovation. Some accommodations already sport a new southwestern resort look. They're decorated in turquoise, mauve, and peach, with splashy floral-print bedspreads and drapes, bureaus topped by large oak-framed mirrors, attractive abstract paintings, and textured beige wallpapers. The older rooms, decorated in earth tones, have sienna ultrasuede walls and photomurals of Las Vegas behind the beds. All offer TVs with pay-movie options and in-house information channels. If you prefer, you can rent a "players suite" with a whirlpool tub in the bedroom and a separate living room with wet bar.

Dining: A major new restaurant is in the planning stage at this writing, though no details were available at press time.

The Treehouse is the Maxim's 24-hour coffee shop, a low-lit facility with many tables overlooking the casino. In addition to the requisite coffee-shop fare, it features daily specials such as a New York steak or prime rib dinner for $4.95.

Jack's Colossal Deli, a cheerful sidewalk cafe with a window wall and red-and-green-striped booths under an awning, is lit by globe street lamps. The booths are separated by planters of philodendrons. There's also a brick-floored ice-cream parlor-like interior room. Service is cafeteria style. The fare includes fresh-baked doughnuts, muffins, and pastries for breakfast. Later in the day you can order tacos, chili, salads, sandwiches, homemade soups, and ice cream. Open 7am to 9pm.

The **Grand Buffet,** served on the mezzanine level, is rather elegant, especially at dinner when candlelit tables are covered in crisp linen and a pianist entertains on a baby grand. Dinner ($5.95) is served nightly from 4 to 10pm. A weekday brunch buffet ($4.95) is served from 10am to 3pm. Saturday and Sunday a champagne brunch ($6.95) is served from 9am to 3pm.

There are two casino cocktail lounges, the **Waterfall** and **Cloud Nine.**

Services: Room service (6 am to midnight), shoeshine.

Facilities: Car-rental desk, tour and show desks, small video-game arcade, gift shop (it also carries resort wear, liquor, luggage, jewelry, and logo items), beauty salon/barbershop, pool and sundeck with seasonal poolside bar.

Sahara Hotel & Casino

2535 Las Vegas Blvd. S., at E. Sahara Ave., Las Vegas, NV 89109. ☎ 702/737-2111 or 800/634-6666. Fax 702/791-2027. 1,945 rms, 90 suites, A/C TV TEL. $55–$85 single or double, $200 suite. Extra person $10. Children under 14 stay free in parents' room. AE, CB, DC, MC, V. Free parking (self and valet).

Fronted by a 222-foot sign spelling out its name in letters 18 feet high and 10 feet wide, the Sahara's come a long way since it opened in 1952 on the site of the old Club Bingo. It's gone from 200 to 2,000-plus rooms with lofty towers, a major showroom, and an impressive array of restaurants, shops, and services. One thing hasn't changed, however; it was the northernmost major hotel on the Strip when it opened, and it still is. At press time, the Sahara was about to change ownership. A major multi-million-dollar renovation will ensue, along with the construction of a sister hotel across the Strip. Hence, some of what you read here may be subject to change. Right now, rooms in the Tunis and Tangiers Towers are decorated in earth tones (beige and rust) with jade accents and grasspaper-look wall coverings embellished by framed floral prints. The largest accommodations—in the Alexandria Tower—are decorated in shades of rust and burgundy. And the original garden rooms, in two-story buildings, are cream and mauve with dark-wood furnishings. All are of the basic hotel room genre. Some Tower rooms have balconies.

Dining: The House of Lords is a plush continental restaurant with a suit of armor in its entrance foyer and a stunning mahogany ceiling within. Seating is in semicircular tufted red leather booths at white-linen-covered tables lit by shaded candle lamps. You'll dine on fancy fare with sorbet served between courses and complimentary petit fours as a finale. Dinner only; entrees $21 to $29.50.

La Terrazza is an intimate Italian dining room on the third floor—a bilevel cream stucco grotto with a wall of windows overlooking the pool, and tables lit by silk-shaded candle lamps. Four pastas are offered with a choice of sauces. Or you might opt for an Italian entree. Dinner only; entrees $12.95 to $29.95.

The Mexican Village—housed in a room that, until recently, was the exotic setting for a Polynesian dinner show—still has a few private dining gazebos that used to comprise VIP seating. Ask for them when you reserve if you have at least three in your party. A meal here might begin with an order of cheese- and jalapeño-stuffed quesadillas, followed by a Mexican version of bouillabaisse, fajitas, or roast pork marinated with garlic and Mexican spices and served with corn tortillas. The adjoining **Acapulco Cantina,** backed by a tropical aquarium, serves margaritas, Mexican beers, and light fare. Dinner only; entrees $8.95 to $12.95.

The **Caravan Coffee Shop,** a 24-hour facility off the casino with windows overlooking the pool, is fronted by a kneeling camel. A mural of an Arab market and photographs of camels and palm trees further enhance the desert theme. Its extensive menu includes all the requisite coffee-shop fare. A steak and lobster dinner with salad, potato, and vegetable is just $7.77. And a steak and eggs breakfast served from 11pm to 6am is $2.95.

The **Turf Club Deli,** next to the Race and Sports Center, features Jewish deli fare—homemade matzoh-ball soup, lox and bagels, pickled herring, and pastrami, corned beef, and brisket on rye. Open 8am to 4pm; everything on the menu is under $6.

The **Oasis Buffet** is detailed in chapter 6. Bar/lounges include two 24-hour casino bars (the **Safari Bar** and the **Sports Book Bar**), plus the **Casbah Lounge** offering top-notch live entertainment daily from 2pm to 6pm and 7pm to 4am.

Services: 24-hour room service.

Facilities: Casino, beauty salon/barbershop, car-rental desk, tour and show desks, shops (see chapter 9), video-game arcade. The Sahara has a large swimming pool and sundeck with a pool shop and poolside bar in nearby thatched-roof structures. A smaller pool shares the same courtyard setting.

Stardust Resort & Casino

3000 Las Vegas Blvd. S., at Convention Center Dr., Las Vegas, NV 89109. ☎ **702/ 732-6111** or 800/634-6757. Fax 702/732-6257. 2,140 rms, 160 suites. A/C TV TEL. Single or double Tower room $75–$150 Sun–Thurs, $75–$300 Fri–Sat; Villa room $40–$70 Sun–Thurs, $60–$100 Fri–Sat; Motor Inn room $24–$36 Sun–Thurs, $45–$65 Fri–Sat; $150–$500 suite. Extra person $10. Children 12 and under stay free in parents' room. AE, CB, DC, MC, V. Free parking (self and valet).

Opened in 1958, the Stardust is a longtime resident of the Strip, its 188-foot, starry sign one of America's most recognized landmarks. Today fronted by a fountain-splashed exterior plaza, the Stardust has kept pace with a growing city. In 1991, it added a 1,500-room tower and a 35,000-square-foot state-of-the-art meeting and conference center—part of a comprehensive $300 million expansion and renovation project. In the 1990s the Stardust is still a brightly shining star on the Strip.

Rooms in the 32-story West Tower are decorated in rich earth tones with black accents and bedspreads and drapes in bold abstract prints. East Tower rooms (my favorites) are light, airy, and spacious, with peach carpeting and attractive sea-foam green floral-print bedspreads, upholstered headboards, and draperies. You can rent an adjoining parlor room with a sofa bed, Jacuzzi tub, refrigerator, and wet bar—a good choice for families. Also quite nice are Villa rooms in two-story buildings surrounding a large swimming pool. Decorated in soft south-western pastels (mauve, beige, aqua), they feature grasspaper-covered walls hung with attractive artwork. Private shaded patios overlooking the pool are a plus here. The least E rooms are in the Stardust's Mo-tor Inn—four two-story white buildings with shuttered windows set far back on the property. They've been cheerfully decorated in southwest-ern resort colors, and if you don't mind being a block from the casino, they represent good value. Motor Inn guests can park at their doors. All Stardust accommodations offer in-room safe, TVs have Spectra-vision movie options and in-house information channels.

Dining: William B's, an elegant steak-and-seafood restaurant, is a clubby crystal-chandeliered precinct with dark oak-paneled walls, candlelit tables, and seating in comfortable upholstered armchairs. It's fronted by a handsome bar/lounge. Flambé desserts are a house specialty. Dinner only; entrees $14.95 to $27.95.

Tres Lobos, designed to resemble the open courtyard of a Mexican hacienda, achieves its south-of-the-border ambience via colonnaded white stucco archways, beamed and vaulted ceilings, ceramic tile floors, murals of Mexico, indoor trees, fountains, statuary, and big planters of greenery. A plush adjoining lounge specializes in many-flavored margaritas. All the usual Mexican fare is offered along with some less typical entrees. Dinner only; entrees $6.95 to $11.95.

Toucan Harry's Coffee Shop, the Stardust's 24-hour facility, is lushly tropical, with grass-green carpeting, abundant faux foliage, mu-rals of tropical birds, overhead fans, bamboo-look chairs (most seating is in roomy booths), and a tented fabric ceiling. In addition to a vast array of sandwiches, salads, and full entrees (including many low-fat, low-cholesterol items), Harry's features a full Chinese menu with more than 50 dishes.

Ralph's Diner reflects America's current nostalgia craze. Fifties rock 'n' roll tunes emanate from an old-fashioned jukebox (there are also jukeboxes at each table), the waitstaff is garbed in classic white diner uniforms, and the decor features a black-and-white checker-board floor and chrome-plated Formica tables. All-American fare is served, an old-fashioned soda fountain turns out desserts, and low-priced blue-plate specials are offered daily. Open 7am to 10pm; everything is under $10 (most are under $7).

Tony Roma's, which you may know from other locations, has a home at the Stardust; more about it—and the Stardust's **Warehouse Buffet**—in chapter 6. **Short Stop,** a snack bar in the race and sports book area of the casino, serves sandwiches and light fare throughout the day. There are eight bars and cocktail lounges in the hotel, including the **Terrace Bar** in the casino with an alfresco seating area overlooking the pool and the **Starlight Lounge,** featuring live music nightly.

Services: 24-hour room service, shoeshine.

Facilities: Casino, beauty salon/barbershop, video-game arcade, car-rental desk, tour and show desks, shops (gifts, candy, clothing, jewelry, logo items, liquor). There are two large swimming pools, one in the Villa section, the other between the East and West Towers. Both have attractively landscaped sundecks and poolside bars; the Towers pool area has three whirlpool spas. Guests can use the Las Vegas Sporting House directly behind the hotel, a state-of-the-art, 24-hour health club; its extensive facilities are detailed in chapter 7.

Tropicana Resort & Casino

3801 Las Vegas Blvd. S., at Tropicana Ave., Las Vegas, NV 89109. ☎ **702/739-2222** or 800/634-4000. Fax 702/739-2469. 1,788 rms, 120 suites (casino use only). A/C TV TEL. $65–$95 single or double. Extra person $10. Children under 18 stay free in parents' room. AE, CB, DC, MC, V. Free parking (self and valet).

The Tropicana, for several decades positioned as a South Seas resort right on the Strip, further enhanced its exotic image in 1995 with a major renovation. Most notably, the resident bird and wildlife population dramatically increased; a colorful Caribbean village facade was erected at the porte-cochere entrance; nightly laser light shows commenced on the Outer Island corner facing the Strip; and pedestrian skywalks were constructed to link the Trop with the MGM Grand, the Excalibur, and the Luxor. Heralded by 35-foot Easter Island heads, a 25-foot waterfall, outrigger canoes, and flaming torchiers, the Trop today comprises a lush landscape of manicured lawns, towering palms, oleanders, weeping willows, and crepe myrtles. There are dozens of waterfalls, thousands of exotic flowers, lagoons, aquariums, and koi ponds. And flamingos, finches, black swans, mandarin ducks, African crown cranes, cockatoos, macaws, toucans, and Brazilian parrots live on the grounds, their effect enhanced by concealed speakers emitting jungle sounds and calypso music. There's even a wildlife walk inside the resort itself, occupying a corridor that connects a pair of towers.

Rooms in the Paradise Tower are traditional, with French provincial furnishings and turn-of-the-century-look wallpapers. Island Tower rooms, more befitting a tropical resort, are decorated in pastel colors like pale pink and seafoam green, with splashy print bedspreads and bamboo furnishings; some have beds with mirrored walls and ceilings. All Trop rooms offer sofas and safes; TVs have Spectravision movies, account review, video checkout, and channels for in-house information and gaming instruction.

Dining: Mizuno's, a beautiful teppanyaki dining room, is detailed in chapter 6, as are the Trop's buffet offerings.

El Gaucho is an elegantly rustic Argentine steak house, with rough-hewn log beams overhead, burgundy leather booths, candlelit ceramic-tile tables, and pecky-pine walls hung with cowhides, antlers, serapes, branding irons, and gaucho gear. Steaks, chops, prime rib, and seafood come with traditional accompaniments. Dinner only; entrees $19.50 to $33.95.

Bella Roma's, a charming Italian ristorante pleasingly decorated in various hues of green, has cream stucco walls hung with impressionist paintings, candlelit tables, and oak-shuttered windows over-looking the treetops of the lushly landscaped pool area. Traditional Italian fare is served along with steaks. Dinner only; entrees $11.50 to $21.95.

Papagayo's is a colorful Mexican eatery behind a wrought-iron gate, where cream stucco walls are adorned with Mexican rugs and paintings by Diego Rivera. Wooden tables are set with brightly hued place mats and napkins; ceramic-tiled room dividers serve as shelves for displaying pottery, cacti, and bowls of gourds; and hanging wrought-iron lanterns provide soft lighting. Dinner only; entrees $7.95 to $14.95.

Calypso's, the Trop's 24-hour coffee shop, is the most cheerful in town. Decorated in bright island colors (turquoise, red, orange, and green), its walls are adorned with paintings and wood cutouts of palm trees, ocean waves, parrots, and macaws. A wall of windows overlooks waterfalls, weeping willows, and palm-fringed ponds filled with ducks and flamingos. Traditional (and very tasty) coffee-shop fare is augmented by interesting items ranging from Caribbean shrimp satay to bacon-stuffed cheese quesadillas. An extensive Chinese menu is available nightly from 6pm to midnight.

The **Players Deli,** sandwiched between the casino and the pool, is a unique cafeteria-cum-gaming room where slot and video poker machines are equipped with handy pullout dining ledges. Gamblers can also snack here at poker tables or in a small keno lounge or sports book. Hot and cold sandwiches, salads, and snack fare (nachos, chicken wings) are featured. Open daily from 10am to 10pm.

Down a level from the casino, in the Atrium Shopping area, is a **Baskin-Robbins** ice-cream and frozen-yogurt parlor and **Antonio's Pizza Deli,** purveying hot dogs, pizza, deli sandwiches, and other light fare. The Trop's buffet room is discussed in chapter 6. The **Coconut Grove Bar** serves the pool area, and the **Tropics Bar** is between the two towers on the wildlife walk.

Services: 24-hour room service, shoeshine.

Facilities: Casino, health club (a range of machines, treadmills, exercise bikes, steam, sauna, Jacuzzi, massage, and tanning room), video-game arcade, tour and show desks, two wedding chapels, car-rental desk, beauty salon and barbershop, business center, travel agent, shops (jewelry, chocolates, women's footwear, logo items, women's fashions, sports clothing, gifts, newsstand).

Three swimming pools (one Olympic size) and three whirlpool spas are located in a 5-acre water park with 30 splashing waterfalls, lagoons, and lush tropical plantings. One pool has a swim-up bar/blackjack table.

INEXPENSIVE

These are basically the lowest priced hotels and motels in town. They include two major Strip properties Circus Circus and Excalibur. Remember that off-season you can sometimes get into hotels in the

"Moderate" to "Very Expensive" categories at budget rates by bargaining with the reservations clerk.

ⓢ Circus Circus Hotel/Casino

2880 Las Vegas Blvd. S., between Circus Circus Dr. and Convention Center Dr., Las Vegas, NV 89109. ☎ **702/734-0410** or 800/444-CIRC or 800/634-3450. Fax 702/734-2268. 2,674 rms, 126 suites. A/C TV TEL. For up to 4 people $36–$40 Sun–Thurs, $50–$55 Fri–Sat, $65 holidays; suite $46 Sun–Thurs, $65 Fri–Sat, $85–$100 holidays and convention times; two-bedroom parlor suite $129. AE, CB, DC, DISC, MC, V. Free parking (self and valet).

A 123-foot clown (his name is Lucky) and a festive pink-and-white circus tent beckon visitors to Circus Circus, a hotel that revolutionized Las Vegas tourism by offering a wealth of entertainment for kids. The midway level features dozens of carnival games, a large arcade (more than 300 video and pinball games), trick mirrors, and ongoing circus acts under the big top from 11am to midnight daily. The world's largest permanent circus according to the *Guinness Book of World Records*, it features renowned trapeze artists, stunt cyclists, jugglers, magicians, acrobats, and high-wire dare-devils. Spectators can view the action from much of the midway or get up close and comfy on benches in the performance arena. There's a "be-a-clown" booth where kids can be made up with washable clown makeup and red foam rubber noses. They can grab a bite to eat in McDonald's (also on this level), and since the mezzanine overlooks the casino action, they can also look down and wave to mom and dad. Circus clowns wander the midway creating balloon animals and cutting up in various ways. Sometimes they even work the front desk.

The thousands of rooms here occupy sufficient acreage to warrant a free Disney World–style aerial shuttle (another kid pleaser) and mini-buses connecting its many components. Accommodations throughout are cheerful, decorated in bright red and blue color schemes. Some have ecru walls adorned with hot-air balloons, others feature striped wallpaper, and all utilize circus-themed art, clown lamps, and so forth. Skyrise Tower rooms offer showers only in the bath. All rooms here have safes; TVs have in-house information and gaming stations. Circus Tower rooms are larger and offer tub baths; however, all accommodations are attractive. You get a lot for your money here. The Manor section comprises five white, three-story buildings out back fronted by rows of cypresses. Manor guests can park at their doors, and a gate to the complex that can be opened only with a room key assures security. All sections of this vast property have their own swimming pools; additional casinos serve the main tower and Skyrise buildings; and both towers provide covered parking garages.

Dining: Popular with locals **The Steak House** is elegant and candlelit, its cherry-paneled walls hung with gilt-framed oil landscapes and other pastoral scenes. Shelves of books and green glass chandeliers create a clubby look. There's an open exhibition kitchen where sides of beef are displayed, and a plush lounge adjoins. Dinner only; entrees $13.95 to $23.95.

The very reasonably priced **Pink Pony** is Circus Circus's cheerful bubble-gum pink and bright red 24-hour eatery, with big paintings of clowns on the walls and pink pony-motif carpeting. It offers a wide array of coffee-shop fare, including a number of specially marked "heart-smart" (low-fat, low-cholesterol) items.

The **Skyrise Dining Room,** another festive 24-hour facility in the Skyrise Tower, has bright red chairs and booths, lots of decorative brass trim, and walls hung with old-fashioned circus posters. Its menu is similar to the Pink Pony's. A 16-ounce prime rib or New York steak dinner here is just $6.95.

There's a brass-railed **Pizzeria** in the main casino, a cheerful setting with roomy red and green booths and red or yellow tables. Hung with colorful banners, it offers pies with a choice of 20 toppings. **Latte Express,** featuring gourmet coffees, adjoins. Two 24-hour eateries—the **Westside Deli** (in the Min Tower's casino) and the **Skyrise Snack Bar** (near the race and sports book)—round out food options here.

In addition there are seven casino bars throughout the Circus Circus complex, notably the carousel-themed **Horse-A-Round Bar** on the midway level. And speaking of the midway level, don't forget **McDonald's.** The **Circus Buffet** is discussed in chapter 6.

Services: Limited room service (continental breakfast and drinks only), shoeshine.

Facilities: Three casinos, wedding chapel, tour and show desks, car-rental desk, unisex hairdresser, three swimming pools, two video-game arcades, shops (see chapter 9), Grand Slam Canyon amusement park.

Adjacent to the hotel is **Circusland RV Park,** with 384 full-utility spaces and up to 50-amp hookups. It has its own 24-hour convenience store, swimming pools, saunas, Jacuzzis, kiddie playground, fenced pet runs, video-game arcade, and community room. The rate is $12 Sunday to Thursday, $16 Friday and Saturday, $18 holidays.

⑤ Excalibur

3850 Las Vegas Blvd. S., at Tropicana Ave., Las Vegas, NV 89109. ☎ **702/597-7777** or 800/937-7777. Fax 702/597-7040. 4,032 rms. A/C TV TEL. For up to 4 people: $49–$69 Sun–Thurs, $59–$89 Fri–Sat. Children under 18 stay free in parents' room, children over 18 pay $10 weekends only. AE, CB, DC, MC, V. Free parking (self and valet).

One of the largest resort hotels in the world, Excalibur (aka "the Realm") is a gleaming white turreted castle complete with moated drawbridge, battlements, and lofty towers. In this Arthurian fantasy world, cocktail waitresses and dealers wear medieval garb; the casino is festooned with armor and heraldic banners; and knights, jesters, madrigal singers, and dancing "bears" roam the premises. The second floor comprises the hotel's Medieval Village—site of Excalibur's restaurants and quaint shops along winding streets and alleyways. On the Village's Jester's Stage, jugglers, puppeteers, and magicians delight guests with free 20-minute performances throughout the day. Another unique Excalibur feature is the Fantasy Faire, below the casino level, housing a large video arcade, dozens of medieval-themed carnival games, and two "magic motion machine" theaters featuring high-tech visual thrills; the thrills include simulated roller coaster and runaway train adventures and an outer space demolition derby directed by George Lucas—

enhanced by hydraulically activated seats that synchronize with the on-screen action. There's enough to entertain kids for hours while mom and dad enjoy the casino.

The rooms maintain the Arthurian-legend motif with walls papered to look like stone castle walls. Oak furnishings are heraldically embellished; torchier sconces frame the mirror; your bedspread has a fleur-de-lis theme; and prints of jousting knights adorn the walls.

Dining: Camelot, Excalibur's fine premier dining room, offers continental fare in a rustic castle setting. Stone walls are hung with replicas of medieval tapestries; ivied stone archways create intimate dining areas, and murals of Camelot's pristine lakes and verdant forests form an idyllic backdrop. Dinner only; entrees $10.95 to $19.95.

Sir Galahad's, a prime rib restaurant, occupies a candlelit "castle" chamber with massive oak beams and wrought-iron candelabra chandeliers overhead. Tudor-style walls are embellished with crossed swords, patinized torchiers, and heraldic crests. The menu features prime rib dinners only. Dinner only; entrees $10.95 to $14.95.

Wild Bill's, a western-themed restaurant and dance hall, features beveled-glass doors punctured by "bullet holes," walls adorned with rodeo murals, and booths separated by large wagon wheels. A rustic bar nestles in one corner, and seating is at bare oak tables overlooking the dance floor (country music is played while you dine). Entrees include steak, ribs, catfish, and burgers. Dinner only; entrees $8.95 to $19.95 (most under $10, burgers and sandwiches $5.95 to $7.95). Sundays a $5.99 breakfast buffet is served from 9am to 1pm.

Lance-a-Lotta Pasta is a flamboyant Italian dining room, with interior awnings and street lamps, fluted columns, and whimsical wall decorations that include a doll carriage, a pitchfork, a sled, immense garlic cloves, and other assorted paraphernalia. Bunches of grapes, strands of pasta, cheeses, and peppers are suspended overhead. Festive Italian music sets the mood. The menu lists pizzas and pastas, subs and hero sandwiches. Open for lunch and dinner; all entrees under $7 at lunch, under $13 at dinner. **Café Expresso,** a window operation off Lance-a-Lotta Pasta, serves espresso, cappuccino, and pastries. It has several tables in the Medieval Village.

The **Sherwood Forest Café,** its entrance guarded by a sentry of lavender dragons (kids love to climb on them), is Excalibur's 24-hour facility. In heraldic mode, it has leaded-glass windows, wrought-iron candelabra chandeliers, faux-stone walls, and adornments that include banners, crests, and cannons. The menu offers the usual Vegas coffee-shop mix of sandwiches, burgers, salads, and serious entrees, but there are some unexpected desserts such as brioche Romanoff—a fresh-baked sweet brioche filled with Grand Marnier-marinated strawberries.

Another heraldic dining room, the **Round Table Buffet,** is described in chapter 6. Other facilities include three snack bars named **Robin Hood** (in the Medieval Village), **Hansel & Gretel** (in Fantasy Faire), and **Little John's** (in the casino). The **Village Pub** is an Alpine-themed bar in the Medieval Village; the **Minstrel's Theatre Lounge,** off the casino, offers live entertainment nightly (during the day movies and sporting events are shown on a large-screen TV); a circular bar called **King's Pavilion** serves the casino; and a snack and cocktail bar serves the North pool.

Services: Limited 24-hour room service (continental breakfast and pizza only), free gaming lessons, shoeshine.

Facilities: Casino, tour and show desks, state-of-the-art video-game arcade, wedding chapel (you can marry in medieval attire), unisex hairdresser, car-rental desk, a parking lot that can accommodate RVs, shops (see chapter 9). There are two large, beautifully landscaped swimming pools complete with waterfalls and water slides and an adjoining 16-seat whirlpool spa.

Westward Ho Hotel & Casino

2900 Las Vegas Blvd. S., between Circus Circus Dr. and Convention Center Dr., Las Vegas, NV 89109. ☎ 702/731-2900 or 800/634-6803. 656 rms, 121 suites. A/C TV TEL. $28 single, $56 double, $76 suite. Extra person $10. MC, V. Free parking at your room door.

Centrally located on the Strip (right next door to Circus Circus), the Westward Ho is fronted by a vast casino, with rooms in two-story buildings that extend out back for several city blocks. In fact, the property is so large that a free bus shuttles regularly between the rooms and the casino 24 hours a day. There are three swimming pools and three whirlpool spas to serve all areas.

The rooms are clean and adequately furnished motel units. A good buy here: two-bedroom suites with $1^1/2$ baths, living rooms with sofa beds, and refrigerators—they sleep up to six people.

There's a 24-hour restaurant in the casino under a stained-glass skylight dome. It serves a buffet breakfast ($4.95), lunch ($5.95), and dinner ($6.95), as well as an à la carte menu featuring traditional coffee-shop fare. Other facilities include a tour desk, free airport shuttle, a gift shop, a casino lounge where a three-piece country band entertains Monday to Saturday from 7pm to 1am, and a deli in the casino serving sandwiches, ribs, and half-pound extra-long hot dogs.

4 On or Near the Strip—Hotels without Casinos

EXPENSIVE

Carriage House

105 E. Harmon Ave., between Las Vegas Blvd. S. and Koval Lane, Las Vegas, NV 89109. ☎ 702/798-1020 or 800/221-2301. Fax 702/798-1020, ext. 112. 154 suites. A/C TV TEL. $115 studio suite for 1 or 2, $145 one-bedroom suite condominium for up to 4, $225 two-bedroom condominium for up to 6. Inquire about low-priced packages. AE, CB, DC, DISC, MC, V. Free parking (self).

Housed in a nine-story stucco building fronted by palm trees, this friendly, low-key resort hotel has a loyal repeat clientele. You enter into a large, comfortably furnished lobby where guests enjoy complimentary Monday afternoon manager's reception with hors d'oeuvres and wine. And the hotel caters to kids with welcome bags of cookies at check-in and gratis VCRs and movies on request; the front desk maintains a nice-sized movie library.

Attractive suites, decorated in teal, peach, and mauve with brass-trimmed lacquer or bleached-oak furnishings, have small sitting areas and fully equipped kitchenettes with refrigerators, microwave ovens, coffeemakers, toasters, and two- or four-burner ranges. Most have dishwashers as well. One-bedroom units have full living rooms and dining areas, with phones, radios, and TVs in both rooms. Two-bedroom/two-bath condominiums have a king-size bed in each bedroom and a queen sofa in the living room. Both rooms and public areas are immaculate. Free local phone calls are a plus.

Dining: Kiefers, perched on the ninth floor, offers a romantic, candlelit setting and superb skyline views via a wall of windows. Its low-key, peach-toned interior features potted ficus trees and seating on plush sofas and bamboo chairs upholstered in raw silk. Tuesday through Saturday a pianist entertains in an adjoining lounge with a small dance floor. The menu highlights steak, seafood, and pasta dishes. Dinner only; entrees $12.95 to $18.95.

Services: Complimentary transportation 7am to 10:30pm to/from airport and major Strip hotels.

Facilities: Tour and show desks, coin-op washers/dryers, Har-Tru tennis court lit for night play (no charge for play, balls, or racquets), swimming pool/sundeck, whirlpool.

MODERATE

La Quinta Motor Inn

3782 Las Vegas Blvd. S., between Tropicana and Harmon aves., Las Vegas, NV 89109. ☎ **702/739-7457** or 800/531-5900. Fax 702/736-1129. 114 rms. A/C TV TEL. All rates include continental breakfast. $55–$65 single, $65–$85 double. Extra person $10. Children 18 and under stay free in parents' room. AE, CB, DC, DISC, MC, V. Free parking at your room door.

La Quinta is a San Antonio, Texas–based chain, and many of its properties can be easily recognized by their mission-style architecture—terra-cotta-roofed stucco buildings with wrought-iron trim. Rooms are southwestern in decor, with Aztec-motif paintings and fabrics. Here, the furnishings are oak, and in-room amenities include TVs with pay-movie options.

There's a nice-sized pool and sundeck, and a big, comfortable 24-hour **Carrows Restaurant** adjoins. Carrows serves everything from breakfast burritos to USDA choice steaks, Italian pastas, and southern fried chicken. Oven-fresh pies here, too. A complimentary breakfast (juice, fruit, muffins, and coffee) is served each morning in La Quinta's pleasant lobby, and there's free transportation to/from the airport. Excalibur and MGM Grand restaurants and casino action are both a block away.

INEXPENSIVE

Algiers Hotel

2845 Las Vegas Blvd. S., between Riviera Blvd. and Sahara Ave., Las Vegas, NV 89109. ☎ **702/735-3311** or 800/732-3361. Fax 702/792-2112. 103 rms, 2 suites. A/C TV TEL. Single or double $35–$45 Sun–Thurs; $49.95–$89.95 Fri–Sat, holidays, and special events . Extra person $10. Children under 12 stay free in parents' room. AE, CB, DC, DISC, MC, V. Free parking (self).

A venerable spot on the Strip, the Algiers opened in 1953. However, a recent multimillion dollar renovation—including landscaping (note the lovely flower beds out back) and a new facade with a 60-foot sign— brought the rooms and public areas up to date. There's no casino here, though you can play video poker in the bar. The Algier's neat two-story, aqua-trimmed peach stucco buildings are complemented by a medium-sized pool and palm-fringed sundeck. Nice-sized rooms are clean and spiffy looking, with birch-wood-look paneling, light-wood furniture, and teal carpets. All have dressing areas.

The cozy **Algiers Restaurant & Lounge** is a local hangout frequented by state and city politicians and journalists. It has a copper-hooded fireplace and walls hung with historic Las Vegas photographs of pretower Strip hotels (Dunes, Sands, Flamingo), Liberace cutting the ribbon at the opening of the Riviera, Clara Bow and Joey Adams with the owner of the now-defunct Thunderbird, and many more. A glassed-in cafe overlooks the pool. The restaurant serves all meals, including many steak and seafood specialties, barbecued baby back ribs, and low-calorie dishes. There are souvenir shops, a jeweler, and a car-rental office out front. Also on the premises is the famed Candlelight Chapel, where many celebrities have tied the knot over the last 3 decades. Local calls are free and you can park at your room door.

The Algiers is a good choice for families—right across the street from Circus Circus with its many child-oriented facilities and a half block from Wet 'n' Wild. It's also within walking distance of the Las Vegas Convention Center.

Center Strip Inn

3688 Las Vegas Blvd. S., at Harmon Ave., Las Vegas, NV 89109. ☎ **702/730-6066** or 800/777-7737. Fax 702/736-2521. 97 rms, 51 suites. A/C TV TEL. Sun–Thurs $29.95 single, $39.95–$49.95 double; Fri–Sat, and holidays $49.95–$89.95 single or double. Suites (for up to 4): $69 Sun–Thurs, $89–$149 Fri, Sat, and special events. All rates include continental breakfast. Mention you read about the Center Strip in Frommer's for a $5 discount Sun–Thurs. AE, CB, DC, DISC, MC, V. Free parking at your room door.

This centrally located little motel is owned and operated by Robert Cohen, who is usually on the premises making sure guests are happy. He's a bit of an eccentric, and his hotel doesn't fit into any expected budget-property pattern. For example, the rooms have video-cassette players, and a selection of about 1,000 movies can be rented for just $2 each. Local calls and use of a fax machine are free. Breakfast consists of bagels, cream cheese, juice, and coffee, and free coffee and snacks are available in the lobby all day. Also available at the front desk: irons, hair dryers, and gratis bath amenities.

The rooms, situated in two-story white stucco buildings, are standard motel units with oak-look furnishings, but they do have small refrigerators, in-room safes, and AM/FM alarm-clock radios. The suites offer kitchenettes, tubs with whirlpool jets, and steam rooms.

There's no on-premises restaurant, but a 24-hour **Denny's** adjoins, numerous hotel restaurants are within easy walking distance, and you can have pizza delivered to your room. You'll also get a coupon for an all-you-can-eat $5.95 buffet for two at the Aladdin across the street. Facilities include a swimming pool and sundeck and a car-rental desk; the front desk can arrange tours.

Cohen also operates two downtown properties—**The Crest Budget Inn** (207 N. 6th St., Las Vegas, NV 89101 ☎ 702/382-5642 or 800/777-1817) and **The Downtowner** (129 N. 8th St., Las Vegas, NV 89101 ☎ 702/384-1441 or 800/777-2566). If you mention this book, you'll pay just $24.95 a night Sunday to Friday, $39.95 Saturday.

Vagabond Inn

3265 Las Vegas Blvd. S., just south of Sands Avenue, Las Vegas, NV 89109. ☎ **702/ 735-5102** or 800/828-8032 or 800/522-1555. Fax 702/735-0168. 126 rms. A/C TV TEL. Double $42–$52 Sun–Thurs, $47–$57 Fri–Sat; King Room $65 Sun–Thurs, $72 Fri–Sat. All rates include continental breakfast. AE, CB, DC, DISC, MC, V. Free parking.

A central location just across the street from Treasure Island, together with clean basic motel rooms nicely decorated in shades of mauve and muted blue, make this a viable choice. One-third of the rooms have patios or balconies, and all offer TVs with pay-movie options. King rooms have wet bars and refrigerators. A wide selection of complimentary bath amenities is available at the front desk, and free coffee is served in the lobby around the clock, as is a daily continental breakfast of juice, fruit, and pastries. Facilities include coin-op washers and dryers. There is a swimming pool but no restaurant. A gratis airport shuttle is a plus, and local calls are free.

5 Convention Center and Paradise Road

HOTELS WITH CASINOS

VERY EXPENSIVE

✪ Las Vegas Hilton

3000 Paradise Rd., at Riviera Blvd., Las Vegas, NV 89109. ☎ **702/732-5111** or 800/ 732-7117. Fax 702/732-5805. 2,900 rms, 274 suites, A/C TV TEL. $89–$269 double, $310–$1,520 suite. Extra person $25. Children of any age stay free in parents' room. Off-season rates may be lower, subject to availability. Inquire about attractively priced golf and other packages. AE, CB, DC, DISC, JCB, MC, V. Free parking (self and valet).

Its 375-foot tower dominating the desert horizon, this dazzling megahotel—fronted by a laser fantasy fountain—occupies 80 acres overlooking the blue lakes and manicured lawns of an adjacent 18-hole golf course. Barbra Streisand and Cary Grant presided at the hotel's 1969 opening, and Elvis Presley made a dramatic return to live performances at the Hilton Showroom the same year. The Hilton is simply magnificent—from its lobby and casino glittering with massive Austrian crystal chandeliers, to its comprehensive resort facilities, plush showroom, and corps of distinguished restaurants—not to mention the largest convention and meeting facilities in the world. You will be impressed.

Rooms are fittingly attractive, decorated in southwestern colors (muted shades of turquoise, mauve, and peach) with verdigris accents and bleached oak furnishings. Paintings of cacti enhance this motif. Some rooms have sofas and/or dressing rooms; most contain in-room safes. All offer TVs (cached in handsome armoires) with HBO, On-Command pay-movie options, an in-house information channel, and video checkout capability.

Dining: Bistro Le Montrachet, the Hilton's premier haute-cuisine French restaurant, is reviewed in chapter 6.

Most dramatic of the Hilton's restaurants is **Benihana Village,** a pagoda-roofed Oriental fantasyland with cascading waterfalls and meandering streams, spanned by quaint wooden bridges. You'll enjoy dancing water displays and fiber-optic fireworks while you dine. The Village houses three restaurants and a lounge.

On one side of the central waterway, the **Garden of the Dragon,** its entrance presided over by a fiery-eyed dragon atop a pagoda, has seating in chinoiserie chairs amid tropical greenery. The menu offers regional Chinese specialties. Dinner only; most entrees $14 to $19 (less for rice, noodle, and vegetable dishes).

Across the stream is the **Seafood Grille,** fronted by a colorful Asian marketplace aclutter with barrels of eggs (above which are animated hens in wooden cages) and displays of fish, fruits, and vegetables. An aquarium graces one wall. Diners sit in bamboo chairs under a pagoda roof, walls are hung with fishing nets, and wooden columns are embellished with Chinese kites. Dinner only; entrees $13.75 to $34.50 (most under $20).

At the far end, occupying two dining levels, is **Benihana,** with a restrained Japanese shoji-screen decor. A samurai-like chef prepares dinner at your grill-centered table, dexterously slicing, dicing, and sautéeing scrumptious morsels of filet mignon, shrimp, and chicken, and flipping them onto your plate. Dinner only; entrees $14.95 to $25.95; combination dinners $28.50 to $30.50.

Near the entrance to this exotic restaurant complex is the **Kabuki Lounge,** an inviting setting for Chinese/Japanese appetizers and cocktails.

The **Hilton Steakhouse** offers a warmly intimate interior. Knotty-pine-paneled walls framed by rich mahogany wainscoting and moldings are hung with attractive abstract paintings, and elegantly appointed tables are lit by brass candle lamps. The menu offers steaks, chops and seafood. Dinner only; entrees $19 to $29.95.

Another beef eatery is the **Barronshire Room,** where an English club ambience is created by high-backed burgundy leather booths and armchairs, crystal chandeliers and sconces, and walls hung with gilt-framed landscape, seascape, and still-life paintings. The restaurant is patterned after the renowned Barronshire Inn in southern England. Dinner only; entrees $18 to $24.95.

The very simpatico **MargaritaGrille** is done up in soft southwestern hues. Mexican music, pots of cacti, and displays of papier-mâché birds and pottery enhance the south-of-the-border ambience. The Grille's bar is quite popular for cocktails and Mexican appetizers. Dinner only; entrees $8.25 to $15.50.

Andiamo, a charming Italian *ristorante,* seats diners amid planters of ficus trees and terra-cotta columns. Decorated in soft hues (peach, beige, muted gray-greens), its cream walls are hung with scenic paintings of Italy. A gleaming copper cappuccino machine sits atop a marble table, and above the brass- and copper-accented exhibition kitchen is a colorful display of Italian food products. All pasta served here is made fresh on the premises. Dinner only; entrees $13.50 to $25.25.

Finally, **The Coffee Shop,** a 24-hour facility, has cream stucco walls adorned with murals of the Old West and Mexican artifacts (rugs, pottery) on display. Lush faux foliage, including hibiscus draped from driftwood beams overhead, gives the room a cheerful ambience. Traditional Las Vegas coffee-shop fare is supplemented by Mexican specialties.

Additional facilities include a branch of **TCBY** and a cappuccino and pastry cart in the lobby. There are seven bar/lounges at the Hilton. In addition, the **Garden Snack Bar** serves the pool deck; the **Paddock Snack Bar** in the race and sports book features pizza, sandwiches, and other light fare items (not oats); and the **Nightclub,** a first-rate casino lounge (details in chapter 10) offers nightly entertainment. See also the buffet listings in chapter 6. *Note:* Children 12 and under dine in any Hilton restaurant for half the listed menu prices.

Services: 24-hour room service (when you order breakfast it comes with a complimentary morning paper), foreign-currency exchange.

Facilities: Casino, car-rental desk, tour desk, travel agency, shops (upscale clothing, shoes, logo items, gifts, candy), small video-game arcade, business service center, multiservice beauty salon/barbershop, jogging trail, 18-hole golf course.

The third-floor roof comprises a beautifully landscaped 8-acre recreation deck with a large swimming pool, a 24-seat whirlpool spa, six Har-Tru tennis courts lit for night play, a pro shop, Ping-Pong, and a nine-hole putting green. Also on this level is a luxurious, 17,000-square-foot, state-of-the-art health club offering Nautilus and Universal equipment, Lifecycles, treadmills, rowing machines, three whirlpool spas, steam, sauna, massage, and tanning beds. Guests are totally pampered: all workout clothing and toiletries are provided; there are comfortable TV lounges; complimentary soft drinks and juices are served in the canteen; and beauty services include manicures, pedicures, salt and soap rubs, facials, and oxygen pep-up.

EXPENSIVE

✪ The Hard Rock Hotel and Casino

4455 Paradise Rd., at Harmon Ave., Las Vegas, NV 89109. ☎ **702/693-5000** or 800/473-ROCK. Fax 702/693-5010. 316 rms, 24 suites. A/C TV TEL. Double $85–$250 Sun–Thurs, $125–$300 Fri–Sat, $250–$350 suite. Extra person $25. Children 12 and under stay free in parents' room. AE, DC, DISC, MC, V. Free parking (self and valet).

Owner Peter Morton, who bills his Hard Rock Hotel and Casino as "Vegas for a new generation," sent out invitations to the property's March 1995 opening inscribed on casino chips bearing the image of Jimi Hendrix. Dozens of glitterati—Kevin Costner, Rob Lowe,

The Smithsonian of Rock 'N' Roll

Fronted by a 90-foot Fender Stratocaster guitar, the Hard Rock is a rock 'n' roll museum displaying a massive collection of rock-legend memorabilia. Some of the exhibits you'll see here include:

- Elvis' gold lamé jacket.
- Guitars from Nirvana, ZZ Top, Bruce Springsteen, Bill Haley (from the movie *Rock Around the Clock*), Eric Clapton, and many others.
- James Brown's shoeshine stand (where he wrote songs when he was a kid) and his "King of Soul" cape and crown.
- The dresses the Supremes wore on the *Ed Sullivan Show.*
- A piece of the plane that carried Otis Redding to his death in the late '60s.
- Pete Townshend's smashed guitar from the *Late Night With David Letterman* show.
- The artist-formerly-known-as-Prince's handwritten lyrics for a song from *Purple Rain.*
- "Maestro of Love" Barry White's Lifetime Achievement Award.
- The white suit worn by Mick Jagger when he was released from a UK jail in the late '60s.
- Greg Allman's favorite biker jacket.
- A collection of surfboards belonging to the Beach Boys.
- The XXL jacket Meat Loaf wore on his last tour.
- Las Vegas hotel menus signed by Elvis and Jimi Hendrix.
- Over 500 merchandising items manufactured with the Beatles' images.
- The piano on which Al Green composed "Take Me to the River."
- "I Hope I Die Before I Get Old"—a poem written by Pearl Jam's Eddie Vedder after Kurt Cobain's suicide.

Patty Smyth, Sandra Bernhard, Stephen Baldwin, Christy Turlington, Jason Patric, Jack Nicholson, Pamela Anderson, and Jon Lovitz, among them—flew in for the festivities, which included concerts by the Eagles and Sheryl Crow. Everything here is rock-themed, from the Stevie Ray Vaughn quote over the entrance ("When this house is a rocking, don't bother knocking, come on in.") to the vast collection of music-legend memorabilia displayed in public areas. The house is always "a rocking" (the pulsating beat emanates from hundreds of speakers throughout the property), and the cheerful casino features piano-shaped roulette tables and guitar-neck-handle slot machines. Even the walls of the bell desk are lined with gold records.

Large, attractive rooms, decorated in earth tones with photographs of rock stars adorning the walls, have beds with leather headboards and French windows that actually open to fresh air (a rarity in Las Vegas). A 27-inch cable stereo TV (most hotel sets are smaller in this town; they want you in the casino, not staring at the tube) offers pay movie options and special music channels.

Dining: The Hard Rock's premier restaurant, **Mortoni's,** is a beauty. Parchment-yellow walls are hung with vintage photographs such as a tuxedoed James Dean at a Hollywood party; Humphrey Bogart, Frank Sinatra, and Grace Kelly at Chasen's in the 1940s; and stills from Las Vegas movies. Candlelit white-linened tables are decorated by pots of African violets, lighting is soft and flattering, and furnishings are butter-soft plush red leather. Large windows overlook the pool area, where, weather permitting, you can dine outdoors at umbrella tables. The fare is Italian, and portions are vast. Dinner only; entrees $12.95 to $23.95 (pastas and pizzas mostly $9 to $14).

At **Mr. Lucky's 24/7**—the hotel's round-the-clock coffee shop displaying rock memorabilia and old Las Vegas hotel signs—California-style entrees and pizzas are offered in addition to the usual Las Vegas steak/sandwich/burger menu.

The **Hard Rock Café** (details in chapter 6) is adjacent to the hotel.

The **Center Bar** in the casino is under a glowing purple dome, from which a globe inscribed with the words "One Love, One World" is suspended. The **Beach Club Bar** serves light fare and frozen drinks poolside. And the **Viva Las Vegas** Lounge, off the casino, has a video wall where four monitors display rapid-paced rock footage.

Services: 24-hour room service, concierge.

Facilities: Small video-game arcade, gift/sundry shop and immense Hard Rock retail store, show desk (for **The Joint** only; tickets to other shows can be arranged by the concierge), health club (offering a full complement of Cybex equipment, stair machines, treadmills, massage, and steamrooms). The Hard Rock has one of the most gorgeous pool areas in Las Vegas, complete with a palm-fringed sandy beach, grassy expanses of lawn, a vast free-form sand-bottomed pool with a water slide and 150 speakers providing underwater music, several whirlpools, and raft rentals. Luxurious poolside cabanas (equipped with TVs, phones, misters, and refrigerators) can be rented for $55 to $75 a day.

MODERATE

Best Western Mardi Gras Inn

3500 Paradise Rd., between Sands Ave. and Desert Inn Rd., Las Vegas, NV 89109. ☎ **702/731-2020** or 800/634-6501. Fax 702/733-6994. 315 minisuites. A/C TV TEL. $40–$72 single or double. Extra person $8. Children 18 and under stay free in parents' room. AE, CB, DC, DISC, JCB, MC, V. Free parking at your room door.

Opened in 1980, this well-run little casino hotel has a lot to offer. A block from the convention center and close to major properties, its three-story building sits on nicely landscaped grounds with manicured lawns, trees, and shrubbery. There's a gazebo out back where guests can enjoy a picnic lunch.

Accommodations are all spacious queen-bedded minisuites with sofa-bedded living room areas and eat-in kitchens, the latter equipped with wet bars, refrigerators, and coffeemakers. Rooms are attractively decorated in muted blues and earth tones, with rust/orange floral-print drapes and bedspreads. All offer TVs with HBO and pay-movie options. Staying here is like having your own little Las Vegas apartment.

Dining: A pleasant restaurant/bar off the lobby, with white-linen-covered tables and fan chandeliers overhead, is open from 6:30am to 11pm daily. It serves typical coffee-shop fare and highlights a 12-ounce prime rib dinner for $8.95.

Services: Free transportation to/from airport and major Strip hotels.

Facilities: Small casino (64 slots/video poker machines), small video-game arcade, car-rental desk, tour and show desks, coin-op washers/dryers, unisex hairdresser, gift shop, RV parking. The inn has a large swimming pool with a duplex sundeck and whirlpool.

⑤ Debbie Reynolds Hotel/Casino/Hollywood Movie Museum

305 Convention Center Dr., between Las Vegas Blvd. S. and Paradise Rd., Las Vegas, NV 89109. ☎ **702/734-0711** or 800/633-1777. Fax 702/734-7548. 197 rms, 7 suites. A/C TV TEL. Single or double $49–$69 Sun–Thurs, $59–$79 Fri–Sat. Rates can go as high as $175 during conventions and peak seasons. Extra person $10. AE, DC, DISC, MC, V. Free parking (self and valet).

In 1993, America's sweetheart—musical-comedy star Debbie Reynolds—took over the 12-story Paddlewheel Hotel, transforming its signature paddlewheel facade into a neon-lit revolving film reel, and inserting color photographs of Hollywood icons into the frames. Why did Debbie buy a hotel? Ever the vivacious entertainer, she had long dreamed of creating a performance space to her own specifications as well as a museum to house her massive collection of Hollywood memorabilia (see chapter 7). Her Hollywood-glamour concept is an exciting one. Not only does she perform in the showroom, but she has created an after-hours lounge where Strip entertainers (many of whom are her friends) can unwind—and take the stage—after their shows.

The lobby here is a minimuseum of Hollywood memorabilia: The Baccarat crystal chandeliers overhead are from the film *The Great Waltz,* the marble-topped console tables were used on the sets of *Camille* and *Marie Antoinette,* and a teak opium bed and side chairs from *The Good Earth* are on display. You can even sit down (an unusual feature for a Las Vegas hotel lobby) on a high-backed burgundy brocade ottoman from the 1932 movie *Grand Hotel.*

Large, attractive rooms are furnished in bleached woods and carpeted in teal, with color-coordinated print bedspreads and draperies. In keeping with the hotel's Hollywood theme, textured beige walls are hung with large black-and-white photographs of movie legends (perhaps Gable and Lombard will be watching over you). Picture windows offer great views of the Strip. All rooms have sizable dressing areas, TVs with Spectravision movie options, and phones with call waiting. Some also offer refrigerators, hair dryers, and coffeemakers. The top three floors house luxurious time-share units; call for details.

Dining: The 24-hour **Celebrity Café** serves as both a hotel coffee shop and a lounge where Debbie and her Strip entertainer friends can hang out and perform until the wee hours on weekend nights.

And **Bogie's Bar,** its back wall lined with Bogart movie stills, serves the casino.

Services: 24-hour room service.

Facilities: Casino, large swimming pool with bilevel sundeck, whirlpool, saunas, gift shop, sightseeing/show/tour desk. A large shopping center—with a drugstore/pharmacy, post office, dry cleaner, and launderette—is just across the street. Guests can enjoy health club privileges nearby.

INEXPENSIVE

Super 8 Motel

4250 Koval Lane, just south of Flamingo Rd., Las Vegas, NV 89109. ☎ **702/794-0888** or 800/800-8000. 294 rms, 6 suites. A/C TV TEL. Sun–Thurs $36 single, $41–$43 double; Fri–Sat $52 single, $56–$58 double. Extra person $8. Children 12 and under stay free in parents' room. Pets $5 per night. AE, CB, DC, DISC, MC, V. Free parking (self).

Billing itself as "the world's largest Super 8 Motel," this friendly property occupies a vaguely Tudor-style stone and stucco building. Coffee is served gratis in a pleasant little lobby furnished with comfortable sofas and wing chairs, and you can help yourself to fresh-popped popcorn all day from a machine in the casino.

Rooms are clean and well maintained. They're standard motel units decorated in three color schemes (burgundy/gray, forest green, or navy/muted blues), with cream stucco walls, oak furnishings, and bedspreads and drapes in splashy floral prints. Some rooms have safes; TVs have both free movie channels and Spectravision pay-movie options.

Dining: The **Ellis Island Restaurant** has a nautical decor composed of tufted red leather booths, dark wood beams and paneling, and a few seagoing artifacts such as ship models and steering wheels on display. Open 24 hours, it offers typical coffee-shop fare at reasonable prices. In the adjoining bar—a librarylike setting with shelves of books and green marble tables—sporting events are aired on TV monitors. There's also a bar in the casino with a karaoke machine.

Services: 24-hour room service, free airport transfer.

Facilities: Casino (race book and 50 slot/poker/21 machines), small kidney-shaped pool/sundeck and adjoining whirlpool, car-rental desk, small video-game arcade, coin-op washers/dryers.

HOTELS WITHOUT CASINOS
EXPENSIVE

✪ Alexis Park Resort

375 E. Harmon Ave., between Koval Lane and Paradise Rd., Las Vegas, NV 89109. ☎ **702/796-3300** or 800/582-2228. Fax 702/796-4334. 500 suites. A/C MINIBAR TV TEL. $105–$250 one-bedroom suite, $175–$400 one-bedroom loft suite, $350–$1,500 larger suite. Extra person $15. Children 18 and under stay free in parents' room. AE, CB, DC, DISC, JCB, MC. V. Free parking (self and valet).

A low-key atmosphere, luxurious digs, and superb service combine to make Alexis Park the hotel choice of many showroom headliners and visiting celebrities. Alan Alda, Alec Baldwin, Jerry Lewis, Whitney Houston, Robert de Niro, Tony Orlando, Dolly Parton, and Shirley MacLaine are just a few of the superstars who've chosen this resort's discreet elegance over the seemingly more glamorous Strip casino/hotels. It's the kind of place where you can get a phone at your restaurant table, or your suit pressed at 3am.

You'll sense the difference the moment you approach the palm-fringed entranceway, fronted by lovingly tended flower beds and a rock waterfall. The elegant lobby, with Saltillo tile flooring, has comfortable sofas and immense terra-cotta pots of ferns, cacti, and calla lilies. And there's notably fine artwork throughout the public areas.

Spacious suites (the smallest is 450 square feet) are decorated in light resort colors with taupe lacquer furnishings. Loft suites have cathedral ceilings. All are equipped with refrigerators, wet bars, two-line phones (one in each room of your suite) with computer jacks, and TVs (also one in each room) with HBO and pay-movie options. More than a third of the suites have working fireplaces and/or Jacuzzi tubs.

Dining: Pegasus, an exquisite award-winning gourmet dining room, is described in chapter 6.

The **Pisces Bistro,** under a 30-foot shallow-domed ceiling with planters of greenery cascading from tiers overhead, provides live entertainment Wednesday to Saturday night (see chapter 10) and serves drinks, pizzas, salads, sandwiches, a few full entrees (steak, seafood, pasta), and desserts—both inside and on a patio overlooking the pool.

Services: 24-hour room service, concierge on duty 8am to midnight, morning newspapers (*Wall Street Journal* and *USA Today*) delivered to your door each morning.

Facilities: Gift shop, unisex hair salon, two Har-Tru tennis courts lit for night play (tennis instruction and clinics available), health club (Paramount six-station machine, StairMasters, Lifecycles, treadmills, whirlpool, massage, steam, and sauna).

Behind the hotel are beautifully landscaped grounds with palm trees and pines, streams and ponds spanned by quaint bridges, gazebos, rock gardens, flower beds, and oleanders. Here you'll find a large fountain-centered swimming pool, two smaller pools, cabana bars, a whirlpool spa, umbrella tables, table tennis, and a nine-hole putting green.

✪ Residence Inn by Marriott

3225 Paradise Rd., between Desert Inn Rd. and Convention Center Dr., Las Vegas, NV 89109. ☎ **702/796-9300** or 800/331-3131. 144 studios, 48 penthouses. A/C TV TEL. $69–$169 studio (for 1 or 2; extra person $10), $89–$219 penthouse (for up to 4). All rates include continental breakfast. AE, CB, DC, DISC, MC, V. Free parking (self).

Marriott's excellent Residence Inns are designed to offer travelers the ultimate in homeyness and hospitality. Staying here is like having your own apartment in Las Vegas. The property occupies 7 acres of perfectly manicured lawns, tropical foliage, and neat flower beds. It's a great choice for families and business travelers.

Accommodations are housed in 24 condo-like, two-story wood and stucco buildings, fronted by little gardens. They're decorated in mauve and gray with peach or teal carpeting and bleached wood furnishings, and most have working fireplaces. Studios have adjoining sitting rooms with sofas and armchairs, dressing areas, and fully equipped eat-in kitchens complete with dishwashers. Every guest receives a welcome basket of microwave popcorn and coffee. TVs have visitor-information channels and VCRs (you can rent movies nearby), and all rooms have balconies or patios. Duplex penthouses, some with cathedral ceilings, add an upstairs bedroom (with its own bath, phone, TV, and radio) and a full dining room.

Dining: A big continental buffet breakfast (fresh fruit, yogurt, cereals, muffins, bagels, pastries) is served each morning in the gatehouse, a delightful cathedral-ceilinged lobby lounge with a working fireplace. There's comfortable seating amid planters of greenery. Daily papers are set out here each morning; there's a large-screen TV and a stereo for guest use; and a selection of toys, games, and books is available for children. Weekday evenings from 5:30 to 7pm, complimentary buffets with beverages (beer, wine, coffee, soda), fresh popcorn, and daily varying fare (soup/salad/sandwiches, tacos, Chinese, barbecue, spaghetti, and so on) are served in the gatehouse. This cocktail-hour spread affords an opportunity to socialize with other guests—a nice feature if you're traveling alone.

Services: Local restaurants deliver food, and there's also a complimentary food-shopping service. Maids wash your dishes.

Facilities: Car-rental desk, barbecue grills, coin-op washers/dryers, sports court (paddle tennis, volleyball, basketball). There's a good-size swimming pool and whirlpool with a sundeck. Guests can use the health club next door at Courtyard Marriott (details below).

MODERATE

Courtyard Marriott

3275 Paradise Rd., between Convention Center Dr. and Desert Inn Rd., Las Vegas, NV 89109. ☎ **702/791-3600** or 800/321-2211. Fax 702/796-7981. 137 rms, 12 suites. A/C TV TEL. Per-room rates are $69–$89 Sun–Thurs, $99 Fri–Sat; suite $109 Sun–Thurs, $119 Fri–Sat. AE, CB, DC, DISC, MC, V. Free parking at your room door.

Housed in three-story terra-cotta-roofed stucco buildings, in an attractively landscaped setting of trees, shrubbery, and flower beds, the Courtyard is a welcome link in the Marriott chain. The concept for these limited-service lower priced lodgings developed in the 1980s, and this particular property opened in 1989. Although the services are limited, don't picture a no-frills establishment. This is a beautiful hotel, with a pleasant plant-filled lobby and very nice rooms indeed.

Like its public areas, the rooms—most with king-size beds—still look spanking new. Decorated in shades of gray-blue, mauve, and burgundy, with sofas and handsome mahogany furnishings (including large desks), they offer TVs with multiple On-Command movie options. All rooms have balconies or patios.

Dining: Off the lobby is a light and airy plant-filled restaurant with glossy oak paneling and tables. It serves buffet breakfasts, as well as à la carte lunches (mostly salads and sandwiches); light fare is available from 5 to 10pm. Adjoining is a comfortable lobby lounge with plush furnishings, a large-screen TV, and a working fireplace. Drinks are served here from 4 to 10pm. You can also enjoy breakfast in this lounge and catch a morning TV news show.

Services: Room service 4 to 10pm, complimentary airport shuttle.

Facilities: Small exercise room, medium-size swimming pool with adjoining whirlpool, picnic tables and barbecue grills, coin-op washers/dryers.

Emerald Springs Holiday Inn

325 E. Flamingo Rd., between Koval Lane and Paradise Rd., Las Vegas, NV 89109. ☎ **702/732-9100** or 800/732-7889. Fax 702/731-9784. 132 rms, 18 suites. A/C TV TEL. Single or double $69–$99 for studio, $99–$115 Jacuzzi suite, $115–$175 hospitality suite. Extra person $15. Children 18 and under stay free in parents' room. AE, CB, DC, DISC, MC, V. Free parking (self).

Housed in three mauve-trimmed peach stucco buildings, Emerald Springs offers a friendly, low-key alternative to casino-hotel glitz and glitter. It's entered via a charming marble-floored lobby with a waterfall fountain and lush faux tropical plantings under a domed skylight. Off the lobby is a comfortably furnished lounge with a large-screen TV and working fireplace. Typical of the inn's hospitality is a bowl of apples for the taking at the front desk. And weeknights from 10:30pm to midnight you can "raid the icebox" at the Veranda Café, which offers complimentary cookies, peanut butter and jelly sandwiches, and coffee, tea, or milk. Although your surroundings here are serene, you're only two blocks from the heart of the Strip.

Public areas and rooms here are notably clean and spiffy. Pristine hallways are hung with nice abstract paintings and have small seating areas on every level, and rooms are beautifully decorated in teal and mauve with bleached-oak furnishings. Even the smallest accommodations (studios) offer small sofas, desks, and armchairs with hassocks. You also get two phones (desk and bedside), an in-room coffeemaker (with gratis coffee), and a wet bar with refrigerator. TVs (concealed in an armoire) have HBO and pay-move options; VCRs are available on request. There's a separate dressing room and a hair dryer in the bath. Suites add a living-room area with a large-screen TV to the above, an eat-in kitchenette with a microwave oven, a larger dressing room, and a Jacuzzi tub. Hospitality suites feature sitting room areas and dining tables, with TVs and phones in every room.

Dining: Just off the lobby (you can hear the splashing of the fountain and waterfall), the **Veranda Café** adheres to the hotel's mauve and teal color scheme. Potted ferns provide a bit of garden ambience, and you can dine alfresco on a covered patio overlooking the pool. It serves buffet breakfasts and à la carte lunches (burgers, salads, deli sandwiches) and dinners (light fare plus entrees). A comfortable bar/lounge with video poker games adjoins.

Services: Concierge, complimentary limousine transportation to and from the airport and nearby casinos between 6:30am and 11pm (van service available 11pm to 6:30am), room service, business services, gratis newspapers available at the front desk.

Facilities: Fitness room, nice sized pool/sundeck and whirlpool in an attractively landscaped setting.

Fairfield Inn by Marriott

3850 Paradise Rd., between Twain Ave. and Flamingo Rd., Las Vegas, NV 89109. ☎ 702/791-0899 or 800/228-2800. Fax 702/791-0899. 129 rms. A/C TV TEL. $56–$70 for up to 5 people. Rates include continental breakfast. AE, CB, DC, DISC, MC, V. Free parking (self).

Marriott developed the Fairfield Inn concept in the mid-1980s to offer a "new standard in economy lodging." This pristine property, opened in 1990, is a pleasant place to stay. It has a comfortable lobby with sofas and armchairs—a simpatico setting in which to plan your day's activities over a cup of coffee (provided gratis all day).

The rooms are cheerful. Units with king-size beds have convertible sofas, and all accommodations offer well-lit work areas with desks; TVs have free movie channels as well as pay-movie options. Local calls are free.

Breakfast pastries, fresh fruit, juice, and yogurt are served in the lobby each morning and many restaurants are within easy walking distance. Facilities include a pool/whirlpool and sundeck with umbrella tables. A free shuttle goes to and from the airport. The front desk proffers warm hospitality.

La Quinta Inn

3970 Paradise Rd., between Twain Ave. and Flamingo Rd., Las Vegas, NV 89109. ☎ 702/796-9000 or 800/531-5900. Fax 702/796-3537. 228 rms, 51 suites. A/C TV TEL. Executive rooms $89 Sun–Thurs, $99 Fri–Sat; double queen rooms $85 Sun–Thurs, $95 Fri–Sat ; $150–$200 suite. Rates include continental breakfast; inquire about seasonal discounts. AE, CB, DC, DISC, MC, V. Free parking (self).

Its four mission-style terra cotta–roofed buildings forming a U around a large courtyard, the La Quinta offers a tranquil alternative to the razzle-dazzle of Strip hotels. Although you're just a minute (and a gratis shuttle ride) from major casinos, you'll feel like you're staying in a countryside retreat. Lovely grounds, with manicured lawns, lovingly tended flower beds, and a charming stone fountain, offer rustic benches, lawn games (croquet, badminton, volleyball), barbecue grills, and picnic tables.

Accommodations are immaculate and attractive. Executive rooms feature one queen-size bed, a small refrigerator, wet bar, and microwave oven. Double queens are larger but have no kitchen facilities. And spacious one- and two-bedroom suites contain large living rooms with sofa beds, dining areas, and full kitchens. Most accommodations have patios or balconies, and all feature baths with oversized whirlpool tubs. TVs offer satellite channels and HBO.

Dining: Continental breakfast (juice, bagels, cereal, muffins, fresh fruit, beverages) is served daily in the **Patio Café.**

Facilities: Car rentals/tours arranged at the front desk, coin-op washers/dryers, medium-size swimming pool and adjoining whirlpool. A free 24-hour shuttle offers pickup and return to and from the airport and several Strip casino hotels.

INEXPENSIVE

⑤ Motel 6

195 E. Tropicana Ave., at Koval Lane, Las Vegas, NV 89109. ☎ **702/798-0728.**
Fax 702/798-5657. 880 rms. A/C TV TEL. For 1 person, Sun–Thurs $29.99, Fri–Sat
$41.99. Extra person $6. Children under 17 stay free in parents' room. AE, CB, DC,
DISC, MC, V. Free parking at your room door.

Fronted by a big neon sign, Las Vegas's Motel 6 is the largest in the
country, and it happens to be a great budget choice. Most Motel 6
properties are a little out of the way, but this one is quite close to
major Strip casino hotels (the MGM is adjacent). It has a big, pleasant lobby, and the rooms, in two-story cream stucco buildings, are
clean and attractively decorated. Some rooms have showers only,
others, tub/shower baths. Local calls are free and your TV offers HBO.

Three restaurants (including a 24-hour **Carrows;** see La Quinta
above) adjoin. On-premises facilities include a large well-stocked gift
shop, vending machines, a tour desk, two nice-size swimming pools in
enclosed courtyards, a whirlpool, and coin-op washers/dryers.

6   Downtown (All Accommodations with Casinos)

INEXPENSIVE

✪ Golden Nugget

129 E. Fremont St., at Casino Center Blvd., Las Vegas, NV 89101. ☎ **702/385-7111**
or 800/634-3454. Fax 702/386-8362. 1,803 rms, 102 suites. A/C TV TEL. Single or
double $49–$150 Sun–Thurs, $80–$150 Fri–Sat, $275–$475 suite. Extra person $20.
AE, CB, DC, DISC, MC, V. Free parking (self and valet).

Gleaming white and gold in the Las Vegas sun, its surrounding streets
lined with tall swaying palms, the Golden Nugget looks more like a
luxurious Côte d'Azur resort than a downtown hotel. And it is. Opened
in 1946, it was the first building in Las Vegas constructed specifically
for casino gambling. When Steve Wynn acquired the property in 1972,
it had a plush Old West/Victorian decor. Over the next decade Wynn
took down all the neon signs, western art, and turn-of-the-century furnishings and created a magnificent first-class European-style resort with
a stunning chandeliered white-marble lobby (no casino games in view),
mirrored ceiling, gleaming brass accents, and lavish floral arrangements
gracing public areas. The Nugget's sun-dappled interior spaces are a
welcome change from the Las Vegas tradition of dim lighting.

Resort-style rooms are fittingly charming—light and airy, with
valanced beds, delightful floral-print bedspreads and draperies, and
furnishings in rattan, bamboo, and light woods.

Dining: Stefano's, off a gorgeous marble-floored courtyard, offers
a festive setting for northern Italian cuisine, complete with singing waiters. Seating is in red-white-and-green-striped satin-upholstered chairs
at candlelit, white-linened tables. Murals of Venice behind trellised
"windows" are designed to look like scenery, Venetian glass chandeliers
are suspended from a coffered ceiling, and baroque elaboration includes
cupids, ornate columns, and gilt-framed mirrors. Dinner only; entrees
$9.95 to $27.25.

Accommodations Downtown

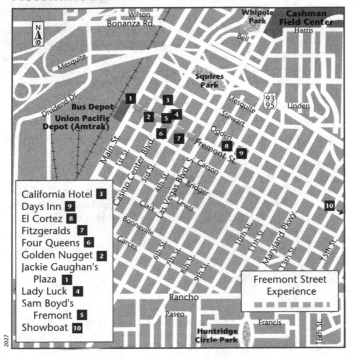

California Hotel **3**
Days Inn **9**
El Cortez **8**
Fitzgeralds **7**
Four Queens **6**
Golden Nugget **2**
Jackie Gaughan's
    Plaza **1**
Lady Luck **4**
Sam Boyd's
    Fremont **5**
Showboat **10**

Freemont Street
Experience

The opulent **Lillie Langtry's** is adorned with beveled and gilt-framed mirrors, gilded wood flowers, Chinese art, and a lovely painting of swans. A gorgeous hand-blown Venetian glass chandelier is suspended from an oak-beamed leather ceiling painted to resemble a sky at sunset. Diners sit in plush booths and banquettes or Louis XV–style armchairs. It's a lovely setting, softly lit and enhanced by a backdrop of piano and harp music. The menu is Chinese. Dinner only; entrees $9 to $14.75 (more for lobster dishes).

California Pizza Kitchen is a plush precinct with a stained-glass dome, black marble tables, a black-and-white marble checkerboard floor, and an exhibition kitchen where white-hatted chefs tend a glowing, oak-burning oven. In addition to pizzas with trendy toppings the menu offers calzones, salads, pasta, and other entrees. Open for lunch and dinner daily; all entrees under $10.

Carson Street Café, the Nugget's 24-hour restaurant, evokes an elegant street cafe of the Champs-Elysées—albeit one overlooking a hotel lobby instead of a Paris street. The jewel-toned interior—under a white-fringed green awning, with upholstered bamboo furnishings, murals of park scenes, potted orange trees, and flower-bedecked tables—couldn't be lovelier. And the food is notably excellent. There are terrific salads, overstuffed deli sandwiches, Mexican and Chinese specialties, and attractively priced specials (a full prime rib dinner for $9.95).

The Golden Nugget has one of the best buffets/Sunday brunches in Las Vegas (see chapter 6). In addition, a 24-hour snack bar in the casino offers deli sandwiches, pizza, and light fare, and there are four casino bars including the elegant **Claude's** and the **38 Different Kinds of Beer Bar.**

Services: 24-hour room service, shoeshine, concierge.

Facilities: Casino, car-rental desk, full-service unisex hair salon, shops (gifts, jewelry, designer fashions, sportswear, logo items), video-game arcade.

The Nugget's top rated health club offers a full line of Universal equipment, Lifecycles, StairMasters, treadmills, rowing machines, Gravitron, free weights, steam, sauna, tanning beds, and massage. Salon treatments include everything from leg waxing to seaweed-mask facials. The spa's opulent Palladian-mirrored foyer is modeled after a salon in New York's Frick Museum.

The entrance to the hotel's immense swimming pool and outdoor whirlpool spa is graced by elegant marble swans and bronze fish sculptures. Fountains, palm trees, and verdant landscaping create a tropical setting, and a poolside bar serves the sundeck.

MODERATE

Days Inn

707 E. Fremont St., at 7th St., Las Vegas, NV 89101. ☎ **702/388-1400** or 800/325-2344 or 800/325-2525. Fax 702/388-9622. 140 rms, 7 suites. A/C TV TEL. $40–$65 for a one-bedded room, $45–$80 for a two-bedded room. Rates for up to 4 people; may be higher during special events. "Super Saver" rate ($39 single or double) if you reserve 30 days in advance via the toll-free number 800/325-2525 (subject to availability). AE, CB, DC, DISC, JCB, MC, V. Free parking (self).

Opened in 1988, this Days Inn still looks quite new. Rooms, in a U-shaped three-story building, are cheerfully decorated in shades of mint and raspberry, with teal carpeting and oak-look furnishings. Brass-framed paintings of palm trees adorn the walls. TVs offer pay movies. On-premises facilities comprise a rooftop pool and sundeck, a few video games, and the **Culinary Restaurant,** serving coffee-shop fare at all meals.

Jackie Gaughan's Plaza Hotel/Casino

1 Main St., at Fremont St., Las Vegas, NV 89101. ☎ **702/386-2110** or 800/634-6575. Fax 702/382-8281. 876 rms, 161 suites. A/C TV TEL. $40 Sun–Thurs, $50–$75 Fri–Sat; $60–$150 suite. Extra person $8. Children under 12 stay free in parents' room. AE, DISC, MC, V. Free parking (self and valet).

Built in 1971 on the site of the old Union Pacific Railroad Depot, the Plaza, a double-towered, three-block-long property, permanently altered the downtown skyline. Las Vegas's Amtrak station is right in the hotel, and the main Greyhound terminal adjoins it.

The spacious North Tower rooms are decorated in muted blue and mauve, with dark wood furnishings in traditional styles and attractive floral-print drapes and bedspreads. All have dressing rooms. King rooms offer plush sofas and full-length mirrors. The South Tower rooms are almost the same, but the furnishings are in lighter woods— oak and pine.

Dining: An upscale continental restaurant, as yet unnamed, is in the works at this time. It will be under a domed skylight, with windows all around offering fabulous views of Glitter Gulch and the Fremont Street Experience. Seating, amid faux palms, will be in plush booths upholstered in tropical fabrics, and a piano bar will adjoin. I toured the site and found it impressive. Dinner only.

The **Plaza Diner,** open 24 hours a day, is right out of the 1950s, with gleaming chrome, Formica-topped pedestal tables, a black-and-white checkerboard floor, red leatherette booths, waitresses in diner uniforms, and a Wurlitzer-style jukebox stocked with oldies. Typical diner fare—everything from a BLT to a stack of hotcakes—is featured, along with Vegas specials such as a full roast prime rib dinner for $5.95, available from 10am to midnight.

At the **Center Stage,** another 24-hour facility, comfortable dark-green tufted-leather booths, wallpapered walls hung with still-life oil paintings, stained-glass windows, and brass candelabra chandeliers combine to create a warmly inviting ambience. Sandwiches, salads, Cajun specialties, and a full breakfast menu are offered. Nothing on the menu is more than $9.25. An 18-ounce porterhouse steak is just $8.95.

Other food and beverage facilities include an ice-cream parlor, **Coffee & Cravings** for gourmet coffees and fresh-baked goods, a 24-hour casino snack bar, several casino cocktail bars, and the **Omaha Lounge** offering live entertainment in the casino almost around-the-clock.

Services: Guest-services desk (also handles in-house shows), tour desk.

Facilities: Casino, car-rental desk, shops (gifts, liquor, jewelry), wedding chapel, beauty salon/barbershop. There's a sports deck with a nice-sized swimming pool, a ¼-mile outdoor jogging track, and four Har-Tru tennis courts.

Lady Luck Casino Hotel

206 N. 3rd St., at Ogden Ave., Las Vegas, NV 89101. ☎ **702/477-3000** or 800/523-9582. Fax 702/477-7021. 630 rms, 162 suites. A/C TV TEL. $45–$55 Sun–Thurs, $55–$90 Fri–Sat; junior suite $55–$75 Sun–Thurs, $70–$105 Fri–Sat. Extra person $8. AE, CB, DC, DISC, MC, V. Free parking (self and valet).

What is today Lady Luck opened in 1964 as Honest John's—a 2,000-square-foot casino with five employees, five pinball machines, and 17 slots. Today that casino occupies 30,000 square feet, and the hotel—including sleek 17- and 25-story towers—is a major Downtown player taking up an entire city block. What it retains from earlier times is a friendly atmosphere—one that has kept customers coming back for decades. Eighty percent of Lady Luck's clientele is repeat business.

Tower rooms are decorated in a variety of attractive color schemes, mostly utilizing muted southwestern hues (peach, mauve, beige, and teal) with handsome oak furnishings. All are equipped with small refrigerators and TVs with pay-per-view movie options. Junior suites in the West Tower have parlor areas with sofas and armchairs, separate dressing areas, and baths with whirlpool tubs. The original Garden Rooms are a little smaller and less spiffy looking in terms of decor; on the plus side, they're right by the pool.

Dining: The **Burgundy Room** evokes Paris in the 1930s, with plush burgundy-velvet-upholstered booths and period artworks on display, including lithographs and original prints by Erté, Poucette, and Salvador Dali as well as art-deco sculptures by Max Le Verrier. Tables, set with pale pink linen cloths, are elegantly appointed and lit by Venetian hurricane lamps. The menu highlights steak, pasta, and fresh seafood. Dinner only; entrees $10.95 to $19.95.

The **Emperor's Room** is also enhanced by museum-quality paintings, sculpture, and screens from the owner's collection, including an exact replica of a work called "Soldiers of Xian" dating from 2000 B.C. It's an elegant setting, with candlelit, white-linened tables and a Persian rug on the floor. A mural on one wall depicts the route of Marco Polo's voyage to the Orient. Cantonese, Mandarin, and Szechuan entrees are offered. Dinner only; most entrees $6.25 to $11.25.

The **Winners' Café** is a southwestern-themed 24-hour coffee shop, with stained-glass windows depicting a desert scene and a hacienda. Stucco walls are hung with colorful serapes and Mexican pottery. A basic coffee-shop menu is augmented by Mexican and Polynesian specialties.

In addition, there are daily buffets (details in chapter 6), and ESPN sports are aired on three TV monitors in the **Casino Bar.**

Services: 24-hour room service, multilingual front desk, and complimentary airport shuttle.

Facilities: Casino, tour and show desks, car-rental desk, gift shop, swimming pool and sundeck.

INEXPENSIVE

California Hotel/Casino & RV Park

12 Ogden Ave., at 1st St., Las Vegas, NV 89101. ☎ **702/385-1222** or 800/634-6255. Fax 702/388-2660. 781 rms, 54 suites. A/C TV TEL. Single or double $40 Sun–Thurs, $50 Fri–Sat, $60 holidays. Extra person $5. Children 12 and under stay free in parents' room. AE, CB, DC, DISC, MC, V. Free parking (self and valet).

This is a hotel with a unique personality. California-themed, it markets mostly in Hawaii, and since 85% of the guests are from the "Aloha State," it offers Hawaiian entrees in several of its restaurants and even has an on-premises food store specializing in Hawaiian foodstuffs. You'll also notice that dealers are wearing colorful Hawaiian shirts. Of course, everyone is welcome to enjoy the aloha spirit here.

The rooms, however, do not reflect either state. Decorated in contemporary-look burgundy/mauve or apricot/teal color schemes, they have mahogany furnishings and attractive marble baths. In-room safes are a plus, and TVs offer pay-per-view movies and keno channels.

Dining: Decorated in forest green, with redwood paneling and a massive stone fireplace, the **Redwood Bar & Grill** looks like an elegant ski lodge. It has tapestried armchairs and booths at candlelit bare oak tables, and green-shaded gaslight-style fixtures provide soft lighting. There's piano bar entertainment in the adjoining lounge. The menu features steak and seafood. A noteworthy special is the 18-ounce porterhouse steak dinner for $10.95. Dinner only; most entrees $12.95 to $24.95.

The brick-floored **Pasta Pirate** evokes a coastal cannery warehouse with a corrugated-tin ceiling and exposed overhead pipes. Tables are candlelit, walls hung with neon signs and historic pages from the *San Francisco Chronicle*. A few other entrees are offered in addition to pasta dishes. You can see food prepared in a display kitchen. Dinner only; pasta dinners $8, entrees $12 to $20.

The **Market Street Café** is the requisite 24-hour facility. This one is rather charming, its walls hung with old-fashioned shop signs and historic photographs of San Francisco. The menu lists all the expected coffee-shop fare, as well as Hawaiian items and specially marked "heart-smart" choices.

The **Cal Club Snack Bar** is a casual cafeteria with an ice-cream parlor decor—a black-and-white checkerboard floor and chrome-rimmed tables. It serves ice-cream sundaes, along with Hawaiian soft drinks (flavors like guava and island punch) and Chinese/Japanese snack fare.

There are two 24-hour casino bars—the **Main Street Bar** and the **San Francisco Pub. Dave's Aloha Bar** on the mezzanine level is a tropical setting for exotic cocktails, liqueur-spiked coffees and ice-cream drinks, and international beers.

Services: Room service (breakfast only).

Facilities: Casino, car-rental desk, small rooftop pool, small video-game arcade, shops (gift shop, chocolates). A food store called **Aloha Specialties** carries kimchee, saimin, macadamia nuts, curries, and numerous flavors of jerky (beef, buffalo, sweet pork, and so on); there are several umbrella tables outside where these snacks can be eaten.

The California also has an attractively landscaped 222-space RV park with pull-through spaces; 192 spaces offer full hookup, and 30 provide electricity and water. Facilities include restrooms, showers, a coin-op launderette, dog run, convenience store, swimming pool, and whirlpool. The rate is $12 per night.

El Cortez Hotel & Casino

600 Fremont St., between 6th and 7th Sts., Las Vegas, NV 89101. ☎ **702/ 385-5200** or 800/634-6703. 107 rms, 200 minisuites. A/C TV TEL. $23–$28 single or double. $32–$40 minisuite. Extra person $3. AE, CB, DC, DISC, JCB, MC, V. Free parking (self and valet).

This small hotel is popular with locals for its casual just-folks Downtown atmosphere and its frequent big-prize lotteries (up to $50,000) based on Social Security numbers. The nicest accommodations are the enormous minisuites in the newer 14-story tower. Decorated in cool earth tones with sienna and teal accents, they feature oak furnishings and attractive leaf-print bedspreads and drapes. Some are just exceptionally large king-bedded rooms with sofas; others have separate sitting areas with sofas, armchairs, and tables plus small dressing areas. The rooms in the original building are furnished more traditionally and with less flair, and they cost less. Local calls are just 25¢.

Roberta's Café, an attractive candlelit restaurant decorated in sienna and teal, has tulip-motif fabric wall coverings and etched-glass panels. A pink glow emanates from recessed lighting in a cove ceiling. The menu features charbroiled steaks and seafood. Dinner only; most entrees $5.95 to $10.95.

There's also a large 24-hour coffee shop called the **Emerald Room** featuring a bacon-and-eggs breakfast with hash browns, toast, and coffee for $1. A "soup-to-nuts" 18-ounce porterhouse steak dinner is $6.45 here; many other full dinners are $4 to $6, and Mexican combination platters are also available. Four bars serve the casino.

On-premises facilities include a small video-game arcade, beauty salon, gift shop, and barbershop.

Under the same ownership is **Ogden House,** just across the street, with rooms that go for just $18 a night.

Fitzgeralds Casino/Hotel

301 Fremont St., at 3rd St., Las Vegas, NV 89101. ☎ **702/388-2400** or 800/274-LUCK. Fax 702/388-2181. 652 rms. A/C TV TEL. Single or double $28–$48 Sun–Thurs, $45–$90 Fri–Sat. Extra person $10. Children under 12 stay free in parents' room. AE, CB, DC, DISC, MC, V. Free parking (self and valet).

At 34 stories, the tallest casino hotel in Nevada, Fitzgeralds is Irish-themed, with pieces of the actual Blarney stone from County Cork at various places in the casino (rub them for luck) and a four-leaf clover logo. Even its rooms—decorated in rust and forest green with dark-stained oak furnishings—look a bit like leprechaun habitats. All have TVs with pay-movie options; corner rooms have dazzling two-sided views of the Fremont Street Experience, and 34 units have Jacuzzis and sofas.

Dining: Oak-paneled and oak-beamed, the American-nostaliga-themed **Cassidy's** has a handsome interior. Cream stucco walls are hung with photographs of America the way it used to be—old cafes, barns, fire stations, diners, and roadhouses. The menu highlights steaks, seafood, and pasta dishes. Dinner only; most entrees $8 to $13.

Molly's Country Kitchen & Buffet is the 24-hour coffee shop, and a very attractive one it is, with booths and chairs upholstered in charcoal gray and planters of greenery creating intimate seating areas. Meals here are *I*; a prime rib dinner offered weekdays from 1 to 11pm is just $4.99. Fitzgeralds also offers buffets at all meals ($4.99 for breakfast and lunch, $6.99 for dinner); on Saturday and Sunday a champagne brunch is $5.99. There's a **McDonald's** on the casino floor, as well as three bars.

Services: Room service 6am to 2pm and 5 to 11pm, complimentary gaming lessons.

Facilities: Casino, tour and show desks, car-rental desk, gift shop.

⑤ Four Queens

202 Fremont St., at Casino Center Blvd., Las Vegas, NV 89101. ☎ **702/385-4011** or 800/634-6045. Fax 702/387-5133. 700 rms, 38 minisuites. A/C TV TEL. Single or double $54–$79 Sun–Thurs, $65–$79 Fri–Sat; minisuite $99–$125. Extra person $10. Children under 2 stay free in parents' room. AE, CB, DC, DISC, MC, V. Free parking (self and valet).

Opened in 1965 as a nonhotel casino, the Four Queens has evolved over the decades into a major Downtown property occupying an entire city block.

Notably attractive rooms are located in 19-story twin towers. Especially lovely are the North Tower rooms, decorated in a southwestern motif and, in most cases, offering views of the Fremont Street Experience. South Tower rooms are done up in earth tones with dark/wood furnishings, leaf-design bedspreads and drapes, and wall-papers in small floral prints. Minisuites, decorated in traditional styles, have living rooms (separated from the bedrooms by a trellised wall) and dining areas, double-sink baths, and dressing areas. All accommodations offer TVs with in-house information and pay-movie channels. Some rooms are equipped with small refrigerators and coffeemakers.

Dining: Hugo's Cellar is a plush continental restaurant with an oak-beamed ceiling, exposed brick walls hung with gilt-framed landscape and still-life paintings, and seating in upholstered armchairs and spacious booths illuminated by amber-bulbed sconces. Every woman receives a red rose as she is seated. Dinner only; entrees $20 to $32.

At **Lailani's Island Café,** a whimsical Hawaiian cafeteria with colorful tropical murals on its walls, diners are entertained by island music, a 3-foot talking macaw, dancing flowers in dugout canoes, a five-headed totem pole with eyes that light up, and a fiber-optic light show overhead. Lunch and dinner; all menu items are under $7, most under $5.

Pastina's Italian Bistro is somewhat more traditional, though it, too, has a vaulted fiber-optic ceiling with shooting stars and swirling galaxies. Diners are seated at marble-topped tables in lacquer chairs or at plush booths upholstered in attractive teal/lavender/purple fabrics. The menu features a choice of pastas and traditional Italian entrees. Dinner only; entrees $4.95–$8.50.

Magnolia's Veranda, a 24-hour dining facility overlooking the casino, has three sections. The veranda part is a casual plant-filled cafe with an oak-beamed ceiling and stained-glass skylight panels. The adjoining courtyard, with Casablanca fan chandeliers overhead and booth seating, is the nonsmoking area. And there's also a rather elegant crystal-chandeliered section decorated in peach and verdigris, with etched-glass booth dividers and murals of New Orleans on the walls. The same menu is offered throughout. Besides the requisite coffee-shop fare, Magnolia's offers Hawaiian specialties. And a great deal is the $4.95 prime rib dinner served from 6pm to 2am.

Hugo's has a cozy lounge with a working fireplace; free afternoon entertainment is featured in the **French Quarter Lounge;** and two bars serve the casino.

Services: 24-hour room service.

Facilities: Gift shop, car-rental desk, tour and show desks, small video-game arcade.

Sam Boyd's Fremont Hotel & Casino

200 E. Fremont St., between Casino Center Blvd. and 3rd St., Las Vegas, NV 89101. ☎ **702/385-3232** or 800/634-6182. Fax 702/385-6229. 428 rms, 24 suites. A/C TV TEL. Single or double $28–$40 Sun–Thurs, $52–$60, Fri–Sat, $60–$75 holidays. Extra person $8. Children under 12 stay free in parents' room. AE, CB, DC, DISC, JCB, MC, V. Free parking (valet).

When it opened in 1956, the Fremont was the first high-rise in downtown Las Vegas. Wayne Newton got his start here, singing in the now-defunct Carousel Showroom. The Fremont's tower rooms are done up in two-color schemes—forest green/rust/cream with floral-print drapes and bedspreads or burgundy/mauve/muted blue with paisley-print fabrics. All have in-room safes and TVs with in-house information channels and pay-movie options.

Dining: The Fremont boasts a gorgeous oak-paneled restaurant called the **Second Street Grill.** Its art-deco interior features a peach-lit recessed ceiling, birch columns, and period alabaster fixtures and sconces. Diners are comfortably ensconced in plush leather booths and oversized chairs at elegantly appointed tables lit by brass candle lamps. A handsome bar adjoins. The fare is upscale continental with international overtones. Dinner only; entrees $13.95–$23.95.

Tony Roma's, A Place for Ribs, offers scrumptious barbecued chicken and smoky, fork-tender baby back ribs. Juicy charbroiled steaks and fresh seafood are additional options. A children's menu is a plus. This is a handsome restaurant, with seating amid planters of greenery and oak-wainscoted forest-green walls hung with historic photographs of Las Vegas. Dinner only; entrees $5.95–$14.25.

The **Lanai Cafe,** a comfortable 24-hour coffee shop softly lit by red neon lighting emanating from a recessed bamboo ceiling, has trompe l'oeil "window" walls painted with backdrops of mountain waterfalls and tropical ocean scenery. A wide-ranging American menu is supplemented by a full Chinese menu. Specials here include a full prime/rib dinner ($5.95) or a steak and lobster tail dinner ($8.88), both served from 5 to 11pm nightly. The **Lanai Express,** a tiny cafeteria featuring American and Chinese fare, adjoins.

The Fremont offers great buffets (see chapter 6 for details). There are bars in the casino, race and sports book, and keno lounge.

Services: Room service at breakfast only.

Facilities: Casino, 24-hour gift shop. Guests can use the swimming pool and RV park at the nearby California Hotel, another Sam Boyd enterprise.

✪ Showboat

2800 Fremont St., between Charleston Blvd. and Mojave Rd., Las Vegas, NV 89104. ☎ **702/385-9123** or 800/826-2800. Fax 702/383-9283. 475 rms, 7 suites, A/C TV TEL. $30–$65 Sun–Thurs, $30–$85 Fri–Sat, $85 holidays; $85–$215 suite. Extra person $10. Children under 12 stay free in parents' room. AE, CB, DC, DISC, MC, V. Free parking (valet and self).

Despite its slightly off-the-beaten-track location, this New Orleans–themed hotel is quite popular for its extensive facilities, friendliness, and totally delightful interior. The Showboat welcomes guests into a charming lobby adorned with flower boxes, murals of Mississippi plantations and riverboats, and stunning Venetian-glass chandeliers. As we go to press, an $18-million renovation is underway, most notably upgrading the casino and public areas. Rooms were redecorated in 1994–1995.

The Showboat has a long history in this town. Opened in 1954, it was the first hotel to offer buffet meals and bingo—not to mention bowling alleys. Today its gorgeous 24-hour bingo parlor is famous—for its flower garden murals and for the highest payouts in town. And the bowling alley—North America's largest—hosts major PBA tournaments.

Spacious rooms are cheerfully decorated in resort hues (peach, coral, teal) with bleached wood furnishings. Dressing areas are equipped with cosmetic mirrors, and baths offer hair dryers and extra phones. TVs have pay-movies and a hotel information station.

Dining: The **Plantation** keeps to the garden theme. One room evokes a veranda with wooden plank floors and white porch railings backed by exquisite botanical murals. Candlelit tables are covered in pale pink linen. The other dining area is more elegant, with Palladian windows and mirrors and ornate Victorian chandeliers. Together they comprise a lovely setting in which to enjoy mesquite-grilled steaks and seafood specialties. Dinner only; entrees $5.95 to $13.95.

Di Napoli diverges from the New Orleans theme, though it, too, is done in pastel hues (peach and apricot) and has a flower-filled fountain and a grape arbor painted on the ceiling. However, Roman wall frescoes, columns, and classical statuary set the stage for this charming candlelit dining room. The menu features California-inspired southern Italian cuisine as well as seafood specialties. Dinner only; most entrees $5.95 to $14.95.

The delightful 24-hour Mardi Gras–themed **Showboat Coffee Shop** extends into the casino with cafe seating. Walls are adorned with lovely murals of the Old South; there's lots of decorate white wood trim; and fan chandeliers whir slowly overhead. The menu offers a wide range of typical American fare ranging from salads, burgers, and sandwiches to full entrees.

There's also a very good buffet here (details in chapter 6), and a snack bar and a bar/lounge are located in the Bowling Center. Several bars serve the casino, including the **Carnival Room,** which features quality lounge acts and occasional big names such as Juice Newton, Sha Na Na, Chubby Checker, and Lacy J. Dalton. When headliners appear, there's a two-drink minimum.

Services: 24-hour room service, shoeshine.

Facilities: Casino, gift shop, beauty salon/barbershop, 24-hour Bowling Center with 106 lanes, bowling pro shop, video-game arcade. The Showboat has an Olympic-size swimming pool in a courtyard setting. There's an in-house babysitting center where you can drop off kids age 2 to 7 at no charge for up to three hours a day. Equipped with TV tapes, a slide, toys, art supplies, and games, its staff members play with the kids and read them stories.

7   A Hostel

July and August are the busiest months for the hostel, though these are the slowest months elsewhere in town. Hence, if you want to stay here because you like hosteling as a way of life, reserve several weeks in advance. On the other hand, if you're considering a hostel only to save money, try bargaining with Strip hotels in their off-season; you might be able to obtain very low rates.

Las Vegas International Hostel

1208 Las Vegas Blvd. S., between Charleston and Oakey blvds., Las Vegas, NV 89104. ☎ **702/385-9955.** Capacity: 60 people. A/C $8.95 in a dorm room with shared bath accommodating 4 people, $19.90 for a private room with shared bath. No credit cards. Free parking.

This American Association of International Hostels (AAIH) facility offers clean but spartan rooms in a two-story building. The upstairs rooms are a tad nicer, with balconies and polished pine floors (ceramic tile downstairs). You get a free sheet and pillowcase and pay $1 for a top sheet, blanket, and towels. Gratis coffee, tea, and lemonade are available in the lounge throughout the day. There are two lounges offering TVs, VCRs (and tapes), stereos, books, and games. Other facilities include barbecue grills, picnic tables, and chaise longues out back, coin-op washers/dryers, a fully equipped kitchen, bicycle racks and lockup, and locker rental (75¢). The hosted arranges excursions to Hoover Dam; Red Rock Canyon; Mount Charleston; Valley of Fire; and Bryce, Zion, and Grand canyons, and the friendly staff is knowledgeable about local sights and restaurants.

Note: Although conveniently located (the Sahara Hotel is just a few blocks away), this stretch of Las Vegas Boulevard South is rather seedy. It may not be a good choice for women traveling alone; and it's not wise for anyone to walk around the area alone at night.

6

Dining in Las Vegas

Many people consider Las Vegas a great restaurant town. It all depends on your point of view. From the vantage point of value for your money it's unbeatable. You can enjoy veritable food orgies at low-priced buffets, many of them offering incredible arrays of good, fresh food, creatively prepared and attractively displayed. At weekend brunch buffets, champagne flows freely as well. And speaking of drinks, they're free at gaming tables in the casinos.

Nor are buffets the only game in town. At many casino-hotel restaurants full dinners are well under $10. At the El Cortez, for instance, a soup-to-nuts dinner with an 18-ounce porterhouse steak is $6.45. And the same hotel features a $1 breakfast of bacon and eggs with hash browns, toast, and coffee. To locate budget fare, check local newspapers (especially Friday editions) and free magazines (such as *Vegas Visitor* and *What's On in Las Vegas*) which are given away at hotel reception desks. Sometimes these sources also yield money-saving coupons.

Now for the negatives. In terms of sophisticated dining, Las Vegas is barely a player. Basically this is a steak and potatoes kind of town. With a few exceptions, the city's bastions of haute cuisine serve everything flambé in cognac cream sauce and feature cherries jubilee and bananas Foster for dessert. Culinary concepts that took hold in close-by California decades ago are just beginning to make a dent in the dining scene here. And the low-priced ethnic eateries you find in most big towns are sparse. Not that I really mind. Las Vegas dining rooms are gorgeous and plushly comfortable, service is gracious, and let's face it, there are many worse things than cognac cream sauce or a really good steak. And things are beginning to change. In 1994 L.A. restaurateur Wolfgang Puck opened two restaurants here and another noted American chef, Mark Miller, installed a Coyote Café at the MGM Grand. Fiore's at the Rio and Charlie Trotter's at the MGM Grand are also on the culinary cutting edge. The future is looking brighter.

These establishments comprise a mix of exceptional hotel dining rooms and noteworthy free-standing restaurants. Among the latter, Las Vegas has far fewer cheap eateries than other cities; they simply can't compete with casino hotels that try to attract gamblers by offering inexpensive food. Las Vegas visitors tend to eat in hotels, and in the hotel section of this book (chapter 5), you'll find dozens of restaurants described at all price levels. Please peruse that chapter as well for dining choices. Many larger hotels have food courts (the one at Caesars Palace is especially nice).

The restaurants in this chapter are arranged first by location, then by the following price categories (based on the average cost of an entree): **Very Expensive,** more than $20; **Expensive,** $15 to $20; **Moderate,** $10 to $15; **Inexpensive,** under $10 (sometimes well under). In expensive and very expensive restaurants, expect to spend no less than twice the price of the average entree for your entire meal with a tip; you can usually get by on a bit less in moderate and inexpensive restaurants. My personal favorites are starred, and those offering especially good value are marked by a **Ⓢ**. Buffets and Sunday brunches are gathered in a separate category at the end of this chapter.

1 Best Bets

- **Best Buffet:** For variety, ambience, overall food quality, and reasonable price, the **Rio's Carnival World Buffet** is the best deal in town.
- **Best Sunday Champagne Brunch:** The *ne plus ultra* of its genre is the **Sheraton Desert Inn's Champagne Brunch** at the Monte Carlo Room. Flawlessly served in an idyllic setting, it begins with a selection of caviars complemented by chilled Stoly and aquavit, and proceeds lavishly to pâté de fois gras, lobster omelets, and free-flowing Moët & Chandon champagne.
- **Best Graveyard Dinner Deals: Binion's Horseshoe** (128 E. Fremont St., Downtown) offers a complete New York steak dinner served with potato, roll, and salad for just $3 from 10pm to 5:45am. The **Sands Shangri-La Café** serves up a 7-ounce steak with eggs, hash browns, and toast for $2.49 from midnight to 6am. And the **Rio's Beach Café** offers a 10-ounce T-bone steak with eggs, potatoes, and toast for $2.99 between 11pm and 7am.
- **Best Cheap Breakfast:** Make your first stop of the day the **Cyclone Coffee Shop** at the **Holiday Inn Boardwalk,** where a $1.29 breakfast includes two eggs, bacon or sausage, hash browns and toast (actually, it's served around the clock, as is a $4.95 all-you-can-eat fish fry with cole slaw and french fries).
- **Best Cheap Eats (Regular Hours):** At the **El Cortez's Emerald Room** an 18- to 20-ounce Porterhouse steak dinner is $6.45 around the clock. Close by, a 12-ounce porterhouse steak dinner is also available at the **Fremont** for just $8.95, served 6 to 10pm Thursday through Monday nights.
- **Best Decor:** Most exquisitely elegant is the Beidermeier interior at **Charlie Trotter's.** And I do love the **Monte Carlo Room** at the Sheraton Desert Inn, with its Palladian windows overlooking the pool and idyllic murals of cavorting Greek youths and nymphs.
- **Best Spot for a Romantic Dinner:** The warmly elegant **Fiore,** with its gorgeous interior and arched windows overlooking the palm-fringed pool, is the most simpatico setting for a leisurely

romantic dinner. Brilliant cuisine, a great wine cellar, and superb service combine to create a memorable evening.

- **Best Spot for a Celebration: Mizuno's** teppanyaki grills are ideal for small parties, with the chef's theatrics comprising a tableside show. And the **Buccaneer Bay Club** at Treasure Island—where everyone rushes to the window when the ship battle begins—is also a very good party venue.
- **Best Wine List:** The distinguished cellar at **Charlie Trotter's** houses 400 selections highlighting the classic food wines of France; Master Sommelier Stephen Geddes is on hand to guide you.
- **Best California Cuisine:** Wolfgang Puck's **Spago**—the very essence of California chic—is always thrilling. I could lunch every day on his signature Chinois chicken salad.
- **Best Chinese Cuisine: Chin's**—where piano bar music enhances an ambience of low-key elegance—offers scrumptious and authentic Cantonese fare including some original creations such as deep-fried battered chicken served with strawberry sauce and fresh strawberries.
- **Best Deli:** There is the New York transplant—the **Stage Deli**—and there is nothing else.
- **Best Italian Cuisine:** Chef Gabriel Crigorescu's northern Italian culinary creations at **Fiore** are unparalleled and sublime.
- **Best Southwestern Cuisine:** The fact that it's the only notable southwestern restaurant in town doesn't make the **Coyote Café** any less impressive. Superstar Santa Fe chef Mark Miller brings contemporary culinary panache to traditional southwestern cookery, and the results are spicy and spectacular.
- **Best Steak and Seafood:** Power-dining precinct **Morton's of Chicago** serves up prime succulent steaks in a comfortable, convivial, and often celebrity-studded setting. And you'll enjoy nothing but the best cuts of beef and the freshest seafood at **The Tillerman,** a gorgeous restaurant with candlelit tables amid an indoor grove of ficus trees and tree-trunk pillars.

2 Restaurants by Cuisine

AMERICAN
Dive! (Fashion Show Mall, On/Near the Strip, *M*)
Hard Rock Café (Hard Rock Hotel, Convention Center/Paradise Road, *M*)

BARBECUE
Tony Roma's (Stardust, On/Near the Strip, *I*)

BRUNCH
Bally's Sterling Sunday Brunch (On/Near the Strip, *VE*)

Key to abbreviations: *I=Inexpensive; M=Moderate; E=Expensive; VE=Very Expensive*

Sheraton Desert Inn's
Champagne Brunch
(On/Near the Strip, *VE*)
Tropicana Sunday Brunch
Buffet (On/Near the
Strip, *E*)

BUFFET

Bally's Big Kitchen Buffet
(On/Near the Strip, *M*)
Caesars Palace Palatium
Buffet (On/Near the
Strip, *M*)
Circus Circus Buffet (On/
Near the Strip, *I*)
Excalibur's Round Table
Buffet (On/Near the
Strip, *I*)
Flamingo Hilton Paradise
Garden Buffet (On/Near
the Strip, *I*)
Sam Boyd's Fremont Paradise
Buffet (Downtown, *I* to *M*)
Golden Nugget Buffet
(Downtown, *I*)
Lady Luck Banquet Buffet
(Downtown, *I*)
Las Vegas Hilton Buffet of
Champions (Convention
Center/Paradise Road, *M*)
Luxor's Manhattan Buffet
(On/Near the Strip, *I*)
MGM Grand Oz Buffet (On/
Near the Strip, *M*)
Mirage Buffet (On/Near the
Strip, *I* to *M*)
Rio's Carnival World Buffet
(On/Near the Strip, *I*)
Sahara Oasis Buffet (On/Near
the Strip, *I*)
Sands Garden Terrace Buffet
(On/Near the Strip, *I*)
Showboat Captain's Buffet
(Downtown, *I*)
Stardust Warehouse Buffet
(On/Near the Strip, *I*)
Treasure Island Buffet (On/
Near the Strip, *I*)
Tropicana Island Buffet (On/
Near the Strip, *I*)

CALIFORNIA

Planet Hollywood (Caesars
Palace, On/Near the
Strip, *M*)
Spago (Caesars Palace,
On/Near the Strip, *VE*)
Wolfgang Puck Café
(MGM Grand, On/Near
the Strip, *M*)

CHINESE

Chin's (Fashion Show Mall,
On/Near the Strip, *E*)
Ho Wan (Sheraton Desert
Inn, On/Near the Strip, *E*)

CONTINENTAL

Bacchanal (Caesars Palace,
On/Near the Strip, *VE*)
Buccaneer Bay Club (Treas-
ure Island, On/Near the
Strip, *VE*)
Pegasus (Alexis Park,
Convention Center/
Paradise Road, *VE*)

DELICATESSEN

Stage Deli (Caesars Palace,
On/Near the Strip, *M*)

FRENCH

Andre's (Downtown, *VE*)
Bistro Le Montrachet (Las
Vegas Hilton, Convention
Center Paradise Road, *VE*)
Monte Carlo Room (Sheraton
Desert Inn, On/Near the
Strip, *VE*)
Palace Court (Caesars Palace,
On/Near the Strip, *VE*)
Pamplemousse (On/Near the
Strip, *E*)

GERMAN

The Rathskeller (Convention
Center/Paradise Road, *I*)

INTERNATIONAL/AMERICAN

Charlie Trotter's (MGM
Grand, On/Near the
Strip, *VE*)

JAPANESE

Ginza (Convention Center/
Paradise Road, *M*)
Mizuno's (Tropicana, On/Near
the Strip, *E*)

MEXICAN

Ricardo's (Out of the Way, *I*)

NORTHERN ITALIAN/PROVENÇAL

Fiore (Rio, On/Near the
Strip, *VE*)

SOUTHWESTERN

Chili's (Convention Center/
Paradise Road, *I*)

Coyote Café (MGM Grand,
On/Near the Strip, *VE*)

STEAK/SEAFOOD

Morton's of Chicago (Fashion
Show Mall, On/Near the
Strip, *VE*)
The Palm (Caesars Palace,
On/Near the Strip, *VE*)
The Tillerman (Out of the
Way, *E*)

SWISS/GERMAN

Alpine Village Inn (Convention Center/Paradise
Road, *M*)

3 On or Near the Strip

VERY EXPENSIVE

Bacchanal

Caesars Palace, 3570 Las Vegas Blvd. S., just north of Flamingo Rd. ☎ 702/
734-7110. Reservations essential. Fixed-price $67.50, plus tax and gratuity. AE, MC,
V. Tues–Sat 6–11pm with seatings at 6 and 9:30pm. ROMAN ORGY CONTINENTAL.

Its pedimented doorways guarded by golden lions, Bacchanal is an
archetypal Las Vegas experience—an imperial Roman feast with
comely "wine goddesses" in harem-girl attire performing sinuous belly
dances, decanting wine from shoulder height into ornate silver chalices,
and—believe it or not—massaging male diners and feeding them
grapes! When not performing, the goddesses repose gracefully around
a fountained pool centered on a gold statue of a graceful wine-pouring
Venus. The setting is palatial: White-columned walls are backed by
murals of ancient Rome; an azure ceiling suggests an open sky, with a
grape arbor looping from beam to beam; and crystal torchiers provide
romantic lighting. The dramatic focus of the evening is a thunder and
lightning storm produced by Zeus to herald the arrival of Caesar and
Cleopatra. Caesar makes a short speech, and the royal pair tour the
room greeting diners. Abandon all reality, ye who enter here.

   Dinner is a sumptuous multicourse feast, including unlimited wine
and champagne. Your first course, presented in a silver and brass
étagère, offers a selection of crudités with a creamy herb dip and an assortment of fresh and dried fruits. This is followed by a cold seafood
medley (shrimp, scallops, and crab claws) in a tangy vinaigrette and
soup du jour. A pasta course varies nightly—perhaps fettuccine Alfredo
or spinach tortellini in lobster sauce. Next comes a salad—a Caesar
salad, of course. Entree choices include filet mignon, roast prime rib,
and Long Island duckling à l'orange, along with nightly specials such
as rack of lamb or stuffed Cornish game hen. They're served with varying side dishes such as herbed potatoes and broccoli hollandaise. The

dramatic finale—a flaming dessert of vanilla ice cream topped with liqueur-soaked fresh fruits—is accompanied by petits fours and tea or coffee.

Buccaneer Bay Club

Treasure Island, 3300 Las Vegas Blvd. S. ☎ **702/894-7350.** Reservations recommended. Main courses $14.95–$25.50. AE, CB, DC, DISC, JCB, MC, V. Nightly 5–10:30pm. AMERICAN/CONTINENTAL.

Its serpentine interior comprising a series of intimate dining nooks, Buccaneer Bay Club is a posh pirate lair, with mullioned windows overlooking the bay, a low beamed ceiling, and rustic stucco walls adorned with daggers and pistols. Treasure chests are displayed in wall niches along with a museum's worth of international plunder— a cane once owned by a maharajah (a gift to Steve Wynn), Moroccan chests inlaid with bone and semiprecious stones, a gilded peacock mirror from Peru, a Spanish conquistador's helmet, an 18th-century Venetian chest inlaid with rare onyx, and an intricately carved 18th-century Chinese opium-bed frame. Diffused lighting emanates from shaded brass table lamps, and classical music creates a sooth-ing audio backdrop. Steve Wynn often drops by with celebrity pals such as Diana Ross, Tom Selleck, Don Johnson, Robin Williams, Steven Spielberg, and Tom Hanks. And, just like everyone else, they rush to the windows when the ship battle begins below. It's part of the fun of dining here.

Begin your meal with an appetizer of chilled lobster médaillons with a piquant brandied Louis sauce. Another excellent choice is a trio of bacon-topped clams casino along with a trio of oysters encased in a smoked salmon/creamed horseradish crust and topped with hollandaise. My favorite entree here is roast rack of lamb—four tender, juicy chops in a balsamic jus reduction sauce with sautéed shallots. Also noteworthy are duckling à l'orange, spit-roasted in Grand Marnier, and crisp-crusted prime rib, which is roasted and then quick-grilled over mesquite and served with a creamy horseradish sauce. All of the above come with potatoes and haricots verts. For dessert order a taster's platter of goodies such as flourless chocolate cake, cappuccino mousse, and a crème brûlée tart.

✪ Charlie Trotter's

The MGM Grand, 3799 Las Vegas Blvd. S. ☎ **702/891-7337.** Reservations required (make them several weeks in advance if possible). Grand tasting menu $85; three-course à la carte menu or vegetarian tasting menu $65. AE, CB, DC, DISC, JCB, MC, V. Wed–Mon 6–11pm. INTERNATIONAL/AMERICAN.

Eminent Chicago restaurateur Charlie Trotter made his debut in Las Vegas in 1995, creating a magnificent new dining precinct at the plush MGM Grand. This is the very pinnacle of haute dining; food, ambience, service, and wines are all impeccable. The luxe Biedermeier interior—its organic curvatures as richly sinuous as a Stradivarius violin's—is an aesthetic tour de force, utilizing contrasting woods, Axminster floral-patterned carpeting, and alabaster chandeliers and sconces. Columned credenzas framing a central promenade display lavish flower arrangements.

Dining on the Strip and Paradise Road

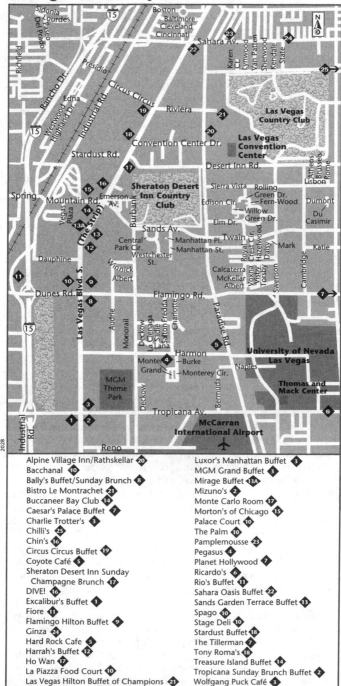

Alpine Village Inn/Rathskellar **20**
Bacchanal **10**
Bally's Buffet/Sunday Brunch **8**
Bistro Le Montrachet **21**
Buccaneer Bay Club **14**
Caesar's Palace Buffet **7**
Charlie Trotter's **3**
Chilli's **25**
Chin's **16**
Circus Circus Buffet **19**
Coyote Café **5**
Sheraton Desert Inn Sunday
  Champagne Brunch **17**
DIVE! **16**
Excalibur's Buffet **1**
Fiore **11**
Flamingo Hilton Buffet **9**
Ginza **24**
Hard Rock Cafe **5**
Harrah's Buffet **12**
Ho Wan **17**
La Piazza Food Court **10**
Las Vegas Hilton Buffet of Champions **21**

Luxor's Manhattan Buffet **3**
MGM Grand Buffet **3**
Mirage Buffet **13A**
Mizuno's **2**
Monte Carlo Room **17**
Morton's of Chicago **15**
Palace Court **10**
The Palm **10**
Pamplemousse **23**
Pegasus **4**
Planet Hollywood **7**
Ricardo's **6**
Rio's Buffet **11**
Sahara Oasis Buffet **22**
Sands Garden Terrace Buffet **13**
Spago **10**
Stage Deli **10**
Stardust Buffet **18**
The Tillerman **7**
Tony Roma's **18**
Treasure Island Buffet **14**
Tropicana Sunday Brunch Buffet **2**
Wolfgang Puck Café **3**

Brilliant chef Guillermo Tellez worked in Trotter's Chicago kitchen for 6 years. His ever-changing degustation (tasting) menus comprise about seven exquisitely complex courses, each one a perfect miniature culinary universe. On a recent visit, dinner included Louisiana oyster accompanied by jalapeño crème fraîche in chilled cucumber dill broth. It was succeeded by caviar-garnished grilled swordfish, then Chilean sea bass with cubes of braised celery root and poached tomatoes in a spicy broth. A highlight was sautéed foie gras, poised on scallion confit and caramelized onions. Grilled free-range organic grass–fed veal and lamb—the heartiest course—came with garlic-potato purée and potato galette, haricots verts, and a ragout of wild mushrooms and sage-infused veal jus. The grand finale was a trio of desserts—moist chocolate-beet cake topped with milk chocolate ice cream, brown-butter strawberry cake in strawberry balsamic sauce crowned with strawberry ice cream, and upside-down polenta pineapple cake with pineapple chips and vanilla bean ice cream. Be sure to consult friendly Master Sommelier Steven Geddes (one of America's most knowledgeable and highly acclaimed wine experts) in selecting wines to complement your meal. The distinguished cellar contains more than 400 selections highlighting the classic food wines of France—many available by the glass and even the half-glass.

✪ Coyote Café

The MGM Grand, 3799 Las Vegas Blvd. S. ☎ **702/891-7349.** Reservations recommended for the Grill Room, not accepted for the Café. Grill Room: Main courses $15–$32; Café: Main courses $6.95–$16.95 (most under $10). AE, CB, DC, DISC, JCB, MC, V. Grill Room: Daily 5:30–10:30pm; Café: Daily 9am–11pm. MODERN SOUTHWESTERN.

In a town where restaurant cuisine often seems stuck in a 1950s time warp, Mark Miller's Coyote Café evokes howls of delight. His robust regional cuisine combines elements of traditional Mexican, Native American, Créole, and Cajun cookery with cutting-edge culinary trends (Miller spent 3¹/₂ years at Chez Panisse). The main dining room is fronted by a lively cafe/bar decorated in adobe hues, which overlooks the MGM's restaurant row and a bank of slot machines. Folk art animals are displayed over the bar, and an open cooking area houses a Mexican *cazuela* (casserole) oven and *comal* grill under a gleaming ceramic tile hood. The adobe-walled Grill Room offers a more tranquil setting. Candlelit tables are set with ocher and rust signature china; decorations include baskets and pottery; etched-glass partitions by Santa Fe artist Kit Carson depict whimsical scenes (such as a coyote and a horse dining in a restaurant), and a warm glow emanates from innovative sconces that filter light through multi-colored Japanese rice paper. A gorgeous flower arrangement is flanked by wine-storage cabinets with hammered-copper doors, and one wall displays woodblock carvings of southwestern cuisine's "Four Magic Plants"—corn, beans, squash, and chilies.

The Grill Room menu changes every 2 weeks. On a recent visit, I began with a heavenly "painted soup"—half garlicky black bean, half beer-infused smoked Cheddar—"painted" with chiptle cream and garnished with salsa fresca and de árbol chili powder. My main course was a salmon fillet crusted with ground pumpkin seeds and corn tortillas topped with roasted chile/pumpkin-seed sauce; it was presented on a bed of spinach-wrapped spaghetti squash studded with pine nuts, corn kernels, scallions, and morsels of sun-dried tomato. Dessert was a chocolate banana torte served on banana crème anglaise and topped with a scoop of vanilla ice cream. The wine list includes many by-the-glass selections, including champagnes and sparkling wines, which nicely complement spicy southwestern fare; Brazilian daiquiris—made with four kinds of rum, Mexican vanilla beans, brown sugar, and fresh pineapple—are a house specialty.

The Café menu offers similar but somewhat lighter fare. Fixed-price southwestern breakfasts ($10.95, including fresh orange juice and coffee) offer entrees such as blue-corn griddle cakes with maple syrup and chicken-apple sausages.

✪ Fiore

Rio Suite Hotel, 3700 W. Flamingo Rd., at I-15. ☎ **702/252-7702.** Reservations recommended. Entrees $21–$32.50. AE, CB, DC, DISC, MC, V. Nightly 6pm–midnight. NORTHERN ITALIAN/PROVENÇAL.

Fiore offers a deliciously simpatico setting for the brilliantly innovative cuisine of chef Gabriel Grigorescu. In his spacious mahogany-ceilinged dining room, with arched windows overlooking a palm-fringed pool, white-linened tables are elegantly appointed with fine silver, flowers, and Villeroy & Boch china in diverse floral patterns. Flower- and fruit-motif carpeting furthers the "fiore" motif, while an exhibition kitchen agleam with copper pots and the glow of wood-burning pizza ovens (nine different hardwoods are used for grilling here) adds warmth and theatricality. Tapestried booths are backed by a mural of the French countryside. I love the interior space, but it's also tempting to dine alfresco on Fiore's lovely flower-bordered flagstone terrace (heated in winter, mist-cooled in summer). Light jazz provides a pleasant musical backdrop.

Grigorescu's seasonally changing menus complement the culinary elegance of northern Italy with the earthy exuberance of southern France. I began a recent dinner here with a cherrywood-baked crunchy herbed risotto cake studded with morsels of shrimp, zucchini, and yellow squash with pomodoro (chopped tomato) sauce. A salad of hearts of palm tossed with haricots verts and warm potato salad in hazelnut vinaigrette was ambrosially topped with fresh seared foie gras. An entree of barbecued Atlantic salmon in honeyed hickory sauce came with grilled polenta and portobello mushrooms, roasted yellow and red Roman tomatoes, and grilled asparagus spears. And roasted Muscovy duck leg and fan of breast (that had been marinated in oranges for 2 days) was lacquered with cherry sauce and accompanied by roasted French chestnuts, fresh Mission figs caramelized in brown sugar, and garlic mashed potatoes.

A "bread hostess" comes by from time to time during your meal, tempting you to fill up on scrumptious fresh-baked pesto, olive, parmesan, potato, squaw, and tomato-basil breads; a dish of herbed olive oil replaces butter. And sorbets splashed with Dom Perignon are served between courses. Fiore's thoughtful list of more than

300 wines—in several price ranges—is international in scope and includes 45 premium by-the-glass selections. Consult your knowledgeable waiter for suggestions. Dine slowly and consider indulging in a cheese course—excellent cheeses are served with seasonal fruits. But do save room for dessert—perhaps a warm chocolate torte on crème anglaise embellished with raspberry stars and chocolate hearts, or an apple soufflé with calvados cream sauce. In addition to an extensive listing of cognacs, ports, and dessert wines, hand-rolled cigars—elegantly presented in a mahogany humidor—are a postprandial option on the terrace.

The Monte Carlo Room

Sheraton Desert Inn, 3145 Las Vegas Blvd. S., between Desert Inn Rd. and Sands Ave. ☎ **702/733-4444.** Reservations recommended. Main courses $26–$37. Fixed-price dinner $37. AE, CB, DC, DISC, JCB, MC, V. Thurs–Mon 6–11pm. FRENCH.

The delightful Monte Carlo Room is equally renowned for its sublime setting and fine French cuisine. The main dining room is romantically decorated in shades of tawny peach, its windows overlooking the palm-fringed pool. Charming murals on classical themes decorate the walls and ceilings. And diners are comfortably ensconced in tapestried banquettes at tables illumined by white taper candles or pink-shaded crystal lamps. A second dining room is similar, though the windows are replaced by mirrors. When Esther Williams had a birthday party here (attended by Debbie Reynolds, Ann Miller, and June Allyson) a teddy bear that sings "Happy Birthday" was acquired for the occasion; since then this birthday bear has been a Monte Carlo tradition.

An excellent appetizer choice is coquille de la marée—chunks of fresh lobster, shrimp, and scallops in Armagnac cream sauce topped with browned duchesse potatoes. Shrimp scampi has never been more scrumptious. And soup choices include a thick, velvety cognac-laced lobster bisque, full of rich flavor, served in a scooped-out round loaf of bread.

For your entree, there's roasted Nevada quail stuffed with foie gras, wild rice, and pine nuts; it's served on a bed of crunchy wild rice, in a rich red wine truffle sauce, and garnished with garlic-toast points, artichoke hearts, and quail eggs. Or consider fresh poached salmon in champagne sauce with white seedless grapes. Steaks and chops are additional choices. A mélange of vegetables and a potato dish (perhaps pommes savoyorde—thin-sliced potatoes layered with cheeses and oven browned) accompany entrees. There's an extensive wine list; consult the sommelier for suggestions. Flaming table-side preparations are a specialty, including desserts such as crêpes Suzette and cherries jubilee. However, I recommend the vanilla soufflé (order with your main course) smothered in crème anglaise and Grand Marnier sauce.

✪ Morton's of Chicago

3200 Las Vegas Blvd. S., in the Fashion Show Mall (take Spring Mountain Rd. off the Strip, make a right at Fashion Show Dr. and follow the signs). ☎ **702/893-0703.** Reservations recommended. Main courses $16.95–$29.95. AE, CB, DC, MC, V. Mon–Sat 5:30–11pm, Sun 5–10pm; bar stays open later. STEAK/SEAFOOD.

Part of a restaurant empire created by former *Playboy* exec Arnie Morton, this gourmet steak house has a warm clublike interior. Ecru walls are hung with LeRoy Neiman prints and photographs of celebrity diners (a keynote of every Morton's is a star-studded clientele), rich mahogany paneling adds a note of substantial elegance, and much of the seating is in roomy gold leather booths, at white-linened tables adorned with fresh flowers. Pewter pig-motif candle lamps (Mr. Morton's whimsical encouragement to make a pig of yourself) cast a soft glow. An exhibition kitchen is hung with copper pots, and wines are stored in a brick-walled rack. Power diners here include Steve Wynn, MGM Grand owner Kirk Kerkorian who comes in at least once a week, and Strip entertainers Penn and Teller.

Waiters in flowing white aprons approach your table with rolling service carts laden with several cuts of meat, a cooked chicken, and a frisky live lobster. What you see is what you get. Start off with an appetizer—perhaps a lump crabmeat cocktail with mustard-mayonnaise sauce. Entree choices include succulent prime midwestern beefsteaks—porterhouse, New York strip sirloin, ribeye, or double filet mignon in béarnaise sauce—prepared to your exact specifications, plus lemon oregano chicken, lamb chops, Sicilian veal, grilled swordfish, whole baked Maine lobster, and prime rib with creamed horseradish. Side orders such as flavorfully fresh al dente asparagus served with hollandaise, or hash browns are highly recommended. Portions are bountiful; plan to share. A loaf of warm onion bread on every table is complimentary. Leave room for dessert—perhaps fresh berries with sabayon sauce or a Grand Marnier soufflé. There is, of course, an extensive wine list. You may want to retreat to a sofa in the cozy mahogany-paneled bar/lounge for after-dinner drinks.

✪ Palace Court

Caesars Palace, 3570 Las Vegas Blvd. S., just north of Flamingo Rd. ☎ **702/ 734-7110.** Reservations essential. Main courses $28–$40. AE, MC, V. Nightly 6–11pm; there are specified seatings at 6, 6:30, 9, and 9:30pm. FRENCH.

Reached via a crystal-ceilinged bronze elevator—or an elegant brass-balustraded spiral staircase—the circular Palace Court is as opulent as a Venetian palazzo. The centerpiece of the room—a towering stained-glass skylight dome (an orange and yellow sunburst) 36 feet in diameter—shelters a grove of ficus trees flanked by classical statuary and flower beds. White-lattice windows draped with peach balloon curtains overlook the hotel's Pompeiian-inspired swimming pool and the mountains beyond. On the opposite wall is a charming mural of the French countryside. White-linened tables—appointed with gold and white Lenox china, vermeil flatware, and hand-blown crystal—are softly lit by shaded brass candle lamps. And the room is further enhanced by bountiful flower arrangements in terra-cotta urns.

Award-winning chef Gerard Vullien trained at Maxim's in Paris and worked under Truisgros. His menus change seasonally. A recent one offered appetizers of poached champagne-glazed Long Island oysters (embellished with beluga caviar, smoked salmon, and julienned leeks) and ravioli stuffed with minced pink prawns, mushrooms, and truffles in lobster bisque sauce. Sorbets are served between courses in frosted glass lilies. Among the entrees, Maine lobster was served with coral (lobster roe) butter and steamed broccoli, and chateaubriand came with peppery red wine/game sauce, a mousseline of spinach, poached pears, and dauphinois potatoes.

There's an extensive, recherché wine list, with 20 by-the-glass selections; consult the sommelier for assistance. Chocolate-dipped and sugar-glazed strawberries are served gratis at the conclusion of your meal. However, that doesn't mean you should forgo dessert. Choices include ambrosial soufflées and a totally satisfying flourless chocolate truffle cake topped with homemade hazelnut ice cream.

End your evening over après-dinner drinks in the romantic adjoining piano bar/lounge. Overlooking the pool, this plushly furnished venue has a stained-glass skylight that retracts for a view of open starlit sky. Off the lounge is an intimate crystal-chandeliered European-style casino for high-stakes players only.

✪ The Palm

The Forum Shops at Caesars Palace, 3500 Las Vegas Blvd. S. ☎ **702/732-7256.** Reservations recommended. Main courses $8.50–$14 lunch, $15–$29 dinner. AE, CB, DC, MC, V. Daily 11:30am–11pm. STEAK/SEAFOOD.

Grandsons of New York's original Palm owners John Ganzi and Pio Bozzi have parlayed the family business into a restaurant empire spanning the country, this Las Vegas branch being one of its more recent manifestations. In the Palm tradition, signature pine-wainscoted ecru walls are plastered with celebrity caricatures of everyone from Wayne Newton to Walt Kelly's Pogo. Diners are seated at crisp white-linened tables and in roomy mahogany booths upholstered in dark green leather; floors are bare oak, and wood-bladed fans whir overhead. A star-studded clientele includes everyone from Tony Curtis (who celebrated a birthday here) to George Foreman (who got a standing ovation from fellow diners).

Another Palm tradition is a bare-bones menu that austerely offers up appetizers (such as shrimp cocktail, clams casino, melon and prosciutto) and entrees (filet mignon, lamb chops, salmon fillet, broiled crabcakes, linguine with clam sauce, prime rib of beef) without frills. By contrast, a listing for string beans aglio e olio (in garlic and oil) seems positively lyrical. Food preparation is simple (nothing is drizzled, infused, or nuanced here). Rather, the emphasis is on fresh fish and seafood, top-quality cuts of meat, and salads using the ripest, reddest, and juiciest tomatoes—all served up in satisfying hungry-man portions. Side dishes of cottage fries and creamed spinach are recommended. The wine list nicely complements the menu, and desserts include big wedges of cheesecake and chocolate pecan pie. At lunch you can choose a $12 fixed-price meal, which includes an entree (perhaps prime rib or batter-fried shrimp), salad, cottage fries, and tea or coffee.

✪ Spago

The Forum Shops at Caesars Palace; 3500 Las Vegas Blvd. S. ☎ **702/369-6300.** Reservations recommended for the dining room; not accepted at the cafe. Dining Room: Main courses $14–$28; Cafe: Main courses $8.50–$16.50. AE, CB, DC, DISC,

MC, Optima, V. Dining Room: Sun–Thurs 6–10:30pm, Fri–Sat 5:30–11pm; Cafe: Daily 11am–1am. ASIAN/ITALIAN-INFLUENCED CALIFORNIAN.

The galaxy of Las Vegas restaurants has been agleam with a bright new star since legendary California chef Wolfgang Puck's movable feast traveled east. His Las Vegas kitchen is under the aegis of an inspired disciple—executive chef David Robins, who adheres to Puck's culinary philosophies but enhances Spago's renowned repertoire of signature dishes with innovative menu items of his own.

Noted restaurant designer Adam Tihany's enchanting interior is fronted by a high-energy casual-chic cafe/bar overlooking the street show of the Forum Shops' classical Roman piazza. This convivial cafe houses a wood-burning pizza oven, which glows candescent under its shining copper hood. A jazz guitarist performs here Sunday afternoons. I love the cafe, but the stunningly theatrical multilevel main dining room is simply breathtaking. Its visual centerpiece, an outer-space-themed mural-sized painting by James Rosenquist, accentuates an alluring otherworldly ambience. To the right, a grand and whimsically railed Brazilian cherrywood staircase—scene of many a dramatic descent—is imbedded with glass mosaics. Stainless-steel and brass "magic carpets" float below the 25-foot ceiling, creating an element of dynamic movement. The lighting plays a stellar role, bouncing off lofty copper columns and enhancing the shimmer of cookware in a 50-foot exhibition kitchen. Most impressive is the play of light upon two glossy wood mezzanine-level doors, transforming them into golden panels flanking a towering brick chimney. Needless to say, Spago is Las Vegas's numero uno celebrity haunt.

The dining room menu changes nightly, but ambrosial appetizers have included such dishes as a quartet of tuna sashimis atop blocks of Japanese rice studded with tiny morsels of cucumber and peppers, served with pickled Asian vegetables. Puckish pasta entrees are divine. I had ravioli stuffed with goat, ricotta, and parmesan cheeses, toasted pine nuts, and fresh herbs. It was topped with a balsamic-glazed ragout of wild mushrooms. And the pièce de résistance was tender moist, crisp-skinned roast Chinese duck that had been marinated with a stuffing of pears and ginger and slow cooked in a Chinese oven in red wine vinegar and soy sauce. It was served with a doughy steamed bun filled with julienned vegetables, plum wine sauce enlivened by an infusion of other fruits, and a garnish of grapefruit slices. Pastry chef Mary Bergin's desserts—such as a caramelized espresso pot de crème textured with coarsely ground espresso beans—make fitting finales. Equally impressive is the extensive and expertly researched wine list. Cafe specialties include Puck's signature Chinois chicken salad and a superb mesquite-fried salmon served with a tangy toss of soba noodles and cashews in a coconut-sesame-chili paste vinaigrette nuanced with lime juice and Szechuan mustard.

EXPENSIVE

✪ Chin's

3200 Las Vegas Blvd. S., in the Fashion Show Mall (turn at the Frontier sign). ☎ **702/733-8899.** Reservations recommended. Main courses $7.95 lunch, $12–$28 dinner. AE, MC, V. Mon–Sat 11:30am–10pm, Sun noon–10pm. CANTONESE.

Chin's offers a tranquil contrast to the neon overkill of the Strip. Its understated decor is almost stark, with bare white walls and white-linened tables. During the day a single flower in a vase graces each table; at night this flower is removed and replaced by a glass oil candle. Other than that, a narrow band of recessed pink lighting is virtually the only adornment. Seating is in comfortable mauve velvet- upholstered armchairs and banquettes. Tuesday through Saturday nights, a pianist plays mellow classics—Cole Porter and the like. I believe you'll find, as I did, that what at first seems a too-cool setting is actually aesthetically refined and soothing.

Chin's cuisine is as pleasing as its ambience—on a par with the finest Chinese restaurants in New York and California. Not-to-be-missed appetizers—served with a trio of sauces—include crispy spring rolls stuffed with finely chopped chicken and vegetables; heavenly shrimp puffs (minced shrimp and mildly curried cream cheese wrapped in wonton skins and deep fried); and a Chinese chicken salad that is a crunchy mix of crisp-fried chicken strips and lettuce tossed with rice noodles, sesame seeds, and coriander in a light dressing with a tang of mustard. At lunch this scrumptious salad is offered as a main course. There are many highly recommended dinner entrees, among them chunks of tender orange roughy wok-fried in black pepper sauce with onions and red and green peppers; barbecued pork fried rice—here a culinary masterpiece comprising a mound of savory rice studded with morsels of pork, crisp scallions, peas, and finely chopped carrots and onions; and Chin's beef—thin slices of wok-sautéed beef that have been marinated for 24 hours in a secret sauce and tossed with rice noodles. A small, but carefully chosen, wine list features French and California wines that complement Chinese cooking. Do order crispy pudding for dessert—a refreshing batter-dipped egg custard splashed with Midori, a melon liqueur.

Ho Wan

(Sheraton) Desert Inn, 3145 Las Vegas Blvd. S. ☎ **702/733-4444.** Reservations suggested. Main courses $10–$35.50 (most under $20). AE, CB, DC, DISC, JCB, MC, V. Nightly 6–11pm. CANTONESE AND SZECHUAN.

Entered via a dragon-motif etched-glass moongate, Ho Wan is heralded by a coral reef aquarium. Within, all is serene elegance. Diners are seated—in plushly upholstered red velvet booths and chairs—at beau-tifully appointed tables graced with fresh flowers. Silk-shaded chande-liers and sconces provide soft lighting; Chinese dishes and objets d'art are displayed in a black lacquer cabinet; and Chinese paintings are set in mahogany-framed wall inserts.

Order up appetizers of pan-fried pot stickers served with four sauces (hot sauce, vinegar, plum sauce, and mustard) and the fabulous Chinese chicken salad—a toss of deep-fried, lightly battered chicken slivers with rice noodles and crisp julienned vegetables in a tangy hoisin/mustard seed vinaigrette. Not on the menu (ask for it) is a de-licious entree of stir-fried shrimp with honey-glazed walnuts and sesame seeds in a mayonnaise-like sauce. And a noteworthy chef's specialty is pan-fried sliced beef rolled with onions and garlic and served with broccoli fleurets. Vegetable dishes here—such as baby bok choy in oyster sauce—merit consideration. For dessert, the flaming fried banana in honey glaze seems an apt Las Vegas finale.

Mizuno's

Tropicana Resort & Casino, 3801 Las Vegas Blvd. S. ☎ **702/739-2222**. Reservations suggested. Full samurai dinners mostly $14.95–$19.95, shogun combination dinners $24.95–$38.95. AE, CB, DC, MC, V. Daily 5–10:30pm. JAPANESE TEPPANYAKI.

This stunning marble-floored restaurant is filled with authentic Japanese artifacts, among them an ancient temple bell, a 400-year-old vase from Tokyo, and antique scrolls and shoji screens. One of the latter depicts the restaurant's theme—the exchange of cultures between the East and West as exemplified by the silk and tea trade. A meandering glass "stream" is lit by tiny twinkling lights to suggest running water; cut-glass dividers are etched with graceful cherry blossoms, irises, and plum trees; and brass palms and walls tiled in gleaming gold add a note of sparkling elegance. Food is prepared at gorgeous sienna marble teppanyaki grill tables where you're seated with other patrons; together you comprise the "audience" for a highly skilled chef, who, wielding cooking knives with the panache of a samurai swordsman, rapidly trims, chops, sautées, and flips the food onto everyone's plates. This being Las Vegas, his dazzling display of dexterity is enhanced by a flashing light show over the grill.

Entrees comprised of tasty morsels of New York strip steak, filet mignon, shrimp, or lobster, or shrimp and vegetable tempura—and various combinations of the above—come with miso soup or consommé (get the tastier miso), salad with ginger dressing, an array of crispy flavorful vegetables stir-fried with sesame seeds and spices, steamed rice, and tea. Though it's a lot of food, an appetizer of shrimp and mushrooms sautéed in garlic butter with lemon soy sauce merits consideration. And a bottle of warm sake is recommended. Ginger or red bean ice cream make for a fittingly light dessert. A great bargain here: a full early-bird dinner served from 5 to 6pm for just $9.95.

Pamplemousse

400 E. Sahara Ave., between Santa Paula and Santa Rita drives, a block east of the Strip. ☎ **702/733-2066**. Reservations essential. Main courses $17.50–$24.50. AE, CB, DC, DISC, MC, V. Two seatings nightly at 6–6:30pm and 9–9:30pm. FRENCH.

Evoking a cozy French countryside inn, Pamplemousse is a series of low-ceilinged rooms and intimate dining nooks with rough-hewn beams. The walls are hung with copperware and provincial pottery. Candlelit tables, beautifully appointed with Villeroy & Boch show plates and fresh flowers, are draped in pale-pink linen. And classical music or light jazz plays softly in the background. It's all very charming and un-Vegasy. There's additional seating in a small garden sheltered by a striped tent. The restaurant's name, which means grapefruit, was suggested by the late singer Bobby Darin, one of the many celebrity pals of owner Georges La Forge. Strip headliners Wayne Newton, Robert Goulet, Siegfried & Roy, and Englebert Humperdinck are regulars.

The menu, which changes nightly, is recited by your waiter. Your meal here begins with a large complimentary basket of crudités (about 10 different crisp, fresh vegetables), a big bowl of olives, and—a nice country touch—a basket of hard-boiled eggs. Appetizers might include lightly floured bay scallops sautéed in buttery grapefruit sauce and soft-shell crab in a butter cognac sauce with fresh herbs and a hint of Dijon mustard. Entrees could be crispy slices of duck breast and banana in a sauce of orange honey, dark rum, and crème de banane (corn-fed duck, raised according to the restaurant's specifications at a Wisconsin farm, is a specialty here) or fresh Norwegian salmon, seared crispy on the outside, juicy pink and tender on the inside, in a light orange beurre blanc with a touch of curry. And filet mignon, New York steak, and rack of lamb are always featured. Entrees are served with a medley of fresh vegetables. Desserts might include homemade dark chocolate ice cream with praline in a sabayon sauce or a classic fruit tart. An extensive, well-rounded wine list complements the menu.

MODERATE

In this category are the restaurants most of us prefer for everyday dining. They offer excellent meals at reasonable prices, often with a fair amount of ambience thrown in for good measure. Once again, depending on what you order, you might enjoy an inexpensive dinner at some of these restaurants. See also the listings for **Bistro Le Montrachet** (p. 128), **Coyote Café** (p. 116) and **Spago** (p. 120), upscale restaurants that are fronted by fairly inexpensive cafes.

DIVE!

3200 Las Vegas Blvd. S., in the Fashion Show Mall. ☎ **702/369-DIVE.** Reservations not accepted. $6.95–$13.95. AE, CB, DC, DISC, MC. V. Sun–Thurs 11am–midnight, Fri–Sat 11am–1am. AMERICAN.

This exuberant restaurant-cum-entertainment concept was the creation of power visionaries Jeffrey Katzenberg, Steve Wynn, and Steven Spielberg. DIVE!'s exterior is designed as a whimsical yellow submarine crashing through a 30-foot wall of water which cascades into an oversized pool erupting with depth-charge blasts. Its gunmetal-gray interior replicates the hull of a submarine with vaulted cylindrical ceilings, porthole-shaped (albeit neon-accented) windows, exposed conduits that burst with steam, pressure gauges, throttles, control panels, sonar screens, and working periscopes. Every half-hour a high-tech show projected on a 16-cube video wall (and 48 additional monitors throughout the restaurant) simulates a fantasy submarine dive (your undersea voyage could, for instance, end up in the swirling waters of a washing machine), with special effects ranging from vibrating seats to flashing safety lights. Overhead, a luxury ocean liner, a manta ray research vessel, exotic fish, a fighting shark, and model subs circumnavigate the room on a computerized track. And even the background music is aquatically themed, featuring songs like "Under the Boardwalk" and "Sea of Love." A DIVE! Gear retail shop is on the premises.

For all the hoopla, DIVE! keeps the focus on food. You can get a really great meal here, and portions are immense. There are, of course, sub sandwiches such as tempura-battered softshell crab served on a

---

🐷 Family-Friendly Dining

Buffets *(see p. 135)*   Cheap meals for the whole family. The kids can choose what they like, and there are sometimes make-your-own sundae machines.

DIVE! *(see p. 124)*   Housed in a submarine and featuring a zany high-tech show every half hour projected on a video wall, this is the most fun family-oriented spot of all.

Hard Rock Café *(see p. 132)*   Kids also adore this restaurant, which throbs with excitement and is filled with rock memorabilia.

Planet Hollywood *(see p. 125)*   This popular chain is not unlike Hard Rock Café, but movie memorabilia replaces the rock artifacts, and numerous video monitors add to the hoopla.

Pink Pony *(see p. 81)*   This bubble-gum pink circus-motif 24-hour coffee shop at Circus Circus will appeal to kids. And mom and dad can linger over coffee while the kids race upstairs to watch circus acts and play carnival games.

Sherwood Forest Cafe *(see p. 83)*   Kids love to climb on the lavender dragons fronting this 24-hour coffee shop at Excalibur, and they also enjoy numerous child-oriented activities while you're on the premises.

---

baguette with lemon-caper mayonnaise. Delicious pizza on a thin lavash-like crust is topped with applewood-smoked chicken drizzled with barbecue sauce, Monterey Jack cheese, cilantro, and scallions. Also excellent—a bottomless bowl of linguine tossed with mussels, clams, and salmon in garlicky white wine/herb butter sauce. Other menu choices include hefty burgers on brioche onion rolls, wood oven-roasted herbed chicken (served with grilled corn on the cob, horseradish-whipped mashed potatoes, and an array of about seven other roasted vegetables), char-grilled steak or salmon, or a slab of barbecued baby back ribs. For dessert order crème brûlée garnished with fresh berries.

Planet Hollywood

Forum Shops at Caesars Palace, 3500 Las Vegas Blvd. S. ☎ **702/791-STAR.** Reservations not accepted. Main courses $6.50–$17.95 (most under $13). AE, DC, MC, V. Sun–Thurs 11am–midnight, Fri–Sat 11am–1am. CALIFORNIAN.

Except for a few reclusive folks who've never heard of O.J. and can't name all four Beatles, by now everyone knows all about celebrity-studded, celebrity-owned (Arnold, Sly, Bruce, and Dem*i*) Planet Hollywood. Its exuberant and cluttery two-level interior, with zebraskin rugs and palm trees, is jam-packed with a veritable museum of Hollywood memorabilia—Clint Eastwood's pistol from *A Fistful of Dollars,* Marlon Brando's *Guys and Dolls* costume, Barbara Eden's genie bottle, James Bond's moon buggy from *Diamonds are Forever,* Clayton Moore's Lone Ranger tunic, chariot wheels from *Ben Hur,* the side of beef Stallone sparred with in *Rocky,* the *Star Trek* control tower, and hundreds more. Touring the premises is part of the fun. Video monitors abound; while you dine, you can watch trailers for soon-to-be-released movies, themed video montages, and footage of Planet Hollywood grand openings around the world. The restaurant is also the scene of frequent autograph signings (Luke Perry, Susan Anton, Cindy Crawford, and many others), memorabilia presentations (such as George Clooney's donation of his *ER* scrubs), and parties (ranging from a benefit for the Agassi Foundation for Youth—Brooke and Andre hosted—to a season premiere party for *Melrose Place*). It's all great fun, even the rest rooms (check it out). Background music is from movie soundtracks.

Best of all, the food is really quite good. There are delicious appetizers: blackened shrimp served with Créole mustard sauce, smoked chicken and cheese nachos, and pot stickers with spicy hoisin dipping sauce. Creole pizza topped with blackened shrimp, andouille sausage, chicken, onions, fresh plum tomatoes, Monterey Jack, and cheddar is superb. Ditto linguine tossed with Thai shrimp, peanuts, and julienned vegetables in spicy sweet chili sauce. Other options include fajitas, burgers, and platters of smoked ribs. There's a full bar; other drink options range from thick malts and shakes to specialty drinks, such as a tropical rum/curacao/pineapple concoction called "Die Harder" (non-alcoholic versions are available for kids). For dessert try white chocolate bread pudding drenched in whiskey sauce and topped with white chocolate ice cream. There's a walkway here directly from the Strip, and three Planet Hollywood merchandise shops are on the premises. Arrive off hours to avoid a wait for seating.

✪ Stage Deli

Forum Shops at Caesars Palace, 3500 Las Vegas Blvd. S. ☎ 702/893-4045. Reservations accepted for large parties only. Main courses $9.95–$13.95, sandwiches $5.95–$12.95. AE, DC, DISC, JCB, MC, V. Sun–Thurs 8am–11pm, Fri–Sat 8am–midnight. KOSHER-STYLE DELI.

New York City's Stage Deli—a legendary hangout for comedians, athletes, and politicians—has been slapping pastrami on rye for more than half a century. Its Las Vegas branch retains the Stage's brightly lit Big Apple essence. The black walls are embellished with subway graffiti and hung with Broadway theater posters, bowls of pickles grace the white Formica tables, and, in the New York tradition, comics Buddy Hackett and Henny Youngman drop by whenever they're in town.

Most of the fare—including fresh-baked pumpernickel and rye, meats, chewy bagels, lox, spicy deli mustard, and pickles—comes in daily from New York. The Stage dishes up authentic 5-inch-high sandwiches stuffed with pastrami, corned beef, brisket, or chopped liver. (I like the soup, half sandwich, and potato salad combo.) Skyscraper sandwich combos are named for celebrities; try a Wayne Newton triple decker (turkey, salami, Swiss cheese, coleslaw, and Russian dressing). Other specialties here: matzoh-ball soup, knishes, kasha varnishkes, cheese blintzes, kreplach, pirogen, and smoked fish platters accompanied by bagels and cream cheese. Or you might prefer a full meal consisting of pot roast and gravy, salad, homemade dinner rolls, potato

---

Factoid

According to the Las Vegas Convention and Visitors Authority, what percentage of vistors are retired?

—26%

---

pancakes, and fresh vegetables. Desserts run the gamut from rugelach cheesecake to Hungarian-style apple strudel, and available beverages include wine and beer, milk shakes, Dr. Brown's sodas and chocolate egg creams.

✪ Wolfgang Puck Café

MGM Grand, 3799 Las Vegas Blvd. S. ☎ 702/895-9653. Reservations not accepted. Main courses $9–$14.50. MC, V. Sun–Thurs 11am–11pm, Fri–Sat 11am–midnight. ASIAN/ITALIAN-INLUENCED CALIFORNIAN.

Lucky Las Vegas has two Wolfgang Puck restaurants—the scintillating Spago at Caesars Forum Shops (see lengthy paean above) and this delightfully whimsical cafe in the sports-themed section of MGM's massive casino. Puck's wife and partner, Barbara Lazaroff, designed the interior, imprinting her signature pizza-slice logo on chair backs, triangular glass sconces, and vibrantly colorful mosaics embedded into walls and glossy granite tables. Black-and-white accents bring unity to this riot of zigzaggy shapes and pulsating color. A large counter seating area faces a display kitchen where chefs tend an oak-burning brick pizza oven.

One of my favorite dishes is Puck's signature Chinois chicken salad tossed with crispy fried wontons, julienned carrots, cabbage, and green onions in a piquant Chinese honey-mustard sauce. Even a half portion is immense—enough for a fairly hearty lunch. Pizzas are also a signature item. Constructed upon a crust topped with fontina and mozzarella cheeses brushed with pesto, they're layered with embellishments such as spicy jalapeño-marinated sautéed chicken, leeks, and cilantro. Also highly recommended is tortellini stuffed with sautéed shiitakes, herbs, and parmesan cheese served with a rich wild mushroom/white wine sauce redolent of shallots and garlic. Or you might prefer rotisserie-barbecued chicken served with garlic mashed potatoes. Wine and beer are available, but I often prefer Puck's fruity tropical iced tea instead. Desserts include a tiramisu that is the ne plus ultra of its genre.

INEXPENSIVE

Tony Roma's—A Place for Ribs

Stardust Resort & Casino, 3000 Las Vegas Blvd. S., at Convention Center Dr. ☎ 702/732-6111. Reservations not accepted. Main courses $8.25–$12.95. Children's portions $4.95. AE, CB, DC, DISC, MC, V. Sun–Thurs 5–11pm, Fri–Sat 5pm–midnight. BARBECUE.

Tony Roma's is a deservedly popular national chain, and the company has voted this Stardust location the very best of its 140 franchises in terms of service, food quality, and cleanliness. It's a comfortable eatery, with seating in leather-upholstered captain's chairs and wood-paneled walls hung with historic photographs of Las Vegas. A tub with brass faucets sits outside, so you can wash your sticky fingers on exiting.

This is a great choice for family dining. The house specialty is meaty, fork-tender baby back ribs barbecued in tangy sauce, but you can also order big, juicy beef ribs, honey- and molasses-basted Carolina-style pork ribs, or spicy Cajun ribs. A sampler plate is available. There are also hearty platters of barbecued shrimp or chicken, burgers, the catch of the day, steaks, and salads. Do try a side order of onion rings (served in a loaf). Entrees come with coleslaw and a choice of baked potato, french fries, or ranch-style beans. The children's menu lists a choice of four meals in a basket—ribs, burgers, chicken fingers, or chicken drumstick and thighs, all served with fries. For dessert there are fresh-baked chocolate, coconut, and banana cream pies, and all bar drinks are available.

4   Off the Strip

VERY EXPENSIVE

Andre's

401 S. 6th St., at Lewis Avenue between Fremont St. and Charleston Blvd. ☎ **702/ 385-5016.** Reservations recommended. Main courses $19.75–$33. AE, CB, DC, MC, V. Nightly from 6pm; closing hours vary. FRENCH/CONTINENTAL.

Owner-chef Andre Rochat has created a rustic country-French setting in a converted 1930s house in Downtown Las Vegas. Low ceilings are crossed with rough-hewn beams, and wainscoted stucco walls (imbedded with straw) are hung with provincial pottery and copperware. Seating is in tapestried chairs and banquettes, and soft lighting emanates from candles and sconces. In addition to a warren of cozy interior rooms, there's a lovely ivy-walled garden patio under the shade of a mulberry tree. This is a major celebrity haunt, where you're likely to see Strip headliners. I was there one night when Tom Hanks, Steven Spielberg, and James Spader joined some pals for a bachelor party.

The menu changes seasonally. On a recent visit, appetizers included jumbo sea scallops rolled in a crunchy macadamia nut crust with citrus beurre blanc and red beet coulis. Sorbets are served between courses. An entree of poached Norwegian salmon in scallion-studded beurre blanc was served with angel hair pasta in a coarsely chopped tomato sauce with a hint of garlic. A fan of pink, juicy slices of sautéed duck comes with a confit of port wine and onions. A medley of vegetables—perhaps pommes lyonnaise, asparagus, broccoli hollandaise, and baby carrots—accompanies each entree. For dessert, I love Andre's classic fruit tarts—flaky butter crusts layered with Grand Marnier custard and topped with fresh, plump berries. An extensive wine list (more than 750 labels) is international in scope and includes many rare vintages; consult the sommelier.

Bistro Le Montrachet

Las Vegas Hilton, 3000 Paradise Rd. ☎ **702/732-5111** or 702/732-5651. Reservations suggested. Restaurant: main courses $23.50–$35; Bistro: main courses $6–$16. AE, CB, DC, DISC, JCB, MC, V. Restaurant: Wed–Mon 6–10:30pm; Bistro: Wed–Mon 5–11pm. FRENCH.

Dining Downtown

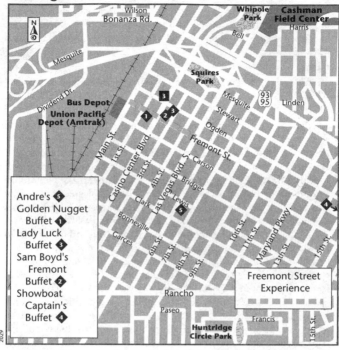

Andre's **5**
Golden Nugget
    Buffet **1**
Lady Luck
    Buffet **3**
Sam Boyd's
    Fremont
    Buffet **2**
Showboat
    Captain's
    Buffet **4**

Freemont Street
Experience

This ultra-elegant French restaurant located in the major Convention Center–area hotel seats diners under a dome bathed in a flattering pink light, an effect enhanced by shaded Chinese lamps casting a soft glow on white-linened tables. These are beautifully appointed with fine crystal and silver, graced with a bowl of roses. Richly paneled mahogany walls are hung with landscapes and still-lifes. A crystal chandelier and beveled mirrors add sparkle. And the room centers on a templelike circle of massive walnut columns wherein a large floral arrangement graces an ornate marble table.

Dishes are exquisitely presented and prepared. You might begin with chilled duck fois gras served on toast points. Also noteworthy are a creamy lobster bisque with tangy-sweet garlic croutons and the salad "Le Montrachet"—a refreshing mélange or Belgian endive, watercress, julienned beets, and enoki mushrooms in a gorgonzola dressing. Entree choices range from roasted breast of Muscovy duck (served with white and black beans and currants in a crème de cassis sauce) to broiled live Maine lobster removed from the shell and served atop herbed Moroccan couscous with crab dressing and drawn butter. Sorbets are served between courses; unique is one made with sweet basil that is quite refreshing to the palate (request it). The restaurant's wine cellar stocks more than 400 wines from vineyards spanning the globe.

Adjoining the dining room—and entered via a wine cellar—is the more casual Bistro, a European-style cafe/bar with seating under an awning. Light gourmet fare—such as saffroned seafood pasta or a salad of grilled rare ahi tuna tossed with tomatoes and artichoke hearts in a balsamic vinaigrette—is featured, along with espresso, cappuccino, and luscious desserts.

Pegasus

Alexis Park Resort, 375 E. Harmon Ave., between Koval Lane and Paradise Rd. ☎ **702/796-3300.** Reservations recommended. Main courses $13.50–$39. AE, DC, MC, V. Nightly 6–11pm. CONTINENTAL.

This low-key luxury resort in the Convention Center/Paradise Road area attracts many visiting celebrities and Strip headliners, and its premier restaurant is a fitting venue for such an upscale clientele. Pegasus has an almost celestial ambience. Its splashing fountains and mist of diffused lighting playing on etched mirrors make me feel like I'm dining in an underwater kingdom. Planters of greenery, pots of ferns, and a large floral centerpiece enhance this serene setting, as does a wall of arched windows overlooking a fountain-splashed rock garden.

Flambé table-side preparations are featured, and sorbets are served between courses. You might begin with a quail egg and mandarin orange salad tossed with sweet mustard dressing. Among the soups, a splendid choice is the velvety cognac-laced lobster bisque. And fresh-shucked oysters Rockefeller here elevate this dish to its delicate apogee. The featured entree is Maine lobster sautéed with black truffles in a Madeira/bordelaise sauce; crowned with almond meringue baked to a golden brown, it is dramatically presented in a flaming veil of fire. Also excellent are boneless quail served with Madeira sauce and wild rice and salmon layered with spinach en croûte in a citrusy white wine-flavored dill sauce. A daily game special is offered each evening. For example, tenderloin of rabbit battered in coconut and sautéed in a Chambord cream sauce. Desserts include flambé selections such as bananas Foster and cherries jubilee along with pastries and cakes from the cart. There's an extensive wine list (mostly French and California) with choices in varying price ranges, and seven or eight premium wines are available by the glass each evening.

EXPENSIVE

✪ The Tillerman

2245 E. Flamingo Rd., at Channel 10 Dr. (just west of Eastern Ave.). ☎ **702/ 731-4036.** Reservations not accepted. Main courses mostly $15.95–$25. AE, CB, DC, DISC, MC, V. Nightly 5–11pm, bar/lounge until midnight. STEAK/SEAFOOD.

Ask any local for a list of favorite restaurants, and you can be sure the Tillerman in east Las Vegas will be on it. How can you go wrong offering flawless food in a stunning arboreal setting? The Tillerman's verdant plant-filled interior is under an oak-beamed, 40-foot cathedral ceiling with retractable skylights. Candlelit dining areas offer seating amid a grove of ficus trees, their woodsy ambience enhanced by exquisite oak paneling and tree-trunk pillars. A circular stained-glass window provides a lovely focal point. There's additional seating on the mezzanine level, where diners enjoy treetop views. All the top Strip performers are regular Tillerman customers.

Owner Tom Kapp personally inspects every piece of meat and fish that comes into the restaurant, and his food sources are worldwide. The menu is likely to offer Chilean sea bass, Norwegian salmon, Australian lobster, farm-raised mussels from Washington State, and Chesapeake Bay oysters, among others. Of equal quality is his dry-aged prime beef, cut on the premises.

Your meal begins with a relish tray and a basket of delicious oven-fresh breads. Also complimentary is a Lazy Susan salad bar served at your table with a choice of homemade dressings, including a memorable chunky blue cheese. Portions are immense, so appetizers are really not necessary, but, then again, they're too good to pass up. Especially notable: ultrafresh plump red médaillons of yellowfin tuna blackened and served almost rare in spicy mustard sauce. Meat entrees include prime center-cut New York strip steak, fork-tender filet mignon, and prime rib. And there are at least a dozen fresh fish/ seafood specials each night. On a recent visit I had a piece of snowy white halibut, charcoal-broiled to perfect brownness and brushed with pecan pesto. Entrees come with a white and wild rice mixture tossed with slivered almonds and chives and fresh vegetables (perhaps thick asparagus spears). Homemade desserts—such as Bavarian cream with strawberries and bananas—change nightly. The wine list highlights California selections and offers six premium wines by the glass each night.

Note: Since the Tillerman doesn't take reservations, arrive early to avoid waiting, or else plan a predinner cocktail in the cozy oak-paneled lounge with a working fireplace.

MODERATE

⑤ Alpine Village Inn

3003 Paradise Rd., between Riviera Blvd. and Convention Center Dr. ☎ **702/ 734-6888.** Reservations recommended. Fixed-price dinners $9.95–19.50; children's portions (under 12 only) about half price. AE, CB, DC, DISC, MC, V. Sun–Thurs 5–10pm, Fri–Sat 5–11pm. SWISS/GERMAN.

A Las Vegas tradition since 1950, this extremely popular family restaurant in the Convention Center/Paradise Road area does not subscribe to the less-is-more theory of interior design. Fresh white napery and red napkins make an immediate cheerful impact. Walls are painted with murals of snowy Alpine scenery, an effect enhanced by snow-covered chalet roofing, twinkling Christmas tree lights, and miniature ski lifts on cables strung across the ceiling. There are Swiss and Austrian cowbells, mounted deer heads, and window boxes filled with geraniums. And the very efficient waitstaff is dressed in Tyrolean costume. Seating is in comfortable burgundy leather booths lit by amber wall lamps.

Dinner is a multicourse feast beginning with a big pewter bowl of crudités served with herbed cottage cheese dip. Next comes a steaming bowl of savory Bavarian chicken soup; a pewter kettle of it is left on your table, so you can ladle out as much as you like. A basket of fresh-baked breads includes scrumptious hot cinnamon rolls. And your salad has a paprika-flavored blue cheese vinaigrette dressing. As an entree, I recommend the roast duckling with sausage stuffing served over wild and brown rice (it comes with orange and cherry sauces) or roast tender chicken with chestnut stuffing. These are accompanied by an array of vegetables and choice of crisp potato pancakes, a baked potato, or Swiss Rösti potatoes (shredded potato mixed with onion, bacon, eggs, and spices, fried in a pancake, and garnished with grated parmesan). If you'd like more than one of the above selections, the waiters generally comply. The finale: homemade apple or peach strudel, served warm (topped with vanilla ice cream if you so desire). Tea or coffee is included. The wine list offers wines by the glass and a large selection of beers, 19 varieties of schnapps, and exotic cocktails.

After dinner, if you can still move, check out the adjoining gift shop's selection of cuckoo clocks, crystal, beer steins, music boxes, cowbells, and Hummel figures. There's also a bar/lounge and a separate downstairs restaurant called the Rathskeller (details below).

Ginza

1000 E. Sahara Ave., between Paradise Rd. and Maryland Pkwy. ☎ **702/732-3080.** Reservations for large parties only. Main courses $12.55–$17.50. AE, MC, V. Tues–Sun 5pm–1am. Free parking in back. JAPANESE.

For almost two decades this charming little restaurant in the Convention Center/Paradise Road area has attracted a devoted clientele of local Japanese and Japanese food aficionados. There's a sushi bar in the front room, and the main dining area has shoji-screen–covered windows, tables sheltered by shingled eaves, rice paper-style lighting fixtures, and cream walls adorned with Japanese fans, paintings, and prints. Four spacious red leather booths are the sole concession to Las Vegas style.

You might begin with a shared appetizer of tempura shrimp and vegetables. Entrees—such as beef, chicken, or salmon sprinkled with sesame seeds in a thick teriyaki sauce—come with soup (miso or egg flower), sunomono (a vinegared Japanese salad), and green tea. Sushi is a highlight, and there are about 30 à la carte selections to choose from. Be sure to try an appetizer or entree portion of Ginza's unique Vegas rolls—salmon, tuna, yellowtail, and avocado rolled with seaweed in sesame-studded rice and quickly deep-fried so the sesame seeds form a scrumptious crust. It's served with lemon soy sauce. Also delicious are seaweed-wrapped California rolls filled with crabmeat, avocado, and cucumber and topped with salmon caviar. The fish is extremely fresh, and everything here is made from scratch. A bottle of sake is recommended. For dessert there's lemon sherbet or ginger and green tea ice cream.

Hard Rock Café

4475 Paradise Rd., at Harmon Ave. ☎ **702/733-8400.** Reservations not accepted. Main courses $8.95–$13.95; burgers & sandwiches $5.50–7.95. AE, DC, MC, V. Sun–Thurs 11am–11:30pm, Fri–Sat 11am–midnight. AMERICAN.

The Hard Rock Café located in the Convention Center/Paradise Road area is an incredible phenomenon. Founder Peter Morton created it so that people would "have a place to go where they could experience the fun of rock 'n' roll, past and present, while enjoying a great meal." And that pretty much describes it. The Las Vegas branch opened in 1990 with an Aerosmith concert. Fronted by an 88-foot guitar and a sidewalk of the stars honoring rock legends, it is, in the Hard Rock tradition, aclutter with rock memorabilia—Roy Orbinson's Harley Davidson, a signed Rolling Stones guitar, Elvis Presley gold records, an outrageous Elton John costume, a Jimi Hendrix concert poster, autographed Jerry Lee Lewis cowboy boots, and so forth. Also in the Hard Rock tradition: It is set up as a place where the average Joe and Jane can come and gape at stars, and, amazingly, stars frequently show up to be gaped at. Sheryl Crow, Michael Keaton, the Ramones, Pat Benatar, and Eddie Van Halen are just a few who've made the scene here.

The menu offers some good salads, such as a crisp tortilla piled high with greens, Cheddar cheese, black beans, guacamole, and sliced grilled chicken. A burger and fries here are as good as they get. And entrees run the gamut from fajitas to Texas ribs in watermelon barbecue sauce served with a salad and fries. Wash it down with anything from a Heineken to a thick chocolate shake. Or skip the latter and indulge in a hot fudge sundae for dessert. An inexpensive children's menu is a plus for families. Don't be frightened by the line outside—it's usually not for the restaurant but the on-premises Hard Rock merchandise store. The Hard Rock Hotel and Casino is next door (see chapter 5).

INEXPENSIVE

Chili's Grill & Bar

2590 S. Maryland Pkwy., between Sahara and Karen aves., in the Sahara Town Square Shopping Center. ☎ **702/733-6462.** Main courses $4.99–$9.99, AE, CB, DC, DISC, MC, V. Mon–Thurs 11am–10pm, Fri–Sat 11am–11pm, Sun 11:30am–10pm. Free parking. SOUTHWESTERN.

Chili's is a national chain, based in Texas, offering superior "bowls of red" and other southwestern specialties. This branch, located in the Convention Center/Paradise Road area, is a sunny, brick-floored restaurant with many plants flourishing in the light streaming in through numerous windows. Seating is in comfortable upholstered booths, ceramic-tiled tables are situated beneath hanging lamps made from old copper chili pots, and walls are adorned with framed posters and photographs of chili cook-offs. This is a great choice for family dining.

Chili is, of course, a specialty, available with or without beans. Equally popular are the fabulous half-pound burgers, made from fresh-ground beef and served with home-style fries and various toppings (I like cheese and chili). Another big item is fried chicken with country gravy, which comes with homemade mashed potatoes (with skins), corn on the cob, and garlic bread. Lighter items include grilled tuna served with tortillas, aioli and salsa dressing, rice, cabbage, and a spicy pinto bean soup. You can even get a plate of steamed vegetables here. Similarly, desserts run the gamut from a brownie topped with ice cream, hot fudge, chopped walnuts, and whipped cream to frozen yogurt. A children's menu, listed on a place mat with games and puzzles, offers full meals for $2.79, including "bottomless fountain drinks."

The Rathskellar

3003 Paradise Rd., between Riviera Blvd. and Convention Center Dr. ☎ **702/ 734-6888.** Reservations recommended. Burgers and sandwiches $4.25–$7.50, main courses $8.75–$11.95. AF, CB, DC, DISC, MC, V. Sun–Thurs 5–10pm, Fri–Sat 5–11pm. GERMAN/AMERICAN.

The Rathskellar is a rollicking downstairs adjunct to the Alpine Village Inn (see above)—a cozy beer hall, with red-and-white checkered table-cloths and a floor strewn with peanut shells (there are bowls of peanuts on every table). A pianist and singer entertain nightly, and everyone sings along. Choices here include a sauerbraten sandwich on pumper-nickel rye served with sweet-and-sour sauce and German potato salad; a hot open-faced turkey sandwich served with mashed potatoes, cranberry sauce, and gravy (salad bar selections included); barbecued pork ribs with baked beans; half-pound burgers; and beer-battered deep-fried buffalo wings with french fries. For dessert, there's apple or peach strudel à la mode. An extensive children's menu makes this a popular choice for family dining.

Ricardo's

2380 Tropicana Ave., at Eastern Ave. (northwest corner). ☎ **702/798-4515.** Res-ervations recommended. Main courses $6–$10.95; lunch buffet $6.95; children's plates $1.95–$3.95, including milk or soft drink with complimentary refills. AE, CB, DC, DISC, MC, V. Mon–Thurs 11am–10pm, Fri–Sat 11am–11pm, Sun noon–10pm. MEXICAN.

This hacienda-style restaurant in east Las Vegas is a great favorite with locals. It has several stucco-walled dining rooms separated by arched doorways—all of them lovely, with candlelit oak tables and booths upholstered in Aztec prints. There's a plant-filled greenhouse area, with Saltillo tile floors and rotating bamboo fans overhead. A tiered terra-cotta fountain and a mission bell grace a garden room with a lofty pine-beamed ceiling. And another area has a ceramic-tiled fireplace (ablaze in winter) and a dark wood coffered ceiling. Strolling Mexican musicians entertain at night.

Start off with an appetizer of deep-fried battered chicken wings served with melted Cheddar (ask for jalapeños if you like your cheese sauce hotter). Nachos smothered with cheese and guacamole are also very good here. For an entree, you can't go wrong with chicken, beef, or pork fajitas served sizzling on a hot skillet atop sautéed onions, mushrooms, and peppers. It comes with rice and beans, tortillas, a selection of salsas, guacamole, and tomato wedges with cilantro. All the usual taco/enchilada/tamale combinations are also listed, along with a variety of burritos. A delicious dessert is helado Las Vegas—ice cream rolled in corn flakes and cinnamon, deep-fried, and served with honey and whipped cream. And do order a pitcher of Ricardo's great margaritas. The same menu is available all day, but a buffet is offered at lunch. The kids' menu—on a place mat with games and puzzles—features both Mexican and American fare.

5 Buffets and Sunday Brunches

Las Vegas is famous for its lavish low-priced buffets. These abundant all-you-can-eat meals—devised by casino hotels to lure guests to the gaming tables—range from lackluster steam-table provender to lovingly prepared and exquisitely presented banquets with free-flowing champagne. Similarly, the settings for buffet meals run the gamut from fluorescent-lit rooms that look like bingo parlors to plush, softly illumined precincts. There are close to 3-dozen hotel buffets in town; the most noteworthy are described below. Except for a few very special weekend champagne brunches, all fall into either the "moderate" or "inexpensive" categories used for restaurants in the preceding sections (based on the cost of the dinner buffets—brunch hours are usually cheaper).

Note: These inexpensive meals are extremely popular. Arrive early (before opening) or late to avoid a long line, especially on weekends.

VERY EXPENSIVE

✪ Bally's Sterling Sunday Brunch
3645 Las Vegas Blvd. S. ☎ **702/739-4111.**

This brunch is served in the clubby elegant precincts of Bally's Steakhouse. Flower arrangements and ice sculptures grace lavish buffet spreads tended by white-hatted chefs. There's a waffle and omelet station, a sushi and sashimi bar, a carving station, and a brimming dessert table. You might choose smoked fish with bagels and cream cheese or help yourself from a mound of fresh shrimp. Entrees vary weekly. On my last visit the possibilities included rolled chicken stuffed with pistachios and porcini mushrooms, beef tenderloin, steak Diane, seared salmon with beet butter sauce and fried leeks, roast duckling with black currant and blueberry sauce, and penne Florentine with pine nuts and smoked chicken in vodka sauce. Of course, there are deli and breakfast meats, vegetables and scrumptious salads, cheeses, raw bar offerings, seasonal fruits and berries, and side dishes such as stuffed potatoes with caviar and sour cream. Champagne flows freely.

Sunday brunch, served from 9am to 2:30pm, is priced at $39. Reservations are suggested.

✪ Sheraton Desert Inn's Champagne Brunch at Monte Carlo Room
3145 Las Vegas Blvd. S. ☎ **702/733-4524** or 800/492-4400.

This is the most lavishly impressive brunch in Las Vegas—and possibly in the nation. Served in the idyllically magnificent Monte Carlo Room (see restaurant listing above), it couples aesthetically stunning displays of the finest gourmet fare with flawless service. Guests are graciously greeted by a maitre d' and offered a selection of caviars served with Stolichnaya or aquavit. They're then taken on a tour of food displays by a server and have the option of helping themselves or indicating selections and having plates prepared for them. The buffet table, backed by charming paintings of cupids, is laden with smoked fish (trout, mussels, sturgeon, Scottish salmon, and mackerel), iced seafood (lobster, cracked crab legs, shrimp, oysters, clams), marvelous salads and antipasti, vegetable dishes, pâté de foie gras, an array of cheeses and cold cuts, a cornucopia of fresh fruits, eggs benedict, break-fast meats, baskets overflowing with fresh- baked breads and breakfast pastries (croissants, danish, scones, muffins, coffee cakes), a quartet of entrees (perhaps scampi fra diavolo with penne in parslied garlic-butter sauce, Petrale sole stuffed with crabmeat in mushroom cream sauce, seasoned melon stuffed with minced pork and black mushrooms, and boneless chicken medallions sautéed in egg-parmesan batter in a wild mushroom shallot sauce). There's also a full sushi bar, a fresh juice bar, an eggs and omelet station, and special stations for waffles/french toast, bananas Foster, and Peking duck with Mandarin pancakes and peppercorn-encrusted tenderloin with Madeira sauce. Waiters pour unlimited Moët & Chandon champagne from a silver bucket by your table, and a tempting array of desserts awaits you at the end. Reserva-tions are required and proper attire is requested (no shorts, T-shirts, or sandals). This is a leisurely affair that should be savored over the course of an entire morning.

The brunch is served Sundays from 9am to 2pm. Price is $50 (tax included, gratuity extra).

✪ Tropicana Sunday Brunch Buffet

3801 Las Vegas Blvd. S. ☎ **702/739-2376.**

This elaborate spread is served in the elegant El Gaucho Steak House (see description under hotel listing in chapter 5). Tables are elegantly appointed, and food displays are embellished with an ice sculpture and a cascade of fresh fruit. Try and get a seat by the wall of windows that overlooks a flamingo pond in the pool area. On my last visit, this im-pressive feast was comprised of sushi, ceviche, raw oysters, cold shrimp, smoked seafood (trout, salmon, whitefish, and sable), caviar, a carving station proferring at least five items (perhaps turkey, roast beef, rack of lamb, salmon Florentine, and roast pork), a waffle and omelet station, a full complement of breakfast meats and potato dishes, cheeses and cold cuts, an extensive salad bar, steak and tuna tartare, fresh vegetables, pasta dishes, numerous entrees (stuffed Maine lobster, filet mignon in burgundy sauce, roast chicken breast stuffed with fruit, red snapper in dill butter sauce, and roast pork with mustard sauce, among others), unlimited champagne, and dozens of desserts (including bananas Foster).

Sunday 9:30am to 2pm ($20.95 for adults, $12.95 for children 10 and under).

MODERATE

✪ Bally's Big Kitchen Buffet

3645 Las Vegas Blvd. S., ☎ **702/739-4111.**

This gorgeous spread is served in a carpeted and crystal-chandeliered dining room with comfortable upholstered armchair seating. Every-thing is extremely fresh and of the highest quality. There's always a prime rib and turkey carving station, a bountiful salad bar, a good choice of fruits and vegetables, entrees (perhaps seafood casserole in a creamy dill sauce, baked red snapper, pork chops sautéed in Cajun spices, barbecued chicken, and broiled steak in peppercorn sauce), pastas, rice and potato dishes, cold cuts, and a vast array of fresh-baked desserts. The brunch buffet includes breakfast fare and all-you-can-eat shrimp, while the dinner buffet adds Chinese selections.

Brunch daily 7:30am to 2:30pm ($17.95); dinner nightly 4:30 to 10pm ($11.95).

✪ Caesars Palace Palatium Buffet

3570 Las Vegas Blvd. S. ☎ **702/731-7110.**

This buffet proffers daily feasts fit for an emperor adjacent to the race and sports book in the Olympic Casino. Named for the 2nd-century meeting place of Rome's academy of chefs, this elegant dining room—with white-linen tables, murals of ancient Rome, and a peach-russet color scheme enhanced by gleaming brass accents—is fronted by an imposing colonnaded pediment. Selections at lunch and dinner include elaborate salad bars, carving stations for roast meats and poultry, a wide array of entrees, fresh-baked breads, desserts, and much, much more. The evening meal includes an elegant seafood station and often highlights Italian, Mexican, and other ethnic specialties. Especially lavish are weekend brunches with omelet stations (in addition to egg dishes), breakfast meats, fresh-squeezed juices, potatoes prepared in various ways, pastas, rice casseroles, carved meats, cold shrimp, smoked salmon, and a waffle and ice-cream sundae bar (they also make flaming desserts such as bananas Foster), in addition to two dessert islands spotlighting cakes and pastries. That's not the half of it.

Breakfast Monday to Friday 7:30–11am ($7.50). Lunch Monday to Friday 11:30am to 2:30pm ($9). Dinner nightly 4:30 to 10pm ($13.25). Saturday brunch 8:30am–2:30pm ($13.25). Sunday brunch, including unlimited champagne, 8:30am to 2:30pm ($15 for adults, $11.25 for children 7 to 12, under 6 free).

✪ Las Vegas Hilton Buffet of Champions

In the Convention Center area at 3000 Paradise Rd. ☎ **702/732-5111.**

This buffet is served in a beautiful gardenlike dining room with pristine white trellises, big planters of flowers, and magnificent white wrought-iron chandeliers and sconces. As the name implies, the room—located near the casino entrance to the race and sports SuperBook—is equally sports themed. Cream walls are adorned with attractive murals and photographs of hockey, football, boxing, and horse racing, and there are bookshelves stocked with sporting literature. All in all, it's one of the loveliest buffet rooms in town. And the fare is fresh and delicious. At lunch and dinner, the tempting array includes a roast beef and turkey carving station; hot entrees such as crabcakes, roast chicken, and pot roast, along with Chinese dishes; gorgeous salads and fresh fruits; many fresh vegetables; and a good selection of homemade desserts plus an ice cream/frozen yogurt sundae station. Dinner additionally features all-you-can-eat crab and shrimp.

Breakfast Monday to Friday 7 to 10am ($5.99); lunch Monday to Friday 11am to 2:30pm ($7.99); dinner nightly 5 to 10pm ($12.99); Saturday ($7.99)/Sunday ($9.99) brunch, including unlimited champagne, 8am to 2:30pm.

The MGM Grand Oz Buffet

3799 Las Vegas Blvd. S. ☎ **702/891-7777.**

This buffet is served in an enchanted garden amid planters of flowers, topiaries, and murals of Oz. This cheerful room has poppy-motif carpeting, white chairs with butterfly backs, leaf chandeliers, and food display tables under big scalloped umbrellas. Breakfast buffets include all the expected fare plus eggs Benedict, biscuits with creamed gravy, and a tempting assortment of fresh-baked pastries. Lunch and dinner feature a large display of fresh fruits and crudités, cooked vegetables, carving stations (roast sirloin or prime rib with creamed horseradish sauce plus roast turkey or ham), a baked potato bar, and close to a dozen entrees (which might include beef teriyaki, seafood Newburg, lamb-stuffed grape leaves, Yankee pot roast, baked mahimahi in pineapple beurre blanc, beef Stroganoff, fajitas, chicken stuffed with almonds and apples, and tortellini Alfredo). For dessert, there's a nice assortment of fresh-baked cakes, pies, and pastries (the chef's specialty is lemon lush) plus an ice cream/frozen yogurt make-your-own-sundae bar. Also available: low-fat, sugar-free desserts! And at all meals you get a full pot of coffee on your table. Breakfast daily 7 to 11am ($6.75), lunch daily 10:30am to 4pm ($7.75), dinner nightly 4 to 10pm ($10.25).

The Circus Circus Buffet

2880 Las Vegas Blvd. S. ☎ **702/734-0410.**

This buffet is housed in a large, cheerful room decorated with whimsical big-top-themed paintings and pink-and-white canvas tenting. There are 45 items at each meal, and plates are oversized to hold plenty. At dinner, for instance, there's a carving station (roast beef and ham), along with numerous entrees (fried fish, fried chicken, lasagne, egg rolls, sweet-and-sour pork, barbecued beef and chicken, and Salisbury steak on a recent visit). Side dishes include a big salad bar, rice and potato dishes, vegetables, and desserts, plus a make-your-own-sundae station and beverages. Four serving lines keep things moving along quickly. At breakfast, fresh- squeezed orange juice is a plus, not to mention oven-fresh biscuits, cheese blintzes, pancakes, and waffles. Selected breakfast items are also served at lunch along with hot entrees.

Breakfast daily 6 to 11:30am ($2.99), lunch daily noon to 4pm ($3.99), dinner nightly 4:30 to 11pm ($4.99).

⑤ Excalibur's Round Table Buffet

3850 Las Vegas Blvd. S. ☎ **702/597-7777.**

The buffet occupies, like all facilities here, a medieval setting. Crossed swords and paintings of knights in armor adorn castlelike faux stone walls, and lighting emanates from vast wrought-iron candelabra chandeliers overhead. The fare served isn't fancy, but it's freshly made, abundant, and inexpensive. Breakfast features fresh-squeezed orange juice and eggs Benedict, along with all the expected morning meal components. Lunch and dinner offer a number of hot and cold entrees (fried chicken, fried fish, stuffed cabbage, stuffed shells, and barbecued baby back ribs on a recent visit), along with dozens of salads, soup, rice and potato dishes, vegetables, fresh fruits, desserts, beverages, and a make-your-own sundae bar. At dinner there's a roast beef and turkey carving station. The plates are large, so you don't have to make as many trips to the buffet tables.

Breakfast daily 7 to 11am ($3.99), lunch daily 11am to 4pm ($4.99), dinner nightly 4 to 10pm ($5.99).

The Flamingo Hilton Paradise Garden Buffet
3555 Las Vegas Blvd. S. ☎ **702/733-7311.**

The buffet here occupies a vast room, with floor-to-ceiling windows overlooking a verdant tropical landscape of cascading waterfalls and a pond filled with ducks, swans, and flamingos. The interior—one of the most pleasant in Las Vegas—is equally lush, though its palm trees and tropical foliage are faux. At dinner, tables are laden with numerous daily-changing entrees—perhaps chicken piccata, pork teriyaki, baked cod in cream sauce, lasagne, barbecued ribs, pot roast, and seafood stew. And these are supplemented by a carving station (roast beef plus turkey or honey-baked ham) and an extensive monthly-changing international food station presenting French, Chinese, Mexican, German, or Italian specialties. A large salad bar, fresh fruits, pastas, vegetables, potato dishes, and a vast dessert display round out the offerings. Lunch is similar, but features a mix of international cuisines as well as a stir-fry station and a soup/salad/pasta bar. At breakfast, you'll find all the expected fare, including a made-to-order omelet station, waffles, eggs Benedict, blintzes, and fresh-baked breads and breakfast pastries (including croissants and doughnuts).

Breakfast daily 6am to noon ($5.95), lunch daily noon to 2:30pm ($6.95), dinner nightly 4:30 to 10pm ($8.95, including two glasses of wine).

✪ Sam Boyd's Fremont Paradise Buffet
Downtown at 200 E. Fremont St. ☎ **702/385-3232.**

This buffet is served in an attractive tropically themed room. Diners sit in spacious booths amid lush jungle foliage—birds of paradise, palms, and bright tropical blooms—and the buffet area is surrounded by a "waterfall" of Tivoli lighting under a reflective ceiling. Island music, enhanced by bird calls and the sound of splashing waterfalls, helps set the tone. Meals here are on the lavish side. A typical dinner features a carving station with three meats (perhaps baked ham, top round, and roast turkey) and six hot entrees (beef Stroganoff, barbecued Thai chicken, fettuccine Alfredo, eggplant parmigiana, salmon ovals with lemon butter, and shrimp fried rice on a recent visit). Fresh salads, soup, cold cuts, vegetables, rice and potato dishes, and desserts ranging from bakery-fresh pies and cakes to make-your-own sundae fixings round out the offerings.

Sunday, Tuesday, and Friday nights the buffet is renamed the **Seafood Fantasy,** and food tables, adorned with beautiful ice sculptures, are laden with lobster claws, crab legs, shrimp, raw oysters, smoked salmon, clams, and entrees such as steamed mussels, shrimp scampi, and scallops Provençale—all in addition to the usual meat carving stations and a few nonseafood entrees. It's great! And finally, the Fremont has a delightful champagne Sunday brunch served by "island girls" in colorful Polynesian garb. It includes not only unlimited champagne, but a full carving station, lox with bagels and cream cheese, an omelet station, and desserts.

Breakfast Monday to Saturday 7 to 10:30am ($3.95). Lunch Monday to Saturday 11am to 3pm ($4.95). Dinner Monday, Wednesday, and Thursday 4 to 10pm and Saturday 4 to 11pm ($7.95). Seafood Fantasy Sunday and Tuesday 4 to 10pm, Friday 4 to 11pm ($11.95). Champagne brunch Sunday 7am to 3pm ($6.95).

✪ The Golden Nugget Buffet
Downtown at 129 E. Fremont St. ☎ **702/385-7111.**

This buffet has often been voted No. 1 in Las Vegas. Not only is the food fresh and delicious, but it's served in an opulent dining room with marble-topped tables amid planters of greenery and potted palms. Mirrored columns, beveled mirrors, etched glass, and brass add sparkle to the room, and swagged draperies provide a note of elegance. Most of the seating is in plush booths. Lunch and dinner feature carving stations (turkey, roast beef, ham) plus five or six entrees (perhaps Calcutta chicken in a curry fruit sauce, sliced leg of lamb, whitefish in salsa, seafood scampi, beer-battered cod, and linguine alla carbonara). The buffet tables are also laden with an extensive salad bar (about 50 items), fresh fruit, and marvelous desserts including Zelma Wynn's (Steve's mother) famous bread pudding. Every night fresh seafood is featured. Most lavish is the all-day Sunday champagne brunch, which adds such dishes as eggs Benedict, blintzes, pancakes, creamed herring, and smoked fish with bagels and cream cheese. *Note:* This stunning buffet room is also the setting for a $2.99 late-night meal of steak eggs with home fries and biscuits with gravy; it's served 11pm to 4am.

Breakfast Monday to Saturday 7 to 10:30am ($5.25). Lunch Monday to Saturday 10:30am to 3pm ($7.50). Dinner Monday to Saturday 4 to 10pm ($9.50). Sunday brunch, including unlimited champagne, 8am to 10pm ($9.95, half price for children under 7).

Harrah's Galley Buffet
3475 Las Vegas Blvd. S. ☎ **702/369-5000.**

The buffet at Harrah's is served in a very pleasant riverboat-themed room with murals of Mississippi paddle wheelers and vintage signs from shipping companies on the wall. A lavish food display under a stained-glass skylight features a full panoply of hot entrees (perhaps braised beef burgundy, teriyaki chicken, stuffed grape leaves, baked cod, pastas, barbecued chicken, and buffalo wings); an array of fresh vegetables and potato dishes, an Asian food station, a fresh fruit and salad bar, and a make-your-own sundae station in addition to a variety of homemade desserts. There's an omelet station at breakfast and a roast beef carving station at dinner.

Breakfast daily 7 to 11am ($4.99), lunch daily 11am to 4pm ($5.99), dinner nightly 4 to 11pm ($7.99). Taxes and beverages are extra.

The Lady Luck Banquet Buffet
Downtown of 206 N. 3rd St. ☎ **702/477-3000.**

This buffet is served in a pretty garden-themed room with trellised dividers separating comfortable leather booths and leaf-design chandeliers overhead. Dinner includes all-you-can-eat prime rib, plus a variety of hot entrees (perhaps baked lasagne, homemade meat loaf, barbecued ribs, grilled mahimahi, and fried chicken). Frequently, there are Chinese, Polynesian, and Italian specialties as well. Offerings additionally include an extensive salad bar, a make-your-own-sundae bar, an array of fresh-baked pies and cakes, and beverages.

Breakfast is served daily 6 to 10:30am ($2.99), lunch daily 10:30am to 2pm ($3.99), and dinner nightly 4 to 10pm ($6.99).

The Luxor's Manhattan Buffet
3900 Las Vegas Blvd. S. ☎ **702/262-4000.**

Here diners are seated in a mazelike assemblage of New York City—themed rooms amid a backdrop of Big Apple landmarks (the Fulton Fish Market, the Stock Exchange, the Chrysler Building, and others). Seating areas range from a sidewalk cafe to an art deco diner. There's an omelet station at breakfast, while other meals feature teppanyaki and carving stations (roast beef with creamed horseradish sauce, turkey or prime rib, and ham). Additional offerings include a vast array of salads and fresh fruit, cold cuts, entrees (such as linguine, stuffed shells, lemon chicken, broiled sea bass in cream sauce, bratwurst, Swiss steak, and stir-fry vegetables), and a make-your-own-sundae bar. The Manhattan Buffet is located on the attraction level.

Breakfast daily 7 to 11am ($3.95), lunch daily 11am to 4pm ($4.95), dinner nightly 4 to 11pm ($6.95).

The Mirage Buffet
3400 Las Vegas Blvd. S. ☎ **702/791-7111.**

The Mirage offers lavish spreads in a lovely garden-themed setting with palm trees, a plant-filled stone fountain, and seating under verdigris eaves and domes embellished with flowers. All meals except breakfast feature a carving station (fresh roast turkey and honey-baked ham at lunch; prime rib is added at brunch and dinner). A typical Mirage buffet meal offers a choice of about a dozen hot entrees, always including a fresh catch of the day and a pasta dish; other selections might range from roast chicken stuffed with wild rice to braised Korean short ribs of beef. The chefs are creative with salads, offering about 25 at each meal—choices such as Thai beef, seafood, niçoise, tabbouleh, Chinese chicken, Créole rice, and tortellini. At brunch champagne flows freely and a scrumptious array of smoked fish is added to the board, along with such items as fruit-filled crêpes and blintzes. And every meal features a spectacular dessert table (the bread pudding in bourbon sauce is noteworthy). For healthful eating there are many light items to choose from, including sugar- and fat-free puddings. And on Sundays a nonalcoholic sparkling cider is a possible champagne alternative.

Breakfast Monday to Saturday 7 to 10:45am ($6.75), Lunch Monday to Saturday 11am to 2:45pm ($8.75). Dinner Monday to Thursday 3 to 9:30pm, Friday and Saturday 3 to 11pm ($10.75). Sunday brunch 8am to 9:30pm ($13). Children under 3 free, reduced prices for children ages 4 to 10.

❂ The Rio's Carnival World Buffet

3700 W. Flamingo Rd. ☎ **702/252-7777.**

The buffet here is located in a festively decorated room with variegated wide sequined ribbons looped overhead and seating amid planters of lush faux tropical blooms. The chairs and booths are upholstered in bright hues—green, purple, red, orange, and turquoise. This is an excellent buffet with cheerfully decorative food booths set up set up like stations in an upscale food court. A barbecued chicken and ribs station offers side dishes of baked beans and mashed potatoes. Other stations proffer stir-fry (chicken, beef, pork, and vegetables), Mexican taco fixings and accompaniments, Chinese fare, a Japanese sushi and teppanyaki grill, a Brazilian mixed grill, Italian pasta and antipasto, and fish and chips. There's even a diner set-up for hot dogs, burgers, fries, and milk shakes. All this is in addition to the usual offerings of most Las Vegas buffets: entrees running the gamut from baked cod in herbed cream sauce to stuffed pork loin with apple dressing and pan gravy, a prime rib carving station, a vast salad bar, soups, fresh fruits, and, at breakfast and brunch, an omelet station. A stunning array of oven-fresh cakes, pies, and pastries (including sugar-free and low-fat desserts) are arranged in a palm- fringed circular display area, and there's also a make-your-own sundae bar. A full cash bar is another Rio plus. Everything is fresh and beautifully prepared and presented.

Breakfast Monday to Friday 7 to 10:30am ($3.99), lunch Monday to Friday 11am to 3pm ($5.99), dinner nightly 3:30 to 10pm ($7.99), Saturday and Sunday brunch 7am to 3:30pm ($7.99; champagne is $1 per glass).

The Sahara Oasis Buffet

2535 Las Vegas Blvd. S. ☎ **702/737-2111.**

This buffet is a vast spread served in an attractive room with a wall of windows overlooking the pool and brass palm trees shading the food display tables. It's not fancy fare, but it is abundant, fresh, and tasty. A typical dinner buffet, for instance; will feature a ham, turkey, and baron of beef carving station, dozens of salads, about eight hot entrees (usually including one or two ethnic dishes each night such as tacos and burritos, Chinese stir-fry, or bratwurst and sauerkraut), vegetables, rice, mashed potatoes, a big dessert display of oven-fresh pies and cakes, and beverages.

Breakfast Monday to Saturday 7 to 10:30am ($4.95), lunch Monday to Saturday 11am to 2:30pm ($5.95), dinner nightly 4 to 10:30pm ($7.95), Sunday brunch 8am to 3pm ($7.95). Children under 12 pay half price for all buffets.

Sands Garden Terrace Buffet

3355 Las Vegas Blvd. S. ☎ **702/733-5000.**

This buffet is served in a casual gardenlike setting with a wall of windows overlooking the pool and seating is at umbrella tables. The room's central focus is a dessert table under a domed skylight. Breakfast fare includes steak and eggs, waffles, omelets, French toast, and blintzes, along with such standards as bacon and eggs, cereal, and juices. At lunch there's a build-your-own taco station; grilled burgers can be embellished with an assortment of trimmings; and entrees range from pizza to rotisserie chicken. Dinner is an all-you-can-eat "seafood spectacular" that also features grilled steak and all other fixings for a complete meal.

Breakfast daily 7 to 11am ($5.99), lunch daily 11:30am to 3pm ($4.99 adults, $3.99 children), dinner nightly 4:30 to 10:30pm ($9.99 adults, $5.99 children).

Showboat Captain's Buffet

Downtown at 2800 Fremont St. ☎ **702/385-9123.**

This buffet occupies a cheerful New Orleans garden–themed room. Centered on a gazebo, it's decorated in raspberry and peach and adorned with lovely still-life paintings of flowers and fruit. There are stunning floral-motif chandeliers overhead; seating is in booths with trellised dividers or at umbrella tables. Lunch and dinner menus offer entrees such as chicken, broiled salmon, tortellini primavera, and char-broiled tenderloin. There is also a carving station serving up roast beef, turkey, and honey-glazed ham. In addition, you will find an extensive salad bar, a vast selection of pastries, and a build-your-own ice-cream (or frozen-yogurt) sundae bar. Wednesday is all-you-can-eat New York strip steak night. A seafood buffet every Friday evening features stuffed crab, fried shrimp, bouillabaisse, crab legs, raw shrimp, and more. And weekend champagne brunch buffets include an omelet station, fruit-stuffed pancakes, and smoked fish with bagels and cream cheese. The Showboat initiated Las Vegas hotel buffets, and its buffets are still among the best in town.

Lunch Monday to Friday 10am to 3:30pm ($3.95); dinner Monday, Tuesday, and Thursday 4:30 to 10pm, Saturday and Sunday 4 to 10pm ($6.45). Wednesday steak buffet 4:30 to 10pm ($7.95). Seafood Spectacular dinner Friday 4:30 to 10pm ($7.95). Saturday and Sunday brunch 8am to 3pm ($5.45).

Stardust Warehouse Buffet

3000 Las Vegas Blvd. S. ☎ **702/732-6111.**

This buffet features, as the name suggests, a raftered warehouse decor, with big restaurant cans of olive oil and chili, sacks of flour, crates of apples, and other provender on display. The tables are covered in laminated burlap potato sacking. It's a pleasant setting for very good buffet meals, featuring a carving station (roast beef, ham, and turkey), a wide variety of salads and hot and cold entrees, fresh fruit, and many fresh-baked breads and cakes. You can also pump your own frozen yogurt.

Breakfast Monday to Saturday 7 to 10:30am ($4.95); lunch Monday to Saturday 10:30am to 3pm ($5.95); dinner nightly 4 to 10pm ($7.95); Sunday brunch 7am to 3:30pm ($6.95).

Treasure Island Buffet

3300 Las Vegas Blvd. S. ☎ **702/894-7111.**

The buffet is served in three internationally themed rooms. The American room—under a central rough-hewn beamed canopy hung with the flags of the 13 colonies—re-creates New Orleans during the era of Jean Lafitte. The Chinese room evokes 17th-century Kowloon—a hotbed of piracy. Diners look through garden "windows" at the Hong Kong harbor. And the Italian room, modeled after a Tuscan villa overlooking a bustling piazza, has strings of festival lights overhead and food displays under a striped awning. All of the rooms are filled with authentic antiques and artifacts typical of their locales and time periods. All three rooms also serve identical fare, including extensive American breakfasts. Dinners offer a wide range of entrees (perhaps halibut in caper cream sauce, beef burgundy, seafood quiche, honey-garlic wings, herb-roasted chicken, and meatloaf) as well as a trio of pastas, a carving station (prime rib, turkey, and a third item such as salmon), a Chinese food station (fried rice, egg rolls, sweet and sour pork, and more), peel-and-eat shrimp, a salad bar, potato and rice side dishes, cheeses and cold cuts, fresh fruits and vegetables, breads, and a large choice of desserts. Lunch is similar, and Sunday brunch includes unlimited champagne.

Breakfast Monday to Saturday 7 to 10:45am ($4.99); lunch Monday to Saturday 11am to 3:45pm ($6.99); dinner nightly 4 to 10:30pm ($8.99); Sunday brunch 7:30am to 3:30pm ($8.99).

Tropicana Island Buffet

3801 Las Vegas Blvd. S. ☎ **702/739-2800.**

This buffet is served in a large and delightful dining room lushly planted with tropical flowers and foliage. There are coral-reef aquariums at the entrance, and the appealing interior keeps to the island theme. Big semicircular booths backed by mirrored walls are separated by bead curtains, and, on the lower level, floor-to-ceiling windows overlook the Trop's stunning palm-fringed pool. Dinners here feature an extensive salad bar, peel- and-eat-shrimp, a carving station for roast turkey and roast beef with creamed horseradish (along with a third meat—perhaps leg of lamb), vegetables, potato and rice dishes, and about five entrees (chicken enchiladas, spicy blackened redfish, barbecued ribs, Cajun pork chops, and linguine Alfredo on a recent visit). An array of luscious fresh-baked desserts always looks especially tempting. A full complement of breakfast fare is available each morning, and weekend brunches include unlimited champagne.

Breakfast Monday to Friday 7:30 to 11:30am ($6.95); dinner nightly 5 to 10:30pm ($9.95); Saturday and Sunday brunch 7:30am to 1:30pm ($9.95).

7

What to See & Do in Las Vegas

Las Vegas is unlike any other tourist Mecca. Here the main attraction is gambling, and if you're staying at one of the casino megahotels, you have not only casino gaming, but accommodations, dining, sightseeing, sports facilities, and entertainment under one roof. The more lavish the hotel, the more Disneyesque its attractions—from the erupting volcano and white tiger habitat at the Mirage to Caesars OMNIMAX™ movies and talking Roman statues. Just strolling the Strip—especially at night when every hotel is spectacularly illuminated in multihued neon—is a mind-boggling experience. There's nothing like it anywhere else in the world.

But there's much more to a Las Vegas vacation than gaming action and headliner entertainment. There are many other points of interest here, ranging from the sublime (magnificent vistas like Red Rock Canyon and Valley of Fire) to the slightly ridiculous (the Liberace Museum). Nearby Hoover Dam is a major sightseeing attraction, and Lake Mead is one of several pristinely beautiful recreation areas. Nevada, and neighboring Arizona, offer stunning scenery, whether you venture just outside Las Vegas or all the way to the Grand Canyon. You can study ancient petroglyphs and learn about Native American cultures dating back 12,000 years, visit ghost towns, raft the Colorado River, hike or ride horseback through canyons, even ski in winter. To my mind, the ideal Las Vegas vacation combines the glitz and glitter of casino hotels with explorations of the area's majestic canyons and desert wilderness. The latter are the perfect antidote to the former. In this chapter, all sightseeing options are described in detail. Check them out—along with "excursions" listed in chapter 11—and plan an itinerary that suits your interests.

Note: Take a look at attractions listed for children, many of which may also interest adults.

SUGGESTED ITINERARIES

The itineraries outlined here are for adults. If you're traveling with kids, incorporate some of the suggestions "Especially for Kids" listed below.

The activities mentioned briefly here are described more fully later in this chapter.

If You Have 1 Day

Go to the Mirage, get tickets for *Siegfried & Roy,* and spend as much time as you like gambling in the casino. While you're here, see the rain forest, tiger and dolphin habitats, and aquarium. Head next door to Caesars, entering via the Forum Shops People Mover. Peruse the shops and statuary, have lunch at Spago, and see an IMAX™ film. Then head in the other direction and catch the ship battle at Treasure Island. Consider spending some time at your hotel swimming pool during the day. Enjoy a leisurely preshow dinner at one of the many restaurants at the Mirage (details in chapters 5 and 6).

If You Have 2 Days

You may wish to procure show tickets for additional days at the outset. On the second day, drive out to Red Rock Canyon. The panoramic 13-mile Scenic Loop Drive is best seen early in the morning when there's little traffic. If you're so inclined, spend some time hiking here. Have lunch at nearby Bonnie Springs Ranch. After lunch enjoy a guided trail ride into the desert wilderness (see chapter 11, "Easy Excursions from Las Vegas," for details). Return to town and loll by the pool with a good book. Suggested evening show: Cirque du Soleil's *Mystère* at Treasure Island.

If You Have 3 Days

On the 3rd day, plan a tour to Hoover Dam. Leave early in the morning. Return to Las Vegas after lunch via Valley of Fire State Park, stopping at the Lost City Museum in Overton en route (see chapter 11 for details). At night, if you still have energy, hit the casinos and/or catch another show—either a headliner favorite or *Country Fever* at the Golden Nugget downtown. This will also provide an opportunity to see the Fremont Street Experience. Another possibility: a romantic evening at the Palace Court piano bar at Caesars Palace (have dinner here first if you feel like splurging).

If You Have 4 Days or More

Instead of returning from your Hoover Dam trip the same day, stay overnight—or longer—at the charming Lake Mead Lodge. Take a dinner cruise on the *Desert Princess,* and spend part of your 4th day enjoying Lake Mead's many recreational facilities before returning to town via Valley of Fire State Park.

As you plan any additional days, consider excursions to other nearby attractions such as Mount Charleston, Goodsprings, or the Grand Canyon. Inquire about interesting tours at your hotel sightseeing desk. Or visit some of the hotels that are sightseeing attractions in their own right—notably the Luxor, Treasure Island, the MGM Grand, and Excalibur.

1 Attractions in Las Vegas

Fremont Street Experience
Fremont St., between Main and Las Vegas Blvd.

For years, the Strip has been experiencing a phenomenal economic and building boom; now, some of the focus of development in this town is about to shift downtown. At press time, a $70 million revitalization project for this area is nearing completion. The Fremont Street Experience is a five-block open-air pedestrian mall—a 90-foot-high "celestial vault" of sculpted steel mesh will shelter a festive, lushly landscaped, strip of outdoor cafes, vendor carts and colorful kiosks purveying food and merchandise, and 50,000 square feet of new indoor retail space. Equipped with more than 2 million lights, the canopy will be utilized for the "Sky Parade"—a dazzling high-tech light and laser show enhanced by a concert hall-quality sound system—that will take place several times nightly. Not only will the canopy provide shade, it will be cooled by a misting system in summer and warmed by radiant heaters in winter. Asphalt on the street is being replaced by a shimmering patterned streetscape lit by runway-type strobe lights. When the project is completed (which should be by the time you're reading this), Fremont Street will be an ongoing festival—the scene of live entertainment, holiday celebrations, and special events. The project will also include parking space for 1,500 vehicles.

Hollywood Movie Museum
Debbie Reynolds Hotel, 305 Convention Center Dr. ☎ 702/7-DEBBIE. Admission $7.95 adults, $5.95 children 3–12. Daily 11am–10pm, with tours every half hour.

Debbie Reynolds has been buying up Hollywood memorabilia for decades. Her $30 million collection—comprising items from more than a half century of American movies—celebrates Hollywood's Golden Age. Changing exhibits showcase some 3,000 costumes—the famous white dress worn by Marilyn Monroe in *The Seven Year Itch,* Elizabeth Taylor's *Cleopatra* headdress, Vivien Leigh's hats from *Gone With the Wind,* Doris Day's mermaid outfit from *Glass Bottom Boat,* the sequined royal-blue swimsuit Esther Williams wore in *Deep in My Heart,* a pair of Judy Garland's ruby slippers from *The Wizard of Oz,* and the dancing shoes of Fred Astaire and Cyd Charisse, among them. Additionally, props, artifacts, and furnishings from classic films (she has a 36,000-square-foot warehouse filled with them) include the dagger used by Errol Flynn in *The Adventures of Don Juan,* Yul Brynner's bullwhip and throne from *The King and I,* Winchester rifles from *Annie Get Your Gun,* and the Ark of the Covenant from *The Ten Commandments.* Museum displays are enhanced by a 35-minute multimedia show presented in a high-tech 80-seat theater that re-creates the intimate ambience of a Hollywood screening room. Guests are greeted by Debbie (on screen), who narrates a nostalgic overview of Hollywood's classic and epic motion pictures. A 30-foot revolving stage, two 10-foot revolving platforms, and lighted dioramas on the side walls permit the dramatic display of film clips, sets, and costumes.

> ### ❓ Did You Know?
>
> - Las Vegas—"sin city"—has more churches per capita than any other city in America.
> - Las Vegas has been called the "Marriage Capital of America." No waiting period or blood test is required, and there are 43 chapels in town where quickie weddings are performed 24 hours a day.
> - Illusionists Siegfried & Roy have sawed a woman in half more times than anyone else.
> - Visitors on a trail ride once brought a horse into the crowded casino of the Thunderbird Hotel. They put a pair of dice between his lips at the craps table, and he threw a natural seven.
> - In 1953, the Sands buried a time capsule on its grounds containing Sugar Ray Robinson's boxing gloves, Bing Crosby's pipe, and a wax impression of Jimmy Durante's nose, among other treasures.

Imperial Palace Auto Collection

Imperial Palace Hotel, 3535 Las Vegas Blvd. S. ☎ **702/731-3311.** Admission $6.95 adults, $3 seniors and children under 12, free for children under 5 and AAA members. Daily 9:30am–11:30pm.

This fascinating museum at the Imperial Palace hotel displays, on a rotating basis, some 750 antique, classic, and special-interest vehicles spanning more than 100 years of automotive history. It's one of the premier collections of its kind. Some 200 vehicles—enhanced by mannequins and period tableaux—are on exhibit at any given time. A 15,000-square-foot room houses the world's largest collection of Model J Duesenbergs (25 vehicles valued at $50 million!), including cars once owned by James Cagney, chewing-gum magnate Phillip K. Wrigley, boxing champion Max Baer, heiress Doris Duke, Father Divine, Tyrone Power, and others. The Duesenberg Room also features a cocktail lounge with 1880s Brunswick furnishings.

In President's Row, JFK's 1962 "bubbletop" Lincoln Continental, Lyndon Johnson's 1964 Cadillac, Eisenhower's 1952 Chrysler Imperial 20-foot-long parade car, Truman's 1950 Lincoln Cosmopolitan with gold-plated interior, FDR's unrestored 1936 V-16 Cadillac, and Herbert Hoover's 1929 Cadillac are on display. Yet another area showcases Adolf Hitler's armored bulletproof and mineproof 1936 Mercedes-Benz 770K, Emperor Hirohito's 1935 Packard, Czar Nicholas II's 1914 Rolls-Royce, former Mexican president Lazaro Cardenas's black 1939 V-12 Packard (armor-plated to resist 50-caliber machine gun bullets), and Argentinean strongman Juan Peron's 1939 straight-8 Packard.

Commercial vehicles of bygone days include antique buses, military transport, taxis (among them, the 1908 French model that appeared in the movie version of *My Fair Lady*), gasoline trucks, fire engines, delivery trucks and vans, dump trucks, and pickup trucks. Other highlights are Al Capone's 1930 V-16 Cadillac, Elvis Presley's powder blue

Attractions in Las Vegas

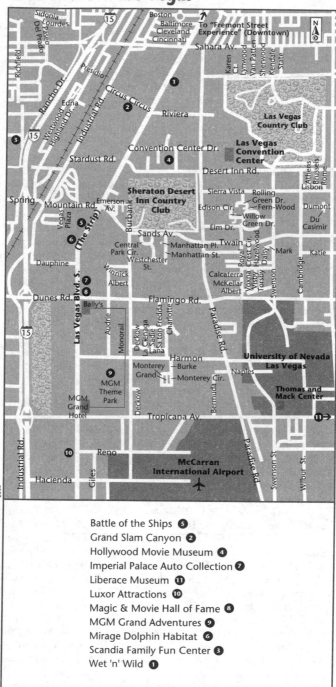

Battle of the Ships ⑤
Grand Slam Canyon ②
Hollywood Movie Museum ④
Imperial Palace Auto Collection ⑦
Liberace Museum ⑪
Luxor Attractions ⑩
Magic & Movie Hall of Fame ⑧
MGM Grand Adventures ⑨
Mirage Dolphin Habitat ⑥
Scandia Family Fun Center ③
Wet 'n' Wild ①

1976 Cadillac Eldorado, Liberace's pale-cream 1981 Zimmer (complete with candelabra), W. C. Field's black 1938 Cadillac V-16 touring sedan with built-in bar, Caruso's 1920 green and black Hudson, Howard Hughes's 1954 Chrysler (because of his phobia about germs, Hughes installed a special air-purification system that cost more than the car itself!), a 1947 Tucker (one of only 51 manufactured before the company went out of business), a 1977 Safarikar with an all-leather exterior and doors that can be extended to ward off attacking jungle animals, and motorcycles that belonged to Steve McQueen, Clark Gable, and Sammy Davis, Jr. A gift shop carries a wide selection of automotive books, scale models, and memorabilia.

Liberace Museum

1775 E. Tropicana Ave., at Spencer St. ☎ **702/798-5595.** Admission $6.50 adults, $4.50 seniors over 60, $3.50 students, $2 children 6–12, free for children under 6. Mon–Sat 10am–5pm, Sun 1–5pm.

This is an only-in-Vegas phenomenon—an entire museum devoted to the career memorabilia of "Mr. Showmanship," Walter Valentino Liberace. Three exhibit areas house his spectacular cars (he owned more than 50 automobiles), antique and custom-made pianos, dazzling costumes and capes, glittering stage jewelry, miniature piano collection (during his lifetime fans gave him more than 3,000 of these), honorary degrees and awards, musical arrangements, and photographs. There's also a re-creation of his office (which contains an inlaid ormolu Louis XV desk originally owned by Czar Nicholas II of Russia) and an ornate bedroom suite. Visitors are greeted at a piano-shaped desk.

Among the fabulous pianos on display here are a 19th-century hand-painted concert grand piano that Chopin played at Versailles, George Gershwin's Chickering concert grand, and Liberace's own mirror-tiled Baldwin concert grand. Then there are the cars, among them a mirrored white Rolls-Royce Phantom V (one of seven made) with a design of galloping horses etched into the mirror tile; a 1975 English cab painted in black-and-white houndstooth; a shocking-pink mirror-tiled Volkswagen with a Rolls-Royce front (it went with his pink fur-trimmed pink-sequined cape); a rhinestone-covered car designed to match a similarly bejeweled piano and costume; and the glittering red, white, and blue bicentennial Rolls-Royce that Liberace drove onstage at New York's Radio City Music Hall in 1976 (he wore matching red-, white-, and blue-spangled hot pants and boots). Dozens of fur- trimmed, feathered, beaded, sequined, and bejeweled costumes include a Czar Nicholas uniform with 22-karat-gold braiding and a blue velvet cape styled after the coronation robes of King George V and covered with $60,000 worth of rare chinchilla! A collection of his crystal, silver, and china includes a set of 22-karat gold-banded Moser crystal glasses from Czechoslovakia—a magnificent service for 12 with 14 glasses for each setting. It is one of only two such handmade collections; the other is owned by Queen Elizabeth. Among the jewelry on display is a candelabra ring with platinum candlesticks and diamond flames and a spectacular piano-shaped ring containing

260 diamonds with keys made of ivory and black jade (a gift from Barron Hilton). Other notable exhibits: a gold replica of Liberace's hands made by the Disney studios, his famed candelabras, and a $50,000 50.6-pound rhinestone—the world's largest—presented to him by the grateful Austrian firm that supplied all his costume stones. There's a gift shop on the premises where you can buy anything from miniature crystal grand pianos to Liberace logo thimbles, along with performance videos, cassettes, and CDs. The museum is 2¹/₂ miles east of the Strip on your right.

⑤ Magic and Movie Hall of Fame

O' Shea's Casino, 3555 Las Vegas Blvd. S., between Sands Avenue and Flamingo Road. ☎ **702/737–1343.** Admission $4.95 adults, $3 children under 12 accompanied by an adult. Wed–Sun 10am–6pm. Magic shows at 2, 3 and 4pm.

This is the best value in town, offering hours of intriguing entertainment for just a few bucks. Admission includes a half-hour show in the Houdini Theatre (note performance hours above) featuring two very talented performers—magician/escapologist Dixie Dooley and ventriloquist Valentine Vox; they are also the owners of much of the collection. After the performance, visitors tour a vast museum that houses props and artifacts of famous magicians such as Houdini (bound with ropes and shackled in leg irons and handcuffs, Houdini once had himself lowered into the East River in a wood packing case that was nailed shut and weighed down with 200 pounds of lead; he freed himself in just 57 seconds!), levitation master Harry Kellar, Sevais Le Roy (who "cremated" a girl on stage), Thurston (his spike cabinet is on display), the Mephistophelian Dante (who popularized the phrases "hocus-pocus" and "abracadabra"), and Carter the Great (Houdini was his assistant as a teenager). Exhibits are enhanced by dozens of video clips of actual performances. Modern-day practitioners are also included; a highlight is a behind-the-scenes video tour with illusionists Siegfried & Roy. Another section contains antique automata, mechanical devices, Gypsy fortune telling booths, vintage arcade games, Nickelodeons, and music boxes, some of them operable by visitors. You'll learn about the history of ventriloquism, which dates back to the 5th century B.C. and was used by ancient diviners to imitate the voices of the dead. Hundreds of antique and modern dummies are on display, and there's entertaining video footage of the greats—Edgar Bergen with Charlie McCarthy and Mortimer Snerd, Arthur Prince with Jim (Prince smoked a cigar while he did his dummy's voice), Valentine Vox (who you've seen in the show), Paul Winchell with Jerry Mahoney, and others. You can attempt ventriloquism yourself in a how-to booth equipped with a dummy and instructions. Movie costumes—such as a dress Liz Taylor wore in *Cleopatra* and Clark Gable's jacket from *Gone With the Wind*—are displayed in another area, along with tableaux of famous movie scenes. The tour winds up in a gift shop where a magician demonstrates many of the wares (magic tricks, juggling equipment, etc.) on sale, providing further entertainment.

Mirage Dolphin Habitat

Mirage Hotel, 3400 Las Vegas Blvd. S. ☎ **702/791-7111.** Admission $3, free for children under 10. Mon–Fri 11am–7pm, Sat–Sun and holidays 9am–7pm. Children under 12 must be accompanied by an adult.

This is no theme park exhibit. The Mirage's dolphin habitat was designed to provide a healthy and nurturing environment and to educate the public about marine mammals and their role in the ecosystem. Mirage owner Steve Wynn is a dedicated environmentalist whose hotel restaurants serve only dolphin-safe tuna and boycott Icelandic fish to protest that nation's whaling practices. No fur is sold in Wynn's hotel boutiques. Specialists worldwide were consulted in creating the habitat, which was designed to serve as a model of a quality secured environment. The pool is more than four times larger than government regulations require, and its 2.5 million gallons of man-made seawater are cycled and cleaned once every 2 hours. The habitat houses seven Atlantic bottlenose dolphins in a lush tropical setting. The facility offers visitors the opportunity to watch dolphins frolicking from above- and below-water viewing areas, and the 15-minute tour is entertaining and informative to adults and children alike. A highlight is a video of a resident dolphin (Duchess) giving birth (to Squirt) underwater. After the tour you can stay in the area and continue watching the dolphins.

While you're at the Mirage, visit the royal white tiger habitat and see the 53-foot, 20,000-gallon simulated coral reef aquarium behind the registration desk. The latter accommodates 1,000 fish and sea creatures—including sharks and rays—indigenous to the Caribbean, Hawaii, Tonga, Fiji, the Red Sea, the Marshall Islands, and Australia.

LUXOR ATTRACTIONS

All of these attractions are located in the **Luxor Las Vegas,** 3900 Las Vegas Blvd. S. ☎ 702/262-4000. A $15 ticket may be purchased, allowing admission to all three attractions for a savings of $6 over individual tickets.

King Tut's Tomb and Museum

Admission $4. Sun–Thurs 9am–11pm, Fri–Sat 9am–11:30pm.

On the Lower Level, this full-scale reproduction of King Tutankhamen's Tomb includes the antechamber, annex, burial chamber, and treasury housing replicas (all handcrafted in Egypt by artisans using historically correct gold leaf and linens, pigments, tools, and ancient methods) of the glittering inventory discovered by archaeologists Howard Carter and Lord Carnarvon in the Valley of Kings at Luxor in 1922. All items have been meticulously positioned according to Carter's records. On display are gilded-wood guardian statues, chariots, funerary beds, alabaster vases, ceramic wine jars, baskets, faience vessels and bead collars, hunting gear, lamps, jewelry, shrines, and mother-of-pearl inlay boxes. Notable artifacts include Tutankhamen's golden throne and sarcophagus (the outer coffin, of solid gold, weighed more than a ton), an ornate canopic gold chest that contained his internal organs, preserved foods to ensure that his spirit would not go hungry in the next world, hundreds of servant statues (to do his bidding in the afterlife), and a model of a royal boat to transport his soul to its next life. Two miniature coffins in the treasury are believed to contain the mummies of two of the king's premature babies. On the west wall is a depiction of 12 baboon deities representing the hours of the night through which the sun and the king must travel before achieving rebirth at dawn. King Tutankhamen ascended the throne in the 14th century B.C. at the age of 9 and died about 10 years later of unknown causes. A 20-minute audio tour (available in English, French, Spanish, and Japanese) is preceded by a 4-minute introductory film.

Nile River Tour
Admission $4. Daily 9am–12:30am.

This 15-minute narrated Nile cruise, departing from the Luxor's casino level, takes you on a journey through ancient Egypt while providing an overview of the hotel. Temple paintings and hieroglyphics along the walls depict Osiris (ruler of the dead), his wife Isis (mistress of magic

The Battle of the Ships

Every 90 minutes between 4 and 11:30pm, a live sea battle between the pirate ship *Hispaniola* and the British frigate HMS *Britannia* takes place on Buccaneer Bay in front of the Treasure Island hotel. Arrive at least half an hour early to get a good viewing spot. The *Hispaniola* is docked by the village banks to unload a cache of ill-gotten goods. As seagulls chatter and waves crash against the shore, a rowboat manned by two pirates hovers into view. An ominous-sounding version of "Rule Britannia" heralds the approach of the HMS *Britannia* stealing around Skull Point. A British officer orders the pirates to lay down their arms and receive a marine boarding party "in the name of His Royal Britannic Majesty, King of England, and all that he surveys." "The only thing we'll receive from you is your stores, valuables, and whatever rum ye might have on board, you son of a footman's goat," responds the pirate captain brazenly. The verbal battle soon escalates to cannon and musket fire. Amid thrilling pyrotechnics, huge masts snap and plunge into the sea and sailors are catapulted into the air. The British captain warns, "Unless you scum want a real taste of His Majesty's naval artillery, I suggest you lower your colors and prepare to be boarded." "Never! To Hades with their rotten hearts," is the pirate rejoinder. The Brits send a broadside into the pirates' powder warehouse, which ignites in magnificent flames and fireworks. But just as the pirates seem to be defeated, the buccaneer captain does an Errol Flynn swing across the ship from bow to stern, grabs a smoldering ember, and fires a final cannonball at the *Britannia,* hitting it dead center. The *Britannia* sways and slowly sinks, as its sailors plunge overboard, but the proud captain defiantly goes down with his ship. This is Las Vegas. The pirates always win!

and motherhood), and Horus (their falcon-headed son, god of the sky); the Temple of Amon, built by Ramses, where Amon (who breathes life into all living things) sits enthroned with his wife, the goddess Mut, and their son Khonsu, the moon god; the Valley of the Queens (Queen Isis is depicted leading Nefertiti to Ra, seated on his throne); the Valley of the Kings, where King Ay, wearing the leopard skin of a priest, is shown performing a ceremony on Tutankhamen's mummy; a servant's burial chamber discovered in Deir el Medina guarded by jackals representing the god Anubis; King Seti I (1318–04 B.C.) shown performing "the blessing of the bread" (he was the father of Ramses II, who is depicted in the next two walls defeating enemies and in the Abu Simbel temple erected in his honor); the tombs of Sakkara and pyramids of Giza (in the double tomb of Amenhotep and his son, we see Egyptians making wine, holding game, and harvesting grain for their journeys in the afterlife); a nobleman and his wife paying homage to Osiris; a barge carrying a mummified body to an entombing place; and, finally, through a fog bank and waterfall to a temple where the "Guardian," an Egyptian god of the future, holds a crystal obelisk—a reference to the above-described attractions.

Secrets of the Luxor Pyramid

Admission "In Search of the Obelisk" $5, "Luxor Live" $4, "The Theater of Time" $4. "Search" Sun–Thurs 9am–11pm, Fri–Sat 9am–11:30pm; "Live" and "Time" Sun–Thurs 10am–11pm, Fri–Sat 10am–11:30pm.

This attraction-floor entertainment comprises a three-page adventure that takes about 90 minutes to complete. A pass granting admission to all three episodes is available for $15, a $3 savings over tickets purchased individually.

In Episode One, "In Search of the Obelisk," motion-simulator technology evokes an action adventure involving a chase sequence inside a pyramid. In a rapidly plummeting elevator (the cable has broken!) you'll descend to an ancient temple 2 miles beneath the Luxor pyramid. Against the orders of militaristic government agent Colonel Claggert, you'll accompany Mac MacPherson and Carina Wolinski (the good guys) in their search for a mysterious crystal obelisk containing the secrets of the universe. In a thrill ride through the temple's maze, you'll experience an explosive battle with evil forces, rescue Carina from the clutches of Dr. Osiris (sinister cult leader of the Enlightened Society for Global Transformation; it is believed he sabotaged the elevator), and narrowly escape death before returning to the surface.

In Episode Two's "Luxor Live" show, you become part of the audience for a live broadcast that begins as a tabloid TV talk show. The topic is the mysterious happenings below the pyramid. Claggert and MacPherson are guests. Remote cameras take us to Egypt (where Wolinski is covering a total solar eclipse) for a 3-D vision. Suddenly the studio set collapses, and the host reveals himself as the High Priest of Paradise before disintegrating into light.

In Episode Three, "The Theater of Time," voyagers (that's us) visit the future via a cosmic time machine that incorporates IMAX™ film projected on a seven-story screen. The fate of the world is in jeopardy as the sinister Dr. Osiris uses the crystal obelisk's power to hijack us (along with Mac and Carina) into his bleak vision of the future aboard his time machine. He forces Carina to activate the obelisk for his own evil purposes. Our mission: to save Carina, reclaim the obelisk, and favorably alter the course of history.

2   Attractions in Nearby Henderson

About 6 miles from the Strip in the town of Henderson are four factories in fairly close proximity to one another. All offer free tours to the public. It's best to see them on a weekday when they're fully operative. To get to Henderson, drive east on Tropicana Avenue, make a right on Mountain Vista, then go 2 miles to Sunset Way; turn left into Green Valley Business Park. You will soon see Ethel M Chocolates, a good place to begin. Use the map in this section to find your way to the other three facilities.

Cranberry World

1301 American Pacific Dr., Henderson. ☎ **702/566-7160.** Free admission. Daily 9am–5pm.

In this Ocean Spray juice processing and distribution plant, visitors view a 7-minute film about cranberry history, harvesting, and the manufacturing processes. Ocean Spray, you'll learn, is also the leading grapefruit grower in the country. The film is followed by a self-guided tour with interactive exhibits, a look at the plant from a view station, and a visit to the juice bar and test kitchen for a free sampling of eight Ocean Spray juices and cranberry-studded baked goods. The tour winds up in the gift shop where you can purchase Ocean Spray products and logo items.

Ethel M Chocolates

2 Cactus Garden Dr., just off Mount Vista and Sunset Way in the Green Valley Business Park. ☎ **702/433-2500** (for recorded information) or ☎ 702/458-8864. Free admission. Daily 8:30am–7pm. Closed Christmas.

Just 6 miles from the Strip is the Ethel M Chocolate Factory and Cactus Garden, a tourist attraction that draws about 2,000 visitors a day. Ethel Mars began making fine chocolates in a little candy kitchen around the turn of the century and her small enterprise evolved to produce not only dozens of varieties of superb boxed chocolates but some of the world's most famous candies—M&Ms, Milky Way, 3 Musketeers, Snickers, and Mars bars.

On a self-guided tour of the plant, you'll see the candy-making process from a glass-enclosed viewing aisle. All of the equipment is marked to aid visitor comprehension. "Kitchen" procedures include the cooking of buttery cream fillings in immense copper kettles, the hand-sorting of nuts, grinding of fresh peanut butter, and fudge making. In one production-line process, little creamy centers are bathed in chocolate and decorated with Ethel M's trademark swirls. On another line chocolate is deposited into molds, vibrated to eliminate air bubbles, cooled, filled (with nuts, creams, and/or liqueurs), and hand boxed. There are actually employees whose job involves the "arduous" task of tasting for quality control. Depending on what's being made the day you visit, you may observe all or little of the above; however, you will see it all in informative video presentations shown along the aisle. The tour winds up in an attractive gift shop where you can sample a free piece of chocolate candy (my favorite is almond butter krisp) and hand-dipped ice cream; here, you can also purchase chocolates and have them shipped anywhere in the United States.

Also on the premises is a 2.5-acre garden displaying 350 species of rare and exotic cacti with signs provided for self-guided tours. It's best appreciated in spring when the cacti are in full bloom. Behind the garden, also with a self-guided tour, is Ethel M's "Living Machine"— a natural waste water–treatment and recycling plant that consists of aerated tanks, ecological fluid beds, a constructed wetlands, reed beds, and a storage pond.

Kidd's Marshmallow Factory

8203 Gibson Rd., Henderson. ☎ **702/564-3878.** Free admission. Mon–Fri 9am–4:30pm, Sat–Sun 9:30am–4:30pm.

This factory has a delicious aroma. Here you can observe the marsh-mallow manufacturing process via large windows—corn starch being rolled smooth on a conveyer belt, then cut into marshmallow shapes which are bounced in a drum, bagged, and boxed into cartons. Signs along the way explain the process. The tour ends in a gift shop where you'll receive free samples and can purchase marshmallow products and logo items. Kidd & Company was founded in Chicago in the 1880s.

Ron Lee's World of Clowns

330 Carousel Parkway, Henderson. ☎ **702/434-3920.** Free admission. Daily 8am–5:30pm.

In this 30,000-square-foot factory, manufacturer Ron Lee creates collector figurines of Hobo Joe and other clowns, as well as Disney and Warner Brothers characters. Visitors can tour the factory, and, via large windows, observe workers making models and rubber molds, soldering parts together, deburring, painting, finishing, and shipping. The procedures are explained on videotapes overhead. On the premises are a carousel, a large gift shop, and a display of clown sculptures and mechanical miniature carousels and ferris wheels. **Jitters,** an upscale cafeteria, features gourmet coffees, sandwiches such as cashew chicken salad on seven-grain bread, and fresh-baked desserts. There's seating inside and on a terrace cooled by misters.

3 Especially for Kids

Las Vegas used to be an adults-only kind of town. These days, it's actively pursuing the family travel trade and offering dozens of child-oriented activities. Personally, I have very mixed feelings about Las Vegas as a family destination. This is a city where every third taxi-cab is topped by a large picture placard advertising the "Topless Girls of Glitter Gulch." Similarly sexy images are everywhere. I wonder, too, about the advisability of exposing young children to the lures of gambling.

Attractions in Henderson

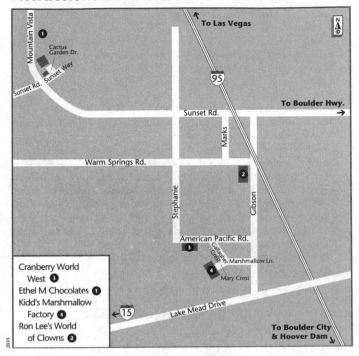

You should also be aware, if you bring your children to Las Vegas, that most of the attractions for them are quite costly. Kids can easily spend $30 an hour (and more) at video-game arcades and carnival midways, and theme parks and motion-simulator rides are overpriced. My feeling is, it would be better—and maybe even cheaper—to hire someone to care for them during your trip. That said, I will add that children love all the flash and excitement. Here's a rundown of the current kid-pleasers both in town and further afield.

Circus Circus (see p. 81) has ongoing circus acts throughout the day, a vast video game and pinball arcade, and dozens of carnival games on its mezzanine level. Behind the hotel is Grand Slam Canyon, detailed below. **Excalibur** (see p. 82) also offers video and carnival games, plus thrill cinemas and free shows (jugglers, puppets, etc.). OMNIMAX™ movies at **Caesars Palace** (see p. 49) are a thrill for everyone in the family; a video-game arcade adjoins the theater. Animated talking statues and motion-simulator rides in the **Forum Shops** are also a kick. The ship battle in front of **Treasure Island** (see box on p. 153) and the erupting volcano at the **Mirage** are sure to please, as will its dolphin habitat (see p. 152), which offers a fun 15-minute tour; while you're here, see the tigers and the sharks. Ditto the attractions at the **Luxor Las Vegas** (see p. 152).

Kids will enjoy **The Magic and Movie Hall of Fame** (see p. 151), but they'll want to leave before you do.

Of moderate interest to youngsters are the quartet of **factory tours in Henderson** (see p. 155), especially Ethel M Chocolates and

Kidd's Marshmallow Factory where free samples sweeten the learning experience.

Appropriate shows for kids include *King Arthur's Tournament* at Excalibur (see p. 200), *Siegfried & Roy* at the Mirage (see p. 207), Lance Burton, currently at the **Hacienda** but moving to **Monte Carlo** when it opens (see p. 202), *Starlight Express* at the Hilton (see p. 204), *EFX* at the MGM Grand (see p. 206), and Cirque du Soleil's *Mystère* at Treasure Island (see p. 212). As a general rule, early shows are less racy than late-night shows. If one of the hotels is featuring a Polynesian show, it's usually a good bet.

Beyond the city limits (see chapter 11 for details on all of these) is **Bonnie Springs Ranch/Old Nevada,** with trail and stagecoach rides, a petting zoo, old-fashioned melodramas, stunt shootouts, a Nevada-themed wax museum, crafts demonstrations, and more. **Lake Mead** has great recreational facilities for family vacations. Finally, organized tours (see p. 161) to the Grand Canyon and other interesting sights in southern Nevada and neighboring states can be fun family activities. Check your hotel sightseeing desk.

Specifically, kid-pleasing attractions are described below.

Grand Slam Canyon Theme Park

2889 Las Vegas Blvd. S., behind Circus Circus Hotel. ☎ **702/734-0410.** Admission $4. Ride tickets $2–$4; unlimited ride ticket $13.95 adults, $9.95 children 3–9, free for over 55 and under 4. Sun–Thurs 10am–6pm, Fri–Sat 10am–midnight.

This indoor amusement park enclosed in a glittering pink-glass dome offers a unique asset in a city where temperatures often soar above 100°F; it's air-conditioned! Themed around the Grand Canyon, its interior evokes southwestern terrain with mountains, sandstone cliffs, and waterfalls. You can have a lot of fun here. Highlights include Canyon Blaster (a really good double-loop, double-corkscrew roller coaster with dark tunnels), Rim Runner (a water flume with a 60-foot free-fall splashdown), and Hot Shots Laser Tag (a futuristic battle game played with laser guns in a dark cavelike chamber equipped with smoke generators and eerie sound effects). About half a dozen rides, a face-painting booth, a sandbox, nets for climbing, and a ball crawl are geared to little kids. Magic/juggling and Wild West–themed bird shows take place throughout the day; a miniature *Jurassic Park* houses animatronic dinosaurs; and there are many carnival midway games in addition to a Sega video-game arcade. Several snack bars and a Mexican restaurant are on the premises.

MGM Grand Adventures

Behind the MGM Grand Hotel, 3799 Las Vegas Blvd. S. ☎ **702/891-7777.** Admission $18.95 adults, $16.95 children 4–12, free for children under 4. (*Note:* Rates vary seasonally.) Daily (hours vary seasonally). Children under 13 must be accompanied by an adult.

This 33-acre facility is divided into geographically themed areas, including a New York street, an Asian Village, and Olde England. New attractions are still being added at this writing. Current highlights include: Lightning Bolt—a roller coaster careening through outer

❓ Did You Know?

- In January, a Las Vegas visitor can ski the snowy slopes of Mount Charleston and waterski on Lake Mead in the same day.
- Former President Ronald Reagan performed at the Last Frontier in 1954. Those who saw him said he was a pretty good song and dance man.
- Edgar Bergen sometimes sat at casino gaming tables making his bets and wiseacre commentary via dummy Charlie McCarthy.
- Marlene Dietrich and Louis Armstrong shared the Riviera stage in 1962 and showed the audience how to do the twist, the dance craze of the decade.
- Bandleader Xavier Cugat and Spanish bombshell singer Charo were the first couple to exchange vows at Caesars Palace, two days after its 1966 opening.
- During a heat wave in the summer of 1953, the Sands moved a roulette table into the swimming pool so gamblers could play in comfort.

space (kind of a mini Space Mountain); Deep Earth Exploration—a motion-simulator journey into the earth's core, complete with rock slides, menacing creatures on a crystallized lake, and an erupting volcano; Backlot River Tour—your canopied boat, which sails past simulated movie sets and production areas, is threatened by swamp creatures, explosions, and bad weather; Over the Edge—a log flume; Grand Canyon Rapids—a simulated white-water-rafting experience; and Parisian Taxis—bumper cars.

Rides are complemented by shows. Plan your show schedule when you enter, and be sure to catch "Dueling Pirates," a humorous stunt show (hero saves fair maiden amid much tumbling, dancing, comedy, acrobatics, dueling, Errol Flynn rope swings, pratfalls, and pyrotechnics) in the 950-seat outdoor Pirate's Cove Theatre. In a show called "You're in the Movies," audience volunteers are costumed and given scripts; their performances are then electronically combined with prefilmed scenes. The "Three Stooges" create hilarious havoc in Dr. Frankenbean's lab in a live show at the Magic Theatre. And there's also a Chinese acrobat show.

Costumed characters (Betty Boop, Popeye, Olive Oyl, Brutus, Tumbleweed, and King LJ—with his lion family) wander the park. There are 11 retail shops, two wedding chapels, and numerous food and beverage outlets, most of which offer open-air seating. Best of the lot is the Kenny Rogers Roasters, an attractive pine-paneled cafeteria specializing in chicken spit-roasted over a hardwood fire.

Emerald City

In the MGM Grand Casino, 3799 Las Vegas Blvd. S. ☎ **702/891-7777.** Admission $5 adults, $4 seniors and children 2–12. Daily 10am to 9:40pm.

This attraction in the Oz-themed section of the casino beckons visitors through Kansas cornfields and along the yellow-brick road to the wizard's castle. En route, you'll meet up with robotics of Dorothy in ruby slippers saying, "There's no place like home" over and over, a talking apple tree, chirping birds, the tin man, scarecrow, and cowardly lion. On the sky dome above, a witch flies across the moon, and a changing light show varies from thunder and lightning to rainbows to starry sky. The path ends at the castle, where a 20-minute magic show takes place three times each hour in the wizard's parlor.

Scandia Family Fun Center

2900 Sirius Ave., at Rancho Dr. between Sahara Ave. and Spring Mountain Rd. ☎ 702/364-0070. Admission free, but there's a fee to play each game. Super Saver Coupons $9.95 (includes 1 round of miniature golf, two rides, and 12 video games); Unlimited Wristband Package $14.95 (includes unlimited bumper boat and car rides, 1 game of miniature golf, and 12 tokens for batting cages or arcade games). Sept–early June: Sun–Thurs 10am–11pm, Fri–Sat until midnight; mid-June–August: Sun–Thurs 10am–midnight, Fri–Sat until 1am.

This family amusement center just a few blocks off the Strip offers three 18-hole miniature golf courses ($4.95 per game, children under 6 free), a state-of-the-art video arcade with 225 machines, miniature car racing and bumper boats ($3.95 per ride, small children ride free with an adult), and automated softball- and baseball-pitching machines for batting practice ($1.25 for 25 pitches).

Wet 'n' Wild

2601 Las Vegas Blvd. S., just north of Sahara Ave. ☎ 702/878-7811. Admission $21.95 adults, half-price seniors over 55, $16.95 children under 10, free for children under 3. Daily mid-Apr–Sept 30, 10am–6 or 8pm (sometimes later). Season and hours vary somewhat from year to year, so call ahead.

When temperatures soar, head for this 26-acre water park right in the heart of the Strip and cool off while jumping waves, careening down steep flumes, and running rapids. Among the highlights: Surf Lagoon, a 500,000-gallon wave pool; Bonzai Bonzai, a roller coaster–like water ride (aboard a plastic sled, you race down a 45-degree-angled 150-foot chute and skip porpoiselike across a 120-foot pool); Der Stuka, the world's fastest and highest water chute; Raging Rapids, a simulated white-water rafting adventure on a 500-foot-long river; Lazy River, a leisurely float trip; Blue Niagara, a dizzying descent inside intertwined looping tubes from a height of six stories; Willy Willy (a hydra-hurricane that propels riders on inner tubes around a 90-foot-diameter pool at 10 miles per hour); Bomb Bay (enter a bomblike casing 76 feet in the air for a speedy vertical flight straight down to a pool target); and the Black Hole (an exhilaratingly rapid space-themed flume descent in the dark enhanced by a bombardment of colorful fiberoptic star fields and spinning galaxy patterns en route to splashdown). There are additional flumes, a challenging children's water playground, and a sunbathing area with a cascading waterfall, as well as video and arcade games. Food concessions are located throughout the park, and you can purchase swimwear and accessories at the Beach Trends Shop.

4 Organized Tours

Just about every hotel in town has a sightseeing desk offering a seem-ingly infinite number of tours in and around Las Vegas. You're sure to find a tour company that will take you where you want to go.

Gray Line   Gray Line (☎ 702/384-1234) offers a rather comprehen-sive roster, including:

- $5^{1}/_{2}$- and 7-hour city tours combining visits to nearby museums with peeks at stars' homes and a bit of Las Vegas history.
- Full-day excursions to Laughlin, Nevada, an up-and-coming mini-Las Vegas 100 miles south with casino hotels on the banks of the Colorado River.
- Half- and full-day excursions to Hoover Dam and Lake Mead (see chapter 11 for details).
- An 8-hour excursion to Red Rock Canyon, including a museum visit.
- An 8-hour excursion to the Valley of Fire that includes lunch at a Lake Mead resort and a drive by Wayne Newton's Ranch.
- A full-day river-rafting tour on the Colorado River from the base of Hoover Dam through majestic Black Canyon.
- A morning or afternoon air tour (and you thought they only had buses) of Grand Canyon.
- A full-day land tour of Hoover Dam and air tour of Grand Canyon.
- A 10-hour Grand Canyon excursion that includes "flightseeing" and river rafting on the Colorado.
- An overnight trip to Grand Canyon.

Call for details or inquire at your hotel sightseeing desk.

THE GRAND CANYON   Generally, tourists visiting Las Vegas don't drive 300 miles to Arizona to see the Grand Canyon, but there are dozens of sightseeing tours departing from the city daily. In addi-tion to the **Gray Line** tours described above, the major operator, **Scenic Airlines** (☎ 702/739-1900 or 800/634-6801), runs deluxe, full-day guided air-ground tours for $189 per person ($149 for chil-dren 2 to 11); the price includes a bus excursion through the national park, a flight over the canyon, lunch, and a screening of the IMAX™ movie *Grand Canyon—the Hidden Secrets.* All Scenic tours include "flightseeing." The company also offers both full-day and overnight tours with hiking. And though all Scenic tours include hotel pickup and drop-off, if you take the Premium Deluxe Tour ($229 for adults, $179 for children) you'll be transported by limo.

INDIVIDUALIZED TOURS   A totally different type of tour is offered by Char Cruze of **Creative Adventures** (☎ 702/361-5565). Char, a charming fourth-generation Las Vegan (she was at the open-ing of the Flamingo), spent her childhood riding horseback through the mesquite and cottonwoods of the Mojave Desert, discovering magi-cal places you'd never find on your own or on a commercial tour.

Char is a lecturer and storyteller as well as a tour guide. She has extensively studied southern Nevada's geology and desert wildlife, its regional history and Native American cultures. Her personalized tours—enhanced by fascinating stories about everything from miners to mobsters—visit haunted mines, sacred Paiute grounds, ghost towns, canyons, and ancient petroglyphs. Depending on your itinerary, the cost is about $100 a day if you use your own car (more, depending on the number of people, if rental transportation is required). It's a good idea to make arrangements with her prior to leaving home.

5 Staying Active

Bring your sports gear to Las Vegas. The city and surrounding areas offer plenty of opportunities for active sports. Just about every hotel has a large swimming pool and health club, tennis courts abound, and there are many highly rated golf courses. All types of water sports are offered at Lake Mead National Recreation Area, there's rafting on the Colorado, horseback riding at Mount Charleston and Bonnie Springs, great hiking in the canyons, and much, much more. Do plan to get out of those smoke-filled casinos and into the fresh air once in a while. It's good for your health and your finances.

Note: When choosing a hotel, check out its recreational facilities, all listed in chapter 5.

BICYCLING   Escape the City Streets (☎ 702/596-2953) rents 21-speed mountain bikes and offers free delivery to all Downtown and Strip hotels. Rates are $25 for the first day, $20 for a half day or consecutive days, $85 for a full week. You must show a major credit card (American Express, MasterCard, or VISA). Inquire about bike trips to Red Rock Canyon and other good biking areas.

BOWLING   The Showboat Hotel & Casino, 2800 E. Fremont St. (☎ 702/385-9153), is famous for housing the largest bowling center in North America—106 lanes—and for being the oldest stop on the Professional Bowlers Tour. A major renovation a few years back made its premises bright and spiffy. Open 24 hours.

BUNGEE JUMPING   At A.J. Hackett Bungy, 810 Circus Circus Dr. between Las Vegas Blvd. S. and Industrial Rd. ☎ 702/385-4321), an elevator in the shape of a rocket takes you to the top of a 200-foot tower—the base for an exhilarating plunge into a large swimming pool below (bring a bathing suit). The price is $59 for your first jump (including a T-shirt), $29 for the second and third jumps; the fourth is free. A videotape of your jump is $19. If you're under 18, parental consent is required. Owner A.J. Hackett, who claims to have been the first commercial developer of bungee jumping (in New Zealand), has overseen more than 500,000 jumps without an accident. Call for hours.

CAMPING   A free comprehensive guide to campsites and RV parks in Nevada (including many in Las Vegas and Lake Mead National Recreation Area) is available from the **Nevada Commission on Tourism,** Capitol Complex, Carson City, NV 89710 (☎ 702/687-4322 or 800/NEVADA-8).

FISHING One doesn't usually think of fishing in the desert, but there are lakes and large ponds. Closest to Las Vegas are the ponds in **Floyd R. Lamb State Park,** 9200 Tule Springs Rd. (☎ 702/486-5413). The park is about 15 miles from the Strip. To get there take I-15 to U.S. 95 north, get off at the Durango exit and follow the signs. You can fish here for catfish, trout, bluegill, sunfish, and large-mouth bass. You will need your own gear, bait, and tackle, as well as a Nevada fishing license, which is available at any sporting goods store (check the Las Vegas yellow pages). There's also fishing at Lake Mead (see listing in chapter 11 for details).

GOLF There are dozens of local courses, including very challenging ones—the Sheraton Desert Inn Country Club and the Mirage Golf Club. Both have hosted many PGA tournaments. Beginner and intermediate golfers might prefer the other courses listed.

The **Angel Park Golf Club,** 100 S. Rampart Blvd., between Charleston Blvd. and Westcliff St. (☎ 702/254-4653), a 36-hole par-70/71 public course, was designed by Arnold Palmer. In addition to the 18-hole Palm and Mountain Courses, Angel Park offers a nightlit Cloud 9 course (12 holes for daylight play, 9 at night), where each hole is patterned after a famous par-3 (including holes from Pebble Beach and Pinehurst). Yardage: Palm Course 6,438 championship, 5,721 regular, 4,565 ladies; Mountain Course 6,783 championship, 6,272 regular, 5,143 ladies. Facilities: pro shop, nightlit driving range, 18-hole putting course, restaurant, snack bar, cocktail bar, beverage cart.

The **Black Mountain Golf & Country Club,** 500 Greenway Rd., in nearby Henderson (☎ 702/565-7933), is an 18-hole, par-72 semi-private course requiring reservations 4 days in advance. Yardage: 6,541 championship, 6,223 regular, 5,478 ladies. Facilities: pro shop, putting green, driving range, restaurant, snack bar, and cocktail lounge.

The **Craig Ranch Golf Club,** 628 W. Craig Rd., between I-15 and Martin Luther King Blvd. (☎ 702/642-9700), is an 18-hole, par-70 public course. Yardage: 6,001 regular, 5,221 ladies. Facilities: driving range, pro shop, PGA teaching pro, putting green, and snack bar.

The **Desert Rose Golf Club,** 5483 Club House Dr., between Nellis Blvd. and Sahara Ave. (☎ 702/431-4653), is an 18-hole, par-71 public course. Yardage: 6,511 championship, 6,135 regular, 5,458 ladies. Facilities: driving range, putting and chipping greens, pro shop, restaurant, and cocktail lounge.

The **Las Vegas Hilton Country Club,** 1911 Desert Inn Rd. (☎ 702/796-0016), is an 18-hole, par-71 public course. Yardage: 6,815 championship, 6,418 regular, 5,761 ladies. Facilities: pro shop, golf school, restaurant, and cocktail lounge. Hilton guests enjoy preferred tee times and rates.

The **Sheraton Desert Inn Golf Club,** 3145 Las Vegas Blvd. S. (☎ 702/733-4290), gets the nod from champions. It's an 18-hole, par-72 resort course. Yardage: 7,066 championship, 6,270 regular, 5,719 ladies. Facilities: driving range, putting green, pro shop, and restaurant. You can reserve 2 days in advance. This is the most famous and demanding course in Las Vegas. *Golf Digest* calls it one of America's top resort courses. The driving range is open to the public, but you must stay at the Sheraton Desert Inn to play the course (or pay a higher fee).

HEALTH CLUBS   Almost every hotel in Las Vegas has an on-premises health club. The facilities, of course, vary enormously. Full descriptions are given of each club in hotel facilities listings in chapter 5.

But none offers the amazing range of facilities you'll find at the **Las Vegas Sporting House,** 3025 Industrial Rd., right behind the Stardust Hotel (☎ 702/733-8999). Opened in 1978, this 65,000-square-foot club is ultraluxurious. UNLV teams and many athletes and Strip head-liners work out here. Facilities include: 10 racquetball/handball courts, two squash courts, two outdoor tennis courts (lit for night play), a full gymnasium for basketball and volleyball, an outdoor pool and sunbath-ing area, a 25-meter indoor pool for lap swimming, indoor and out-door jogging tracks, treadmills, Lifecycles, Virtual Reality bikes, stair machines, free weights, and a simulated skate machine. In addition, there are full lines of Cybex, Universal, and Paramount machines, along with some Nautilus equipment; sauna, steam, and Jacuzzi; a pro shop; men's and women's skin care and hair salons; massage; free babysitting service while you work out; restaurant, bar, and lounge. Aerobics classes are given at frequent intervals throughout the day. Cost for a single visit is $15 if you're staying at a local hotel; reduced weekly and monthly rates are available. Open daily 24 hours.

HORSEBACK RIDING   The **Mt. Charleston Riding Stables** (☎ 702/872-7009, 702/386-6899 from Las Vegas), under the auspices of the Mount Charleston Resort, offer glorious scenic trail rides to the edge of the wilderness. They depart from stables on Kyle Canyon Road. Since the schedule varies, it's best to call in advance for details. The stables also offer sleigh rides in winter and hayrides in summer. Riding stables at **Bonnie Springs Ranch** (☎ 702/875-4191) also offer guided trail rides daily. Rates are $16.50 per hour.

HIKING   Except in summer, when the temperature can reach 120° in the shade, the Las Vegas area is great for hiking. The best hiking season is November through March. Great locales include the incred-ibly scenic Red Rock Canyon, Valley of Fire State Park, and Mount Charleston (see individual headings in chapter 11 for details).

JET SKIING   **Las Vegas Adventure Tours (LVAT)** (☎ 800/553-5452) offers jet-ski rides on Lake Mead. Call LVAT, too, about horseback riding, hot-air ballooning, and all-terrain-vehicle desert tours.

RACQUETBALL   There are courts in several locations around town.
The **Las Vegas Athletic Club East,** 1070 E. Sahara Ave., at Mary-land Pkwy. (☎ 702/733-1919), has seven courts open 24 hours a day, 7 days a week. Rates: $10 per person, per day; $25 per week. Call to reserve a court.
The **Las Vegas Athletic Club West,** 3315 Spring Mountain Rd., between I-15 and Valley View Blvd. (☎ 702/362-3720), has eight courts open weekdays 5am to 11pm; weekends 8am to 8pm. Rates: $10 per person, per visit; $25 per week.

The **Las Vegas Sporting House,** 3025 Industrial Rd., right behind the Stardust Hotel (☎ 702/733-8999), has 10 racquetball/handball courts open 24 hours a day, 7 days a week. Rates are $15 per visit if you're staying at a local hotel.

The **University of Nevada, Las Vegas (UNLV),** 4505 Maryland Pkwy., just off Swenson St. (☎ 702/895-3150), has eight racquetball courts open weekdays 6am to 9:45pm, Saturdays 8:30am to 5:30pm, Sundays 10:30am to 5:30pm. Hours may vary somewhat each semester. Rates: $2 per person, per hour. Call before you go to find out if a court is available. You must pick up a guest pass in the Physical Education Building.

RIVER RAFTING Black Canyon Inc. (☎ 702/293-3776) offers daily raft trips on the Colorado River from February 1 through the end

---

Desert Hiking Tips

Hiking in the desert is exceptionally rewarding, but it can be dangerous. Some safety tips:

1. Do not hike alone.

2. Carry plenty of water and drink it often. Don't assume spring waters are safe to drink. A gallon of water per person, per day is recommended for hikers.

3. Be alert for signs of heat exhaustion (headache, nausea, dizziness, fatigue, and cool, damp, pale, or red skin).

4. Gauge your fitness accurately. Desert hiking may involve rough or steep terrain. Don't take on more than you can handle.

5. Check weather forecasts before starting out. Thunderstorms can turn into raging flash floods, which are extremely hazardous to hikers.

6. Dress properly. Wear sturdy walking shoes for rock scrambling, long pants (to protect yourself from rocks and cacti), a hat, sunscreen, and sunglasses.

7. Carry a small first-aid kit.

8. Be careful when climbing on sandstone, which can be surprisingly soft and crumbly.

9. Don't feed or play with animals, such as wild burros in Red Rock Canyon.

10. Be alert for snakes and insects. Though they're rarely encountered, you'll want to look into a crevice before putting your hand into it.

11. Visit park or other information offices before you start out and acquaint yourself with rules and regulations and any possible hazards. It's also a good idea to tell them where you are going, when you will return, how many are in your party, and so on. Some park offices offer hiker-registration programs.

12. Follow the hiker's rule of thumb: "Take only photographs, and leave only footprints."

of November. Trips include 3 hours of scenic rafting and lunch. You'll see waterfalls gush from majestic canyon walls, pass tranquil coves, spy bighorn sheep on sheer cliffs, and spot blue herons, cormorants, and falcons. Knowledgeable guides provide a lot of fascinating area history and geology. Each raft is piloted by an experienced navigator. Rates, including Las Vegas hotel pickup and return, are $69.95 per person, $64.95 if you drive to and from the put-in point.

ROCK CLIMBING   Red Rock Canyon, just 19 miles west of Las Vegas, is one of the world's most popular rock-climbing areas. In addition to awe-inspiring natural beauty, it offers everything from bouldering to big walls. If you'd like to join the bighorn sheep, Red Rock has more than 1,000 routes to inaugurate beginners and challenge accomplished climbers. Experienced climbers can contact the Visitor Center (☎ 702/363-1921) for information.

If you're interested in learning or improving your skills, an excellent rock-climbing school and guide service called **Sky's the Limit** (☎ 702/363-4533 or 800/733-7597) offers programs for beginning, intermediate, and advanced climbers. No experience is needed. The school is accredited by the American Mountain Guides Association.

TENNIS   Tennis buffs should choose one of the many hotels in town that have tennis courts.

Caesars Palace (☎ 702/731-7786) has four outdoor hard courts that are open to the public, as well as a pro shop. Hours are 8am to 7pm daily. Rates are $25 per hour, per court for nonguests; $15 for guests (you can stay longer if no one is waiting). Reservations are required.

The **Flamingo Hilton** (☎ 702/733-3444) has four outdoor hard courts (all lit for night play), and a pro shop. They are open to the public Monday to Friday from 7am to 8pm, Saturday and Sunday from 7am to 6pm. Rates are $16 per hour for nonguests, $12 for guests. Lessons are available. Reservations are required.

The **Las Vegas Hilton** (☎ 702/732-5648) has six outdoor hard courts (all lit for night play). However, they are not open to the public. Hours are 6am to 10:30pm. There is no charge.

The **Riviera** (☎ 702/734-5110) has two outdoor hard courts (both lit for night play) that are open to the public, subject to availability; hotel guests have priority. They are open 24 hours. There is no charge, but reservations are required.

The **Sheraton Desert Inn** (☎ 702/733-4557) has five outdoor hard courts (all lit for night play) and a pro shop. They are open to the public. Hours are daybreak to 10pm. Rates are $10 per person for a daily pass (you book for an hour but can stay longer if no one is waiting); they are free for guests. Reservations are necessary.

In addition to hotels, the **University of Nevada, Las Vegas (UNLV),** 4505 Maryland Pkwy., just off Swenson St. (☎ 702/895-0844) has a dozen courts (all lit for night play) that are open weekdays from 6am to 9:45pm, on weekends from 8am to 9pm. Rates are $5 per person, per day on weekdays; $10 weekends. You should call before going to find out if a court is available.

6   Spectator Sports

The **Sam Boyd Stadium** at the University of Nevada, Las Vegas (UNLV), Boulder Hwy. and Russell Rd. (☎ 702/895-3900), is a 32,000-seat outdoor stadium. The UNLV Rebels play about six football games here each year between September and November. And the stadium is also used for motorsports and supercross events, truck and tractor pulls, high school football games, and the Las Vegas Bowl in December. For information and to charge tickets, call the above number or Ticketmaster (☎ 702/474-4000).

The **Thomas and Mack Center,** also on the UNLV campus at Tropicana Ave. and Swenson St. (☎ 702/895-3900), is an 18,500-seat facility used for a variety of sporting events. It is home to the UNLV's Runnin' Rebels (basketball), who play 16 to 20 games during a November to March season. Las Vegas Thunder (International Hockey League) plays about 40 games here between October and early April (call 702/798-PUCK for information). Other events here include major boxing tournaments, NBA exhibition games, rodeos, truck and tractor pulls, and major tennis matches. For information and to charge tickets, call the stadium number or TicketMaster (☎ 702/474-4000).

The **Las Vegas Stars,** a AAA baseball team, play from April through August at the 10,000-seat **Cashman Field Center,** 805 Las Vegas Blvd. N. (☎ 702/386-7200 for tickets and information). Tickets are priced at $7 to $15.

The **Aladdin's** 7,000-seat **Theatre for the Performing Arts** is occasionally used for professional boxing and wrestling matches.

Caesars Palace (☎ 702/731-7110 or 800/634-6698) has a long tradition of sporting events, from Evel Knievel's attempted motorcycle jump over its fountains in 1967 to Grand Prix auto races. The hotel's tennis courts have been the site of many championship tournaments, and—an interesting side note—one Caesars' employee used to sneak his talented son onto the courts here to practice. That was little Andre Agassi, who later played championship tournaments legitimately on those same courts. Mary Lou Retton has tumbled in gymnastic events at Caesars, and Olympians Brian Boitano and Katarina Witt have taken to the ice, as has Wayne Gretzky (he led the L.A. Kings to victory over the New York Rangers in a preseason exhibition game). In 1992 Evander Holyfield defeated Larry Holmes here—one of 117 world-championship boxing contests that have taken place here since the hotel opened. In the spirit of ancient Rome, Caesars awards riches and honors to the "gladiators" who compete in its arenas.

The **MGM Grand's Garden Events Arena** (☎ 702/891-7777 or 800/929-1111) is a major venue for sporting events: professional boxing matches, rodeos, tennis, ice-skating shows, World Figure Skating Championships, and more.

The Mirage (☎ 702/791-7111 or 800/627-6667) features championship boxing matches several times a year.

8

About Casino Gambling

Most people don't come to Las Vegas simply to visit the Liberace Museum. The Las Vegas economy depends upon gambling, and even the hotels here conceive of themselves basically as casinos with rooms. Visitors range from cautious types who play nickel slots for an hour and fret about losing a few dollars to flamboyant high rollers risking hundreds—if not thousands—of dollars on a roll of the dice, a good blackjack hand, or a spin of the roulette wheel. These diverse gamblers have just one thing in common: secretly, every one of them expects to win. It's this elusive dream that keeps people coming back, trying out elaborate systems, reading books on how to beat the odds, betting excitedly when a craps table gets hot, and dropping spare change into slot machines.

Of course, there is no system that really beats the odds. And if there were, the casinos would be on it faster than a New York minute. The best system is to decide how much you're willing to risk, learn the rules of any game you're playing, and, if you have the fortitude, walk away with moderate winnings. Many good players hold out for a 50% profit. Keep in mind that it's extremely easy to get carried away trying to recoup losses. I've personally seen tragic cases of average folks losing large sums, and, desperate to win them back, making larger and larger bets until they've gambled away cars, homes, and savings.

The first part of this chapter tells you the basics of betting. Knowing how to play the games not only improves your odds but makes playing more enjoyable. In addition to the instructions below, you'll find dozens of books on how to gamble at all casino hotel gift shops, and many casinos offer free gaming lessons on the premises. The second part of this chapter describes all the major casinos in town.

1 The Games

BACCARAT

The ancient game of baccarat—or *chemin de fer*—is played with eight decks of cards. Firm rules apply, and there is no skill involved other than deciding whether to bet on the bank or the player. Any beginner can play, but check the betting minimum before you sit down. The cards are shuffled by the croupier and then placed in a box that is called the "shoe."

BACCARAT RULES

PLAYER'S HAND

Having

0–1–2–3–4–5	Must draw a third card.
6–7	*Must stand.*
8–9	Natural. Banker cannot draw.

BANKER'S HAND

Having	**Draws** When giving Player 3rd card of:	**Does Not Draw** When giving Player 3rd card of:
3	1–2–3–4–5–6–7–9–10	8
4	2–3–4–5–6–7	1–8–9–10
5	4–5–6–7	1–2–3–8–9–10
6	6–7	1–2–3–4–5–8–9–10
7	*Must stand.*	
8–9	Natural. Player cannot draw.	

If the player takes no third card, the banker must stand on 6. No one draws against a natural 8 or 9.

Players may wager on "bank" or "player" at any time. Two cards are dealt from the shoe and given to the player who has the largest wager against the bank, and two cards are dealt to the croupier acting as banker. If the rule calls for a third card (see rules on chart shown here), the player or banker, or both, must take the third card. In the event of a tie, the hand is dealt over.

The object of the game is to come as close as possible to the number 9. To score the hands, the cards of each hand are totaled and the *last digit* is used. All cards have face value. For example: 10 plus 5 equal 15 (score is 5); 10 plus 4 plus 9 equal 23 (score is 3); 4 plus 3 plus 3 equal 10 (score is 0); and 4 plus 3 plus 2 equal 9 (score is 9). The closest hand to 9 wins.

Each player has a chance to deal the cards. The shoe passes to the player on the right each time the bank loses. If the player wishes, he or she may pass the shoe at any time.

Note: When you bet on the bank and the bank wins, you are charged a 5% commission. This must be paid at the start of a new game or when you leave the table.

BIG SIX

Big Six provides pleasant recreation and involves no study or effort. The wheel has 56 positions on it, 54 of them marked by bills from $1 to $20 denominations. The other two spots are jokers, and each pays 40 to 1 if the wheel stops in that position.

All other stops pay at face value. Those marked with $20 bills pay 20 to 1; the $5 bills pay 5 to 1; and so forth.

BLACKJACK

The dealer starts the game by dealing each player two cards. In some casinos they're dealt to the player faceup, in others facedown, but the dealer always gets one card up and one card down. Everybody plays against the dealer. The object is to get a total that is higher than that of the dealer without exceeding 21. All face cards count as 10; all other number cards except aces count as their number value. An ace may be counted as 1 or 11, whichever you choose it to be.

Starting at his or her left, the dealer gives additional cards to the players who wish to draw (be "hit") or none to a player who wishes to "stand" or "hold." If your count is nearer to 21 than the dealer's, you win. If it's under the dealer's, you lose. Ties are a push and nobody wins. After all the players are satisfied with their counts, the dealer exposes his or her facedown card. If his two cards total 16 or less, the dealer must "hit" (draw an additional card) until reaching 17 or over. If the dealer's total goes over 21, he or she must pay all the players whose hands have not gone "bust." It is important to note here that the blackjack dealer has no choice as to whether he or she should stay or draw. A dealer's decisions are predetermined and known to all the players at the table.

HOW TO PLAY   Here are eight "rules" for blackjack.

1. Place the amount of chips that you want to bet on the betting space on your table.

2. Look at the first two cards the dealer starts you with. If your hand adds up to the total you prefer, place your cards *under your bet money,* indicating that you don't wish any additional cards. If you elect to draw an additional card, you tell the dealer to "hit" you by making a sweeping motion with your cards, or point to your open hand (watch your fellow players).

3. If your count goes over 21, you go "bust" and lose—even if the dealer also goes "bust" afterward. Unless hands are dealt faceup, *you then turn your hand faceup on the table.*

4. If you make 21 in your first two cards (any picture card or 10 with an ace), you've got blackjack. *You expose your winning hand immediately,* and you collect $1^{1}/_{2}$ times your bet—unless the dealer has blackjack, too, in which case it's a push and nobody wins.

5. If you find a "pair" in your first two cards (say, two 8s or two aces) you may "split" the pair into two hands and treat each card as the first card dealt in two separate hands. *Turn the pair faceup on the table,* place the original bet on one of these cards, then place an equal amount on the other card. *Split aces are limited to a one-card draw on each.*

6. You may double your original bet and make a one-card draw after receiving your initial two cards. *Turn your hand faceup* and you'll receive one more card facedown.

7. Anytime the dealer deals himself or herself an ace for the "up" card, you may insure your hand against the possibility that the hole card is a 10 or face card, which would give him or her an automatic blackjack. To insure, you place an amount up to one-half of your bet on the "insurance" line. If the dealer does have a blackjack, you do not lose, even though he or she has your hand beat, and you keep your bet and your insurance money. If the dealer does not have a blackjack, he or she takes your insurance money and play continues in the normal fashion.

8. *Remember!* The dealer *must* stand on 17 or more and *must* hit a hand of 16 or less.

PROFESSIONAL TIPS   Advice of the experts in playing blackjack is as follows.

1. *Do not* ask for an extra card if you have a count of 17, 18, 19, 20, or 21 in your cards, no matter what the dealer has showing in his or her "up" card.

2. *Do not* ask for an extra card when you have 12, 13, 14, 15, 16, or more . . . if the dealer has a 2, 3, 4, 5, or 6 showing in his or her "up" card.

3. *Do ask* for an extra card or more when you have a count of 12 through 16 in your hand . . . if the dealer's "up" card is a 7, 8, 9, 10, or ace.

There's a lot more to blackjack-playing strategy than the above, of course. So consider this merely as the bare bones of the game.

A final tip: Avoid insurance bets; they're sucker bait!

CRAPS

The most exciting casino action is always at the craps tables. Betting is frenetic, play fast-paced, and groups quickly bond yelling and screaming in response to the action.

THE TABLE   The craps table is divided into marked areas (Pass, Come, Field, Big 6, Big 8, and so on), where you place your chips to bet. The following are a few simple directions.

Pass Line   A "Pass Line" bet pays even money. If the first roll of the dice adds up to 7 or 11, you win your bet; if the first roll adds up to 2, 3, or 12, you lose your bet. If any other number comes up, it's your "point." If you roll your point again, you win, but if a 7 comes up again before your point is rolled, you lose.

Don't Pass Line   Betting on the "Don't Pass" is the opposite of betting on the Pass Line. This time, you lose if a 7 or an 11 is thrown on the first roll, and you win if a 2 or a 3 is thrown on the first roll.

If the first roll is 12, however, it's a push (standoff), and nobody wins. If none of these numbers is thrown and you have a point instead,

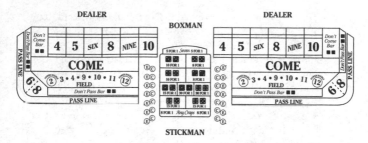

in order to win, a 7 will have to be thrown before the point comes up again. A "Don't Pass" bet also pays even money.

Come   Betting on "Come" is the same as betting on the Pass Line, but you must bet *after* the first roll or on any following roll. Again, you'll win on 7 or 11 and lose on 2, 3, or 12. Any other number is your point, and you win if your point comes up again before a 7.

Don't Come   This is the opposite of a "Come" bet. Again, you wait until after the first roll to bet. A 7 or an 11 means you lose; a 2 or a 3 means you win; 12 is a push, and nobody wins. You win if 7 comes up before the point. (The point, you'll recall, was the first number rolled if it was none of the above.)

Field   This is a bet for one roll only. The "Field" consists of seven numbers: 2, 3, 4, 9, 10, 11, and 12. If any of these numbers is thrown on the next roll, you win even money, except on 2 and 12, which pay to 2 to 1 (at some casinos 3 to 1).

Big 6 and 8   A "Big 6 and 8" bet pays even money. You win if either a 6 or an 8 is rolled before a 7.

Any 7   An "Any 7" bet pays the winner five for one. If a 7 is thrown on the first roll after you bet, you win.

"Hard Way" Bets   In the middle of a craps table are pictures of several possible dice combinations together with the odds the casino will pay you if you bet and win on any of those combinations being thrown. For example, if 8 is thrown by having a 4 appear on each die, and you bet on it, the bank will pay 10 for 1; if 4 is thrown by having a 2 appear on each die, and you bet on it, the bank will pay 8 for 1; if 3 is thrown, the bank pays 15 for 1. . . . You win at the odds quoted if the *exact* combination of numbers you bet on comes up. But you lose either if a 7 is rolled or if the number you bet on was rolled any way other than the "Hard Way" shown on the table. In-the-know gamblers tend to avoid "Hard Way" bets as an easy way to lose their money. And note that the odds quoted are *not* 3 to 1, 4 to 1, or 8 to 1; here the key word is *for*—that is, 3 for 1 or 8 for 1.

Any Craps   Here you're lucky if the dice "crap out"—if they show 2, 3, or 12 on the first roll after you bet. If this happens, the bank pays for 8 for 1. Any other number is a loser.

Place Bets   You can make a "Place Bet" on any of the following numbers: 4, 5, 6, 8, 9, and 10. You're betting that the number you choose will be thrown before a 7 is thrown. If you win, the payoff is as follows: 4 or 10 pays at the rate of 9 to 5; 5 or 9 pays at the rate of 7 to 5; 6 or 8 pays at the rate of 7 to 6 "Place Bets" can be removed at any time before a roll.

SOME PROBABILITIES   Because each die has six sides numbered from 1 to 6—and craps is played with a pair of dice—the probability of throwing certain numbers has been studied carefully. Professionals have employed complex mathematical formulas in searching for the answers. And computers have data-processed curves of probability.

Suffice it to say that 7 (a crucial number in craps) will be thrown more frequently than any other number over the long run, for there are six possible combinations that make 7 when you break down the 1 to 6 possibilities on each separate die. As to the total possible number of combinations on the dice, there are 36.

Comparing the 36 possible combinations, numbers—or point combinations—run as follows:

> *2 and 12* may be thrown in *1 way only.*
> *3 and 11* may be thrown in *2 ways.*
> *4 and 10* may be thrown in *3 ways.*
> *5 and 9* may be thrown in *4 ways.*
> *6 and 8* may be thrown in *5 ways.*
> *7* may be thrown in *6 ways.*

So 7 has an advantage over all other combinations, which, over the long run, is in favor of the casino. You can't beat the law of averages. Players, however, often have winning streaks—a proven fact in ESP studies—and that's when the experts advise that it's wise to increase the size of bets. But when a losing streak sets in, stop playing!

KENO

This is one of the oldest games of chance. Originating in China, the game can be traced back to a time before Christ, when it operated as a national lottery. Legend has it that funds acquired from the game were used to finance construction of the Great Wall of China.

Keno was first introduced into the United States in the 1800s by Chinese railroad construction workers. Easy to play, and offering a chance to sit down and converse between bets, it is one of the most popular games in town—despite the fact that *the house percentage is greater than that of any other casino game!*

To play, you must first obtain a keno form, available at the counter in the keno lounge and in most Las Vegas coffee shops. In the latter, you'll usually find blank keno forms and thick black crayons on your table. Fill yours out, and a miniskirted keno runner will come and collect it. After the game is over, she'll return with your winning or losing ticket. If you've won, it's customary to offer a tip, depending on your winnings.

Looking at your keno ticket and the keno board, you'll see that it is divided horizontally into two rectangles. The upper half (in China the yin area) contains the numbers 1 through 40, the lower (yang) half contains the numbers 41 through 80. You can win a maximum of

	PRICE PER WAY	PRICE PER GAME
$50,000.00 LIMIT TO AGGREGATE PLAYERS EACH GAME		
MARK NUMBER OF SPOTS OR WAYS PLAYED	NO. OF GAMES	TOTAL PRICE

WINNING TICKETS MUST BE COLLECTED IMMEDIATELY AFTER EACH KENO GAME IS CALLED.

1	2	3	4	5	6	7	8	9	10
11	12	13	14	15	16	17	18	19	20
21	22	23	24	25	26	27	28	29	30
31	32	33	34	35	36	37	38	39	40

WE PAY ON MACHINE ISSUED TICKETS - TICKETS WITH ERRORS NOT CORRECTED BEFORE START OF GAME WILL BE ACCEPTED AS ISSUED.

41	42	43	44	45	46	47	48	49	50
51	52	53	54	55	56	57	58	59	60
61	62	63	64	65	66	67	68	69	70
71	72	73	74	75	76	77	78	79	80

WE ARE NOT RESPONSIBLE FOR KENO RUNNERS TICKETS NOT VALIDATED BEFORE START OF NEXT GAME.

$50,000—even more on progressive games—though it's highly unlikely (the probability is less than a hundredth of a percent). Mark up to 15 out of the 80 numbers; bets range from about 70¢ on up. A one-number mark is known as a one-spot, a two-number selection is a two-spot, and so on. After you have selected the number of spots you wish to play, write the price of the ticket in the right hand corner where indicated. The more you bet, the more you can win if your numbers come up. Before the game starts, you have to give the completed form to a keno runner—or hand it in at the keno lounge desk—and pay for your bet. You'll get back a duplicate form with the number of the game you're playing on it. Then the game begins. As numbers appear on the keno board, compare them to the numbers you've marked on your ticket. After 20 numbers have appeared on the board, if you've won, turn in your ticket immediately for a payoff—before the next game begins. Otherwise, you will forfeit your winnings, a frustrating experience to say the least.

On a straight ticket that is marked with one or two spots, all of your numbers must appear on the board for you to win anything. With a few exceptions, if you mark from 3 to 7 spots, 3 numbers must appear on the board for you to win anything. Similarly, if you mark 8 to 12 spots, usually at least 5 numbers must come up for you to win the minimum amount. And if you mark 13 to 15 spots, usually at least 6 numbers must come up for a winning ticket. To win the maximum amount ($50,000), which requires that all of your numbers come up, you must select at least 8 spots. The more numbers on the board matching the numbers on your ticket, the more you win. If you want to keep playing the same numbers over and over, you can replay a ticket by handing in your duplicate to the keno runner; you don't have to keep rewriting it.

In addition to the straight bets described above, you can split your ticket, betting various amounts on two or more groups of numbers. To do so, circle the groups. The amount you bet is then divided by the number of groups. You could, if you so desired, play as many as 40 two-spots on a single ticket. Another possibility is to play three groups of four numbers each as eight spots (any two of the three groups of four numbers can be considered an eight spot). It does get a little complex, since combination betting options are almost infinite. Helpful casino personnel in the keno lounge can help you with combination betting.

POKER

Poker is *the* game of the Old West. There's at least one sequence in every western where the hero faces off against the villain over a poker hand. In Las Vegas poker is a tradition, although it isn't played at every casino.

There are lots of variations on the basic game, but one of the most popular is Hold 'Em. Five cards are dealt face up in the center of the table and two are dealt to each player. The player uses the best five of seven, and the best hand wins. The house dealer takes care of the shuffling and the dealing and moves a marker around the table to alternate the start of the deal. The house rakes 1% to 10% (it depends on the casino) from each pot. Most casinos include the usual seven-card stud and a few have hi-lo split.

If you don't know how to play poker, don't attempt to learn at a table. Find a casino that teaches it in free gaming lessons.

Pai-gow poker (a variation on poker) has become increasingly popular. The game is played with a traditional deck plus one joker. The joker is a wild card that can be used as an ace or to complete a straight, a flush, a straight flush, or a royal flush. Each player is dealt seven cards to arrange into two hands—a two-card hand and a five-card hand. As in standard poker, the highest two-card hand is two aces, and the highest five-card hand is a royal flush. The five-card hand *must* be higher than the two-card hand (if the two-card hand is a pair of sixes, for example, the five-card hand must be a pair of sevens or better). Any player's hand that is set incorrectly is an automatic lose. The object of the game is for both of the player's hands to rank higher than both of the banker's hands. Should one hand rank exactly the same as the banker's hand, this is a tie (called a "copy"), *and the banker wins all tie hands*. If the player wins one hand but loses the other, this is a "push," and no money changes hands. The house dealer or any player may be the banker. The bank is offered to each player, and each player may accept or pass. Winning hands are paid even money, less a 5% commission.

ROULETTE

Roulette is an extremely easy game to play, and it's really quite colorful and exciting to watch. The wheel spins, and the little ball bounces
around, finally dropping into one of the slots, numbered 1 to 36, plus
0 and 00. You can bet on a single number, a combination of numbers,
or red or black, odd or even. If you're lucky, you can win as much as
35 to 1 (see the table). The method of placing single-number bets, col-
umn bets, and others is fairly obvious. The dealer will be happy to show

ROULETTE CHART KEY	ODDS	TYPE OF BET
		Straight Bets
A	35 to 1	*Straight-up:* All numbers, plus 0 and 00.
B	2 to 1	*Column Bet:* Pays off on any number in that horizontal column
C	2 to 1	*First Dozen:* Pays off on any number 1 through 12. Same for second and third dozen.
D	Even Money	
		Combination Bets
E	17 to 1	*Split:* Pays off on 11 or 12.
F	11 to 1	Pays off on 28, 29, or 30.
G	8 to 1	*Corner:* Pays off on 17, 18, 20 or 21.
H	6 to 1	Pays off on 0, 00, 1, 2, or 3.
I	5 to 1	Pays off on 22, 23, 24, 25, 26 or 27.

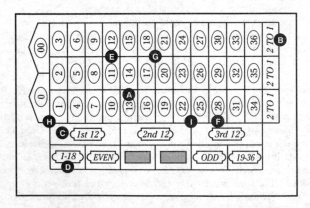

you how to "straddle" two or more numbers and make many other interesting betting combinations. Each player is given different-colored chips so that it's easy to follow the numbers you're on.

A number of typical bets are indicated by means of letters on the roulette layout depicted here. The winning odds for each of these sample bets are listed. These bets can be made on any corresponding combinations of numbers.

SPORTS BOOKS

Most of the larger hotels in Las Vegas have sports book operations—they look a lot like commodities-futures trading boards. In some, almost as large as theaters, you can sit comfortably and watch ball games, fights, and, at some casinos, horse races on huge TV screens. To add to your enjoyment, there's usually a deli/bar nearby that serves sandwiches, hot dogs, soft drinks, and beer. As a matter of fact, some of the best sandwiches in Las Vegas are served next to the sports books. Sports books take bets on virtually every sport.

2   The Casinos

Each casino has its own personality and special features. The following is a rundown of each, including exact gaming facilities:

BALLY'S   Bally's casino is one of the most cheerful on the Strip—a large (it's the size of a football field), brightly lit facility with lots of colorful signs and confetti-motif carpeting. There's a Most Valuable Player Slot Club, offering members room discounts, free meals and show tickets, and invitations to special events, among other perks. The casino hosts frequent slot tournaments, and free gaming lessons are offered. Gaming facilities include a keno lounge, a state-of-the-art race and sports book, blackjack tables, craps, roulette, baccarat, minibaccarat, Caribbean stud (Bally's innovated this now popular Las Vegas game), pai-gow, a Big Six wheel, let-it ride tables, and 1,565 slot/video poker machines (with more to come). There are also blackjack tables and slot/video poker machines in Bally's Avenue Shoppes.

BARBARY COAST   The Barbary Coast has a cheerful 1890s-style casino ornately decorated with $2 million worth of gorgeous stained-glass skylights and signs, as well as immense crystal-dangling globe chandeliers over the gaming tables. It's worth stopping in just to take a look around when you're in the central "four corners" area of the Strip. The casino has a free Fun Club for slot players. Participants earn points toward gifts and prizes. Gaming facilities include a race and sports book, keno, blackjack tables, craps, roulette, minibaccarat, pai-gow poker, and 550 slot/video poker machines.

CAESARS PALACE   Caesars has two interconnecting deluxe gaming rooms—the high-end **Forum Casino** (with the action under crystal-fringed black domes) and the slightly more casual **Olympic Casino.** A notable facility in the latter is the state-of-the-art Race and Sports Book, with huge electronic display boards and giant video screens. (Caesars pioneered computer-generated wagering data that can

In 1994, according to the Las Vegas Convention and Visitors
Authority, the average visitor to Las Vegas . . .

—had been to Las Vegas 8.8 times in the last 5 years

—stayed 4 days

—set aside $479 for gambling

be communicated in less than half a second and sophisticated satellite
equipment that can pick up virtually any broadcast sporting event in
the world). The domed VIP slot arena of the Forum Casino (minimum
bet is $5, but you can wager up to $1,500 on a single pull!) is a plush,
crystal-chandeliered precinct with seating in roomy adjustable chairs.
All slot players can accumulate bonus points toward gifts and gratis
show tickets, meals, and rooms by joining the Emperors Club. Club
membership also lets you in on grand prize drawings, tournaments, and
parties. Most upscale of the Caesars gaming room is the intimate
European-style casino adjoining the **Palace Court** restaurant. Total
facilities in all three casinos contain craps tables, blackjack, roulette,
baccarat, minibaccarat, let-it-ride poker, Caribbean stud, pai-gow
poker, 2 Big Six wheels, more than 2,000 slot/video poker machines,
and a keno lounge.

CALIFORNIA HOTEL/CASINO   The California caters to a largely
Hawaiian clientele, hence, dealers in its attractive marble and
crystal-chandeliered casino wear colorful aloha shirts. This friendly
facility actually provides sofas and armchairs in the casino area—
an unheard-of luxury in this town. Players can join the Cal Slot
Club and amass points toward gifts and cash prizes or participate in
daily slot tournaments. Gaming facilities include a keno lounge,
sports book, blackjack tables, craps, roulette, minibaccarat, pai-
gow poker, let-it-ride, Caribbean stud, and over 1,000 slot and video
poker machines.

CIRCUS CIRCUS   This vast property has three full-size casinos that,
combined, comprise one of the largest gaming operations in Nevada
(more than 100,000 square feet). The main casino is the one entered
via the front door off the Strip. And there are additional gaming
facilities in the Circus Circus Main Tower and Skyrise buildings.
Circus Circus fun books offer coupons for free $10,000 cash slot
pulls. And there's no cost to join the Ringmaster Club and earn points
while playing a variety of casino games that are redeemable for cash,
discounted rooms and meals, and other benefits. Circus Bucks progressive slot machines here build from a jackpot base of $500,000,
which players can win on a $2 pull. Gaming facilities include a
10,000-square-foot race and sports book with 30 video monitors ranging from 13 to 52 inches, 40-seat and 89-seat keno lounges, poker
tables, blackjack, craps, roulette, a Big Six wheel, let-it-ride poker,
pai-gow poker, dice, Caribbean stud poker, and 2,400 slot and video
poker machines.

DEBBIE REYNOLDS HOTEL/CASINO   Debbie has installed marquee lights in the casino and adorned its walls with oversized black-and-white photographs of stars such as Audrey Hepburn, Clark Gable, Charlie Chaplin, Lucille Ball, Gary Cooper, Gregory Peck, and Ginger Rogers. Gaming facilities include 178 slot/video poker machines and 2 blackjack tables.

SHERATON DESERT INN   This is one of my favorite Las Vegas casinos—a low-key setting typical of the hotel's country-club elegance. And it is being revamped at this writing as the hotel strives to achieve an even more plush, upscale profile. Crystal chandeliers here replace the usual neon glitz, and gaming tables are comfortably spaced. The ambience is reminiscent of intimate European gaming houses. Since there are fewer slot machines here than at most major casinos, there's less noise in ringing bells and clinking coins. Most table games have a $5 minimum. Facilities include a race and sports book, a poker room, blackjack tables, craps, pai-gow, pai-gow poker, minibaccarat, baccarat, roulette wheels, and 375 slot/video poker machines. A sophisticated casino lounge featuring name artists like Keely Smith is a plus.

EL CORTEZ   This friendly Downtown casino features frequent big-prize drawings (up to $50,000) based on your Social Security number. It's also popular for low limits (10¢ roulette and 25¢ craps). Gaming facilities include a race and sports book, keno, blackjack tables, craps, roulette, minibaccarat, and 1,500 slot/video poker machines.

EXCALIBUR   As you might expect, the Excalibur casino is replete with suits of armor, stained-glass panels, knights, dragons, and velvet and satin heraldic banners, with gaming action taking place beneath vast iron and gold chandeliers fit for a medieval castle fortress. A popular feature here is Circus Bucks—a progressive slot machine that builds from a jackpot base of $500,000 that players can win on a $3 pull. Excalibur's 100,000-plus square feet of gaming facilities also include a race and sports book, a keno lounge, a poker room, blackjack tables, minibaccarat, Caribbean stud poker, craps, roulette, pai-gow poker, Big Six wheels, and 2,630 slot/video poker machines. There's also a nonsmoking area.

FITZGERALDS   At this 47,000-square-foot Irish-themed casino, guests are greeted by Leprechaun Mr. O'Lucky, and they can rub pieces of the actual Blarney stone from Country Cork for good luck. Blackjack, craps, and keno tournaments are frequent events here. The Fitzgerald Card offers slot players cash back and VIP privileges with accumulated points. Several slot machines offer cars as prizes; fun books provide two-for-one gaming coupons; and there are some nonsmoking

Impressions

Stilled forever is the click of the roulette wheel, the rattle of dice, and the swish of cards.
—Short-sighted editorial in the *Nevada State Journal* after gambling was outlawed in 1910

gaming tables. Facilities include a sports book, a keno lounge, black-jack, craps, let-it-ride poker, roulette, survival dice, "21" Superbucks, Caribbean stud, and 1,100 slot and video poker machines.

FLAMINGO HILTON   The Flamingo's large, Caribbean-themed casino, brilliantly lit by pink and orange neon lights that mirror its landmark facade, has "faux" skylights overhead through which chinks of painted sky are visible. Actual daylight streams in as well from windows and glass doorways on the Strip. There are slots here offering Cadillacs and Continentals as jackpots. Players Club slot bettors qualify for free meals, shows, and other play-based incentives. Free gaming lessons are offered weekdays. Gaming facilities include a keno lounge, race and sports book, poker room, 40 blackjack tables, craps, roulette, minibaccarat, pai-gow poker, sic bo, a Big Six wheel, and 2,100 slot/video poker machines.

FOUR QUEENS   The Four Queens' casino is pleasant and cheerful looking, with Mardi Gras–motif carpeting, light beige slot machines, and gaming tables under turn-of-the-century–style globe chandeliers. The facility boasts the world's largest slot machine (more than 9 feet high and almost 20 feet long; six people can play it at one time!) and the world's largest blackjack table (it seats 14 players). The Reel Winners Club offers slot players bonus points toward cash rebates. Slot, blackjack, and craps tournaments are frequent events, and there are major poker tournaments every January and May. The casino also offers exciting multiple-action blackjack (it's like playing three hands at once with separate wagers on each). Gaming facilities include a keno lounge, sports book, blackjack tables, craps, roulette, pai-gow poker, Caribbean stud, let-it-ride poker, and 1,021 slot/video poker machines.

SAM BOYD'S FREMONT HOTEL & CASINO   This 32,000-square-foot casino offers a relaxed atmosphere and low gambling limits ($2 blackjack, 25¢ roulette). Casino guests can accumulate bonus points redeemable toward cash by joining the Five Star Slot Club, and take part in frequent slot and keno tournaments. Gaming facilities include two keno lounges, a race and sports book, 16 blackjack tables, craps, roulette, Caribbean stud progressive poker, let-it-ride poker, pai-gow poker, and 1,000 slot/video poker machines.

GOLDEN NUGGET   This luxurious Downtown resort has a gorgeous casino reminiscent of the opulent gaming houses of Europe. Tables are located beneath stained-glass panels, and neon glitz is replaced by tivoli lighting. Slot players can earn bonus points toward complimentary rooms, meals, shows, and gifts by joining the 24 Karat Club. Gaming facilities include an attractive and comfortable keno lounge, a race and sports book, blackjack tables ($1 minimum bet), craps, roulette, baccarat, pai-gow, pai-gow poker, red dog, a Big Six wheel, and 1,136 slot/video poker machines.

HACIENDA HOTEL & CASINO   Styled after a Mexican hacienda, this lovely 35,000-square-foot casino has white stucco walls adorned with colorful paintings of flowers, fruit, and tropical birds. Slot players can join Club Viva! to earn points toward free stays, meals, show tickets, gifts, and tournament invitations. The Hacienda hosts many special events, including blackjack and slot tournaments. Gaming facilities: keno lounge, race and sports book, blackjack tables, craps, roulette, poker, pai-gow poker, Caribbean stud (progressive jackpot), and 1,050 slot/video poker machines.

HARD ROCK HOTEL AND CASINO   The Hard Rock's cheerful 30,000-square-foot circular casino, where you can place your bets to a high-energy beat, is a big favorite with the under-35 crowd. Note the chandelier at the entrance made from 32 gold saxaphones. Roulette tables are piano-shaped, slot machines have guitar-neck handles, win-a-Harley slots are equipped with motorcycle seats for players, and Elton John's bejeweled piano overlooks another bank of slots. Most original, however, is a bank of slots that make gambling an act of charity; environmentally committed owner Peter Morton (the Hard Rock's motto is "Save the Planet") donates profits from specified slots to organizations dedicated to saving the rain forests. A Back Stage Pass allows patrons to rack up discounts on meals, lodging, and gift shop items while playing slots and table games. The race and sports book here provides comfortable seating in leather-upholstered reclining armchairs. Gaming facilities (with selected nonsmoking tables) include blackjack tables, roulette, craps, Caribbean stud, minibaccarat, let-it-ride, pai-gow poker, and 802 slot/video poker machines.

HARRAH'S   Mirroring its exterior, Harrah's casino is Mississippi riverboat-themed, with gaming tables under gorgeous crystal chandeliers, facades of French Quarter homes, and dealers attired as riverboat gamblers. At 80,000 square feet, this is one of the larger facilities in town, and an additional 22,000 square feet will be added by 1997. It is the scene of numerous year-round slot and keno tournaments offering big prizes.

Other special features include a Sports Pit where gamblers can view athletic events on 35-inch TV monitors while playing blackjack; if you get a same-suit blackjack here, you can shoot hoops for prizes. Free hotdogs and peanuts are served to players, and, on weekends, there are sometimes cheerleaders. Another zany area is the balloon-festooned Party Pit (in action daily from noon to 4pm), where rock music is played, dealers sing and dance, players get prizes and party favors, and card games include a version of war (just like you played it when you were a kid). If you win a slot jackpot at Harrah's, entertainers (women dressed as riverboat belles, men as gamblers or Huck Finn) come by, play the song "Celebration," take your picture with a Polaroid camera, and present you with a medal and a package of "lucky dust." Slot and table game players can earn bonus points toward complimentary rooms, meals, and show tickets by acquiring a Harrah's Gold Card in the casino. Facilities include a sports book, keno lounge, poker room, blackjack, craps, roulette, minibaccarat, pai-gow poker, red dog, casino war, let-it-ride, a Big Six wheel, and 1,907 slot and video poker machines. There are nonsmoking areas, and free gaming lessons are offered weekdays.

IMPERIAL PALACE   The 75,000-square-foot casino here reflects the hotel's pagoda-roofed Asian exterior with a dragon-motif ceiling

---

Impressions _____

I am, after all, the best hold 'em player alive. I'm forced to play this tournament, you understand, to demonstrate this fact.
                    —Casino owner Bob Stupak on why he entered Binion's
                                    Horseshoe World Series of Poker

---

and giant wind-chime chandeliers. Visitors can get free Scratch Slotto cards for prizes up to $5,000 in cash (cards and free passes to the auto collection are distributed on the sidewalk out front). A gaming school offers lessons in craps and blackjack, and slots tournaments take place daily. The Imperial Palace boasts a 230-seat race and sports book, attractively decorated with oil murals of sporting events. The room is tiered like a grandstand, and every seat has its own color monitor. Other gaming facilities include a keno lounge, blackjack tables, craps, roulette, minibaccarat, pai-gow poker, Caribbean stud, a Big Six wheel, and 2,000 slot/video poker machines.

JACKIE GAUGHAN'S PLAZA HOTEL/CASINO   The Plaza has a lively and attractive crystal-chandeliered casino whose gaming facilities include a keno lounge (featuring double keno); race and sports book, blackjack tables, craps, roulette, baccarat, Caribbean stud, pai-gow poker, poker, pan, let-it-ride, and 1,572 slot/video poker machines. Cautious bettors will appreciate the $1 blackjack tables and penny slots here.

LADY LUCK   I like to gamble at the Lady Luck casino, a friendly Downtown facility. Dazzling neon signs, marquee lights, and balloons attached to slot machines make for a festive setting. The Mad Money Slot Club offers scrip, cash, meals, accommodations, and prizes as incentives. Liberal game rules are attractive to gamblers. You can play "fast action hold 'em" here—a combination of 21, poker, and pai-gow poker. Other gaming facilities include a keno lounge, blackjack tables, craps, roulette, minibaccarat, pai-gow poker, and 800 slot/video poker machines.

LAS VEGAS HILTON   Austrian crystal chandeliers make the Hilton's 67,000-square-foot casino one of the city's most elegant. Especially plush are the baccarat room—under a gorgeous crystal chandelier, its walls adorned with beautiful period paintings—and the VIP slot area where personnel are attired in tuxedos. Both areas offer gracious service to players. The Hilton's Race and Sports SuperBook is, at 30,500 square feet, the world's largest race and sports book facility. It, too, is a luxurious precinct equipped with the most advanced audio, video, and computer technology available, including 46 TV monitors, some as large as 15 feet across. In fact, its video wall is second in size only to NASA's. By joining Club Magic, a slot club, you can amass bonus points toward cash prizes, gifts, and complimentary rooms, meals, and show tickets. In addition to the above, gaming facilities include a keno lounge, blackjack tables, craps, roulette, baccarat, pai-gow, pai-gow poker, Caribbean stud, a Big Six wheel, and 1,130 slot/video poker machines.

LUXOR LAS VEGAS   This massive 100,000-square-foot casino—with red ceiling, carpeting, and gaming tables—evokes ancient Egypt with reproductions of artifacts and hieroglyphics found in the tombs and temples of Luxor and Karnak. Larger-than-life gold statues represent tomb guardians. In a variation on a horserace game, Egyptian boats race around a pyramid. And King Tut heads and sphinxes adorn slot areas. The Luxor's slot/video poker machines are equipped to change up to $100 in bills. There's a nonsmoking slot area. The Gold Chamber Club offers rewards of cash, merchandise, meals, and special services to slot and table players. And sports action unfolds on 17 large-screen TVs and 128 personalized monitors in Luxor's race and sports book. Additional gaming facilities include a keno lounge, blackjack tables, craps, roulette, poker (including Texas hold'em), baccarat, minibaccarat, pai-gow, Big Six wheels, Caribbean stud, and 2,500 slot/video poker machines.

MGM GRAND   The world's largest casino (171,500 square feet—that's bigger than Yankee Stadium!) is divided into four themed areas: Emerald City has a seven-story replica of the wizard's castle, a yellow-brick road, a 63-color rainbow, fluffy white clouds over gaming tables, and an animated robotic cast of Oz characters; you can win a $125,000 house on "there's-no-place-like-home" quarter slots. Hollywood is glitzy, with red and yellow marquee lights. The sports casino houses a big poker room, a state-of-the-art race and sports book, and the Turf Club Lounge. And the French Riviera–themed Monte Carlo casino has a luxurious marble-columned and gold-draped private high-end gaming area where French roulette is tended by European croupiers. Other unique MGM casino offerings include: a Fred Astaire robot accompanied by showgirls performing numbers such as *Puttin' on the Ritz*, a bank of astrologically themed slot machines where you can play your own sign, and, since Chrysler is a hotel sponsor, a number of win-a-car slots. The MGM Players Club offers guests prizes ranging from complimentary meals to $10,000 cash, not to mention MGM Grand stock. Gaming lessons are available. Gaming facilities include a race and sports book, keno lounge, over 100 blackjack tables, craps, roulette, French roulette (the only one in the United States), baccarat, minibaccarat, pai-gow, pai-gow poker, Caribbean stud, let-it-ride, Big Six wheels, and 3,500 slot/video poker machines.

MAXIM   This friendly, but dimly lit, 25,000-square-foot casino presents plaques to big slot winners. Its slot machines offer a red Grand Cherokee Laredo Jeep as a prize. Pick up a fun book here for a free $1,000 slot pull. Gaming facilities include a keno lounge, sports book, blackjack tables, craps, roulette, Caribbean stud, let-it-ride poker, pai-gow poker, and 848 slot/video poker machines.

THE MIRAGE   Entered via a tropical rain forest, this 95,400-square-foot casino is designed to resemble a Polynesian village with gaming areas under separate roofs to create a more intimate ambience. Facilities include a separate poker room and a plush European-style *salon privé* for high rollers at baccarat, blackjack, and roulette; an elegant dining room serves catered meals here. Slot players can join the Club Mirage and work toward bonus points for cash rebates, special room rates, complimentary meals and/or show tickets, and other benefits. The elaborate race and sports book offers theater stereo sound and a movie theater–size screen. Other gaming facilities here: a keno lounge, over 75 blackjack tables, craps, roulette, baccarat, minibaccarat, pai-gow, pai-gow poker, Big Six wheels, and more than 2,250 slot and video poker machines.

THE RIO　This Brazilian-themed resort's 85,000-square-foot casino is aglitter with neon and marquee lights. Rio Rita—a Carmen Miranda look-alike in a towering fruit-covered hat—presides over the casino from a thatched hut filled with colorful stuffed parrots. She greets visitors, congratulates winners, announces contests and promotions, and runs frequent slot, craps, and blackjack tournaments. In an area called Jackpot Jungle, slot machines amid lush foliage and live palms are equipped with TV monitors that present old movies and in-house information while you play. And in the high-end slot area ($5 to $100 a pull), guests enjoy a private lounge and gratis champagne. There are nonsmoking slot and gaming table areas. Facilities include a keno lounge, race and sports book, 40 blackjack tables, craps, roulette, baccarat, minibaccarat, pai-gow, Caribbean stud, survival dice, let-it-ride, a Big Six wheel, and 2,200 slot and video poker machines.

THE RIVIERA　The Riviera's 100,000-square-foot casino— one of the largest in the world—is also one of the most attractive on the Strip. A wall of windows lets daylight stream in (most unusual), and the gaming tables are situated beneath gleaming brass arches lit by recessed pink neon tubing. The casino's Slot and Gold (seniors) clubs allow slot players to earn bonus points toward free meals, rooms, and show tickets. The race and sports book here offers individual monitors at each of its 250 seats, and this is one of the few places in town where you can play the ancient Chinese game of *sic bo* (a fast-paced dice game resembling craps). Additional facilities include a large keno parlor, 42 blackjack tables, craps, roulette, baccarat, pai-gow poker, Caribbean stud, let-it-ride poker, Big Six wheels, and more than 1,400 slot/video poker machines.

THE SAHARA　In keeping with the hotel's desert theme, this 56,275-square-foot casino is watched over by statues of turbaned soldiers with scimitars at the ready. Not to worry, though; the dealers are friendly. The Sahara runs frequent slot tournaments and other events. Gaming facilities include a race and sports book, keno lounge, blackjack tables, craps, roulette, baccarat, poker, let-it-ride poker, pai-gow poker, red dog, Caribbean stud, 1 Big Six wheel, 6 pan tables, and slot/video poker machines. *Note:* This is the only Strip casino that offers pan, a card game.

THE SANDS   This 45,000-square-foot casino is a lively one, with a Charlie Chaplin look-alike roaming the premises and occasionally working the Big Six wheel. Part of the casino is adazzle with crystal-fringed red neon. The remainder (a newer section), lit by coral and blue recessed neon lights, has a wall of windows and open-air doors that beckon Strip pedestrians and bring the unusual phenomenon of daylight into the casino. The Sands offers free gaming instructions and fun books, hosts daily slot and weekly blackjack tournaments, and claims a minimum 97% return on all slots (more on some). There's a special "fun pit" bounded by balloons where minimum bets are $1 to $5 and bettors enjoy the patter of entertaining dealers, Caribbean music, and special chances to win a car. The Sandsational Bonus Slot Club gives players bonus points toward free meals, discounts, perks, and prizes. Gaming facilities include a keno lounge, a state-of-the-art race and sports book, blackjack tables, craps, roulette, poker, baccarat, minibaccarat, pai-gow, pai-gow poker, Caribbean stud, a Big Six wheel, and 1,100 slot/video poker machines.

SHOWBOAT   The Showboat's casino is undergoing a massive renovation at this writing. At its completion, it will have a Mardi Gras/Bourbon Street theme, and its ceiling will be raised to 25 feet. Gorgeous flower murals and trellised arches laced with flowery vines embellish the Showboat's enormous 24-hour bingo parlor—a facility also noted for high payouts. Slot players can join a club to accumulate bonus points toward free meals, rooms, gifts, and cash prizes. And if you're traveling with kids ages two to seven, you can leave them at an in-house babysitting facility free for 3 hours while you gamble. Older kids can be dropped at the Showboat's 106-lane bowling center. In addition to bingo, gaming facilities include a keno lounge, race and sports book, blackjack tables, craps, roulette, let-it-ride, pai-gow, Caribbean stud, and over 1,000 slot and video poker machines.

THE STARDUST   This casino features 90,000 square feet of lively gaming action, including a 250-seat race and sports book with a sophisticated satellite system and more than 50 TV monitors airing sporting events and horse racing results around the clock. Adjacent to it is a sports handicapper's library offering comprehensive statistical information on current sporting events. Stardust Slot Club members win cash rebates, with credit piling up even on nickel machines. Free rooms, shows, meals, and invitations to special events are other possible bonuses. Other gaming facilities: a large, well-lit keno lounge, a poker room, an elegant baccarat lounge, over 40 blackjack tables, craps, roulette, minibaccarat, pai-gow poker, Caribbean stud poker, let-it-ride poker, a Big Six wheel, and over 2,000 slot and video poker machines. If you're a novice, avail yourself of the gratis gaming lessons.

Impressions

The most exciting thing in craps is to win. The next most exciting thing is to lose.

—Nick the Greek

TREASURE ISLAND   Treasure Island's huge casino is one of the most elegant in Las Vegas. It is, however, highly themed. Niches— amid the rough-hewn oak beams of a woven-rattan ceiling—contain treasure chests overflowing with pirate loot; the carpeting is also littered with buccaneer booty; and ships' figureheads, a plush poker room hung with nautical paintings, and blackjack tables with eyepatch-wearing parrots further enhance the Caribbean pirate ambience. Especially luxurious are a high-limit baccarat/blackjack area (where players enjoy a buffet of hot hors d'oeuvres) and a high-limit slot area. Slot club members can earn meals, services, show tickets, and cash rebates. There are nonsmoking gaming tables in each pit. A race and sports book boasts state-of-the-art electronic information boards, and TV monitors at every seat as well as numerous large-screen monitors. Other facilities include a keno lounge, over 50 blackjack tables, craps, roulette, poker, minibaccarat, midibaccarat, pai-gow, pai-gow poker, Caribbean stud, let-it-ride, a Big Six wheel, and over 2,000 slot and video poker machines.

TROPICANA   The Trop casino is simply gorgeous, with gaming tables situated beneath a massive stained-glass archway, art nouveau lighting fixtures, and acres of tropical foliage. In summer it offers something totally unique—swim-up blackjack tables located in the hotel's stunning 5-acre tropical garden and pool area. Slot and table game players can earn bonus points toward rooms, shows, and meals by obtaining an Island Winners Club card in the casino. A luxurious high-end slot area called Fortune Cove has machines that take up to $100 on a single pull. Numerous tournaments take place here, and free gaming lessons are offered weekdays. Facilities include a sports book, keno lounge, poker room, blackjack tables, craps, roulette, baccarat, pai-gow poker, let-it-ride, Caribbean stud, minibaccarat, pai-gow, and 1600 slot and video poker machines.

WESTWARD HO HOTEL & CASINO   This small but centrally located strip casino hosts many slot tournaments, and slot players who obtain Preferred Customer cards can amass credits toward complimentary rooms, meals, and shows, among other benefits. Gaming facilities include 14 blackjack tables, craps, roulette, a Big Six wheel, and 1,000 slot/video poker machines.

9

Las Vegas Shopping

Unless you're looking for souvenir decks of cards and miniature slot machines, Las Vegas is not exactly a shopping mecca. It does, however, have several noteworthy malls that can amply supply the basics. And many hotels also offer comprehensive shopping arcades, most notably Caesars Palace (details below).

1 The Malls

Boulevard Mall

3528 S. Maryland Pkwy., between Twain Ave. and Desert Inn Rd. ☎ 702/735-8268. Mon–Fri 10am–9pm, Sat 10am–7pm, Sun noon–5pm.

The Boulevard's 144-plus stores and restaurants are arranged in arcade fashion on a single floor occupying 1,131,000 square feet. In terms of size, it's the largest in Nevada, and, when it opened in 1968, it was the first fully enclosed air-conditioned mall in the state. It's geared to the average consumer (not the carriage trade), with anchors like Sears, J. C. Penney, Woolworth, Macy's, Dillard's, and Marshalls. Other notables include branches of the Disney Store, The Nature Company, and Sesame Street; Colorado (for outdoor clothing and gear); Howard & Phil's Western Wear; and African & World Imports. There's a wide variety of shops offering moderately priced shoes and clothing for the entire family, books and gifts, jewelry, and home furnishings, plus over a dozen fast-food eateries. In short, you can find just about anything you need here.

Fashion Show Mall

3200 Las Vegas Blvd. S., at the corner of Spring Mountain Rd. ☎ 702/369-8382. Mon–Fri 10am–9pm, Sat 10am–7pm, Sun noon–6pm.

This luxurious and centrally located mall—one of the city's largest—opened in 1981 to great hoopla. Designers Adolfo, Geoffrey Beene, Bill Blass, Bob Mackie, and Pauline Trigere were all on hand to display their fashion interpretations of the "Las Vegas look."

The mall comprises more than 150 shops, restaurants, and services. It is anchored by Neiman-Marcus, Saks Fifth Avenue, Macy's, Robinsons-May, and Dillard's. Other notable tenants: Abercrombie & Fitch, the Disney Store, the Disney Gallery, The Discovery Channel Store, Lillie Rubin (upscale women's clothing), The Gap, Benetton, Uomo, Banana Republic, Victoria's Secret, Caché, Williams-Sonoma

Grand Cuisine, The Body Shop, Mondi (upscale women's clothing), Waldenbooks, Louis Vuitton, and Sharper Image. There are several card and book shops, a wide selection of apparel stores for the whole family (including large sizes and petites), 9 jewelers, 21 shoe stores, and gift and specialty shops. There are dozens of eating places (see chapter 6 for specifics). Valet parking is available, and you can even arrange to have your car hand washed while you shop.

The Meadows

4300 Meadows Lane, at the intersection of Valley View and U.S. 95. ☎ **702/ 878-4849.** Mon– Fri from 10am to 9pm, Sat and Sun until 6pm.

Another immense mall, the Meadows comprises 144 shops, services, and eateries, anchored by four department stores—Broadway, Dillard's, Sears, and J.C. Penney. In addition, there are 15 shoe stores, a full array of apparel for the entire family (including maternity wear, petites, and large sizes), an extensive food court, and shops purveying toys, books, CDs and tapes, luggage, gifts, jewelry, home furnishings (The Bombay Company, among others), accessories, and so on. Fountains and trees enhance the Meadows' ultramodern, high-ceilinged interior, and a 1995 renovation added comfortable conversation/seating areas and made the mall lighter and brighter. It is divided into five courts, one centered on a turn-of-the-century carousel (a plus for kids). A natural history–themed court has a "desert fossil" floor, and an entertainment court is the setting for occasional live musical and dramatic performances. You can rent strollers and get purchases gift wrapped at the Customer Service Center.

FACTORY OUTLETS

Las Vegas has two big factory outlets just a few miles past the southern end of the Strip. If you don't have a car, you can take a no. 301 or 302 CAT bus from anywhere on the Strip and change at Vegas World for a no. 303.

Belz Factory Outlet World

7400 Las Vegas Blvd. S., at Warm Springs Rd. ☎ **702/896-5599.** Mon–Sat 10am– 9pm, Sun 10am–6pm.

Belz houses 72 air-conditioned outlets, including 25 clothing stores and many shoe stores. It offers an immense range of merchandise at savings up to 75% off retail prices. Among other emporia, you'll find Adolfo II, Levi's, Nike, Dress Barn, Oshkosh B'Gosh, Leggs/Hanes/ Bali, Aileen, Bugle Boy, Carters, Oneida, Springmaid, Danskin, Van Heusen, Burlington, and Geoffrey Beene here. And since this is Las Vegas, laser shows are presented every hour on the hour.

Factory Stores of America

9155 Las Vegas Blvd. St., at Serene St. ☎ **702/897-9090.** Mon–Sat 10am–8pm, Sun 10am–6pm.

A 30-acre open-air mall with Spanish-style architecture, this is the only outlet center in the country with a casino bar/lounge on its premises. Its 51 stores include Corning/Revere, Izod, Mikasa, American

Factoid

In the last couple of years, one star has been seen in two very different films set in Las Vegas. In the first, the comedy *Honeymoon in Vegas,* he shares the spotlight with several hundred Elvis impersonators. In the second, the deadly serious *Leaving Las Vegas,* he plays a down-and-out screenwriter who goes to Vegas for one last binge. Who is the actor?
—Nicolas Cage

Tourister, Van Heusen, B.U.M. Equipment, Spiegel, London Fog, VF (sportswear), Book Warehouse, Geoffrey Beene, Adolfo II, and Arrow Shirts. Come here for clothing, housewares, toys, shoes, china, and much, much more.

2 Hotel Shopping Arcades

Just about every Las Vegas hotel offers some shopping opportunities. The following have the most extensive arcades. *Note:* The Forum Shops at Caesars—as much a sightseeing attraction as a shopping arcade—are in the must-see category.

BALLY'S Bally's Avenue Shoppes number around 20 emporia offering pro-team sports apparel, toys, men's, women's, and children's clothing, logo items, gourmet chocolates, liquor, jewelry, nuts and dried fruit, flowers, handbags, and T-shirts. In addition, there are several gift shops, art galleries, and a poolwear shop. There are blackjack tables and slot and video poker machines right in the mall, as well as a race and sports book. You can dispatch the kids to a video arcade here while you shop.

CAESARS PALACE Caesars has always had an impressive arcade of shops called the **Appian Way.** Highlighted by an immense white Carrara marble replica of Michelangelo's *David* standing more than 18 feet high, its shops include the aptly named Galerie Michelangelo (original and limited-edition artworks), jewelers (including branches of Ciro and Cartier), a logo merchandise shop, and several shops for up-scale men's and women's clothing. All in all, a respectable grouping of hotel shops, and an expansion is in the works.

But in the hotel's tradition of constantly surpassing itself, in 1992 Caesars inaugurated the fabulous **Forum Shops**—an independently operated 240,000-square-foot Rodeo-Drive-meets-the-Roman-Empire affair complete with a 48-foot triumphal arch entranceway, a painted Mediterranean sky that changes as the day progresses from rosy-tinted dawn to twinkling evening stars, acres of marble, lofty scagliola Corinthian columns with gold capitals, and a welcoming Goddess of Fortune under a central dome. Its architecture and sculpture span a period from 300 B.C. to A.D. 1700. Storefront facades—some topped with statues of Roman senators—resemble a classical Italian streetscape, with archways, piazzas, ornate fountains, and a barrel-vaulted ceiling.

The "center of town" is the magnificent domed Fountain of the Gods, where Jupiter rules from his mountaintop surrounded by Pegasus, Mars, Venus, Neptune, and Diana. And at the Festival Fountain, seemingly immovable "marble" animatronic statues of Bacchus (slightly in his cups), a lyre-playing Apollo, Plutus, and Venus come to life for a seven-minute revel with dancing waters and high-tech laser-light effects. The shows take place every hour on the hour.

More than 70 prestigious emporia here include Louis Vuitton, Plaza Escada, Bernini, Christian Dior, A/X Armani Exchange, bebe, Cache, Gucci, Ann Taylor, and Gianni Versace, along with many other clothing, shoe, and accessory shops. Other notables include: a Warner Brothers Studio Store (a sign at the exit reads THATIUS FINITUS FOLKUS), The Disney Store, Kids Kastle (beautiful children's clothing and toys), Rose of Sharon (classy styles for large-size women), Sports Logo (buy a basketball signed by Michael Jordan for $1,500!), Field of Dreams (more autographed sports memorabilia), Museum Company (reproductions ranging from 16th-century hand-painted Turkish boxes to ancient Egyptian scarab necklaces), West of Santa Fe (western wear and Native American jewelry and crafts), Antiquities (neon Shell gas signs, 1950s malt machines, Americana; sometimes "Elvis" is on hand), Endangered Species Store (ecology-themed merchandise), Brookstone (one-of-a-kind items from garden tools to sports paraphernalia), and Victoria's Secret. There's much more—including jewelry shops and art galleries. And a 225,000-square-foot expansion is in the works that will add 37 stores and two restaurants by 1997.

While you shop, send the kids downstairs for spine-tingling Motion-Simulator Cinema Rides in 3-D. Four 5-minute shows simulate a flight into outer space to destroy a runaway nuclear missile, a submarine race through the ancient ruins of Atlantis, a bicycle ride through a haunted graveyard, and a roller coaster adventure. Price is $5 for one film, $8 for a double feature. Children must be at least 42 inches high.

Dining choices range from a burger and malt at Boogie's Diner to a pastrami on rye at the Stage Deli, from a thick, juicy steak at The Palm to Wolfgang Puck's sublime Spago creations. Several Forum Shops restaurants are described in chapter 6.

The shops are open Sunday to Thursday from 10am to 11pm, Friday and Saturday 10am to midnight. An automated walkway transports people from the Strip to the shopping complex. Heralded by a marble temple housing four golden horses and a charioteer, it is flanked by flaming torchiers and fronted by a waterfall cascading over a bas-relief of the god Neptune—you can't miss it! Often a gladiator with sword and shield is there to greet you at the other end. Valet parking is available.

CIRCUS CIRCUS   About 15 on-premises shops offer a wide selection of gifts and sundries, logo items, toys and games, jewelry, liquor, resort apparel for the entire family, T-shirts, homemade fudge/candy/ soft ice cream, and, fittingly, clown dolls and puppets. At Amazing Pictures you can have your photo taken as a pinup girl, muscleman, or other persona. There are additional shops in Grand Slam Canyon, the hotel's amusement park.

A Las Vegas Specialty Store

Gambler's Book Shop, 630 S. 11th St., just off Charleston Blvd.
☎ 702/382-7555 or 800/522-1777.

Here you can buy a book on any system ever devised to beat casino odds. Owner Edna Luckman carries more than 4,000 gambling-related titles, including many out-of-print books, computer software, and videotapes. She describes her store as a place where "gamblers, writers, researchers, statisticians, and computer specialists can meet and exchange information." On request, knowledgeable clerks provide on-the-spot expert advice on handicapping the ponies and other aspects of sports betting. The store's motto is "knowledge is protection."

Open: Mon–Sat 9am–5pm.

EXCALIBUR   The shops of "The Realm," for the most part reflect the hotel's medieval theme. Ye Olde Candlemaker, for example, vends intricately sculptured candles, Heraldry offers sewn and painted family crests. Dragon's Lair features items such as miniature castles and pewter swords and shields, and the White Wizard creates clay wizards and other magical characters while you watch. Other shops carry more conventional wares— gifts, candy, jewelry, women's clothing, and Excalibur logo items. A child pleaser is Kids of the Kingdom, which displays licensed character merchandise from Disney, Looney Tunes, Garfield, and Snoopy. Wild Bill's carries western wear and Native American jewelry and crafts. And at Fantasy Faire you can have your photo taken in Renaissance attire.

FLAMINGO HILTON   A shopping arcade here accommodates men's and women's clothing stores, gift shops, and a variety of other emporia selling beachwear, southwestern crafts, liquor, Ethel M Chocolates, dried fruits and nuts, logo items, children's gifts and novelties, toys, and games.

HARRAH'S   Just outside the hotel, Harrah's offers a 6,000-square-foot New Orleans–style shopping complex called **Jackson Square.** Shops include Maison Rose for women's fashions (some items for men and children, too), Louisiana Limited (an old-fashioned general store for Louisiana/Las Vegas gifts), Holiday Jazz (liquor, snacks); and Cajun Spice (New Orleans gourmet items). Inside the hotel are a gift shop, logo shop, a florist, a jewelry shop, and a store featuring casual clothing for the whole family.

LUXOR HOTEL/CASINO   This hotel's unique retail outlets together comprise a kind of Egyptian bazaar. Especially noteworthy is The Source, on the arena level, where you'll find museum-quality Egyptian antiquities such as an alabaster portrait of Ptolemy V (205 B.C.) for $3,000 or a bronze Isis statue (664-525 B.C.) for $10,000. More affordable are beautiful Egyptian jewelry (both reproductions and Egypt-inspired designs), gift items (mother-of-pearl inlay boxes and tables, paintings, pottery, scarabs, and amulets), and books about ancient Egypt. An extensive selection of Egyptian-themed art, jewelry, apparel featuring King Tut and Nefertiti, pottery, musical instruments, and logo items can be found at the Scarab Shop, the Park Avenue Shop, and the rock-walled Innerspace (the latter also offers oils and incense, crystals, and New Age music). A more typical hotel gift/newspaper/magazine shop is Sobek's Sundries.

THE MGM GRAND　The hotel's Star Lane Shoppes include more than a dozen upscale emporia lining the corridors en route from the monorail entrance. The Knots Shop carries designer ties by Calvin Klein, Gianni Versace, and others. El Portal features luggage and hand-bags—Coach, Dior, Fendi, Polo Ralph Lauren, and other exclusive lines. Replicas of Marilyn Monroe's jewelry and *Gone With the Wind* T-shirts are among the movie-memorabilia merchandise at Hollywood & Grand. Similar in concept is Grand 50's, carrying *Route 66* jackets, Elvis T-shirts, photos of James Dean, and other mementoes of the 1950s. MGM Grand Sports sells signed athletic uniforms, baseballs autographed by Michael Jordan, and the like; it is the scene of occa-sional appearances by sports stars such as Floyd Patterson and Stan Musial. You can choose an oyster and have its pearl set in jewelry at The Pearl Factory. Other Star Lane Shoppes specialize in Oz-themed merchandise, Betty Boop-themed merchandise, *EFX* wares, children's clothing, decorative magnets, MGM Grand logo items and Las Vegas souvenirs, seashells and coral, candy, and sunglasses. Refreshments are available at a Häagen-Dazs ice cream counter and Yummy's Coffees and Desserts. In other parts of the hotel retail shops include a *Wizard of Oz* themed gift shop, Front Page (for newspapers, books, magazines, and sundries), a spa shop selling everything from beachwear to top-of-the-line European skin care products, a liquor store, a candy store, Kenneth J. Lane jewelry, and Marshall Rousso (men's and women's clothing). In addition, theme park emporia sell Hollywood memorabilia, cameras and photographic supplies, MGM Grand and theme park logo products, toys, fine china and crystal, animation cels, collectibles (limited-edition dolls, plates, figurines), Hollywood-themed clothing and accessories, and western wear. At Arts and Crafts you can watch artisans working in leather, glass, wood, pottery, and other ma-terials, and at Photoplay Gallery, you can have your picture taken as *Time* magazine's man or woman of the year.

THE RIVIERA　The Riviera has a fairly extensive shopping arcade comprising art galleries, jewelers, a creative photographer, and shops specializing in women's shoes and handbags, clothing for the entire family, furs, gifts, logo items, toys, phones and electronic gadgets, and chocolates.

THE SAHARA　The Sahara Shopping Arcade includes a Marshall Rousso's for women's apparel. Other shops carry children's clothing and toys, menswear, T-shirts, luggage and handbags, brass, flowers, logo items, jewelry, and gifts.

TREASURE ISLAND   Treasure Island's shopping promenade—doubling as a portrait gallery of famed buccaneers (Blackbeard, Jean Lafitte, Calico Jack, Barbarosa)—has wooden ship figureheads and battling pirates suspended from its ceiling. Emporia here include the Treasure Island Store (your basic hotel gift/sundry shop, also offering much pirate-themed merchandise), Loot n'Booty (stocked with exotic wares from India, Morocco, and other ports, as well as ship models and ships in bottles), Candy Reef (an old-fashioned candy store with beaded-silk Victorian lighting fixtures overhead), Captain Kid's (children's clothing, logo items, and toys), and Damsels in Dis'Dress (women's sportswear and accessories). The Mutiny Bay Shop, in the video-game arcade, carries logo items and stuffed animals. In the casino are the Buccaneer Bay Shoppe (logo merchandise) and the Treasure Chest (a jewelry store; spend those winnings right on the spot). And the Crow's Nest, en route to the Mirage monorail, carries Cirque du Soleil logo items. Similar wares are sold within the showroom.

10

Las Vegas Nights

No city in the world offers more excitement after dark than Las Vegas. In addition to casino gambling (see chapter 8), you have your choice of dozens of shows ranging from lavish production spectaculars to superstar entertainment. There are also comedy clubs, female impersonators, mind-boggling magicians, Broadway shows, and sexy revues, not to mention free lounge shows.

On my last visit, the following big-name entertainers were performing at hotel showrooms: George Carlin, Susan Anton, Fleetwood Mac, Pat Benatar, Bernadette Peters, Louie Anderson, Gladys Knight, The Righteous Brothers, Neil Sedaka, Debbie Reynolds, Buddy Hackett, Engelbert Humperdinck, Don Rickles, and Tony Bennett.

There were—and are—at least a dozen elaborate production shows in town, including magic/illusion shows, all featuring high-tech lighting and laser effects, sexy showgirls in feathered and sequined costumes, and great choreography. These shows cost a lot of money to produce, and so they have long runs. I've described every show now running in Las Vegas in detail, and though most will still be on when you read this book, some will no doubt have closed. Things change.

Casino lounge shows, which are either free or charge a one-drink minimum, also offer first-rate entertainment. Many of the headliners you see on major stages started out as lounge acts. You could have a great time just going from lounge to lounge without spending very much money.

Admission to shows runs a wide gamut, from about $16.95 for *An Evening at La Cage* (a female impersonator show at the Riviera) to more than $75 for top headliners or *Siegfried & Roy*. Prices may include two drinks or dinner.

To find out who will be performing during your stay, you can call the various hotels featuring headliner entertainment, using toll-free numbers. Or call the Las Vegas Convention and Visitors Authority (☎ 702/892-0711) and ask them to send you a free copy of *Showguide*.

Every hotel entertainment option is described below, with information on ticket prices, what is included in the price (drinks, dinner, taxes, and/or gratuities), showroom policies (as to assigned or maître d' seating and smoking), and how to make reservations. Whenever possible, reserve in advance, especially on weekends and holidays. If the showroom has maître d' seating (as opposed to assigned seats), you may want to tip him to upgrade your seat. A tip of $15 to $20 per couple will usually do the trick at a major show, less at a small showroom. An alternative to tipping the maître d' is to wait until the captain shows you to your seat. Perhaps it will be adequate, in which case you've saved some money. If not, you can offer the captain a tip for a better seat. If you do plan to tip, have the money ready; maître d's and captains tend to get annoyed if you fumble around for it. They have other people to seat. You can also tip with casino chips (from the hotel casino where the show is taking place only) in lieu of cash. Whatever you tip, the proper etiquette is to do it rather subtly—a kind of palm-to-palm action. There's really no reason for this, since everyone knows what's going on, but being blatant is in poor taste. Arrive early at maître d' shows to get the best choice of seats.

If you buy tickets for an assigned-seat show in person, you can look over a seating chart. Avoid sitting right up by the stage if possible, especially for big production shows. Dance numbers are better viewed from the middle of the theater. With headliners, you might like to sit up close.

Note: All of these caveats and instructions aside, most casino-hotel showrooms offer good visibility from just about every seat in the house.

Not to be missed: the incomparable *Siegfried & Roy* at the Mirage and the Cirque du Soleil's enchanting *Mystère* at Treasure Island. Best value for the money: *Country Fever* at the Golden Nugget.

1   The Major Production Shows

This alphabetical list of major production shows currently playing in Las Vegas gives the name of the hotel where the production resides and a brief description of the type of entertainment. Look under the names of the hotels in the next two sections for a more complete description of the show and its ticket policies.

- *Cirque du Soleil—Mystère,* at the Treasure Island (unique circus performance)
- *Copacabana Dinner Show,* at the Rio (Latin-themed review)
- *Country Fever,* at the Golden Nugget (country music review)
- *Country Tonite,* at the Aladdin (country music review)
- *Enter the Night,* at the Stardust (Las Vegas–style review)
- *Crazy Girls,* at the Riviera (sexy Las Vegas–style review)
- *Debbie Reynolds,* at the Debbie Reynolds Hotel (a Las Vegas review featuring Debbie)
- *EFX,* at the MGM Grand (musical review featuring Michael Crawford and amazing special effects)
- *An Evening at La Cage,* at the Rivera (review featuring female impersonators)
- *Folies Bergère,* at the Tropicana (Las Vegas–style review)
- *Forever Plaid,* at the Flamingo Hilton (off-Broadway–style review, featuring early '60s music)
- *Great Radio City Spectacular,* at the Flamingo Hilton (Las Vegas–style review, featuring the Radio City Music Hall Rockettes)
- *Jubilee,* at Bally's (Las Vegas–style review, featuring topless showgirls)
- *King Arthur's Tournament,* at Excalibur (medieval-themed review)

- *Lance Burton: World Champion Magician,* at the Hacienda (magic show and review)
- *Legends in Concert,* at the Imperial Palace (review featuring celebrity impersonators)
- *Siegfried & Roy,* at the Mirage (magical extravaganza, featuring trained animals)
- *Spellbound,* at Harrah's Las Vegas (magic-themed review)
- *Splash II,* at the Riviera (aquatic review)
- *Starlight Express,* at the Las Vegas Hilton (Andrew Lloyd Weber's Broadway show)
- *Symphony in White,* at Excalibur (afternoon show featuring the Lipizzaner stallions)
- *Xposed,* at Jackie Gaughan's (sexy Las Vegas–style review)

2   Entertainment at Hotels: On or Near the Strip

Aladdin Hotel & Casino

3667 Las Vegas Blvd. S., between Flamingo Rd. and Harmon Ave. ☎ **702/736-0419** or 800/637-8133.

The 7,000-seat **Theatre for the Performing Arts**—a major Las Vegas entertainment venue—hosts headliner concerts featuring acts like Kenny Rogers, Pearl Jam, the Allman Brothers, Yanni, Alan Jackson, the Scorpions, Sawyer Brown, Luther Vandross, Tears for Fears, Meatloaf, and Dwight Yokum. These alternate with Broadway shows (with touring-company casts) such as *Phantom of the Opera, Nutcracker on Ice, Dreamgirls,* and *Cats* and professional boxing and wrestling matches. There is a bar in the theater.

- **Showroom Policies:** Nonsmoking with preassigned seating.
- **Price:** $13–$100, depending on the performer/show/event (tax included; drinks extra).
- **Show Times:** Vary with the performer or show.
- **Reservations:** Policy varies with the performer, theatrical production, or event. Most shows can be reserved via **Ticketmaster** (☎ 702/474-4000 or your local outlet) or the Aladdin Theatre box office as soon as they are announced.

In its other showroom, the Aladdin presents *Country Tonite,* a lively revue with plenty of singin', fiddlin', guitar strummin', and foot-stompin' western dances. Highlights include Karen Brownlee's rendition of the legendary Patsy Kline's "Sweet Dreams," a lasso-and gun-twirling exhibition, cloggers, a "Devil Went Down to Georgia . . ." fiddling contest, and the antics of ventriloquist Sammy King and his Mexican parrot dummy. The show ends in a patriotic finale, with American flags flanking the stage and the cast performing "America the Beautiful," "All Gave Some, Some Gave All," "God Bless the USA," "Stand Up," and "We Shall Be Free."

- **Showroom Policies:** Nonsmoking with maître d' seating.
- **Price:** $17.95 adults, $11.95 for children under 12 (tax and drinks extra). With buffet adults pay $21.95, children $14.95.

- **Show Times:** Wed–Mon 7:15 and 10pm.
- **Reservations:** You can reserve up to 2 weeks in advance by calling 702/736-0240.

The Aladdin's **casino lounge** features live entertainment daily from about 3pm to as late as 5am—Top 40, country, Motown, and even big-band sounds. Often the group booked reflects the show at the Theatre for the Performing Arts. If, for instance, a top country star is playing there, a C&W band will be in the lounge. Off-hours sporting events are aired on a large-screen TV. No cover or drink minimum.

Alexis Park Resort
375 E. Harmon Ave. ☎ **702/796-3300.**

The very upscale Alexis Park offers live entertainment in its beautiful **Pisces Bistro**—a candlelit room under a 30-foot domed ceiling crossed with rough-hewn beams; balconied tiers are cascaded with greenery. When the weather permits, it's lovely to sit at umbrella tables on a terra-cotta–patio overlooking the pool. Live music is featured Wednesday through Saturday nights from 8pm till about midnight; a versatile pianist and vocalist perform everything from show tunes to oldies to Top 40. Light fare is available, along with specialty drinks and wines by the glass. No cover or minimum.

✪ Bally's
3645 Las Vegas Blvd. S. ☎ **702/739-4567** or 800/237-7469.

The 1,000-seat **Jubilee Theater**—with its vast stage, excellent design (not a bad seat in the house), and state-of-the-art technical equipment—presents a classic Las Vegas spectacular called *Jubilee*. It features dazzling sets and lighting effects and a magnificently costumed cast (many outfits were designed by Bob Mackie) of close to 100 singers and dancers. There are beautiful topless showgirls in sequins and feathers and hunky guys in studded-leather thongs. The show ranges from nostalgia numbers—honoring the songs and stars of yesteryear (a tribute to Elvis comprises the most up-to-date music)—to lavish production extravaganzas built around such themes as Samson and Delilah (culminating in the fiery destruction of the temple), the

---

Headliner Stadiums

Two arenas are worth a special mention since they often feature major entertainers. **Sam Boyd Stadium,** the outdoor stadium at the University of Nevada, Las Vegas (UNLV), has been host to such major acts as Paul McCartney, U2, the Eagles, and Metallica. **Thomas & Mack Center,** the university's indoor arena, has a more comprehensive concert schedule, including such names as Billy Joel, Michael Bolton, Elton John, ZZ Top, George Strait, and Garth Brooks. Both are located on the **UNLV campus** at Boulder Highway and Russell Road (☎ 702/895-3900). Ticketmaster (☎ 702/474-4000) handles ticketing for both arenas.

sinking of the *Titanic* (involving 5,000 gallons of water cascading through the set), and a World War I air battle. Interspersed with these are specialty acts (comics, acrobats, et al.). And the finale—a tribute to Fred Astaire and Ginger Rogers, Cole Porter, Jerome Kern, and George Gershwin—culminates in a parade of showgirls modeled after the Ziegfeld Follies.

- **Showroom Policies:** Nonsmoking with preassigned seating.
- **Price:** $44 (tax included, drinks extra).
- **Show Times:** Sun–Mon at 8pm, Tues–Thurs and Sat at 8 and 11pm; dark Fri.
- **Reservations:** You can reserve up to 6 weeks in advance.

Superstar headliners play the 1,400-seat **Celebrity Room.** Dean Martin inaugurated the facility, Today, frequent performers include Barbara Mandrell, The Oak Ridge Boys, Engelbert Humperdinck, Bernadette Peters, David Lee Roth, Harry Blackstone, George Carlin, Andrew Dice Clay, Paul Anka, Anne Murray, Louie Anderson, and Penn & Teller.

- **Showroom Policies:** Nonsmoking and preassigned seating.
- **Price:** $25–$45, depending on the performer (tax included, drinks extra).
- **Show Times:** There are one or two shows a night at varying times (this also depends on the performer).
- **Reservations:** You can reserve up to 6 weeks in advance.

Caesars Palace

3570 Las Vegas Blvd. S. ☎ **702/731-7333** or 800/445-4544.

You can make quite a night of it—or two or three—at Caesars. This is one hotel that doesn't stint on entertainment. In fact, just walking around the premises is quite a thrill.

From its opening in 1966, Caesar's 1,200-seat **Circus Maximus Showroom** has presented superstar entertainment—everyone from Judy Garland to Frank Sinatra. Many current headliners started out here as opening acts for established performers, among them Richard Pryor for singer Bobbie Gentry, Jay Leno for Tom Jones, and the Pointer Sisters for Paul Anka. In addition to the hundreds of headliners who have sparkled in the spotlight here, Caesars entertainment history includes many long-running theatrical productions. Theodore Bikel starred in a long run of *Fiddler on the Roof,* and Tony Randall performed *The Odd Couple* for the first time in a Caesars Palace production, launching a hit run on Broadway and a top-rated television show.

These days the format is headliners only, and the current lineup of luminaries includes Julio Iglesias, David Copperfield, Howie Mandel, Clint Black, Jerry Seinfield, Natalie Cole, Chicago, Burt Bacharach and Dionne Warwick, and Johnny Mathis. The luxurious showroom keeps to the Roman theme. Illuminated shields along the wall are replicas of those used by the legions of Caesar, and plush royal purple booths are patterned after Roman chariots (these can be reserved if you're willing to pay extra for tickets).

- **Showroom Policies:** Nonsmoking with preassigned seating.
- **Price:** $45–$75, depending on the performer (including tax, gratuity extra, drinks optional).
- **Show Times:** One or two shows nightly; times depend on performer.
- **Reservations:** You can reserve up to a month in advance via credit card.

Live bands play Top 40 dance tunes aboard **Cleopatra's Barge Nightclub,** a replica of the majestic ships that sailed the Nile in ancient Egypt. This waterborne dance club is also afloat on "the Nile," complete with oars, ostrich-feather fans, statues of ancient pharaohs, furled sails, and a canopied royal box. You board via gangplanks, and hydraulic mechanisms rock the barge gently. There's seating on the main barge, aboard two adjacent lesser craft, and on the dock. Nubian-inspired waitresses in diaphanous togas bring drinks. In the early days of this facility, Caesars found it necessary to construct a dockside fence to keep awestruck sightseers from falling into the river. There's no cover or minimum. Open Tuesday to Sunday 10pm to 4am.

In addition to the above, two casino facilities—the **Olympic Lounge** and the **La Piazza Lounge** offer live entertainment nightly. And there's an ultraelegant piano bar/lounge adjacent to the **Palace Court** restaurant—one of my favorite Las Vegas nightspots. No entry or drink minimum at any of these facilities.

The Carriage House

105 E. Harmon Ave. ☎ **702/739-8000.**

Kiefer's, the hotel's rooftop restaurant, has a plushly furnished adjoining piano bar/lounge with a dance floor. Windowed walls offer great views of the Las Vegas neon skyline, making this a romantic setting for cocktails and hors d'oeuvres. There's piano music Tuesday to Saturday from 8pm to midnight. No cover or minimum.

✪ Debbie Reynolds Hotel

305 Convention Center Dr. ☎ **702/737-3224.**

The very talented and boundlessly energetic Debbie Reynolds projects a warmth and relaxed stage presence seen only in the most seasoned of pros. And her beautiful 500-seat state-of-the-art Star Theatre (son Todd Fisher designed it) is filled to bursting with devoted fans at every performance. Debbie, as cute and exuberant as ever, sings, shows clips from her famous movies (like *Singin' in the Rain* and *The Tender Trap*), does impressions (her repertoire includes Katharine Hepburn, Bette Davis, Mae West, Zsa Zsa Gabor, Dolly Parton, Edith Bunker, and Barbra Streisand), cracks jokes, tells stories about her Hollywood heyday, and mingles with the audience. She is ably assisted by the Uptown Country Singers who perform popular country music songs and sing and dance with Debbie. The show ends with a tribute to the big-band era. After each performance Debbie meets fans in the showroom to sign autographs and pose for pictures.

- **Showroom Policies:** Nonsmoking with maître d' seating.
- **Price:** $34.95 (includes tax, two drinks, and gratuity).

- **Show Times:** Tues–Sat 8pm, Sun matinee 3pm.
- **Reservations:** You can reserve by phone up to 3 days in advance.

Every Friday and Saturday night from 10pm to 2am, an informal "show" called *Jazz & Jokes with Debbie Reynolds and Friends* takes place in the comfortable Celebrity Café. Basically, it's an intimate after-hours place where Strip entertainers, who are usually too keyed up to go home immediately after their shows, can hang out and unwind with Debbie. And being entertainers, they love to take the mike and belt out a few numbers. Among those who have already dropped by are Tony Bennett, blues singer Bobby Jones, Keely Smith, and comedian Steve Rossi. At its best this is great impromptu entertainment with a chance to star-gaze at close quarters. There is a $5 cover, plus a 2-drink minimum.

In addition, a pianist entertains in the casino Tuesday through Saturday from 3 to 7pm on Harold Lloyd's vintage Steinway. A life-size Mae West mannequin stands beside it, and nearby are mannequins of Laurel and Hardy.

(Sheraton) Desert Inn

3145 Las Vegas Blvd. S. ☎ **702/733-4444** or 800/634-6906.

The Desert Inn has a long history of superstar entertainment. Frank Sinatra's Las Vegas debut took place in the hotel's Painted Desert Room in 1951, and other early performers included Maurice Chevalier, Noël Coward, Buster Keaton, and Marlene Dietrich. Jimmy Durante once broke the piano board on a new spinet and yelled to the audience, "Mr. Hughes, it was broke when I got it!" And on one memorable night the entire Rat Pack (Dean Martin, Frank Sinatra, Joey Bishop, Sammy Davis, Jr., and Peter Lawford) invaded the stage when Eddie Fisher was performing! Today this historic showroom has been renamed the **Crystal Room.** Its major headliners include Taylor Dane, Tony Bennett, Smokey Robinson, The Temptations, The Everly Brothers, Gladys Knight, and Buddy Hackett.

- **Showroom Policies:** Nonsmoking with maître d' seating.
- **Price:** $35–$50, depending on the performer (including two drinks; tax and gratuity extra).
- **Show Times:** Tues–Sun 9pm.
- **Reservations:** Nonguests can reserve 3 days in advance, hotel guests can book shows when making room reservations.

The Desert Inn's **Starlight Theatre** is the most sophisticated casino lounge in town. It features name performers such as Sam Butera and Keely Smith, along with talented newcomers. It's a romantic setting for cocktails and dancing. No cover; occasionally there's a drink minimum. Open for entertainment Tuesday to Sunday 4pm to 2am.

Excalibur

3850 Las Vegas Blvd. S. ☎ **702/597-7600.**

Excalibur's primary entertainment offering is in keeping with its medieval theme. *King Arthur's Tournament* is a colorful tale of gallant knights and fair ladies—of romance, magic, medieval games, and pageantry—enlivened by pyrotechnics, lasers, fiber optics, and fancy lighting effects. Bursts of fireworks herald the presence of Merlin the

Impressions

*If I stand still while I'm singing, I'm a dead man. I might as well go
back to driving a truck.*
                                    —Legendary Las Vegas headliner Elvis Presley

magician in his star-spangled blue robe, and lasers add flash and drama
to sword fights and jousting contests. The story is about the battle
between the evil black knight and the heroic white knight for the
princess's hand in marriage. Each section of the arena is given a knight
to cheer, and the audience is encouraged to hoot, holler, and pound on
the tables (kids adore it). Knightly battles are complemented by lively
dances, equestrian acrobatics, tumblers, jugglers, and stunt riders. And
the show culminates, of course, in the victory of the white knight and
his marriage to King Arthur's fair daughter in a magnificent court wedding. Dinner, served during the show by "serfs" and "wenches," is a
robust affair eaten in lusty medieval style without utensils. It includes
a pot of creamy chicken soup, Cornish game hen, stuffed baked potato,
vegetable, biscuits, apple tart, and beverage.

* **Showroom Policies:** Nonsmoking with assigned seating.
* **Price:** $29.95 (including dinner, beverage, tax, and gratuity).
* **Show Times:** 6 and 8:30pm "knightly."
* **Reservations:** You can reserve up to 6 days in advance by
  phone via credit card.

In the same vast arena, Excalibur presents *Symphony in White,* starring the world-famous Lipizzaner stallions. Developed in Moorish
Spain from three superior equine breeds (Spanish Andalusian, Arabian,
and the swift and sturdy Karst of the Adriatic coast), these regal white
horses were trained in the elegant and graceful movements of dressage
and haute école and shown in Vienna's magnificent riding halls. The
Excalibur show is in that centuries-old tradition. Riders in the military
uniforms of imperial Austria present their stallions in a dignified pro-
cession set to classical music, and put them through a variety of complex movements—leaps, kicks, battlefield maneuvers, and historic
equestrian arts.

* **Showroom Policies:** Nonsmoking; seating is on a first-come
  basis.
* **Price:** $6.95 (including tax).
* **Show Times:** Mon–Fri 2pm, Sat–Sun noon and 2pm. Dark Wed.
* **Reservations:** Tickets can be purchased up to 3 days in advance
  at Excalibur ticket booths.

The medievally decorated **Minstrel's Theatre Lounge** offers live
20th-century bands nightly till about midnight weekdays, 3:40am
Friday and Saturday. No cover or minimum. See the hotel listing in
chapter 5 for other Excalibur entertainment possibilities.

Flamingo Hilton
3555 Las Vegas Blvd. S. ☎ **702/733-3333.**

The *Great Radio City Spectacular* begins with early movie footage of New York's Radio City Music Hall, a prelude to the synchronized shapely leg-kicking appearance of the world's most famous chorus line—the Rockettes. Highlights include a tribute to Fred Astaire, whose movies all debuted at Radio City; a Busby Berkley-esque Strauss waltz number with big white feather fans; a stunningly costumed and imaginatively choreographed dance to Ravel's *Bolero,* the charming "Parade of the Wooden Soldiers" from the Radio City Christmas show, and a "Stairway to the Stars" grand finale. Co-starring with the Rockettes are a series of guest hosts (at this writing Susan Anton, but that will change) who perform between dance numbers. Also featured are illusionists Tim Kole and Jenny Lynn. Another segment features Stacy Moore & His "Mess of Mutts," a comic dog troupe. Moore's highly trained canines are all abandoned animals he rescued from shelters and dog pounds. The dinner show menu features a choice of coq au vin, steak, roast prime rib, or poached salmon.

- **Showroom Policies:** Nonsmoking with maître d' seating.
- **Price:** Dinner show based on main-course price ($45.50–$53.55, including tax and gratuity; cocktail show $28.29 (includes two drinks, tax, and gratuity).
- **Show Times:** Dinner show 7:45pm nightly, cocktail show 10:30pm.
- **Reservations:** You can reserve 2 weeks in advance.

Bugsy's Celebrity Theatre presents the off-Broadway hit *Forever Plaid.* The plot line is bizarre, to say the least. The Plaids, an early 1960s harmony quartet on the order of The Four Freshmen, are killed on their way to their first big gig (at the Airport Hilton) when their car is broadsided by a busload of parochial-school girls en route to see the Beatles' U.S. television debut on "The Ed Sullivan Show." After 30 years, they've mysteriously returned to Earth (it has to do with the power of harmony and expanding holes in the ozone layer) to finally perform the show they never got to do in life. This totally weird context is just an excuse for a zany musical stroll down memory lane consisting of 29 oldies—songs like "Rags to Riches," "Sixteen Tons," "Love is a Many-Splendored Thing," "Three Coins in the Fountain," and "No, Not Much." If you're sentimental about that era, you'll love it.

- **Showroom Policies:** Nonsmoking with maître d' seating.
- **Price:** $17.95 (drinks and tax extra).
- **Show Times:** Tues–Sun 7:30 and 10:30.
- **Reservations:** Tickets can be reserved a week in advance.

Hacienda Casino & Resort

3950 Las Vegas Blvd. S. ☎ **702/739-8911.**

Note: The recent purchase of the Hacienda by Circus Circus will probably result in an eventual change in their entertainment offerings. Lance Burton will be at the Fiesta Theatre through March of 1996 and possibly longer; however, when the Monte Carlo opens, he will move there.

Magician extraodinaire Lance Burton was a player in the Tropicana's *Folies Bergère* for 9 years before creating his own show—*Lance Burton: World Champion Magician*—for the Hacienda's **Fiesta Theatre** in 1991. Lance is a charismatic performer (he looks a little like Elvis) and a first-rate magician who levitates birds and sexy showgirls, has himself executed onstage, makes women appear and disappear, flies into the air, and amusingly spoofs Strip superstar illusionists Siegfried & Roy. The show keeps a lively pace with dance numbers, sword fights, a hilarious comic juggler, and Lance's really expert showmanship.

- **Showroom Policies:** Nonsmoking with reserved seating.
- **Price:** $29 (includes tax, drinks extra).
- **Show Times:** Tues–Sat, 7:30 and 10:30pm, Sun 7:30pm.
- **Reservations:** Tickets can be reserved up to 2 weeks in advance by phone.

The **Bolero Lounge** in the casino offers live music (oldies and mellow rock bands) nightly from 9pm to 3am. No cover or minimum.

The Hard Rock Hotel and Casino
4455 Paradise Rd. ☎ **702/693-5000** or 800/693-7625.

The Eagles were the first act to play **The Joint,** the Hard Rock's 1,400-seat state-of-the-art live concert venue. Other performers during the hotel's opening festivities were Melissa Etheridge (with Al Green), B.B. King, Iggy Pop, Duran Duran, and Sheryl Crow. And since then the facility has presented Ziggy Marley, Hootie & the Blowfish, the Black Crowes, Stephen Stills, Todd Rundgren, Seal, James Brown, and Bob Dylan.

- **Showroom Policies:** Smoking permitted; seating preassigned or general, depending on the performer.
- **Price:** $20 to $100, depending on the performer (drinks and tax extra).
- **Show Times:** 8:30pm (nights of performance vary).
- **Reservations:** You can reserve up to 30 days in advance.

✪ Harrah's Las Vegas
3475 Las Vegas Blvd. S. ☎ **702/369-5111** or 800/392-9002.

Harrah's fast-paced and very entertaining magical extravaganza, *Spellbound,* is enlivened by a pulsating rock music score, a troupe of talented dancers in sexy costumes, and futuristic laser and lighting effects. The stars of the show—magician Mark Kalin and his beautiful assistant Jinger—combine great charm with thrilling artistry. Mark puts Jinger into a box and runs flaming swords through her (when he opens it, she is gone), transforms her into a slinky black panther (and himself into a tiger), lets her climb through his body, impales her on the point of a sword, and levitates her (passing a flaming hoop over her supine form). Joining Kalin and Jinger is the astounding Human Design—a superb trio, two of them Olympic athletes—whose slow-motion act, creating the illusion of ever-changing statues, is an amazing display of strength, controlled synchronized movement, and acrobatic skill. The show also features a comedian and exotic jungle animals.

- **Showroom Policies:** Nonsmoking with preassigned seating.
- **Price:** $29.65 (includes one drink, tax, and gratuity).
- **Show Times:** Mon–Sat 7:30 and 10:30pm.
- **Reservations:** You can charge tickets up to 30 days in advance via credit card.

The Improv at Harrah's, an offshoot of Budd Friedman's famed comedy club (the first one opened in 1963 in New York City), presents about four comedians per show in a 400-seat showroom. These are talented performers—the top comics on the circuit who you're likely to see on Leno and Letterman. You can be sure of an entertaining evening.

- **Showroom Policies:** Nonsmoking with preassigned seating.
- **Price:** $15.35 (includes tax, drinks extra).
- **Show Times:** Tues–Sun 8 and 10:30pm.
- **Reservations:** You can charge tickets up to 30 days in advance via credit card.

In addition to the above, the **Court of Two Gators,** a New Orleans–themed courtyard-style bar/lounge off the casino, features live bands for dancing Tuesday to Sunday from 8pm to 2am. The music ranges from mellow jazz to oldies. Monday night football games are aired in season; the rest of the year Monday is karaoke night. No cover or minimum.

Finally, on selected summer nights live rock and country bands entertain outside the hotel on the ship's bow. Admission is free.

Imperial Palace

3535 Las Vegas Blvd. S. ☎ **702/794-3261** or 800/351-7400, ext. 5.

An extravaganza called *Legends in Concert* has been playing at the 800-seat **Imperial Theatre** since May 1983. It has appeared on Broadway and, in 1991, toured the Russian cities of Moscow and St. Petersburg. Performers impersonate superstar entertainers with actual singing (no lip-synching), paying tribute to Michael Jackson, Whitney Houston, Liberace, Marilyn Monroe, the Blues Brothers, Buddy Holly, Neil Diamond, Paul McCartney, Cher, Madonna, Tom Jones, Elton John, Dolly Parton, and Barbra Streisand, among others. The roster of stars impersonated changes weekly, so you may not see all of the above, but I can guarantee an Elvis sighting nightly. The show utilizes dazzling high-tech lighting and laser effects, and singers are backed by a live onstage orchestra. Photographic blowups of the stars being imitated flank the stage.

- **Showroom Policies:** Nonsmoking, with maître d'seating.
- **Price:** $29.50 (includes two drinks or one Polynesian cocktail such as a mai tai or zombie; tax and gratuity extra).
- **Show Times:** Mon–Sat 7:30 and 10:30pm.
- **Reservations:** You can make reservations by phone up to a month in advance.

Las Vegas Hilton

3000 Paradise Rd. ☎ **702/732-5755** or 800/222-5361.

In 1993 the Hilton transformed its famed showroom (where Elvis played 837 sold-out shows in 10 years) into a gorgeous 1,500-seat oval theater to house Andrew Lloyd Webber's musical extravaganza on roller skates, *Starlight Express*. It's a dazzling high-energy, high-tech production, with futuristic sets and costumes, state-of-the-art sound and lighting effects, pyrotechnics, lasers, and a pulsating score that incorporates rock, country, jazz, and rap music. The fantasy of a nine-year-old boy playing with his model trains, *Starlight Express* is a love story, a sports story featuring a series of exciting train races enhanced by movie footage, and an inspirational tale of the triumph of the human spirit. Key characters include Rusty, a shy, well-intentioned steam engine who fears modern technology has passed him by; the Elvis-like Greaseball, a sleek diesel engine; Electra, a high-tech electric engine with an androgynous rock-star persona; and Rusty's dad, Poppa, a wise old steam engine. Needless to say, this modern version of "the little engine that could" is a great show choice for kids.

- **Showroom Policies:** Nonsmoking with preassigned seating.
- **Price:** $19.50–$45 (tax and drinks extra); $19.50 for children under 12.
- **Show Times:** Sun, Tues, and Fri–Sat 7:30 and 10:30pm; Wed–Thurs 9pm; dark Mon.
- **Reservations:** You can reserve by phone 3 months in advance.

The Hilton also boasts the 9,900-seat **Hilton Center,** a convention facility that is sometimes used for big-name concerts. The Beach Boys, Dennis Miller, and Rita Rudner have played here in recent years, and both Montel Williams and Donahue have used the Center stage for live shows. Information is available through the above-listed phone numbers.

The Nightclub—a plush balconied art deco lounge with color-changing etched-glass panels lit by fiber optics—is equipped with state-of-the-art sound and lighting systems. It features soul music, R&B, and contemporary dance tunes (there's a dance floor)—acts like King Cotton, Motor City Magic, Lil' Elmo & the Cosmos, Earl Turner, and the Royal Crown Revue. Open 3pm to 5am daily; no cover, one-drink minimum.

When sports action is over at the **SuperBook** every night, contemporary soft rock videos are aired on the largest of its monitors, and the room takes on a nightclub atmosphere. No cover or minimum. Drinks and food are available.

And the plush **Hilton Casino Lounge** features live music for dancing nightly through 3am. No cover; one-drink minimum.

Luxor Las Vegas
3900 Las Vegas Blvd. S. ☎ **702/262-4900.**

At press time, the Luxor's 1,100-seat oval arena—previously the setting for an Egyptian-themed extravaganza—is being converted into a classic Las Vegas showroom. No decision had yet been made on the entertainment that will take place here. Call for details.

The plush **Nefertiti's Lounge,** on the banks of the Nile in the casino, features live bands for dancing nightly from 8pm to 3am (no cover or minimum); off-hours sporting events are aired on a large-screen TV.

Impressions

I've built my own world here. Wayne's world.
—Las Vegas superstar Wayne Newton talking about his 52-acre estate,
Casa de Shenandoah, 5 miles out of town

☼ MGM Grand

3799 Las Vegas Blvd. S. ☎ **702/891-7777** or 800/929-1111.

Not surprisingly, this megahotel houses several entertainment facilities. Most notably, the 1,700-seat Grand Theatre presents *EFX*, a "multi-media mega-musical" extravaganza starring Michael Crawford (of *Phantom* fame) and a cast of 70 singers, dancers, acrobats, stunt people, and aerial artists. As the majestic *EFX* Master, Crawford takes us on a surrealistic high-tech journey through time and space to "worlds beyond imagination." He enters the vast stage soaring through clouds to introduce the masters of the four forces that govern *EFX:* Magic, Laughter, Spirit, and Time. In the persona of Merlin (backed by an elaborate stage set of a castle in an enchanted forest, complete with a mountain waterfall), he teaches young King Arthur about the magic of the natural world, and engages in a deadly wizard's duel of magical powers with the sorceress Morgana. He next presents an inter-galactic circus of wonders starring alien performers (two-headed women, peacocks of Pluto, and other strange creatures) who arrive onstage in a rainbow-hued spaceship. Next, Crawford appears as Houdini (many of whose famous illusions are re-created) at a seance led by Houdini's wife on the anniversary of his death. Finally, as H.G. Wells, he takes us on a mesmerizing 3-D journey through time—from the primitive world to the future. The $40-plus million production utilizes state-of-the-art scenery, lighting (there's enough electrical power here to power 1,440 homes!) and sound systems, mind-boggling spe-cial effects, phantasmagorical costumes, lasers, pyrotechnics, vibrating seats, and magnificent 3-D movie footage—not to mention anima-tronic fire-breathing dragons.

- **Showroom Policies:** Nonsmoking with preassigned seating.
- **Price:** $70 (including one drink, tax, and gratuity).
- **Show Times:** Fri-Wed 7:30 and 10:30pm. Dark Thurs.
- **Reservations:** You can reserve any time in advance.

The 15,222-seat **MGM Grand Garden Events Arena** is a major venue for sporting events. It also hosts big-name concerts. Barbra Streisand returned to the stage here after an absence of 25 years on New Year's Eve 1993. Others who have played the Arena include Luther Vandross, Janet Jackson, The Rolling Stones, Bette Midler, Billy Joel, Elton John, and Whitney Houston. Grand Garden Events tickets are generally also available through Ticketmaster (702/474-4000).

- **Showroom Policies:** Nonsmoking with preassigned seating.
- **Price:** Varies with event or performer.
- **Show Times:** Vary with event or performer.

- **Reservations:** Advance-reservations policy varies with event or performer.

The 650-seat **Hollywood Theatre** hosts headliners such as Don Rickles, Sheena Easton, Tom Jones, Manhattan Transfer, the Righteous Brothers, Dennis Miller, Rita Rudner, and Randy Travis. It has also featured occasional live telecasts of "The Tonight Show" with Jay Leno.

- **Showroom Policies:** Nonsmoking with preassigned seating.
- **Price:** Usually $35–$50, varies with performer (tax and drinks extra).
- **Show Times:** Vary with performer; there's usually a show at 9pm.
- **Reservations:** Tickets can be ordered anytime in advance as soon as they become available.

Entertainment lounges include the plush **Center Stage Lounge,** a tiered casino facility situated beneath a large dome that features high-energy Top 40 bands for dancing nightly from about 5pm to 2 or 3am (no cover; one-drink minimum). At the **Betty Boop Lounge,** off the casino, a Foster Brooks robot entertains customers with a 35-minute comedy set (no cover or minimum). In addition, the **Flying Monkey Bar** (backed by the Oz castle) and the **Santa Fe Lounge** offer live music nightly.

Maxim

160 E. Flamingo Rd. ☎ **702/731-4423** or 800/634-6987.

The Maxim houses a very attractive nightclub called **Comedy Max** featuring three comics nightly. Every seat is good.

- **Showroom Policies:** Nonsmoking, maître d' seating.
- **Price:** $16.25 (includes two drinks, tax, and gratuity). For $19.95 you can enjoy a buffet dinner as well.
- **Show Times:** 7, 9, and 10:30pm nightly.
- **Reservations:** You can reserve up to a week in advance by phone.

✪ The Mirage

3400 Las Vegas Blvd. S. ☎ **702/792-7777** or 800/627-6667.

The most spectacular hotel on the Strip also has the ultimate entertainment package featuring illusionists par excellence *Siegfried & Roy.* Not to mince praise, I'd as soon go to India and not visit the Taj Mahal as miss S&R in Las Vegas. For more than 2 decades, the Las Vegas show starring this dynamic duo has been the top show in town, playing to sellout audiences twice a night. Leave it to Steve Wynn to give them carte blanche (and $25 million) to build the 1,500-seat **Siegfried & Roy Theatre** to their own specifications. Producer Ken Feld contributed another $30 million to the new spectacle—making it the most expensive theatrical attraction ever staged. Singer Michael Jackson wrote and produced a song just for the show! The luxurious and very comfortable theater—designed so that no seat is more than 100 feet from the edge of the stage—features the world's most advanced computerized lighting and audio system. And the cast includes a company of 60 dancers and 2 dozen wild animals. Among the latter are the rare royal white tigers that have become an S&R trademark; they freely roam the stage during the show. These sorcerers supreme make elephants disappear, transform beautiful women into tigers, ride horses sideways and backwards, impale themselves on swords, are captured by aliens, levitate, set the stage on fire, and leap through flaming hoops. Enchanting dreamlike dance numbers feature demons, gossamer-winged fairies, and armies of human and mechanized soldiers in gold and silver armor battling a fire-breathing dragon. The laser and lighting effects, costumes, scenery, and choreography are unparalleled. Don't miss this awe-inspiring world of wonders.

- **Showroom Policies:** Nonsmoking with preassigned seating.
- **Price:** $78.35 (includes two drinks, souvenir brochure, tax, and gratuity).
- **Show Times:** Performances are Thurs–Tues at 7:30 and 11pm, except during occasional dark periods.
- **Reservations:** Tickets can be purchased on day of performance only. Box office opens at 8am. Arrive early.

The **Lagoon Saloon** in the tropical rain forest atrium offers live entertainment—reggae, light jazz, Top 40, and Cole Porter classics—for dancing till 2am Sunday to Wednesday, 3am Thursday to Saturday. Seating—in parrot-motif chairs at umbrella tables—is under an arbor of bougainvillea amid waterfalls and lagoons, and the bar top is a glass-covered beach strewn with seashells. Tropical drinks are a specialty. There's no admission; a two-drink minimum is in effect Friday and Saturday only.

In addition, a pianist plays show tunes and classic melodies nightly in the **Baccarat Bar,** adjacent to the baccarat pit off the casino. No cover or minimum. Jacket and tie are required for men.

Rio Suite Hotel & Casino

3700 W. Flamingo Rd. ☎ **702/597-5970** or 800/634-6787.

The Rio's deluxe **Copacabana Showroom**—a state-of-the-art theater in the round with tiered seating at individual tables—is the setting for the *Copacabana Dinner Show.* Exotic, upbeat, and pulsating with Latin rhythms, it stars a Carmen Miranda–like Rio Rita in a parade of elaborate tropical costumes. As you dine, a Latin band plays music for dancing, and the gorgeous scenery of Brazil is projected onto two 96-foot video walls. Acts include a Latin dance exhibition and lavish song and dance numbers. Food presentation, under the auspices of the zany Chef Rico, is a big part of the show. Chefs ascend from a recessed central stage, and as a cadre of waiters serves dinner, sexy dancers with carrot, corn, tomato, eggplant, and radish hats and lettuce-leaf fans are tossed into a vast salad bowl. At the end of the show, the audience—led by a cast member—congas out of the showroom and into the casino.

- **Showroom Policies:** Nonsmoking with preassigned seating.
- **Price:** $45.37 (includes dinner, tax, and gratuity; cocktails extra).
- **Show Times:** Tues–Sat, 6 and 8:30pm.
- **Reservations:** You can reserve by credit card up to 30 days in advance.

Club Rio, an upscale after-hours club, utilizes the luxurious Copacabana Showroom. A DJ plays Top 40 tunes and other high-energy sounds from 11pm to 3am nightly, and there's occasional live entertainment as well. Guests view music videos (and see themselves) on high-tech video walls. There's a $10 cover charge (for men only), no drink minimum.

The very simpatico **Ipenama Bar,** tropically themed with lush plantings and upholstered bamboo furnishings, features live music—reggae and Brazilian sounds. Cocktail waitresses wear sexy Ipenama girl costumes, and tropical drinks (such as the "Copa Banana"—banana liqueur, blackberry brandy, dark rum, and grenadine) are featured. No cover or minimum. The **Mambo Bar** in the casino—under thatched roofing with rice-paper fans overhead and bamboo furnishings—features live bands for dancing nightly (except Monday) from 9pm to 3am. During the day, sporting events are aired. No cover or minimum.

Riviera Hotel & Casino
2901 Las Vegas Blvd. S. ☎ **702/734-9301** or 800/634-6753.

The Riviera presents four big shows nightly, making it the Strip leader in entertainment offerings. Most lavish is *Splash II*—a lively revue that has been playing to sell-out audiences in the **Versailles Theatre** since 1985. As the name implies, the show is an aquacade extravaganza with an onstage 20,000-gallon tank surrounded by dancing fountains and waterfalls. A uniquely thrilling number features four stunt motorcyclists racing inside a 13$^1/_2$-foot sphere. There are gorgeous showgirls, mermaids, seahorses, and starfish, as well as divers, water ballet, comedy, magic, the world's fastest juggler, an exotic bird show, and acrobatic skits, all of which lead up to a spectacular finale—a musical excursion to the lost city of Atlantis. The show is enhanced by state-of-the-art lighting and laser technology.

- **Showroom Policies:** Nonsmoking with assigned seating.
- **Price:** $31.75–$53.75, the latter for best seats in the house (includes tax; drinks and gratuity extra).
- **Show Times:** 7:30 and 10:30pm nightly.
- **Reservations:** You can reserve by phone up to a month in advance.

An Evening at La Cage is based on the premise that "boys will be girls," with transvestite performers doing lip-synch impersonations of Diana Ross, Tina Turner, Aretha Franklin, Patti LaBelle, Peggy Lee, Cher, Shirley MacLaine, Roseanne Barr, Carol Channing, Bette Midler, Dionne Warwick, and Liza Minnelli. Frank Marino is "mistress of ceremonies" in the persona of comedienne Joan Rivers. And a performer in half-drag sings "Unforgettable" as both Nat and Natalie Cole. The show has lots of hilarious spicy schtick, and an overweight

Impressions

By creating a series of enchanted moments, we hope our audience will recall the time in their lives when they felt that anything was possible.
—Siegfried & Roy

Tammy Wynette does a comic version of "Help Me Make It Through the Night." There's also a first-rate Michael Jackson impersonator in the show, though having a female impersonator portray a male performer brings new meaning to the concept of androgyny. The show is presented in a small theater on the third-floor **Mardi Gras Plaza.**

- **Showroom Policies:** Nonsmoking with maître d' seating.
- **Price:** $16.95 (includes two drinks; tax and gratuity extra).
- **Show Times:** Wed–Mon 7:30 and 9:30pm, with an extra 11:15pm show Wed and Sat.
- **Reservations:** Tickets can be purchased at the box office only, in advance if you wish.

Crazy Girls—Sensuality, Passion & Pudgy!, presented in another intimate Mardi Gras Plaza theater, is probably the raciest revue on the Strip. It features sexy showgirls with perfect bodies in erotic song and dance numbers enhanced by innovative lighting effects. Think of *Penthouse* poses come to life. Comic relief is provided by the chubby Pudgy.

- **Showroom Policies:** Nonsmoking with maître d' seating.
- **Price:** $14.95 (includes two drinks; tax and gratuity extra).
- **Show Times:** Tues–Sun 8:30 and 10:30pm, with an extra midnight show Sat.
- **Reservations:** Tickets can be purchased at the box office only, in advance if you wish.

✪ The Riviera Comedy Club (formerly Budd Friedman's Improv)

Showcases four comedians nightly on the second floor of the Mardi Gras Plaza. Once a month, usually on the last weekend, the club hosts a late-night XXXTREME Comedy Showcase for shock and X-rated comedians. Other frequent special events include the *All Gay Comedy Revue* and Bill Kirchenbauer's Legends of Comedy (a talented troupe of impersonators who portray George Burns, Lucy and Desi, Sam Kinison, Bob Hope, and other comic legends).

- **Showroom Policies:** Nonsmoking with maître d' seating.
- **Price:** $13.95 (includes two drinks; tax and gratuity extra).
- **Show Times:** 8 and 10pm nightly, with an extra show at 11:45pm Fri and Sat.
- **Reservations:** Tickets can be purchased at the box office only, in advance if you wish.

Bottoms Up, billed as a "laughter-noon delight," combines vaudeville, burlesque, and musical comedy into a lively hour-long revue. Shows are presented on the second level of the Mardi Gras Plaza.

- **Showroom Policies:** Nonsmoking with maître d' seating.
- **Price:** $9.95 (drinks, tax, and gratuity extra).
- **Show Times:** Fri–Wed 2 and 4pm.
- **Reservations:** Tickets can be purchased at the box office only, in advance if you wish.

The elegant **Bistro Lounge** in the casino offers live entertainment through 3am nightly—Top 40 groups, jazz, and country. No cover; two-drink minimum.

Sahara Hotel & Casino

2535 Las Vegas Blvd. S. ☎ **702/737-2878.**

Since the Sahara was just completing a change of ownership at presstime—one that will involve major changes in all areas of the hotel and casino—scant details were available.

At this writing, plans are for the hotel's Congo Theatre to present major headliner performers (call or check local listings for specifics).

- **Showroom Policies:** Nonsmoking, maître d' seating.
- **Price:** $20–$40 (tax included, drinks extra).
- **Show Times:** Wed–Sun at 8pm.

The Sahara's Casbah Lounge (in the casino) presents live entertainment ranging from oldies to C&W daily from 2 to 6pm and 7pm to 4am. No cover, two-drink minimum.

Sands Hotel Casino

3355 Las Vegas Blvd. S. ☎ **702/733-5453** or 800/446-4678.

The famed **Copa Room** (in its early days the venue for "Rat Packers" Frank Sinatra, Sammy Davis, Jr., Dean Martin, and Joey Bishop) recently changed its format from production shows to headliners such as Frankie Valli, Neil Sedaka, and Gladys Knight.

- **Showroom Policies:** Nonsmoking with maître d' seating.
- **Price:** $18–$40 (tax, drinks, and gratuity extra).
- **Show Times:** Vary with the performer.
- **Reservations:** Policy varies with performer; you can usually reserve at least a week in advance by phone.

The Copa also presents a very popular afternoon show called *Viva Las Vegas,* combining comedy, singing, dancing, and magic. The acts change from time to time, but keep pretty much the same mix, and, of course, there are always leggy showgirls in fabulous costumes.

- **Showroom Policies:** Nonsmoking with maître d' seating.
- **Price:** $10 (tax and one drink included; gratuity extra).
- **Show Times:** Mon–Fri at 1 and 3:30pm.
- **Reservations:** You can reserve only 1 day in advance by phone.

In addition, the Sands's elegant crystal-chandeliered 1,100-seat **Celebrity Theatre** hosts headliners, many of them comics, such as Elayne Boosler, Louie Anderson, Rita Rudner, George Wallace, Steven Wright, and Rosie O'Donnell. On the other hand, you might catch James Brown here.

- **Showroom Policies:** Nonsmoking with maître d' seating.
- **Price:** $18–$40 (tax and drinks extra).
- **Show Times:** Vary with the performer.
- **Reservations:** Policy varies with the performer; you can usually reserve at least a week in advance by phone.

And live entertainment is featured in the **Winners Circle Lounge** daily from 1:15pm to 4am. Changing musical groups offer country, rock, Broadway hits, oldies, or Top 40 tunes. No cover or minimum.

The main character in Paul Verhoven's *Showgirls* gets a job in the
production show of a major Strip hotel. Which one?

—The Stardust

Stardust Resort & Casino

3000 Las Vegas Blvd. S. ☎ **702/732-6111** or 800/824-6033.

The **Stardust Theatre** has traditionally offered top-flight entertainment, and its current show is one of the very best in town. *Enter
the Night* is a high-tech, sophisticated version of the classic Las Vegas
spectacular—a multimedia production extraordinaire with awe-
inspiring laser and lighting effects, stunning sets and costumes, gorgeous showgirls, enchanting dance numbers, and great music that
runs the gamut from original songs to Fats Waller tunes. Performers
range from world champion ice skaters to Argentinean gaucho dancers; especially impressive is an incredibly choreographed number
in which six performers dance with laser lights. This show never
flags but moves from height to height, concluding with a massive
finale.

- **Showroom Policies:** Nonsmoking with preassigned seating.
- **Price:** $26.90 (includes two drinks and tax; gratuity extra).
- **Show Times:** Sun–Mon 7:30 and 10:30pm Wed–Sat 8pm.
- **Reservations:** You can reserve up to a month in advance by
  phone.

The **Starlight Lounge** in the casino offers contemporary live music (small bands and singers) daily from 4pm to 2am. Other times this
comfortable cocktail lounge transmits sporting events on a multiscreen
TV. No cover or minimum.

✪ Treasure Island at the Mirage

3300 Las Vegas Blvd. S. ☎ **702/894-7723** or 800/392-1999.

The superbly talented international **Cirque du Soleil** troupe stages
Mystère, its most ambitious production to date, at Treasure Island's
state-of-the-art 1,541-seat theater in the round. Under a lofty ceiling
laced with catwalks and painted to suggest a parchment world map, the
huge stage includes a circus ring, a 28-foot revolving turntable, and
sail-like screens used to project mists of kaleidoscopic color and form.
A cast of 70 artists—acrobats, clowns, actors, comedians, stilt-walkers,
ventriloquists, singers, dancers, and musicians—perform with the grace
of a ballet company and the precision of Olympic athletes. This sur-
real postmodern circus, combining high-tech special effects, seemingly
superhuman ability, and commedia dell'arte whimsy, is like nothing
you've ever seen before. The curved silver rods of a juggling act become
figures in a dance, acrobats scamper up and down poles with the
agility of chimps, Japanese Taiko drummers rap out primal rhythms,
iridescent-plumed trapeze artists on bungee cords soar like birds, and
opaque white Apollonian "human statues" bathed in chartreuse light
perform feats of strength and balance in mesmerizing slow motion.

Throughout the show, the audience is caught up in a dazzling mystical dream world. The music is haunting, the choreography and conception brilliantly creative, the lighting exquisite, costumes and sets ethereal. Cirque du Soleil is flawless.

- **Showroom Policies:** Nonsmoking with preassigned seating.
- **Price:** $48 adults, $24 for children under 12 (drinks and tax extra).
- **Show Times:** Wed–Sun 7:30 and 10:30pm.
- **Reservations:** You can reserve by phone via credit card up to 90 days in advance (do reserve early since it often sells out).

The comfortable **Captain Morgan's Lounge,** across from the registration desk and overlooking the casino, offers piano bar entertainment from late afternoon through 1 or 2am. Note the skull-and-bone chandeliers, gilded versions of originals in the Roman catacombs.

Tropicana Resort & Casino

3801 Las Vegas Blvd. S. ☎ **702/739-2411** or 800/468-9494.

The Trop's famous *Folies Bergère* is the longest running production show in town and one of the few remaining dinner shows. It's the quintessential Las Vegas extravaganza with a French accent—an enchanting mix of innovative scenery, lively music, bare-breasted showgirls in lavish feathered/rhinestoned/sequined costumes, and fast-paced choreography. Scene I is set in a turn-of-the-century Parisian music hall. Scene II salutes American music—gospel, blues, movie melodies, the big-band and swing eras—culminating in a medley of oldies from the '50s through the '90s. A highlight is a kaleidoscope dance number (they do it with mirrors). And Scene III once more celebrates the belle époque, leading up to a colorful can-can finale. Acts are punctuated by acrobatic numbers and comedy routines. *Note:* If you'd like to take a backstage tour of the Folies set, they are scheduled Tuesday, Thursday, and Friday at noon and 1pm, Wednesday and Saturday at 1 and 3pm. Tickets cost $3.50; call the above phone number for details.

- **Showroom Policies:** Nonsmoking with maître d' seating.
- **Price:** $22.95 (includes two drinks; tax and gratuity extra). You can have dinner at the 7:30pm show (admission is based on your entree price ($28.95–$32.95; tax and gratuity extra).
- **Show Times:** Fri–Wed 7:30 and 10:30pm.
- **Reservations:** You can charge tickets in advance via credit card.

A second Tropicana entertainment venue is the **Comedy Stop** (☎ **702/739-2714**), featuring three nationally known comedy headliners nightly.

- **Showroom Policies:** Smoking permitted with maître d' seating.
- **Price:** $12.95 (includes two drinks; tax and gratuity extra).
- **Show Times:** 8 and 10:30pm nightly.
- **Reservations:** You can charge tickets in advance via credit card.

The **Atrium Lounge** in the casino offers a variety of live music nightly from 5pm to 1:45am. No cover; one-drink minimum.

There are **laser light shows** nightly in front of the hotel beginning at 9pm.

3   Entertainment at Hotels: Downtown

Four Queens

202 E. Fremont St. ☎ **702/385-4011.**

The **French Quarter Lounge** of this delightful Downtown hotel presents live entertainment (usually superstar impersonators or oldies bands) every afternoon, when there is no cover or drink minimum. Monday night shows feature big bands and jazz artists such as Joe Williams, Si Zentner, Charlie Byrd, Mose Allison, Kenny Burrell, and Dorothy Donegan. Performances are at 7:30, 9:30, and 11:30pm. There's a one-drink minimum (about $4). Tuesday through Sunday there's karaoke at night in the lounge.

✪ Golden Nugget

129 E. Fremont St. ☎ **702/386-8100** or 800/777-4658.

The Golden Nugget has redecorated its showroom walls with a display of western paraphernalia and neon cacti, steer heads, and cowboy boots. It's the setting for *Country Fever*—the best foot stompin', hand-clappin' country music show in town—featuring a cast of tremendously talented singers and dancers, including bare-buttocked showgirls in fringed country thongs and cowboy boots (This is Las Vegas!). They're backed up by an outstanding nine-piece band called The Posse. Country superstar impersonators—dare I say it—actually outperform the singers they're imitating: George Strait, Reba McEntire, and Garth Brooks. A highlight is the exuberant T.J. Weaver's definitive rendition of "Friends in Low Places." *Country Fever* also features a thrilling gospel choir and a first-rate stand-up comic, Kirby St. Romaine. This high-energy show goes from height to height; country music fans will go wild, and nonbelievers may be converted.

- **Showroom Policies:** Nonsmoking with maître d' seating.
- **Price:** $22.50 (including a pitcher of beer, sangria, or soda and a basket of popcorn shrimp and chicken tenders); tax and gratuity extra).
- **Show Times:** Sat–Thurs 7:15 and 10:15pm.
- **Reservations:** You can reserve as far in advance as you like.

Jackie Gaughan's Plaza Hotel/Casino

1 Main St. ☎ **702/386-2444** or 800/634-6575.

At press time, a new show was about to open here, so I've yet to see it. Racily titled *Xposed,* it is billed as a "fast-paced, steamy, adults-only revue, featuring talented singers and dancers as well as hilarious comedy." Use your imagination.

- **Showroom Policies:** Smoking permitted, maître d' seating.
- **Price:** $19.95 (includes one drink; tax and gratuity extra).
- **Show Times:** Sat–Thurs 8 and 10pm.
- **Reservations:** You can reserve up to a week in advance by phone.

11

Easy Excursions from Las Vegas

Anyone who has seen the cascades of neon along the strip would agree that the Las Vegas way is to do things on a grand scale. What most visitors to Las Vegas don't realize is that the sense of being amid the extraordinary only shifts gears at the city limits; seeing the stark grandeur of the surrounding desert is an unforgettable experience in its own right. Also within easy reach are some of the country's most imposing man-made and natural wonders, such as the Hoover Dam and Red Rock Canyon; ghost towns, and other places where you can experience the flavor of the Old West; and innumerable opportunities for outdoor recreation—from white-water rafting to precipitous downhill skiing to desert hiking—all in a landscape like none other.

The following excursions will take you from 20 to 60 miles out of town. Every one of them offers a memorable travel experience.

1 Goodsprings—A Ghost Town

35 miles SW of Las Vegas

The shadowy phenomenon of ghost towns—once-flourishing areas that were later deserted and abandoned—has always been an intriguing and romantic image. Many of these towns began with one lone traveler who serendipitously stumbled upon mineral-rich rocks while out on another pursuit—perhaps tracking game or strayed livestock. He would mark off his area, stuff his pockets and knapsacks with specimens, and rush off to register his claim. Soon adventurers, drifters, and raggedy prospectors would flock to the area, set up meager lodgings, break out picks and shovels, and get to work. If the yield was promising, word would spread quickly, and entrepreneurs would arrive with provisions. A main street would develop around a general merchandise store, followed by other shops and the inevitable mining-camp saloons, gambling houses, and red-light district. Eventually a real town would emerge.

But then the mines would begin drying up. Little by little, businesses would fold, and the population would dwindle. Vandalism, wind, and fire would ravage the remaining structures, leaving only ghost-inhabited remnants of what had been. And so the town died. Nevada has at least 40 such towns, of which Goodsprings is the closest to Las Vegas.

Founded in the 1860s, and named for Joseph Good, a prospector, Goodsprings flourished as a silver and lead mining town around the turn of the century. During World War I, the Goodsprings Hotel was advertised in New York newspapers as "the finest in the West," and people from Las Vegas flocked here to shop, gamble, and see shows. The thriving metropolis had a population of 2,000, nine bars, several restaurants, a theater, churches, homes, and businesses. A narrow-gauge railroad carried ore from the surrounding mines to the Union Pacific tracks at nearby Jean. As the biggest town in Nevada, Goodsprings was a regular stop for Barnum & Bailey.

Shortly thereafter, mining days ended and the town began its decline. It has had only one brief brush with fame since. On January 16, 1942, Goodsprings made headlines because it was the closest town to Potosi Mountain where a plane, lost in a storm, crashed with movie star Carole Lombard on board. Her husband, Clark Gable, stayed briefly at the Goodsprings Hotel while awaiting further news. By 1967 Goodsprings's population had shrunk to 62. The hotel had burned to the ground, and one of its last remaining businesses, a general store, was torn down. Today it is an authentic ghost town—an eerie relic of Nevada's boom-and-bust mining era. All that remains of the once-thriving town is the rotting machinery of mining companies, discarded wrecks of old, abandoned cars—and the still-extant Pioneer Saloon.

ESSENTIALS

By car, follow I-15 south out of Las Vegas and turn onto Nev. 161 west at the Jean-Goodsprings turnoff. The first thing you'll pass—about a half mile before you get to the town itself—is a cemetery.

WHAT TO SEE AND DO

Stop at the cemetary and poke around a bit. It's a down-at-the-heels sort of place where perpetual care has not been a big thing. A couple of markers are wood, weathered almost to the point of illegibility. Most of the standard headstones are in a segment of the yard that has been fenced off by a low rail. All of these stones belong to the Fayle family, who were prominent Goodsprings citizens in the town's heyday. Surprisingly, there are some recent graves of desert-rat bikers here. In the area near the cemetery, you can search for Native American arrowheads, spearheads, and other artifacts.

The heart of Goodsprings is the **Pioneer Saloon** (☎ 702/ 874-9362), which from its dusty, run-down exterior does not look operative. It has, however, been a going concern since 1913. The only complete decorative-metal building left standing anywhere in the United States, the saloon has pressed-tin walls (interior and exterior) and ceiling. If you're nostalgic about old-time western saloons, you'll love the Pioneer. It's heated by a potbelly stove in winter and cooled by a swamp cooler in summer. Many of its fixtures and furnishings (even the curtains) are original to the saloon. Bartenders at the century-old cherry and mahogany bar regale customers with anecdotes about Goodsprings's past. A copy of the 1916 *Goodsprings Gazette* that

Excursions from Las Vegas

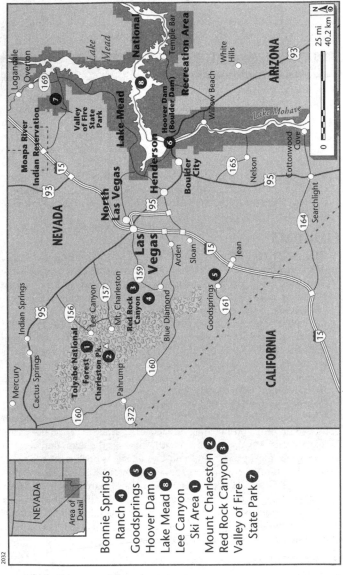

Bonnie Springs
Ranch **4**
Goodsprings **5**
Hoover Dam **6**
Lake Mead **8**
Lee Canyon
Ski Area **1**
Mount Charleston **2**
Red Rock Canyon **3**
Valley of Fire
State Park **7**

carries an advertisement for the saloon is displayed on one wall; while you're looking at the walls, note the bullet holes—legacy of a long-ago gunfight over a poker game. In addition to authentic ambience, the Pioneer offers such diverse entertainments as a pool table, dart board, jukebox, and poker machines. Personally, I found it thrilling to play pool in a ghost town. The Pioneer is open daily from 10am to midnight.

These days, Goodsprings may be making something of a comeback. Two big casino hotels, the **Gold Strike** and **Nevada Landing,** have been erected nearby, and the population is now up to about 110.

2 Hoover Dam and Lake Mead

30 miles SE of Las Vegas

This is one of the most popular excursions from Las Vegas, visited by 2,000 to 3,000 people daily. Wear comfortable shoes; the dam tour involves quite a bit of walking. The best plan would be to tour the dam in the morning, have lunch in Boulder City, take the Lake Mead dinner cruise, and stay a night or two at Lake Mead Lodge (details below) enjoying the area's scenic beauty and recreation facilities. Drive back to Las Vegas through the Valley of Fire, which is about 60 magnificently scenic miles from Lake Mead (purchase gas before your start!).

ESSENTIALS

GETTING THERE   By Car   Take U.S. 93 south from Las Vegas (it's a continuation of Fremont Street Downtown). As you near the dam, you'll see a five-story parking structure tucked into the canyon wall on your left. Park here and take the elevators or stairs to the walkway leading to the new Visitor Center.

If you would rather go on an **organized tour, Gray Line** (☎ 702/384-1234) offers several Hoover Dam packages, all of them including admission and a tour of the dam. The 5¹/₂-hour **Hoover Dam Express** excursion, departing daily at 8am and noon, also includes a stop at Cranberry World; price is $22.95 for adults, $20.45 for children 10 to 16 and seniors over 62, $17.95 for children under 10. The full-day **Deluxe Hoover Dam & City Highlights Tour,** departing daily at 10am and returning at 6pm, includes a stop at the Heritage Museum to view mining and ranching artifacts of frontier days, Boulder City (for spectacular views of Lake Mead), lunch at the dam, and visits to Ron Lee's World of Clowns and Cranberry World; adults $26.60, children 10 to 16 and seniors $24.10, under 10 $21.60. Most elaborate is the **Grand Hoover Dam Tour,** also departing daily at 10am and returning at 6pm, which includes the World of Clowns and a 1¹/₂-hour paddlewheeler cruise on Lake Mead; adults $36.50, children 10 to 16 and seniors $34.10, under 10 $31.60. You can inquire at your hotel sightseeing desk about other bus tours.

HOOVER DAM

Until Hoover Dam was built, much of the southwestern United States was plagued by two natural problems—parched, sandy terrain that lacked irrigation for most of the year and extensive flooding in spring and early summer when the mighty Colorado River, fed by melting snow from its source in the Rocky Mountains, overflowed its banks and destroyed crops, lives, and property. On the positive side, raging unchecked over eons, the river's turbulent, rushing waters carved the Grand Canyon.

Lake Mead & Vicinity

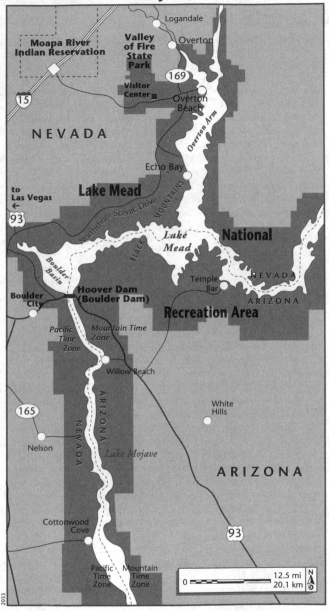

In 1928, prodded by the seven states through which the river runs during the course of its 1,400-mile journey to the Gulf of California, Congress authorized construction of a dam at Boulder Canyon (later moved to Black Canyon) under the auspices of the Bureau of Reclamation, U.S. Department of the Interior—the agency that still

Impressions

Everybody knows Las Vegas is the best town by a dam site.
                        —Masthead slogan of the *Las Vegas Review Journal*

operates it today. The Senate's declaration of intention was that "A mighty river, now a source of destruction, is to be curbed and put to work in the interests of society." Construction began in 1931. Because of its vast scope, and the unprecedented problems posed in its realization, the project generated significant advances in many areas of machinery production, engineering, and construction. An army of more than 5,200 laborers was assembled, and work proceeded 24 hours a day. Completed in 1936, 2 years ahead of schedule, the dam stopped the annual floods and conserved water for irrigation, industrial, and domestic use. Equally important, it became one of the world's major electrical generating plants, providing low-cost, pollution-free hydroelectric power to a score of surrounding communities. Hoover Dam's $175-million cost has been repaid with interest by the sale of inexpensive power to a number of California cities and the states of Arizona and Nevada. The dam is a government project that paid for itself—a feat almost as awe-inspiring as its engineering.

The dam itself is a massive curved wall, 660 feet thick at the bottom and tapering to 45 feet where the road crosses it at the top. It towers 726.4 feet above bedrock (about the height of a 60-story sky-scraper) and acts as a plug between the canyon walls to hold back up to 9.2 trillion gallons of water in Lake Mead—the reservoir created by its construction. Four concrete intake towers on the lake side drop the water down about 600 feet to drive turbines and create power, after which the water spills out into the river and continues south. All the architecture is on a grand scale, with beautiful art deco elements unusual in an engineering project. Note, for instance, the monumental 30-foot bronze sculpture, *Winged Figures of the Republic,* flanking a 142-foot flagpole at the Nevada entrance. According to its creator, Oskar Hansen, the sculpture symbolizes "the immutable calm of intellectual resolution, and the enormous power of trained physical strength, equally enthroned in placid triumph of scientific achievement."

The dam has become a major sightseeing attraction along with Lake Mead—America's largest man-made reservoir and a major Nevada recreation area.

Seven miles northwest of the dam on U.S. 93, you'll pass through **Boulder City,** which was built to house managerial and construction workers. Sweltering summer heat (many days it is 125°F) ruled out a campsite by the dam, whereas the higher elevation of Boulder City offered lower temperatures. The city emerged within a single year, turning a desert waste into a community of 6,000 with tree-shaded lawns, homes, churches, parks, restaurants, hotels, and schools. By 1934 it was Nevada's 3rd-largest town. Today, it continues to thrive with a population of 13,500; you might plan on having lunch here at **Totos,** a very good and reasonably priced Mexican restaurant at 806 Buchanan Blvd. (☎ 702/293-1744); it's in the Von's shopping center. About 300 yards past Boulder City, at the top of a slight incline, Lake Mead comes into view.

TOURING THE DAM

The **Hoover Dam Visitor Center,** a vast three-level circular concrete structure with a rooftop overlook, opened in 1995. You'll enter the Reception Lobby, where you can buy tickets, peruse informational exhibits, photographs, and memorabilia, and view three 12-minute video presentations in a rotating theater (respectively, about the importance of water to life, the events leading up to the construction of Hoover Dam, and the construction itself as well as the many benefits it confers). Additional exhibition galleries are in the works at this writing. Those on the Plaza Level will house interactive displays on the environment, habitation and development of the Southwest, the people who built the dam, and related topics. Galleries on the Overlook Level, yet another floor up, will demonstrate the benefits of Hoover Dam and Lake Mead to the states of Arizona, Nevada, and California. The Overlook Level additionally provides an unobstructed view of Lake Mead, the dam, the power plant, the Colorado River, and Black Canyon. You can visit an exhibit center across the street where a 10-minute presentation in a small theater focuses on a topographical map of the 1,400-mile Colorado River and the 14 dams and diversions along it. This building also houses a turbine and generator model and an information desk, and serves as a ticket purchase point for Lake Mead cruises. A gift shop and food concession are under construction in the parking structure.

Thirty-minute tours of the dam depart from the Reception Lobby every few minutes daily, except Christmas and Thanksgiving. The

---

Hoover Dam Factoids

- The amount of concrete used in the construction of the dam could pave a standard highway from San Francisco to New York.
- The minimum wage paid on the project was $4 a day.
- Ninety-six men died while building, excavating, blasting, and scaling mountains during construction, and on-the-job injuries totaled about 1,500 a month.
- In summer, the canyon rocks are so hot you could literally fry an egg on them.
- Lake Mead contains enough water to cover the entire state of Pennsylvania to a 1-foot depth.
- The dam was originally called Boulder Dam because of its first-designated canyon site, then renamed Hoover Dam in 1930 to honor Herbert Hoover's years of work making the project a reality. Unofficially it was renamed Boulder Dam by FDR who did not wish to honor Hoover; it finally regained the name Hoover Dam under Truman, who, in 1947, asked the 80th Congress to find out just what the "dam" name really was. Both names are still in popular usage.

Visitor Center opens at 8:30am, and the first tour departs soon after. The last tour leaves at 5:40pm, and the center closes at 6:30pm. Admission is $5 for adults, $2.50 for senior citizens and children 10 to 16, free for children under 10. More extensive hard-hat tours can be arranged by calling in advance (☎ 702/294-3522).

The tour begins with a 530-foot elevator descent deep into the dam's interior to one of the many galleries used for maintenance and inspection. There are more than 2 miles of galleries inside the dam at various levels. From the gallery, you'll proceed into the power plant, downstream through the thickness of the dam. Note, en route, the terrazzo floors that are inlaid with basketry and pottery designs of southwestern Native American tribes. The power plant consists of two similar wings, each 650 feet long, on either side of the river. From the visitor's balcony of the Nevada wing, you'll see eight huge hydroelectric generators (nine from the Arizona wing). These generators are driven by individual turbines located 40 feet below the floor. Water is delivered from the reservoir to the turbines (through canyon walls) via massive 30-foot-diameter pipes called penstocks. You'll learn about the manufacture of these generating units, each of which produces sufficient electrical energy to supply the domestic needs of a city of 95,000 people. Units lighted at the top are in operation. After visiting the generating room below, you'll go outside to see a tunnel through the 600-foot canyon wall that provides access to vehicles entering the power plant area. However, heavy equipment is lowered by a cableway that has a capacity of 150 tons! Looking up, you can see the control room for the cable operation. During construction, entire railroad cars loaded with materials were lowered into the canyon via this cableway. The drumlike tanks on the deck above are electrical transformers. Moving on to the Arizona wing, your guide (with the aid of a diagram) will explain construction procedures of the four tunnels that were drilled and blasted through solid rock and used to divert the river around the damsite. These diversion tunnels averaged 4,000 feet in length and 56 feet in diameter. When construction work advanced beyond the point where it was no longer necessary to divert water around the damsite, the tunnels were permanently sealed off. You'll also learn about the four intake towers which control the supply of water drawn from Lake Mead for the power plant turbines, and the spillways which, one on each side of the lake, control its maximum depth and ensure that no flood will ever overflow the dam. Finally, visitors stand in one of the diversion tunnels and view one of the largest steel water pipes ever made (its interior could accommodate two lanes of automobile traffic).

LAKE MEAD NATIONAL RECREATION AREA

Under the auspices of the National Park Service, the 1.5-million-acre Lake Mead National Recreation Area was created in 1936 around Lake Mead (the reservoir lake resulted from the construction of Hoover Dam) and later Lake Mohave to the south (formed with the construction of Davis Dam). Before the lakes emerged, this desert region was brutally hot, dry, and rugged—unfit for human habitation. Today it is one of the nation's most popular playgrounds, attracting about 9 million visitors annually. The two lakes comprise 290.7 square miles.

At an elevation of 1,221.4 feet, Lake Mead itself extends some 110 miles upstream toward the Grand Canyon. Its 550-mile shoreline, backed by spectacular cliff and canyon scenery, forms a perfect setting for a wide variety of water sports and desert hiking.

INFORMATION   The **Alan Bible Visitor Center,** 4 miles northeast of Boulder City on U.S. 93 at Nev. 166 (☎ 702/293-8990) can provide information on all area activities and services. You can pick up trail maps and brochures here, view informative films, and find out about scenic drives, accommodations, ranger-guided hikes, naturalist programs and lectures, birdwatching, canoeing, camping, lakeside RV parks, and picnic facilities. The center also sells books and videotapes about the area. It's open daily 8:30am to 4:30pm. For information on accommodations, boat rentals, and fishing also, call **Seven Crown Resorts** (☎ 800/752-9669).

ACTIVITIES   Hiking   The best season for hiking is November through March (too hot the rest of the year). Some ranger-guided hikes are offered via the Alan Bible Visitor Center, which also stocks detailed trail maps. Three trails—ranging in length from three-quarters of a mile to 6 miles—originate at the Visitor Center. The 6-mile trail goes past remains of the railroad built for the dam project. Be sure to take all necessary desert-hiking precautions (see details in chapter 7).

Camping   Lake Mead's shoreline is dotted with campsites, all of them equipped with running water, picnic tables, and grills. Available on a first-come, first-served basis, they are administered by the **National Park Service** (☎ 702/293-8990). There's a charge of $8 per night at each campsite.

Boating and Fishing   A store at **Lake Mead Resort & Marina** under the auspices of Seven Crown Resorts (☎ 702/293-3484 or 800/752-9669), rents fishing boats, ski boats, personal watercraft, and patio boats. It also carries groceries, clothing, marine supplies, sporting goods, waterskiing gear, scuba and fishing equipment, and bait and tackle. You can get a fishing license here ($45.50 a year, $30.50 for 10 days, $17.50 for 3 days, $8.50 for children 12 to 15, under 12 free). The staff is knowledgeable and can apprise you of good fishing spots. Largemouth bass, striped bass, channel catfish, crappie, and bluegill are found in Lake Mead, rainbow trout, largemouth bass, and striped bass in Lake Mohave. You can also arrange here to rent a fully equipped houseboat at **Echo Bay,** 40 miles north.

Other convenient Lake Mead marinas offering similar rentals and equipment are **Las Vegas Bay** (☎ 702/565-9111), which is even closer to Las Vegas, **Callville Bay** (☎ 702/565-8958), which is the least crowded of the five on the Nevada Shore.

Scuba Diving   October to April, there's good visibility, lessened in summer months when algae flourishes. A list of good dive locations, authorized instructors, and nearby dive shops is available at Alan Bible Visitor Center. There's an underwater designated diving area near Lake Mead Marina.

Rafting   Rafting trips on the Colorado River are offered February 1 through November 30 by **Black Canyon, Inc.,** 1297 Nevada Hwy. in

Boulder City (☎ 702/293-3776 or 800/696-7238). Twelve-mile trips begin at the base of Hoover Dam. You'll see canyon waterfalls and wildlife (bighorn sheep, wild burros, chuckwalla lizards, mallards, grebe, and the occasional golden eagle) and stop at a quiet cove for a picnic lunch. There are stunning rock formations en route, and the area is rich in history—southern Paiute rock shelters and 1920s river-gauging stations and cableways. Guides are quite knowledgeable about local lore. Prices (including lunch): $64.95 for adults, $35 for children ages 5 to 12, under 5 free. Bus transportation back to Las Vegas is available. Even if you don't go rafting, stop by Black Canyon Inc.'s Boulder City headquarters to see exhibits about the area and a film on Hoover Dam. Their office also functions as an information center and tour operator for a wide array of area activities (Grand Canyon flights, jetskiing, skydiving, and more).

Canoeing   The Alan Bible Visitor Center can provide a list of out-fitters who rent canoes for trips on the Colorado River. There's one catch, however: A canoeing permit ($5 for one; $10 for 2 to 5 canoes) is required in advance from the Bureau of Reclamation. Call 702/293-8204 Monday through Thursday for information.

Lake Cruises   A delightful way to enjoy Lake Mead is on a cruise aboard the *Desert Princess* (☎ 702/293-6180), a Mississippi-style paddle wheeler. Cruises depart year-round from the Hoover Dam Ferry Terminal, which is near Lake Mead Lodge (see below). At some time in the near future (possibly already as you read this), they will also depart from a dock right at the Hoover Dam Visitor Center; a ticket booth will be on the premises. It's a relaxing, scenic trip (enjoyed from an open promenade deck or one of two fully enclosed, climate-controlled decks) through Black Canyon and past colorful rock forma-tions known as the "Arizona Paint Pots" en route to Hoover Dam, which is lit at night. Options include buffet breakfast cruises ($21 adults; $10 children under 12), narrated midday cruises (light lunch fare available; $14.50 adults; $6 children), cocktail/dinner cruises (April 1 through October 31 only; $29 adults, $15 children, or $19 adults, $8 children without dinner), and sunset dinner/dance cruises with live music ($43 adults, children not allowed). Dinner cruises include a meal of salad, hot garlic bread, entree, fresh vegetable, rice pilaf or parsleyed red potatoes, dessert, and tea or coffee; it's served in a pleasant, window-filled, air-conditioned dining room. There's a full bar on board. Call for departure times.

WHERE TO STAY

Lake Mead Lodge

322 Lakeshore Rd., Boulder City, NV 89005. ☎ **702/293-2074** or 800/752-9669. 45 rms. A/C TV. Early Mar–late Nov $50–$65, the rest of the year $35–$50. Extra person $6. Children under 5 stay free in parents' room. DISC, MC. V.

If you aren't properly outfitted for camping at Lake Mead (see above), it's heavenly to spend a few nights relaxing at this tranquil lakeside resort, enjoying the area's numerous recreational activities and, per-haps, a leisurely dinner cruise. It's an easy drive from Hoover Dam. The rooms, housed in terra-cotta roofed cream-brick buildings, are comfortable and attractive with wood-paneled ceilings and walls of white-painted brick or rough-hewn pine. All offer full baths and cable TVs, and most have patios overlooking the lake. A lovely pool glitters in its lakeside setting, surrounded by mountains and beautifully land-scaped grounds planted with pines, palm trees, and flowering oleander bushes. Weathered-wood roped dock posts add a nautical look to the resort. You might want to relax with a good book in one of the gazebos on the property. About a half mile down the road is the ma-rina, where you can while away a few hours over cocktails on a lakeside patio. The marina is headquarters for boating, fishing, Lake Mead cruises, and water sports and it also houses a large shop (see details above under "Boating and Fishing"). And Boulder Beach, also an easy walk from the lodge, has waterfront picnic tables and barbecue grills.

Dining/Entertainment: There's a nautically themed restaurant called **Tale of the Whale** (☎ 702/293-3484) at the marina, its rough-hewn pine interior embellished with harpoons, figureheads, ship lanterns, ropes, pulleys, and steering wheels. Open from 7am to 9pm Sunday to Thursday, till 10pm Friday and Saturday, it serves hearty breakfasts; sandwiches, salads, and burgers at lunch; and steak-and-seafood dinners, all at moderate prices. Sometimes there's live music Friday and Saturday nights.

3 Valley of Fire State Park

60 miles NE of Las Vegas

Most people visualize the desert as a vast expanse of undulating sands punctuated by the occasional cactus or palm-fringed oasis. The desert of America's southwest bears little relation to this Lawrence of Arabia image. Stretching for hundreds of miles around Las Vegas in every direction is a seemingly lifeless tundra of vivid reddish earth, shaped by time, climate, and subterranean upheavals into majestic canyons, cliffs, and ridges.

The 39,000-acre Valley of Fire State Park, typifying the mountain-ous red Mojave Desert, derives its name from the brilliant sandstone formations that were created 150 million years ago by a great shifting of sand and continue to be shaped by the geologic processes of wind and water erosion.

Although it's hard to imagine in the sweltering Nevada heat, for billions of years these rocks were under hundreds of feet of ocean. This ocean floor began to rise some 200 million years ago and the waters became more shallow. Eventually the sea made a complete retreat, leav-ing a muddy terrain traversed by ever diminishing streams. A great sandy desert covered much of the southwestern part of the American continent until about 140 million years ago. Over eons, winds, mas-sive fault action, and water erosion sculpted fantastic formations of sand and limestone. Oxidation of iron in the sands and mud—and the effect of groundwater leaching the oxidized iron—turned the rocks the many hues of red, pink, russet, lavender, and white that can be seen today. Logs of ancient forests washed down from far away highlands and became petrified fossils which can be seen along two interpre-tive trails.

Human beings occupied the region—a wetter and cooler one—as far back as 4,000 years ago. They didn't live in the Valley of Fire, but during the Gypsum period (2000 B.C. to 300 B.C.), men hunted bighorn sheep (a source of food, clothing, blankets, and hut coverings) here with a notched stick called an atlatl that is depicted in the park's petroglyphs. Women and children caught rabbits, tortoises, and other small game. In the next phase, from 300 B.C. to A.D. 700, the climate became warmer and dryer. Bows and arrows replaced the atlatl and the hunters and gatherers discovered farming. The Anasazi people began cultivating corn, squash, and beans, and communities began replacing small nomadic family groups. These ancient people wove water-tight baskets, mats, hunting nets, and clothing. Around A.D. 300 they learned how to make sun-dried ceramic pottery. Other tribes, notably the Paiutes, migrated to the area. By A.D. 1150 they had become the dominant group. Unlike the Anasazis, they were still nomadic and used the Valley of Fire region seasonally. These were the inhabitants white settlers found when they entered the area in the early- to mid-1800s. The newcomers diverted river and spring waters to irrigate their farmlands, destroying the nature-based Paiute way of life. About 300 descendants of those Paiute tribespeople still live on the Moapa Indian Reservation (about 20 miles northwest) that was established along the Muddy River in 1872.

ESSENTIALS

GETTING THERE   By Car   From Las Vegas take I-15 north to Exit 75 (Valley of Fire turnoff). However, the more scenic route is to take I-15 north, then travel Lake Mead Blvd. east to North Shore Rd. (Nev. 167), and proceed north to the Valley of Fire exit. The first route takes about an hour, the second 1¹/₂ hours.

Numerous **sightseeing tours** go to Valley of Fire. **Gray Line** (☎ 702/384-1234), has a 7-hour tour from Las Vegas, including lunch, that costs $28.50 per person. Inquire at your hotel tour desk.

Valley of Fire can also be visited in conjunction with Lake Mead. **From Lake Mead Lodge,** take Nev. 166 (Lakeshore Scenic Dr.) north, make a right turn on Nev. 167 (North Shore Scenic Dr.), turn left on Nev. 169 (Moapa Valley Blvd.) west—a spectacularly scenic drive—and follow the signs. Valley of Fire is about 60 miles from Lake Mead.

WHAT TO SEE AND DO

There are no food concessions or gas stations in the park; however, you can obtain meals or gas on Nev. 167 or in nearby **Overton** (15 miles northwest on Nev. 169). Overton is a fertile valley town replete with trees, agricultural crops, horses, and herds of cattle—quite a change in scenery.

At the southern edge of town is the **Lost City Museum,** 721 S. Moapa Valley Blvd. (☎ 702/397-2193), commemorating an ancient Anasazi village that was discovered in the region in 1924. Its population reached one of the highest levels of Native American culture in the United States. Artifacts dating back 12,000 years are on display, as are clay jars, dried corn and beans, arrowheads, seashell necklaces, and willow baskets of the ancient Pueblo culture that inhabited this region between A.D. 300 and 1150. Other exhibits document the Mormon farmers who settled the valley in the 1860s. A large collection of local rocks—petrified wood, fern fossils, iron pyrites, green copper, and red iron oxide—along with manganese blown bottles turned purple by the ultraviolet rays of the sun are also displayed here. The museum is surrounded by reconstructed wattle and daub pueblos. Admission $2, free for children under 18. The museum is open daily from 8:30am to 4:30pm. Closed Thanksgiving, Christmas, and New Year's Day.

Information headquarters for Valley of Fire is the **Visitor Center** on Nev. 169, 6 miles west of North Shore Rd. (☎ 702/397-2088). It's open 7 days a week from 8:30am to 4:30pm. Exhibits on the premises explain the origin and geologic history of the park's colorful sandstone formations, describe the ancient peoples who carved their rock art on canyon walls, and identify the plants and wildlife you're likely to see. Postcards, books, slides, and films are on sale here, and you can pick up hiking maps and brochures. Rangers can answer your park-related questions.

There are hiking trails, shaded picnic sites, and two campgrounds in the park. Most sites are equipped with tables, grills, water, and rest rooms. A fee ($8 per night, per vehicle) is charged for use of the campground, and it costs $4 to enter the park.

Some of the notable formations in the park have been named for the shapes they vaguely resemble—a duck, an elephant, seven sisters, domes, beehives, and so on. Mouse's Tank is a natural basin that collects rainwater, so named for a fugitive Paiute called Mouse who hid there in the late 1890s. And Native American petroglyphs etched into the rock walls and boulders—some dating as far back as 3,000 years ago—can be observed on self-guided trails. Petroglyphs at Atlatl Rock and Petroglyph Canyon are both easily accessible. Always awe-inspiring, the park is especially beautiful in early spring when the desert blooms with wildflowers—mallow, desert marigold, and indigo bush—in dramatic contrast to the predominant earth tones. Other desert life forms include bighorn sheep, ground squirrels, bats, kit foxes, jackrabbits, gila monsters, rattlesnakes, and lizards. And numerous birds—cactus and rock wrens, ravens, finches, and sage sparrows, as well as migrant species—are best observed in the early morning or late afternoon. In summer, when temperatures are usually over 100°, you may have to settle for driving through the park in an air-conditioned car.

4 Mount Charleston and Lee Canyon Ski Area

Mount Charleston: 40 miles NW of Las Vegas; Lee Canyon: 47 miles NW of Las Vegas

In summertime, the mountains that encircle Toiyabe National Forest are as much as 30° to 40° cooler than the sweltering desert city. These mountains, once an island in an ancient sea, are today a cool oasis in the desert. The highest peak towers 11,918 feet above sea level. It's a beautiful drive. Nev. 157 winds up for about 21 miles through gorgeous canyon scenery, and, as you ascend, desert vegetation—cactus, yucca, creosite bush, and Joshua trees—gives way to stands of juniper, dense ponderosa forest, aspen firs, and bristlecone pine. The highway ends at the lovely **Mount Charleston Resort.** You can plan a day around lunch here, with activities like hiking, camping, bird watching, and horseback riding. In winter, there are sleigh rides, and you can ski at nearby **Lee Canyon.** In summer, there are hayrides, scenic chair-lift rides in the ski area, barbecues, and a music festival.

It's a twilight-zone feeling to come from hot and air-conditioned Las Vegas to this sometimes snowy region where you can sit in front of a blazing fire sipping a hot buttered rum. Both the Mount Charleston Resort and the Mount Charleston Hotel serve as information centers for area activities. In addition to the below-listed attractions, see "Staying Active" in chapter 7.

ESSENTIALS

GETTING THERE   By Car   Take I-15 north and stay in the Reno Lane to U.S. 95 north. Make a left on Nev. 157.

During ski season you can catch a **bus** to the Lee Canyon Ski Area. Departure points vary each year. For details, call 702/646-0008. There is no bus transportation to Mount Charleston.

WHAT TO SEE AND DO

Under the auspices of the Mount Charleston Resort are the **Mt. Charleston Riding Stables** (☎ 702/872-7009 or 702/386-6899 from Las Vegas), offering marvelously scenic trail rides to the edge of the wilderness. These depart from stables on Kyle Canyon Road. Since the schedule varies, it's best to call in advance for details. Weather permitting, the stables also offer horse-drawn sleigh rides Thanksgiving Day through March ($7 for adults, $4 for children 10 and under) and hayrides Memorial Day through Labor Day ($5 for adults, $3 for children).

Forty pine-sheltered and secluded picnic groves are equipped with barbecue grills.

There are numerous **hiking trails,** ranging from short panoramic walks to waterfalls near the restaurant/lounge to more difficult hikes farther afield. A popular 5-mile trail beginning at Lee Canyon Highway takes you through a canyon of aspen and into forested areas of ponderosa, white fir, and bristlecone pine. There are picnic areas and campsites along some trails. For information on camping and hiking trails, contact the **U.S. Forest Service,** 2881 S. Valley View Blvd., Suite 16, Las Vegas, NV 89102 (☎ 702/873-8800). For camping information and reservations, you can also call 800/280-CAMP. Both the Mount Charleston Resort and the Mount Charleston Hotel can provide trail maps.

The **Las Vegas Ski and Snowboard Resort,** at the end of Nev. 156 (☎ 702/646-0008), has a base elevation of 8,510 feet which, along with an extensive snow-making system, provides an almost ideal climate and snow cover for skiing Thanksgiving Day through Easter Day. Facilities include a lodge, a complete ski school, an extensive ski-rental shop, a snowboard park, a coffee shop, and a lounge with blazing fire-place and sundeck. Three double chair lifts carry skiers over 40 acres of well-maintained slopes (in summer, you can ride them for scenic views Friday through Monday). And summer weekends, the resort is the scene of a country/bluegrass and rock music festival.

WHERE TO STAY

The Mount Charleston Hotel

2 Kyle Canyon Rd. (on Nev. 157). ☎ **702/872-5500** or 800/794-3456. 60 rms. 3 suites. A/C TV TEL Single or double Sun–Thurs $39–$59, Fri–Sat $69–$89; $155 suite. Extra person $5. Children under 12 stay free in parents' room. Inquire about ski packages. AE, CB, DC, DISC, MC, V.

Nestled in the mountains, this three-story property offers lodgings in a rustic log and stone building. Its lobby, with massive stone fire-places, mounted deer heads, and a lofty beamed pine ceiling, resembles a ski lodge. The accommodations aren't fancy, but they're attractively deco-rated in earth tones and forest green; cathedral ceilings and balconies make third-floor rooms especially desirable. And nicest of all are the suites with convertible sofas in the living rooms, larger balconies, and wood-burning stone fireplaces. Facilities include a Jacuzzi and sauna in a windowed room, a small video-game arcade, and a gift shop. Room service is available from 8am to 9pm.

Dining/Entertainment: The hotel's hexagonal **Canyon Dining Room** has a lot of rustic charm. Decorated in forest green and peach, it has two working fireplaces, windows all around overlooking beau-tiful mountain scenery, and heavy wrought-iron chandeliers suspended from a cathedral pine ceiling. At night it's romantically candlelit. All meals are available here including full and continental breakfasts. Lunch fare includes moderately priced burgers, sandwiches, fajitas, pizzas, and salads (everything's under $9). And dinner entrees ($8.95 to $19.95) offer a choice of lighter fare (pizzas and pasta dishes) along with a steak-and-seafood menu. Like the restaurant, the simpatico adjoining lounge—scene of live music Tuesday through Sunday nights (Monday, football games are aired in-season)—has a full window wall and a working fireplace.

Mount Charleston Resort

End of Nev. 157. ☎ **702/386-6899** or 800/955-1314. 24 cabins. Sun–Thurs stan-dard cabin (for one or two) $105, deluxe (for up to four) $135; Fri–Sat standard cabin $160, deluxe $200. Extra person $10. All include full or continental breakfast. AE, CB, DC, DISC, MC, V.

These charmingly rustic pine log cabins, built right into the mountain-side to proffer stunning scenic views, are a delight. Beautifully deco-rated with southwestern and Native American artifacts (Paiute drums and decorative blankets, sheepskin rugs, steer horns), they have peaked ceilings beamed with rough-hewn logs, oak parquet floors, and lots of windows. Knotty-pine furnishings are complemented by oversized king beds and attractively upholstered armchairs and sofas, each room has a working gas fireplace and a whirlpool tub big enough for two, and in-room amenities include fan chandeliers and coffeemakers (coffee, tea, and cocoa are provided). A big plus: each cabin has a furnished mountain-view terrace which provides an ideal setting for the gratis continental breakfast (fresh-baked croissants, muffins, coffee, grapefruit, and juice) delivered to your room with the morning paper each day. Or you can opt for a full American or Mexican breakfast (also gratis) in the resort's restaurant (see details below). In addition to breakfast, a fresh fruit basket is delivered to your cabin every afternoon, and warm chocolate-chip cookies arrive about 7pm. This serene getaway is the perfect antidote to Las Vegas glitz and glitter, and, for couples, it would be hard to come by a more romantic setting.

WHERE TO DINE

Mount Charleston Resort

End of Nev. 157. ☎ **702/386-6899** or 800/955-1314. Reservations recommended. Breakfast main courses $4.50–$9.75; lunch main courses $3–$9.75; dinner main courses $13.50–$19.50. AE, CB, DC, DISC, MC, V. Sun–Thurs 8am–9pm, Fri–Sat until 10pm; the bar/lounge is open 24 hours. AMERICAN/CONTINENTAL.

This warmly inviting mountain chalet centers on a vast hooded fireplace stacked high with massive ponderosa pine and cedar logs. Wagon-wheel chandeliers are suspended from a lofty beamed ceiling, and large windows provide magnificent vistas. Mid-May to the end of October, you can sit at umbrella tables on a patio nestled in the wooded mountains, and you'd be hard pressed to find a more exquisitely peaceful setting. The lounge isn't fancy; it's a casual, kickback kind of place. At night, however, it is romantically candlelit, and there's dancing to live music weekends and holidays. At lunch weekends and holidays, a Bavarian oompah-pah band called the Dummkopfs entertains.

The restaurant serves all meals, beginning with hearty country breakfasts (available through 5pm) such as eggs with wild-game sausages, hash browns, homemade biscuits, and gravy. Mexican breakfasts (eggs wrapped in tortillas with chili and cheddar) are another tempting option. At lunch there are sandwiches, salads, and full entrees ranging from Dijon-honey-glazed broiled salmon with rice pilaf and vegetable to broiled pork chops served with applesauce, vegetable, and fries. Dinner entrees include wild-game specialties such as marinated elk steak topped with snow crabmeat, asparagus, and sauce béarnaise. Other choices include steaks, pasta dishes, and seafood. Everything is fresh and cooked on the premises, including homemade breads and desserts. At night the bar here is quite popular. Come by after dinner for a hot buttered rum or Mount Charleston coffee—a Jamaican blend spiked with brandy and Scotch liqueur, topped with homemade vanilla ice cream and a dollop of real whipped cream.

In 1995, the resort built 24 lovely cabins on its grounds; see details above.

5 Red Rock Canyon

19 miles W of Las Vegas

Less than 20 miles from Las Vegas, Red Rock Canyon is worlds away experientially—a magnificent unspoiled vista which, in its timeless beauty, is the perfect balm for your casino-jaded soul. You can simply drive the panoramic **13-mile Scenic Drive** (open daily 7am till dusk) or explore in depth. There are many interesting sights and trailheads along the drive itself. The wider **National Conservation Area** offers hiking trails and internationally acclaimed rock-climbing opportunities (especially notable is the 7,068-foot Mt. Wilson, the highest sandstone peak among the bluffs). There are picnic areas along the drive and also in nearby **Spring Mountain Ranch State Park** 5 miles south. Since Bonnie Springs Ranch (see the next section) is just a few miles away, it makes a great base for exploring Red Rock Canyon.

ESSENTIALS

GETTING THERE   By Car   You simply drive west on Charleston Blvd., which becomes Nev. 159. Look for the Visitor Center on your right.

You can also go on an **organized tour.** Numerous companies, including **Ray & Ross** (☎ 702/646-4661 or 800/338-8111) and **Gray Line** (☎ 702/384-1234), run bus tours to Red Rock Canyon (and also Bonnie Springs Ranch). Inquire at your hotel tour desk.

Finally, you can go **by bike.** Not very far out of town (at Rainbow Blvd.), Charleston Blvd. is flanked by a bike path that continues for about 11 miles to the Visitor Center/Scenic Drive. The path is hilly but not difficult if you're in reasonable shape. However, exploring Red Rock Canyon by bike should be attempted only by exceptionally fit and experienced bikers. For bike rental information, see chapter 7.

Just off Nev. 159, you'll see the **Red Rock Canyon Visitor Center** (☎ 702/363-1921). It's open daily from 8am to 4:30pm, and you can pick up information on trails; there are also history exhibits on the canyon. A visit to Red Rock Canyon can be combined with a visit to Bonnie Springs Ranch.

ABOUT RED ROCK CANYON

The geologic history of these ancient stones goes back some 600 million years. Over eons, the forces of nature have formed Red Rock's sandstone monoliths into arches, natural bridges, and massive sculptures painted in a stunning palate of gray-white limestone and dolomite, black mineral deposits, and oxidized minerals in earth-toned sienna hues ranging from pink to crimson and burgundy. Orange and green lichens add further contrast, as do spring-fed areas of lush foliage. And formations like Calico Hill are brilliantly white where groundwaters have leached out oxidized iron. Cliffs cut by deep canyons tower 2,000 feet above the valley floor.

During most of its history, Red Rock Canyon was below a warm shallow sea. Massive fault action and volcanic eruptions caused this seabed to begin rising some 225 million years ago. As the waters receded, sea creatures died and the calcium in their bodies combined with sea minerals to form limestone cliffs studded with ancient fossils. Some 45 million years later, the region was buried beneath thousands of feet of windblown sand. The landscape was as arid as the Sahara. As time progressed, iron oxide and calcium carbonate infiltrated the sand, consolidating it into cross-bedded rock. Shallow streams began carving the Red Rock landscape, and logs that washed down from ancient highland forests fossilized, their molecules gradually replaced by quartz and other minerals. These petrified stone logs, which the Paiute Indians believed were weapons of the wolf god, Shinarav, can be viewed in the Chinle Formation at the base of the Red Rock Cliffs. About 100 million years ago, massive fault action began dramatically shifting the rock landscape here, forming spectacular limestone and sandstone cliffs and rugged canyons punctuated by waterfalls, shallow streams, and serene oasis pools. Especially notable is the Keystone Thrust Fault, dating back about 65 million years when two of the earth's crustal plates collided, forcing older limestone and dolomite plates from the ancient seas over younger red and white sandstones. Over the years, water and wind have been ever creative sculptors, continuing to redefine this strikingly beautiful landscape.

Red Rock's valley is home to more than 45 species of mammals, about 100 species of birds, 30 reptiles and amphibians, and an abundance of plant life. Ascending the slopes from the valley, you'll see cactus and creosote bushes, aromatic purple sage, yellow-flowering blackbrush, yucca and Joshua trees, and, at higher elevations, clusters of forest-green piñon, juniper, and ponderosa pines. In spring, the desert blooms with fiery red globe mallow, magenta monkeyflowers, pink-blossomed redbud trees, pristine white forget-me-nots, golden desert marigolds, and lavender phacelia. Among the animal denizens of the canyon are bighorn sheep, antelope ground squirrels, mule deer, kangaroo rats, lizards, California jackrabbits and desert cotton-tails, gray and kit foxes, tortoises, coyotes, bobcats, rattlesnakes, reclusive gila monsters, even mountain lions. Burros and wild horses are not indigenous but descended from animals that were set free by, or escaped from, miners in the 1800s. And commonly observed birds include eagles and hawks, roadrunners, turkey vultures, loggerhead shrike, cactus wrens, quail, mourning doves, broad-tailed hummingbirds, woodpeckers, horned larks, western bluebirds, American robins, northern mockingbirds, yellow warblers, sage sparrows, and peregrine falcons.

Archeological studies of Red Rock—which turned up pottery fragments, remains of limestone roasting pits, stone tools, pictographs (rock drawings), and petroglyphs (rock etchings), along with other ancient artifacts—show that humans have been in this region since about 3000 B.C. (some experts say as far back as 10,000 B.C.). You can still see remains of early inhabitants on hiking expeditions in the park. The Anasazi (also known as the "Basketmaker" people and "the Ancient Ones") lived here from the 1st century A.D. Originally hunter-gatherers, they learned to farm maize, squash, and beans and began forming communities. From pit houses, they progressed to elaborate structures of up to 100 rooms and became known as the Pueblo Indians. They departed from the area (no one knows why) about A.D. 1150, and the Paiutes—who were still essentially hunter-gatherer nomads—became the dominant group. Until the mid-1800s, the Paiutes lived here in perfect harmony with nature—a harmony destroyed when white settlers arrived and began felling the pine forests for timber, introducing grazing livestock that destroyed food and medicinal plant sources, and decimating the Native American population with European diseases to which they had no immunity. By the 1880s, the Paiutes were forced onto reservations, their culture and way of life in shambles.

In the latter part of the 19th century, Red Rock was a mining site and later a sandstone quarry that provided materials for many buildings in Los Angeles, San Francisco, and early Las Vegas. By the end of World War II, as Las Vegas developed, many people became aware of the importance of preserving the canyon. In 1967 the Secretary of the Interior designated 62,000 acres as Red Rock Canyon Recreation Lands under the auspices of the Bureau of Land Management, and later legislation banned all development except hiking trails and limited recreational facilities. In 1990 Red Rock Canyon became a National Conservation Area, further elevating its protected status; its current acreage is 197,000.

Today Red Rock Canyon affords visitors the opportunity to experience nature's grandeur and serenity—to leave the stresses of daily life behind and get in touch with greater realities.

WHAT TO SEE AND DO

First, you'll want to stop off at the Visitor Center. There you can view exhibits, enhanced by an audio tour, that tell the history of the canyon and depict its plant and animal life. You'll also see a fascinating video here about Nevada's thousands of wild horses and burros, protected by an Act of Congress since 1971. At the Center, you can obtain trail maps, brochures, permits for hiking and backpacking, and other information about the canyon. Call ahead to find out about ranger-guided tours as well as informative guided hikes offered by groups like the Sierra Club and the Audubon Society. Hiking trails range from a 0.7-mile loop stroll to a waterfall at Lost Creek (a spring that flows year-round) to much longer and more strenuous treks involving rock scrambling. A popular 2-mile round-trip hike leads to Pine Creek Canyon and the creekside ruins of a historic homesite surrounded by ponderosa pine trees. On trails along Calico Hills and the escarpment, look for "Indian marbles," a local name for small rounded sandstone rocks that have eroded off larger sandstone formations. And, if you're traveling with children, ask about the free *Junior Ranger Discovery Book* filled with fun family activities. Books and videotapes are on sale here, including a guidebook identifying more than 100 top-rated climbing sites. After you tour the canyon, drive over to Bonnie Springs Ranch (details in the next section) for lunch or dinner. See chapter 7 for further details on biking and climbing.

6 Bonnie Springs Ranch/Old Nevada

About 24 miles W of Las Vegas, 5 miles past Red Rock Canyon

Bonnie Springs Ranch/Old Nevada is a kind of Wild West theme park with accommodations and a charmingly rustic restaurant. If you're traveling with kids, a day or overnight trip to Bonnie Springs is recommended, but there's much for adults, too. It could even be a romantic getaway, offering horseback riding, gorgeous mountain vistas, proximity to Red Rock Canyon, and temperatures 5 to 10 degrees cooler than on the Strip.

ESSENTIALS

GETTING THERE   If you are traveling **by car,** a trip to Bonnie Springs Ranch can be combined easily with a daytrip to Red Rock Canyon; it is about 5 miles. But you can also stay overnight.

For those without transportation, there are **Ray & Ross shuttle buses** to and from Las Vegas. Call 702/646-4661 or 800/338-8111 for details.

For additional information, you can call **Bonnie Springs Ranch/ Old Nevada** at 702/875-4191.

WHAT TO SEE AND DO AT BONNIE SPRINGS RANCH

Old Nevada attractions are detailed below. However, even if you just come out here for lunch, you can enjoy several things free of charge. A **small zoo** on the premises is home to dozens of animals—burros, mouflon sheep, buffalo, steer, raccoons, ferrets, ducks, red squirrels, coyotes, coatis, an Arctic fox (donated by singer Wayne Newton), porcupines, wolves, bobcats, guinea pigs, and rabbits. There are always baby animals, and llamas, potbelly pigs, deer, and miniature goats roam free and can be petted and fed.

There's also an **aviary** housing peacocks (including a rare white peacock), Polish chickens, peachface and blackmask lovebirds, finches, parakeets, ravens, ducks, pheasants, and geese.

Riding stables offer guided trail rides into the mountain area on a continuous basis throughout the day (from 9am to 3:15pm spring through fall, until 5:45pm in summer). Children must be at least 6 years old to participate. Cost is $17.50 per hour.

And scenic 20-minute **stagecoach rides** offered weekends and holidays cost $5 for adults, $3 for children under 12.

WHAT TO SEE AND DO IN OLD NEVADA

Old Nevada (☎ 702/875-4191) is a microcosm of a mid-1800s western Nevada town, its main street lined with weathered-wood buildings fronted by covered verandas. It has a rustic turn-of-the-century **saloon** complete with red flocked wallpaper and wagon-wheel chandeliers overhead. Country music is played in the saloon during the day, except when **stage melodramas** take place (at frequent intervals between 11:30am and 5pm). In response to cue cards held up by the players, the audience boos and hisses the mustache-twirling villain, sobs in sympathy with the distressed heroine, laughs, cheers, and applauds. It's quite silly, but lots of fun; kids adore it. Drinks and snacks can be purchased at the bar.

Following each melodrama a **western drama** is presented outside the saloon, involving a bank robbery, a shootout, and the trial of the bad guy. A judge, prosecuting attorney, and defense attorney are chosen from the audience, the remainder of whom act as jury. The action always culminates in a hanging. We're not talking Neil Simon or anything, but the dialogue is quite funny.

Throughout the area, cowboys continually interact with visiting kids. There are also ongoing **stunt shootouts** in this wild frontier town, and some rather unsavory characters languish in the town jail.

A **wax museum** displays tableaux with replicas of John C. Frémont and Kit Carson (who actually stopped at this site in the 1840s), an animated Abraham Lincoln reading the proclamation that made Nevada a state, early trailblazers and mountain men, Brigham Young, 19th-century Paiute chief Old Winnemucca, and early Nevada madam Julia Bulette, among others. A 9-minute film on Nevada history is shown in the wax museum throughout the day.

In the **Old Nevada Photograph Shoppe** you can have a tintype picture taken in 1890s Wild West costume with a 120-year-old camera. There are replicas of a turn-of-the-century church and stamp mill, the latter used for crushing rocks to separate gold and silver from the earth. Movies (one about nearby Red Rock Canyon, one a silent film) are shown in the **Old Movie House** throughout the day from 10:30am to 5pm. You can test your skills in a **shooting gallery,** peek into an old-fashioned **dentist/barbershop** (and surprise a man in his bath), see a **Bootleg Hill still,** and tour the remains of the **old Comstock lode silver mine.** The **Trading Post,** a museum and gift shop, displays a variety of 19th-century items (a switchboard, a craps table and slot machine, cash registers, radios, Victrolas, typewriters, a printing press, shotguns, and the remains of a New Mexico drugstore with many old-fashioned remedies). Other Old Nevada shops sell hand-blown glass, old-fashioned candy, Native American items (rugs, moccasins, silver and turquoise jewelry, baskets), and western wear and gear. Eateries in Old Nevada are discussed below. There's plenty of parking; weekends and holidays, a free shuttle train takes visitors from the parking lot to the entrance.

Admission to Old Nevada is $6.50 for adults, $5.50 for seniors 62 and over, $4 for children ages 5 to 11, and free for children under 5. The park is open daily from 10:30am to 5pm November through April, and until 6pm the rest of the year.

WHERE TO STAY AND DINE

Bonnie Springs Motel

Nev. 159. ☎ 702/875-4400. 50 rms, including 13 suites and 5 fantasy rms. A/C TV TEL Standard room (based on double occupancy) $55–$65 Sun–Thurs, $65–$75 Fri–Sat; fantasy suite $110 Sun–Thurs, $125 Fri–Sat; family suite $85 Sun–Thurs, $95 Fri–Sat. An optional breakfast trail ride for motel guests is $17.50 per person; it departs at 9am every morning. Staying at the motel also entitles you to discounted tickets for Old Nevada. AE, MC, V.

The motel, housed in two-story weathered-wood buildings, is, like Old Nevada, evocative of a 19th-century western town. Even standard rooms offer scenic mountain views and are delightfully decorated with pine-plank-motif carpets, floral-print calico drapes and bedspreads, and handcrafted pine furnishings. Some rooms are equipped with electric fireplaces, and all feature inviting individual touches—perhaps an antique oak mirror stand with a ceramic bowl and jug, Indian rugs, a Mexican serape artfully draped on a branch, lamps with ruffled calico shades, or Victorian-style lighting fixture/fans overhead. All rooms have full baths, in-room coffee makers, and patios overlooking the mountains. There are beautiful family suites with fully equipped kitchens, bedrooms, living rooms (with convertible sofas), and dressing areas; these are equipped with two phones and two TVs. Fantasy rooms are romantic settings with sumptuous Jacuzzi tubs and mirrors over the bed. For instance, a Gay '90s room, decorated in mauve tones, is furnished with velvet-upholstered period chairs. It has a quaint bathtub on brass feet (in addition to an oversized faux-marble Jacuzzi), a lovely porcelain sink with hand-painted floral motifs, and a pink and black lace canopy over the bed. Other fantasy rooms are Chinese, Native American, Old West, and Spanish themed.

Dining: The **Bonnie Springs Ranch Restaurant** is cozily rustic, with rough-hewn pine walls, a beamed ceiling, and glossy cedar-slab tables. A wall of windows overlooks a serene pond with ducks and swans, and an aluminum-hooded wood-burning fireplace is ablaze in winter. Menus, printed on whiskey bottles, offer hearty breakfasts such as a chili-and-cheese omelet with ranch potatoes and homemade biscuits or thick slabs of Texas toast. Sandwiches, salads, burgers, and barbecued beef are featured at lunch ($2.50 to $5.75). And dinner entrees ($11.25 to $15.25) include barbecued chicken and pork ribs, steaks, and seafood.

IN OLD NEVADA

The **Miner's Restaurant,** another rustic western setting, is right in town and has unfinished pine-plank floors, a beamed ceiling, and ruffled curtains. Inexpensive snack fare (sandwiches, burgers, pizza, hot dogs) is served, along with fresh-baked desserts. There are tables out on the porch. In summer, you can also get beer and soft drinks in a similarly old-fashioned **Beer Parlor.**

Index

FROMMER'S COMPLETE TRAVEL GUIDES

(Comprehensive guides to sightseeing, dining and accommodations, with selections in all price ranges—from deluxe to budget)

FROMMER'S $-A-DAY GUIDES

(Dream Vacations at Down-to-Earth Prices)

FROMMER'S COMPLETE CITY GUIDES

(Comprehensive guides to sightseeing, dining, and accommodations in all price ranges)

FROMMER'S FAMILY GUIDES

(Guides to family-friendly hotels, restaurants, activities, and attractions)

FROMMER'S WALKING TOURS

(Memorable strolls through colorful and historic neighborhoods, accompanied by detailed directions and maps)

FROMMER'S AMERICA ON WHEELS

(Guides for travelers who are exploring the U.S.A. by car, featuring a brand-new rating system for accommodations and full-color road maps)

FROMMER'S SPECIAL-INTEREST TITLES

Arthur Frommer's Branson!	P107	Frommer's Where to	
Arthur Frommer's New World		Stay U.S.A., 11th Ed.	P102
of Travel (avail. 11/95)	P112	National Park Guide, 29th Ed.	P106
Frommer's Caribbean		USA Today Golf	
Hideaways (avail. 9/95)	P110	Tournament Guide	P113
Frommer's America's 100		USA Today Minor League	
Best-Loved State Parks	P109	Baseball Book	P111

FROMMER'S BEST BEACH VACATIONS
(The top places to sun, stroll, shop, stay, play, party, and swim—with each beach rated for beauty, swimming, sand, and amenities)

California (avail. 10/95)	G100	Hawaii (avail. 10/95)	G102
Florida (avail. 10/95)	G101		

FROMMER'S BED & BREAKFAST GUIDES
(Selective guides with four-color photos and full descriptions of the best inns in each region)

California	B100	Hawaii	B105
Caribbean	B101	Pacific Northwest	B106
East Coast	B102	Rockies	B107
Eastern United States	B103	Southwest	B108
Great American Cities	B104		

FROMMER'S IRREVERENT GUIDES
(Wickedly honest guides for sophisticated travelers and those who want to be)

Chicago (avail. 11/95)	I100	New Orleans (avail. 11/95)	I103
London (avail. 11/95)	I101	San Francisco (avail. 11/95)	I104
Manhattan (avail. 11/95)	I102	Virgin Islands (avail. 11/95)	I105

FROMMER'S DRIVING TOURS
(Four-color photos and detailed maps outlining spectacular scenic driving routes)

Australia	Y100	Italy	Y108
Austria	Y101	Mexico	Y109
Britain	Y102	Scandinavia	Y110
Canada	Y103	Scotland	Y111
Florida	Y104	Spain	Y112
France	Y105	Switzerland	Y113
Germany	Y106	U.S.A.	Y114
Ireland	Y107		

FROMMER'S BORN TO SHOP
(The ultimate travel guides for discriminating shoppers—from cut-rate to couture)

Hong Kong (avail. 11/95)	Z100	London (avail. 11/95)	Z101